David W. Kritt
Editor

Constructivist Education in an Age of Accountability

Editor
David W. Kritt
College of Staten Island
City University of New York
Staten Island, New York
USA

ISBN 978-3-319-88164-5 ISBN 978-3-319-66050-9 (eBook)
https://doi.org/10.1007/978-3-319-66050-9

Softcover re-print of the Hardcover 1st edition 2018

Printed on acid-free paper

This Palgrave Macmillan imprint is published by Springer Nature
The registered company is Springer International Publishing AG
The registered company address is: Gewerbestrasse 11, 6330 Cham, Switzerland

Constructivist Education in an Age of Accountability

Contents

Part I Introduction 1

1 Teaching As if Children Matter 3
David W. Kritt

2 The Place for Dewey's Constructivism of Intelligent Action in the American Meritocracy of Thorndike 21
Brian D. Cox

3 The Confucian Concept of Learning 57
Liqing Tao

Part II Engaged Learning for Understanding 71

4 Pedagogic Doublethink: Scientific Enquiry and the Construction of Personal Knowledge Under the English National Curriculum for Science 73
Keith S. Taber

5 **The Practice Turn in Learning Theory and Science Education** 97
Ellice A. Forman

6 **How Constructivism Can Boost Success in STEM Fields for Women and Students of Color** 113
Oscar E. Fernandez

7 **Reconceptualizing Accountability: The Ethical Importance of Expanding Understandings of Literacy and Assessment for Twenty-First-Century Learners** 127
Kathryn Hibbert and Luigi Iannacci

8 **Where DAP Is Due: Constructing Community Across Difference with the Dialogue Arts Project** 143
Adam Falkner

9 **A Constructivist Perspective on Games in Education** 163
Linda G. Polin

10 **Social Studies, Common Core, and the Threat to Constructivist Education** 189
Alan Singer, Eustace Thompson, and Catherine DiMartino

11 **Toward a Resolution for Teacher-Student Conflict: Crafting Spaces of Rigorous Freedom with Classroom Debate** 211
Dmitri Seals

12 **Activity Settings as Contexts for Motivation: Reframing Classroom Motivation as Dilemmas Within and Between Activities** 231
Michael Middleton, Alison Rheingold, and Jayson Seaman

13 **Expeditionary Learning, Constructivism, and the Emotional Risks of Open-Ended Inquiry** 267
Amy L. Heath and Peter Smagorinsky

Part III Implications for the Future of Public Education 283

14 **Learning, Teaching, and Social Justice: Eleanor Duckworth's Perspective** 285
Yeh Hsueh

15 **How Documentation of Practice Contributes to Construction and Reconstruction of an Understanding of Learning and Teaching** 301
Linda R. Kroll

16 **Reimagining Research and Practice in Education** 317
Stanton Wortham

17 **School Learning as Compliance or Creation** 327
David W. Kritt

Index 347

List of Contributors

Brian D. Cox is Associate Professor in the Department of Psychology, Hofstra University, Hempstead, NY, USA.

Catherine DiMartino is Associate Professor, Department of Administrative and Instructional Leadership, St. John's University, Queens, NY, USA.

Adam Falkner is a Ph.D. Candidate in English and Education, Teachers College, Columbia University, New York, NY, USA. He is the founder and Executive Director of the Dialogue Arts Project.

Oscar E. Fernandez is Assistant Professor, Department of Mathematics, Wellesley College, Wellesley, MA, USA.

Ellice A. Forman is Professor, Department of Instruction and Learning, University of Pittsburgh, PA, USA.

Amy Heath is Clinical Assistant Professor, Department of Language and Literacy Education, The University of Georgia, Athens, GA, USA.

Kathryn Hibbert is Associate Professor of Education and Director of the Interdisciplinary Centre for Research in Curriculum as Social Practice, University of Western Ontario, London, Ontario, Canada.

Yeh Hsueh is Associate Professor in Educational Psychology and Research, University of Memphis, TN, USA.

Luigi Iannacci is Associate Professor, School of Education, Trent University, Peterborough, Ontario, Canada.

David W. Kritt is Associate Professor of Learning and Development in the School of Education at the College of Staten Island/City University of New York, USA.

Linda R. Kroll is the Holland Professor of Early Childhood Education and Associate Dean of the School of Education at Mills College in Oakland, California, USA.

Michael Middleton is Dean of the School of Education at Hunter College/City University of New York, USA.

Linda Polin is Davidson Professor of Education & Technology in the Graduate School of Education and Psychology at Pepperdine University, W. Los Angeles, CA, USA.

Alison Rheingold is an Instructional Strategist for high schools in Holyoke, Massachusetts, Public Schools, USA.

Dmitri Seals is a Ph.D. Candidate in Education, University of California, Berkeley, USA. He was Director of the Bay Area Urban Debate League program in Oakland and subsequently launched the Silicon Valley Urban Debate League in San Jose.

Jayson Seaman is Associate Professor, Department of Kinesiology (Outdoor Education), University of New Hampshire, Durham, NH, USA. He is Editor in Chief of the *Journal of Experiential Education.*

Alan Singer is Professor, Department of Teaching, Learning, & Technology, Hofstra University in Hempstead, NY, USA. He frequently blogs at the *Huffington Post.*

Peter Smagorinsky is Distinguished Research Professor, Department of Language and Literacy Education, The University of Georgia, Athens, GA, USA.

Keith S. Taber is Professor of Science Education, University of Cambridge, England, UK.

Liqing Tao is Associate Professor in the Department of Curriculum & Instruction, College of Staten Island/City University of New York, USA.

Eustace Thompson is Professor and Chair of the Department of Teaching, Learning, and Technology at Hofstra University, Hempstead, NY, USA.

Stanton F. Wortham is Dean of Education at Boston College, Boston, MA, USA.

List of Figure

Fig. 11.1 Sample flow tracking arguments and rebuttals across six speeches in a debate round 224

List of Tables

Table 9.1	From learning theory to pedagogy	170
Table 9.2	How games can help	173
Table 9.3	How virtual worlds support learners	183

PART I

Introduction

CHAPTER 1

Teaching As if Children Matter

David W. Kritt

As this book was going to press, Betsy DeVos had begun her tenure as Secretary of Education. Prior to that, she headed the All Children Matter Political Action Committee. Her agenda was not to improve public schools, but to shrink public services, protect students from exposure to liberal ideologies, and monetize education. It is easy to foresee the future if this trend goes unchecked: The affluent will be able to purchase access to the best schools and tutelage available, while schools for the middle class will be further diminished and the poor will continue to receive subpar educations with equally poor life choices for all but a token few. Dismantling public schools and making the populace less aware of the entire scheme of things and their place in it, but with sufficient skills to meet corporate needs, is the barely concealed ultimate goal.

These are contentious times in Education and the continuing press of neo-liberal reforms has evoked disparate responses. One is to cede superior wisdom to those who wield extensive test data, funding, and momentum. A second is to accommodate all practice to the standards of accountability and instruction currently in place not because of belief in the approach, but because it is mandated. This is especially rampant among new teachers, and probably the best way to ensure continued employment. A third position is

D.W. Kritt (✉)
School of Education, College of Staten Island, City University of New York, Staten Island, NY, USA

D.W. Kritt (ed.), *Constructivist Education in an Age of Accountability*, https://doi.org/10.1007/978-3-319-66050-9_1

vehemently denying all legitimacy to testing and resisting it in every way possible (e.g., refusing to teach to the test and parents opting out of tests), but this stance is only pursued by activist parents and teachers secure in their positions. These responses tend to omit careful consideration of what should be happening in classrooms. Moving the educational dialogue forward in a progressive direction requires an account of how we got where we are, both in terms of policy and the deeply ingrained folk knowledge underlying common educational practice.

This chapter will examine the educational reforms of recent years to set a context for juxtaposing theories of learning and development with educational politics as they affect teacher education and classroom practices. Because the reforms are tied directly to funding, certification of teachers, and accreditation of schools, their impact is immense. Although the fervor for testing has cooled to some degree in response to pressures from both teachers and parents, its determinant influence on schools persists.

Educational Reforms

A great deal of scrutiny of education goes under the banner of "standards," exerting pressure upon teachers and students to produce tangible results. The current spate of mandates for accountability began with No Child Left Behind (NCLB; U.S. Department of Education, 2002), which promised that within 12 years all students nationwide would achieve "proficiency" or above on a number of indicators, as measured by test scores. Now, over 12 years later, no one would concede that this goal has been met.

One of the most beautiful—and cynical—statements about education reform was coined when NCLB was introduced, demanding high standards that mitigate "the soft bigotry of low expectations" (U.S. Department of Education, 2003). But such solutions, if we take them at face value, seem to assume this can be achieved in the same way that manufacturing practices are designed to achieve acceptable quality in goods.

Although the metaphor used to frame the problem with education was inaccurate, the "low expectations" statement introduced at least a shadow of a doubt that someone else knew more. This has been a successful tactic. Most educators, unable to adequately deflect the sly attacks on their integrity, knowledge, judgment, and orientation to current realities, have acquiesced to whatever comes down from the City, State, or Federal government agencies.

The Race to the Top (U.S. Department of Education, 2009) extended the NCLB initiative, linking compliance with prescribed practices to federal funding. It continued widespread reliance on high-stakes standardized testing, setting outcome goals with insufficient attention to how children think, individual differences, and the context of any particular classroom. Patterns of mind are not shaped in nine-month, academic year, increments. Neither intellectual curiosity nor the development of sustained interest are short-term goals. Reports of progress or problems along the way should inform ongoing instructional interventions, rather than being considered attainments, credits, or debits in a ledger. The press of immediate measurable results is analogous to an emphasis on quarterly earnings rather than long-term investment in infrastructure. Yet education is not simply a commodity or service to be delivered as efficiently as possible. It is a sacred pact between a society and its children.

A perceived problem with NCLB was the state-by-state variability in the knowledge students were expected to acquire. In order to assure a greater number of students are able to demonstrate content mastery learning in Mathematics and English Language Arts (ELA), and that their performance is measurable and comparable to those of students across the country, curriculum standards and tests aligned to them appeared on the scene. The Common Core State Standards are not officially mandated by the federal government; they originated with two organizations: the Council of Chief State School Officers and the National Governors Association. The curriculum guidelines claim to be a response to the disparate educational preparation of children, seeking equity by promising to offer the same curriculum to all students at a particular grade level, ignoring differences and hoping they will disappear. But real equality of opportunity means circumventing barriers that accompany growing up within an impoverished family in a marginalized community.

Instead, coverage of topics in ELA and Mathematics for students in grades K–12 was delineated. Common Core has been implemented by 42 states and the District of Columbia. Larry Cuban, a noted Stanford University School of Education Professor Emeritus and blogger, wryly asserts that it will be declared a success regardless of student outcomes, simply because it has been so widely adopted (Cuban, 2013).

Common Core curriculum guidelines include reference to making connections between prior experiences and new ones, a shift from passive to active learning, a push toward deeper understanding, and efforts to encourage analytical and critical thinking (e.g., engage NY, n.d.). Yet in practice, it often functions as a deficit model of fixing those who don't immediately get it right and teaching to the test. Curriculum guidelines prescribe how mathematics problems should be set up, the questions that should be asked, and how problems should be solved; it is claimed this will ensure conceptual understanding. There is no recognition or support for students who devise their own understanding, even if they consistently arrive at correct solutions. From a constructivist point-of-view, rigidly prescribing steps for problem solution is antithetical to exploration of the material, working out relations and distinctions, weighing alternate interpretations, and considering possibilities. In English classes, there is less emphasis on fiction and more on nonfiction. Acquiring factual evidence from text is granted more attention than the reader's response or interpretation. Individual and cultural differences are ignored.

Common Core's assumptions, goals, and methods markedly contrast with the progressive education tradition of Dewey, Piaget, Vygotsky, Freire, and numerous others. Mandates only pay lip service to these principles while undermining the value of both students and teachers actively creating understandings. And the gap between avowed values and the emphasis on test data is a great frustration to many educators.

Learning Theory and "Objective" Research

There are divergent conceptions of what thinking and learning are, and these necessarily color all other ideas about what schools should be doing. Even at the height of its popularity, constructivism was overshadowed by an old and entrenched tradition of school practices; direct instruction, memorization of "the basics" (e.g., multiplication tables, verb conjugations, rules, and formulas), repetitive practice, and modeling (i.e., in the simplistic sense of expecting students to copy a demonstration) remain popular. This influence may be traced to theories of learning by association (Hume, 1777/1975; Locke, 1690/1975; Pavlov, 1927/1960), rewards, and punishments (e.g., Skinner, 1951/2014; Watson, 1925/1970). Another type of learning theory that has a prominent place in classrooms focuses on the replication and retention of input from observed behavior (e.g., Bandura, 1962). A long experimental tradition focused on verbal learning of paired associates—often random words or nonsense syllables placed in spatial or temporal contiguity (Anderson & Bower, 1979, Chap. 14; Ebbinghaus, 1885/1962; Kling & Riggs, 1971, Chap. 19)—has been especially influential in schools. Rote learning was prescribed as useful in forming connections that were assumed to become consolidated and more complex with repeated use.

Through the years, learning theory has been updated and refined, but retains an emphasis on the external environment and observable behavior, both relatively easy to measure. At heart, there is an assumption that a mechanistic relation between stimuli and responses, physical or temporal contiguity, will yield meaningful (or functional, to be more precise) relations. Analyses began by breaking behavior into atomistic bits that could be measured and counted; this was viewed as more scientific because it has been "purified" of all its messy humanness.

The quest for certainty suggests the need for rigorous methods. The sort of "objective" research accepted as justification biases the questions that are asked and the types of solution that will be entertained. During the George W. Bush administration, the government's Educational Research Information Center (www.ERIC.gov) was reorganized into the Institute of Education Sciences (IES, n.d.) to highlight quantitative research using large sample sizes and standardized testing instruments. Studies utilizing methodologies such as qualitative case study were excluded; the rationale was an emphasis on higher quality "real" data (Kolata, 2013). The embrace of science was used to exclude consideration of education in a wider societal context. Viewing the enterprise in a positivistic scientific manner meant that only data about student and teacher performance, curriculum, textbooks, and use of specific technology would inform national policy.

Research formulated in accordance with specific assumptions about schooling, especially narrow concern with the performance of students and teachers, deflects attention from issues of diversity and achieving social justice in schools. Failures in education are defined as deficiencies in individuals; critiques of structural causes (e.g., Aronowitz, 2008; Varenne & McDermott, 1998) are dismissed as ideological, lacking an objective basis.

Test scores are designated as "student performance," a reductive measurement that has gained acceptance as the sufficient index of thinking and learning, and as a valid and reliable predictor of future success (itself a loaded term). A further proposal based on outsized faith in test scores was their use to assess teachers, despite insufficient support for extending the use of results in this way (Darling-Hammond, Amrein-Beardsley, Haertel, & Rothstein, 2011; Kupermintz, 2003). And there have been proposals for Schools of Education to be held responsible for the performance of in-service teachers who were their graduates.

Skewed in this way, the research apparatus may find culprits to blame but will never yield real educational improvement. With both questions and answers focusing on test performance, that is the entire universe of possibility; no other successes or failures are acknowledged. Beyond the circularity of teaching to the test, in widespread use among schools desperate to remain in good standing, there is selective use of research. Politicians and education entrepreneurs do not play by the same rules as responsible scientists. Despite the rhetoric, current educational practices and reforms are not "research-based best-practices"; if we take the phrase at face value, it must be concluded that there has been insufficient research, conducted on paltry samples considering how widely they are to be applied.

The forgone conclusion that better research and development, always forthcoming, will convincingly demonstrate the superiority of current reforms is supported by the way problems are posed. But the real issue is not about research methodology. It is how and why the current educational reforms have been deployed. Proposed free-market solutions seem to converge on conclusions that would privatize the enterprise, tapping a vast potential market. Charter schools, privately run but publicly subsidized, are often exempt from the objective assessments required of public schools. They institutionalize exclusivity by offering opportunities only for those selected, leaving the majority of students in public schools that have been further diminished. Other so-called reform efforts seek to circumvent both college preparation of teachers and teachers' unions, further refashioning education as a profit center.

Within the classroom, the stated intent of reforms is to facilitate careful analysis of problem spaces. This is predicated upon deep disciplinary ways of knowing in mathematics, science, and language, with an emphasis on specific desired performances and pedagogy formulated in terms of optimal steps toward problem solution. In contrast, constructivism offers a view of learning and thinking that puts an active agent at its center. Beyond developmentally appropriate practices acknowledging the functioning of immature minds, central concerns include imperfect everyday understandings of situations, bridging resultant conceptual gaps, and addressing learner's resistance to formalized modes of thought (cf. Gardner, 1991; Vygotsky, 1934/1987).

The Varieties of Constructivist Education

Constructivism is many things to many people, as will be evident in the following pages. What is clear is that it is not the mindless enterprise derided by its severest critics: a laissez-faire approach that simply lets children do whatever they want, encouraging them by heaping praise no matter what the outcome. Certainly many current proponents share a learner-centered approach, but not without serious guidance; the differences of opinion mostly concern type of support and when it should be offered. If there are remnants of looseness, they derive from rejection of rigid technologies (broadly conceived) of education, premised on faith that everyone can and should learn in the same way, providing content has been delivered in a straight-forward, efficient manner. Instead of well-defined formats and narrowly defined accountability, constructivist education relies upon observation to determine how a student thinks and learns so that teachers know when to allow more time for working things out and when targeted intervention is needed.

The primary tenets of constructivist education are those of John Dewey (1916/1997), whose pragmatic philosophy emphasized learning-by-doing and involvement in authentic activities. Dewey's thought has influenced a wide range of instructional practices. Perhaps central to all constructivist approaches is recognition that learning is not reception of transmitted information and internal accretion. It is transactional, abetted by a dialectic of cognitive integration.

Although not directly concerned with the education of children, since its introduction to the USA in the 1960s, Piaget's theory of cognitive development has had an influence in pre-K, elementary, and secondary classrooms. Piaget's central metaphor for development is the adaptive organism, which he extended to characterize thinking (Gallagher & Reid, 1982; Piaget, 1974). A natural tendency is to impose our frameworks for understanding onto whatever we encounter. But sometimes this does not work—situations challenge the conceptions we bring to them and our thoughts must adapt. This is not a passive adaptation, but an active one (Inhelder, Sinclair, & Bovet, 1974/2014). As Piaget noted, "to learn is to invent." An insightful extension is that working on relations between things you already know is more important than simply acquiring new information (Duckworth, 1973/2006). Obsessed as we all are by the Internet, too much information is readily acquired with little meaningful framework for understanding. Such a context of acquisition brings the need for integrating knowledge to the forefront.

Vygotsky's influence on education in the USA began later, achieving substantial interest after publication of the translation of *Mind in Society* (1978). Much of his work directly addressed teaching and learning and many found the focus on social and culturally embedded human activity a needed corrective to the a-contextual rationality of a solitary individual figuring out how things work. Attention shifted to interactions with proximal others and engagement with historically developed tools, both physical and symbolic, as well as traditional and institutionalized ways of doing things (Arievitch, 2017; Cole, 1996; John-Steiner, 1985/1997; Lave & Wenger, 1991; Stetsenko, 2017).

Some theorists, researchers, and practitioners saw a fundamental incommensurability between Piaget and Vygotsky. Others saw a complementarity, with each theory's strengths better explaining some aspects of development than the other (e.g., Glassman, 1994; Glick, 1983). Despite significant theoretical struggles and differing emphases (e.g., on individual or social process), partisans borrow freely, often in unacknowledged ways, to consider learning and development in terms of fully human agents acting within a context. It is likely that, by playing off each other, both theories and their adherents are enriched, yielding a multifaceted framework for working with children and youth in and out of classrooms.

Although differently conceptualized, both Piagetian/structuralist and Vygotskian/cultural-historical approaches to constructivism recognize the importance of qualitative differences in thought in early and middle childhood, into early adolescence, and concur that understanding how children think and learn should guide instruction. Developmentally appropriate practice has been universally accepted; although in practice this may not be a refined understanding of the child's thought, nonetheless it is much preferable to instruction that proceeds solely from the organization of the subject matter.

The hands-on use of materials to assist student conceptualization and problem solving continues to be a popular classroom practice; ongoing theoretical controversies include emphasis on involvement with physical objects or participation in humanly meaningful activities, as well as the virtues of working with actual materials or representational simulacra on computer screens.

Because the emphasis is on the active rather than passive, constructivist approaches tend to focus on overt activity. One unfortunate consequence is that in too many cases, this is reduced to fetishistic performance rituals—is there a "hands-on" component, are students working in groups or on projects? Surface features of classroom activity obscure the fact that the absence of observable action does not necessarily indicate passivity. Solitary reading is an active process, with comprehension influenced by extant frames of understanding and integration of the old and new. And obvious activity in the classroom can be "hands on" but not "minds on" (Driver, 1983/2001; Wells, 1999, p. 213). Learning is a subtle process, extending across time and performances, to yield consolidated understandings.

Collaborative group work is widely evident in classrooms, but as commonly implemented, the emphasis is on covering subject matter. Interaction processes are granted less attention than resultant products, and empty performances within a group are expected to work via some inexplicable magic. Yet the organization of a working group is not foolproof and replicable, like assembly line production. Scant attention is granted thought patterns and personalities of group members. Too often it is taken on blind faith that peers—working on a joint (assigned) challenge and with no background in facilitation—will be able to assist each other in ways that teachers do not. Only at its best does discourse among individuals struggling to complete a task afford comparison of one's own perspective with others to create deeper understanding.

If Children Mattered

In practice, with so much attention on test scores, too many classroom activities continue to emphasize transmission of information as the primary mode of knowledge acquisition. And there is also persistent faith in student performance that replicates what has been demonstrated by the teacher. But contrary to the impulse of many novices, teaching is not primarily telling, explaining, and showing-how.

Scaffolding, at its best coaching based on careful observation of how a student approaches a problem, is an ubiquitous buzzword in education. But it is frequently inexpertly implemented. There is too much reliance on modeling, with the expectation of repetition and retention of observed behavior (e.g., Bandura, 1962) rather than assisting students by cuing or presenting crucial steps toward solution in a way that requires overcoming obstacles (e.g., Rogoff & Wertsch, 1984).

Variation in constructivist viewpoints regarding the degree of students' responsibility for their own learning may be placed on a continuum. At one extreme, students freely explore how to approach a problem. At the other, the emphasis is on the teacher sequentially isolating variables necessary for understanding. Working between these poles, as many have (e.g., Brown & Campione, 1994), has the potential to invigorate thought about teaching and learning. But this is far from typical teacher practice. With the current pressures of Common Core and testing, teachers often begrudgingly acknowledge the right way to do things, but regret that they have too many constraints and students and too little time to do it. Unfortunately, in many classrooms, the only student talk that is welcome is when they give the correct answer. A focus on curriculum coverage and improving test performance has eclipsed student-centered classroom practice.

In addition to instruction, assessment weighs heavily on the classroom teacher. Assessment as a form of quality control is more applicable to manufactured products than developing individuals. The overall effect is to divert attention from optimal human development and personal fulfillment, whether as butcher or baker, scientist or artist or assistant manager on the way up in an organization. There are no easy universally applicable formulas.

Good teachers assess daily student performances in a formative way, using informal evidence to suggest the most effective way to involve students in classroom activities. Teachers must carefully observe their students and how they approach problems, but this is only truly useful if they develop a framework for appreciating what they see and using it as an impetus for educational intervention. At best, educators create cultures in their classrooms where students are not afraid to try out ideas and explain them. In such a milieu, misconceptions and mistakes will be seen as opportunities to build upon what students think they know, encouraging exploration of uncertainties and providing guidance toward deeper understandings.

Constructivist Education in an Age of Accountability

Bureaucratic dictates set policy, but teachers can assert agency in their classrooms. NCLB, Race to the Top, All Children Matter, and so on, lofty but empty slogans, have been bandied about with much fanfare. The words themselves sound just about right, but they obscure what is actually being done, which is the antithesis of what is claimed. The race is to a standardized uniformity in providing minimal requirements and any child who cannot thrive on that thin gruel is left behind. The new regime may proclaim that all children matter, but, as George Orwell might put it, some children are "more equal than others."

This book is a symposium of interesting minds. Their visions of better educational practice are strong and contain many deep threads of intellectual kinship. Although the varieties of constructivist thought have often been seen as discrete strains, especially at a time when educational thought is embattled not by rival camps but from external sources, strength can and should be built among the differences.

The chapters in this book examine the competing demands of accountability and meaningfully engaged learning, contributing to the public debate about schools in a way that provides real insight into the process of education. Each author in this volume brings a distinctive flavor, and the reader has a rich array from which to sample, note variances, and create new fusions. Although they represent a range of disciplines and perspectives, there is clear consensus that the challenge currently facing educators is how to teach as if students really mattered.

Brian Cox, author of a forthcoming comprehensive history of Psychology, reintroduces readers to two figures emblematic of a major chasm in educational thought. Dewey is the patron saint of progressive education in the USA, while Edward Thorndike is godfather of the quest for measurable certainty that has wrought the current mania for testing. Cox traces similar roots, good intentions, and the origins of divergence.

Liqing Tao came of age at a time of Cultural Revolution in China. He presents a deep understanding of traditional Confucian values whose influence has quietly persisted. Confucius was by no means a revolutionary. But his concern with nurturing a thoughtful populace and wise leaders for a strong and stable society may provide some ingredients of a much-needed tonic for current times.

Science, Technology, Engineering, and Mathematics, or STEM, is highlighted in current educational initiatives. It is valued by industry and government, and students fluent in its language are all but assured of a well-rewarded future. Yet relatively few students excel in these areas. The three chapter authors in this section address this issue from different but complementary angles.

Keith Taber critiques the implementation of standards for science education in the UK. More directly and overtly an official national curriculum than Common Core and various governmental funding incentives for rigorous assessment, the British educational system and its impact on preparing a new generation of scientists provides a cautionary tale. He presents a convincing case that if we value scientific inquiry and discovery, a rigidly constrained education is the wrong path.

Ellice Forman discusses some central features of a better science education. If science is more than recitation of established fact, we must educate a generation that not only adequately knows scientific facts, but can also do science; hence, the practice turn. Integral to her stance, she provides a new understanding of a favored term of educational jargon, modeling, considering the contribution of tangible representations of structures and relationships to the development of scientific thought.

Oscar Fernandez, an emerging voice in mathematics and mathematics education, confronts a longstanding issue head-on: women and students of color are under-represented in advanced mathematics classes and STEM fields. He reviews research to present a case that the traditional lecture format of STEM courses is less effective than small group, problem-based learning. In both his writings and his practice, he suggests a way forward using pedagogy informed by constructivism.

Literacy, beyond its rudiments of decoding and initial comprehension, adherence to grammatical conventions, and a contested and changing canon of authors, is many splendored things. This collection provides a taste of that range.

Kathryn Hibbert and Luigi Iannacci critique tests of literacy. They passionately plea for a broader definition that respects multiliteracies. Assessments sensitive to culture, identity, and semiotic diversity enlarge what is commonly acknowledged by educators; this, they argue, has significant implications for classroom teaching and learning.

Adam Falkner demonstrates the vital importance of writing for the expression of identity and to reflect upon one's own experience, as well as for overall school success. He draws upon experience, insight, and participant observation to provide a rich portrait of youth writing "creative autoethnographies" and engaging in dialogue about them. This is a personal, deeply meaningful approach with high school students working to explicate their own perspectives, appreciate those of others, and take risks in discussing them.

Linda Polin's chapter may be considered as further extending traditional views of literacy, focusing on the potential of virtual world game play for a broad range of learning and development. She presents the case that complex, multifaceted, and immersive gaming environments are contexts that challenge, hone skills, and provide opportunities for the creation of meaning.

Although not the focus of testing, disciplinary knowledge about societal functioning and the often implicit lessons of involvement in school activities are a very important part of any student's education. Such lessons are helpful in negotiating daily life and vital for fully participating in a democratic society.

Alan Singer, Eustace Thompson, and Catherine DiMartino present a fierce repudiation of the impact of Common Core on Social Studies disciplines. The guidelines for curriculum de-contextualize knowledge by emphasizing text-dependent questions and avoiding discussion of democratic values. The authors discuss exemplary projects in elementary, middle school, and high school that involve students in activities at the heart of participating in a democratic society.

Michael Middleton, Alison Rheingold, and Jayson Seaman use a fine-grained analysis to focus on relational identities that come into play during participation in learning activities. Mutual work to address challenges and resolve problems contributes greatly to the creation of students' classroom goals and their construction of understanding. Such processes compel us to look beyond teaching procedures to appreciate small group learning as a fully human activity.

Dmitri Seals presents a compelling case that debate is a powerful educational tool of vital importance to a democratic society, strengthening a sense of personal agency and respect for teamwork in the course of intensive preparation for a public, competitive academic performance.

Amy Heath and Peter Smagorinsky introduce an immersive type of learning and a case study of an individual participant. The program is steeped in constructivist justifications, but its implementation was flawed; it clearly did not have the intended effect on the student observed, a female African American middle school student. Their portrayal of her experience serves as a stark reminder that even the best of intentions are not adequate in themselves and that constructivist approaches cannot be blind to difference.

Educating all children is a public good, but it is increasingly clear that systems of public education will not continue to exist, let alone flourish, without sustained vigilance and protection. What schools need, what teachers should do, what students should learn are always determined with specific priorities in mind. As a response, we must revitalize rich traditions, extend them in new ways, and re-conceptualize how knowledge about teaching and learning is generated and disseminated. Accepted truths should be interrogated in an ongoing fashion, not universally prescribed and institutionalized.

Yeh Hsueh, a former student of Eleanor Duckworth, has woven together quintessential statements and recent reflections of this pioneering educator and educational theorist in a way that assesses the current educational landscape and looks toward the future. This chapter examines Duckworth's views on education in a rapidly changing world and school reforms that disempower both teachers and students. Her focus on students developing understanding through active exploration incorporates deep concerns for social justice.

Linda Kroll considers teaching itself as a constructive activity. A more complete appreciation of teaching and learning requires looking beyond curriculum and the material that is tested. She discusses teacher preparation rooted in an inquiry stance that privileges reflection and restructuring of understandings—both those of teachers and their students—and ongoing interrogation of classroom practices. A central insight of this approach is that the representation of what is being learned, its process as well as conclusions or achievements, can be an enlightened form of assessment that contributes to further learning for all involved.

Stanton Wortham provides a cultural-historical activity theory perspective on how research has been used in education and how it should be used. The "flow" of research evidence into practice must be understood in relation to the activities of researchers and practitioners, as well as "political struggles" over what it means to be "evidence-based" and how this is interpreted in practical application. Such framing infuses ideas as they are disseminated between researchers and practitioners and incorporated into classroom activities. This critique of widespread ideas about implementation adds an important perspective to current educational discourse.

Education can enrich or diminish students in terms of whether they are held to be inherently important or only instrumentally so, the types of thought promoted, and how it makes them feel about themselves and the world. My final chapter is a call to arms: If we are going to do this, let's do it right.

References

Anderson, J. R., & Bower, G. H. (1979). *Human associative memory.* Hillsdale, NJ: Lawrence Erlbaum Associates.

Arievitch, I. M. (2017). *Beyond the brain: An agentive activity perspective on mind, development, and learning.* Rotterdam, The Netherlands/New York: Sense Publishers.

Aronowitz, S. (2008). *Against schooling: For an education that matters.* Boulder, CO: Paradigm Publishers.

Bandura, A. (1962). Social learning through imitation. In M. R. Jones (Ed.), *1962 Nebraska symposium on motivation* (pp. 211–269). Lincoln, NE: University of Nebraska Press.

Brown, A. L., & Campione, J. C. (1994). Guided discovery in a community of learners. In K. McGilly (Ed.), *Classroom lessons: Integrating cognitive theory and classroom practice* (pp. 229–270). Cambridge, MA: MIT Press/Bradford Books.

Cole, M. (1996). *Cultural psychology: A once and future discipline.* Cambridge, MA: Harvard University Press.

Cuban, L. (2013). *How common core standards will succeed.* Retrieved December 7, 2016, from https://larrycuban.wordpress.com/2013/08/15/why-common-core-standards-will-succeed/

Darling-Hammond, L., Amrein-Beardsley, A., Haertel, E.H., & Rothstein, J. (2011, September 14). *Getting teacher evaluation right: A background paper for policy makers.* Washington, DC: Research briefing, Dirksen Senate Office Building. Retrieved March 8, 2016, from http://files.eric.ed.gov/fulltext/ED533702.pdf

Dewey, J. (1916/1997). *Democracy and education: An introduction to the philosophy of education.* New York: Free Press.

Driver, R. (1983/2001). *The pupil as scientist?* Milton Keynes, UK: Open University Press.

Duckworth, E. (1973/2006). *"The having of wonderful ideas" and other essays on teaching and learning* (3rd ed.). New York: Teachers College Press.

Ebbinghaus, H. (1885/1962). *Memory: A contribution to experimental psychology.* New York: Dover.

Engage NY. (n.d.) *Common core curriculum/NYS P-12 common core learning standards.* Retrieved December 7, 2016, from https://www.engageny.org/resource/new-york-state-p-12-common-core-learning-standards

Gallagher, J., & Reid, D. K. (1982). *The learning theory of Piaget and Inhelder.* Monterey, CA: Brooks/Cole.

Gardner, H. (1991). *The unschooled mind: How children think and how schools should teach.* New York: Basic Books.

Glassman, M. (1994). All things being equal. The two roads of Piaget and Vygotsky. *Developmental Review, 14*, 186–214.

Glick, J. (1983). Piaget, Vygotsky, and Werner. In S. Wapner & B. Kaplan (Eds.), *Toward a holistic developmental psychology* (pp. 35–52). Hillsdale, NJ: Lawrence Erlbaum Associates.

Hume, D. (1777/1975). *A treatise of human nature.* Oxford, UK: Clarendon Press.

Inhelder, B., Sinclair, H., & Bovet, M. (1974/2014). *Learning and the development of cognition*. New York: Psychology Press.

Institute of Education Sciences. (n.d.). *About IES: Connecting research, policy and practice*. Retrieved March 21, 2017, from https://ies.ed.gov/aboutus/

John-Steiner, V. (1985/1997). *Notebooks of the mind: Explorations of thinking*. New York: Oxford University Press.

Kling, J. W., & Riggs, L. A. (1971). *Woodworth & Schlossberg's Experimental Psychology* (3rd ed.). New York: Holt, Rinehart and Winston.

Kolata, G. (2013, September 2). Guesses and hype give way to data in study of education. *New York Times*. Retrieved March 21, 2017, from https://mobile.nytimes.com/2013/09/03/science/applying-new-rigor-in-studying-education

Kupermintz, H. (2003). Teacher effects and teacher effectiveness: A validity investigation of the Tennessee value added assessment system. *Educational Evaluation and Policy Analysis, 25*(3), 287–298.

Lave, J., & Wenger, E. (1991). *Situated learning: Legitimate peripheral participation*. New York: Cambridge University Press.

Locke, J. (1690/1975). *An essay concerning human understanding*. Oxford, UK: Clarendon Press.

Pavlov, I. P. (1927/1960). *Conditional reflexes*. New York: Dover.

Piaget, J. (1974). *Biology and knowledge: An essay on the relations between organic regulations and cognitive processes*. Chicago: University of Chicago Press.

Rogoff, B., & Wertsch, J. (Eds.). (1984). *Children's learning in the "zone of proximal development"*. San Francisco: Jossey Bass.

Skinner, B. F. (1951/2014). *Science and human behavior*. Cambridge, MA: The B.F. Skinner Foundation.

Stetsenko, A. (2017). *The transformative mind: Expanding Vygotsky's approach to development and education*. New York: Cambridge University Press.

U.S. Department of Education. (2002). *Executive summary: The no child left behind act of 2001*. Retrieved January 26, 2016, from http://www2.ed.gov/nclb/overview/intro/execsumm.html

U.S. Department of Education. (2003, March 12). *Paige blasts "soft bigotry of low expectations"* [Press release]. Retrieved January 26, 2016, from http://www2.ed.gov/news/pressreleases/2003/03/03122003.html

U.S. Department of Education. (2009). *Executive summary: Race to the top program*. Retrieved January 26, 2016, from http://www2.ed.gov/programs/racetothetop/executive-summary.pdf

Varenne, H., & McDermott, R. P. (1998). *Successful failure: The school America builds*. Boulder, CO: Westview.

Vygotsky, L. S. (1934/1987). Thinking and speech (trans: Minnick, N.). In R. Rieber & A. Carton (Eds.), *The collected works of L.S. Vygotsky: Volume 1, Problems of general psychology* (pp. 39–285). New York: Plenum.

Vygotsky, L. S. (1978). *Mind in society: The development of higher psychological processes.* Cambridge, MA: Harvard University Press.
Watson, J. B. (1925/1970). *Behaviorism.* New York: W.W. Norton.
Wells, G. (1999). *Dialogic inquiry: Toward a sociocultural practice and theory of education.* New York: Cambridge University Press.

CHAPTER 2

The Place for Dewey's Constructivism of Intelligent Action in the American Meritocracy of Thorndike

Brian D. Cox

American educators have long been pulled in different directions by two twentieth-century legacies: E. L. Thorndike is often portrayed as a technocratic proto-behaviorist, in favor of atomized habit-focused education. At best, he is believed to advocate standardization, accurate psychometrics, and scientific administration; at worst, he is portrayed as furthering the twin evils of rote memorization and eugenics. By contrast, the tradition fostered by John Dewey is where many teachers' hearts lie: He is seen as promoting a fundamentally social, discovery-based, hands-on construction of knowledge through hypothesis testing and creativity. If teachers do their jobs right, students experience what Dewey called "a freeing of activity" or "growth" toward deeper inquiry. Moreover, especially in his classic *Democracy and Education*, Dewey was prescient about the ways in which the hierarchical, often autocratic or corporate nature of educational bureaucracies can deaden the excitement of creative learning.

Dewey and Thorndike were almost exact contemporaries—Dewey was born earlier than Thorndike and outlived him; they were both inspired by the work of Darwin and William James, and they both taught at Columbia University for over 40 years. Each believed himself to be a progressive

B.D. Cox (✉)
Department of Psychology, Hofstra University, Hempstead, NY, USA

D.W. Kritt (ed.), *Constructivist Education in an Age of Accountability*,
https://doi.org/10.1007/978-3-319-66050-9_2

educator, dedicated to replacing the waning rote-based Latinate system known as Formal Discipline with a modern approach based on adaptation to current circumstances. Each was considered, in his own way, as an authority on American Education. This chapter is a historical interpretation of why they diverged from each other, how both views became so commonplace as to be woven into the fabric of our unconscious assumptions about how children should be taught, how they (and their teachers) might be tested, and even what kind of democracy they are to be brought up to live and participate in.

Similar Beginnings

John Dewey (1859–1952) and Edward Lee Thorndike (1874–1949) started life in similar circumstances. Both were New Englanders born into Calvinist Evangelical faiths who revised those beliefs when they left home, but not before their religious upbringings had left their marks. Thorndike's father was a Methodist minister. In Methodism, ordained preachers seldom stay longer than three years at a given church, so the Thorndike children became remarkably self-sufficient, sustained in their path by a mania for reading and a staunchly, perhaps excessively pious mother. Thorndike complained to his future wife that "no sane person" could follow his mother's dicta (Joncich, 1968).

Dewey's mother was an equally firm evangelical, and his education at University of Vermont was equally Calvinist, but with a twist: "The Burlington Philosophy" was based on a book written by the Romantic poet Samuel Taylor Coleridge, that through an idiosyncratic reading of Kant claimed that Christianity and human reason cannot conflict. Coleridge's (1829/1873) *Aids to Reflection, in the Formation of a Manly Character, on the Several Grounds of Prudence, Morality, and Religion* formed the basis for the entire Vermont curriculum, unifying all courses under its umbrella. The curriculum, anticipating Dewey's later philosophy, was meant to unfold as a process of "natural development and growth"; it disdained formal examinations, and was capped by a senior course celebrating the unity of all knowledge. It is no wonder that when he went for graduate study at Johns Hopkins, Dewey was drawn to the work of another great synthesizer, G. W. F. Hegel: "Hegel's synthesis of subject and object, matter and spirit, the divine and the human, was ... no mere intellectual formula; it operated as an immense release" (Dewey, 1930, as cited in Menand, 2001, p. 267). Although he would later, as we shall see, throw Hegel over in favor of

William James' Pragmatism, Dewey would resist dualisms (mind vs. body, Platonic idealism vs. manual practice, individual vs. social) all his life. Moreover, he understood, in a way that James did not, the propensities of social structures for good (to create meaning or to create democracy) and ill (to thwart genuine inquiry with the deadening hand of bureaucratic educational administration).

Thorndike and Dewey shared one other almost subconscious tendency from their Calvinist upbringing: Their Protestant Work Ethic (Weber, 1905/2002). In Calvinism, one's salvation is set, from the beginning of time, only by God's grace and not one's works. To assuage one's anxiety over whether or not he or she is saved, one works in his or her divinely inspired calling in a way that the Elected of God would act, continuously without praise or relief, presumably faithfully furthering God's plan. Max Weber's famous article suggests that Calvinists should plan and act for the future as if they had free will, even if they may not, taking responsibility for their actions without expecting fate to go their way (Poggi, 1983).

United with the Victorian notion of progress, such a work ethic pervaded so completely the society of the late nineteenth century that one needed not to be religious to feel its constant pull. Both men were ambitious, but understood individual responsibility was balanced with duty to their professions and society. However much either would rebel against these tenets—neither man was conventionally religious in his mature thought (Richardson & Slife, 2013)—both men had internalized these norms and became indefatigable, prolific workers. Thorndike authored, coauthored, or supervised 50 books, and some 500 works overall (Woodworth, 1952; Russell, 1949). *The Collected Works of John Dewey* edited by Jo Ann Boydston of Southern Illinois Press runs to 37 large volumes. But I emphasize Calvinism here for another reason: American individualism and drive to succeed is unconsciously founded on it, as is the empire of testing and ranking. As we shall see, even Dewey at his most socialist based his views on the democratic right of individual Americans to freely choose their social groups.

The Influence of William James

When Thorndike was a junior at Wesleyan, he read some chapters of William James' masterpiece *The Principles of Psychology* (1890/1983); more than 40 years later, he recalled it as the most stimulating book he had ever read, and the only one other than novels he had purchased with his own money as an undergraduate (Thorndike & Murchison, 1936). He then set his sights on graduate work with James, even as James himself was shifting back to Philosophy from Psychology. Dewey was in his 30s when *The Principles* came out, and had already published a Hegelian-flavored Psychology textbook (Dewey, 1887), which William James predictably disliked. Nevertheless, Dewey was to say that James' textbook "worked its way more and more into all my ideas and acted as a ferment to transform old beliefs" (Dewey, 1930, p. 24).

The Principles was the most popular psychology text for its generation because of its transitional nature: On the one hand, James took great care to build his Psychology from philosophical first principles, including, for example, the issues of mind–body dualism, and determinism versus free will. But James had also read Darwin's works in his 20s, and had been considering the effect of Darwinian ideas on Philosophy since the early 1870s (Menand, 2001). He had been taught the latest materialistic experimental physiology of the brain at Harvard's then new Lawrence Scientific School and at the Medical School, and during occasional forays to Europe. He was familiar with the Wundtian "New Psychology" of experimental self-observation, but disliked it intensely. James considered Wundt's focus on rigorous training of graduate students to look intensely at their own consciousness under rigid control to be a fool's errand; the fluidity of consciousness is such that trying to keep it still for inspection would be no more successful than squeezing tightly a bar of wet soap. Rather, James considered consciousness as a mechanism of continuous adaptation to local threats, novelties, and challenges.

It is perhaps too much to say of James' text that he put psychology on a scientific footing, but what he did do was to methodically dismantle the world of ideas as a separate world that goes back to Plato, and the mind as a storehouse of ideas that goes back to Locke. He replaced it with a world of moment-to-moment nervous impulses in a naturally selected brain. He replaced Cartesian dualism with the new dualism of parallelism: As a physiologist, one can study the nervous system from the outside as a series of neurochemical electrical signals, or from the inside the conscious mind as a flow of experience itself. Psychology, now anchored in the material world, was for James the study of that flow of experience, a science of mental life. Every moment of experience is caused by the brain, and that experience is always flowing, always on. In the same way that one can never step in the same river twice, the stream of consciousness is always new; one's consciousness selects out of the stream any thought that solves a momentary problem for an organism, whatever thought is needed for adaptation to the world at that moment. The metaphor for the mind is no longer that of a storehouse of ideas, but of sequential nervous impulses experienced consciously as the flow of time. James brilliantly points out that Darwin's mechanisms are not purposeful in themselves—consciousness did not evolve *in order to allow us to* choose, but once it did evolve by Darwinian capriciousness, it *did in fact* allow us to make choices. Humans have evolved away from having a brain that produces the rigid instincts of the lower animal kingdom to having a brain that is supremely flexible. Without the processes of learning, which are essentially repeated successful episodes of adapting saved up as habit, such a fluid consciousness is not such a lucky accident—such a flexible brain would surely result in humans being eaten by predators. Choice followed by consequences produces learning. Learning repeatedly produces habit, which replaces the need for instinct, in James' view, and increases adaptation to local conditions. A Jamesian mind encourages survival of the fittest thoughts (James, 1890/1983).

Learning as Adaptation to Context: Thorndike's Survival of the Fittest Behavior

From a talk given by Conwy Lloyd Morgan at Harvard on a speaking tour, Thorndike saw that lower animals learn through trial and error: The random pecking by chickens around sweet and sour kernels gradually becomes less random, and then errorless in pecking sweet kernels. What looks like intelligent behavior started out as anything but. Thorndike was therefore always very cautious in ascribing higher cognition to animals, even while he strongly believed in the advanced cognitive abilities of humans (see below). Through his classic dissertation work on trial and error behavior in chickens at Harvard, and then studies of cats escaping from ingenious "puzzle boxes" at Columbia, he formulated the Law of Effect (Thorndike, 1898, 1911): Random behaviors emitted to reach a goal such as food or freedom become "stamped in" if that goal is reached, but "stamped out" if they fail. Of course, these principles became known as positive reinforcement and positive punishment in operant behaviorism; the dissertation also pioneered such notions (under different names) as shaping and fading, stimulus generalization, and the like, but Thorndike preferred the term "connectionism." Connectionism implied that actions—behavioral *or cognitive*—followed by "satisfiers" or "annoyers" would lead eventually to better and better adaptation by an organism to its current environment. In other words, the Law of Effect promotes survival of the fittest behaviors.

Thorndike agreed wholeheartedly with William James that *humans are cognitive beings. Humans select and evaluate things from their environment:*

> All man's behavior is selective. Man does not, in any useful sense of the words, ever absorb, or re-present, or mirror, or copy the situation uniformly. Even when he seems most subservient to the external situation . . . it appears that his sense organs have shut off important features of the situation from him. (Thorndike, 1906, p. 22)

The stimulus was never a "given" to Thorndike, but a result of cognitive selection: The mind's most frequent act is to connect one thing with another, but its highest performance is to think a thing apart from its elements (Thorndike, 1906, p. 133). A teacher can aid his or her pupils first by making it easier for them to see and then select the most adaptive response to stimuli selected consciously out of what Thorndike called the "gross total stimulus situation." He strongly recommended that mathematics not be taught as a closed abstract system, but with reference to the world in which the students will inhabit. For example, there should be many word problems with units of measurement attached to quantities, such as feet, inches, or pounds, and no student should be made to solve a problem that involves, say, seventeen-eighteenths of a dollar. In this way, the teacher is increasing a child's adaptation to context.

Second, once useful connections and strategies have been established, they should be practiced (followed by praise, esteem, or reward—or simply by the self-reinforcement of repeated success) until the response is automatic. Following James, Thorndike believed that such practice of basic skills allows their deployment to become subconscious, thus freeing up the conscious mind to deal with novel or sudden situations, or to increase creativity and the effectiveness of rational thought. This is not rote practice, but adaptive practice. In his massive, three-volume *Educational Psychology* (1911–1913), he demonstrated this idea by showing graphs suggesting that, with extensive practice, telegraph operators' speed and accuracy take tremendous nonlinear leaps once operators learn to process words instead of letters or dots. Practice done right encourages higher-level thinking.

Finally, Thorndike emphasized that one should teach connections in such a way that it ensures that older connections do not have to be broken to learn new ones, that care is taken to build knowledge in a way that minimizes having to go backward in order to go forward. For example, the traditional transitions in mathematics from counting to adding to multiplication of whole numbers to multiplication of fractions can be managed more easily by focusing a child's attention not on counting, but on rules, demonstrated in many settings that themselves differ in step-by-step fashion en route to the desired skill.

Critics of Thorndike's educational psychology, especially, for example, the Gestaltists, accused him of encouraging "piecemeal" or "rote" learning (see Cox, 1997). Nothing could be further from the truth:

> The psychologists of to-day [sic] do not wish to make the learning of arithmetic a mere matter of acquiring thousands of disconnected habits, nor to decrease by one jot the pupil's genuine comprehension of its general truths. They wish him to reason not less than he has in the past, but more. They find, however, that you do not secure reasoning in a pupil by demanding it, and that his learning of a general truth without the proper development of organized habits back of it is likely not to be a rational learning of that general truth, but only a mechanical memorizing of a verbal statement of it. (Thorndike, 1913b, p. 7)

In fact, Thorndike saw himself as in the forefront of overturning the old classical system of education that he saw as having too much rote learning of information that had lost its usefulness. By the twentieth century, teachers in Latin Schools were fighting a rear-guard action in the USA. What had been the lingua franca of the educated world for several hundred years was justifying its existence not by the intrinsic worth of its subject matter, but by how learning Latin, or other difficult subjects, like Greek or Geometry, would provide a foundation for learning other subjects. The discipline and rigor used in such classes, it was said, would easily translate to other material, in much the same way that lifting weights would provide the muscles to lift any object. This approach, known as mental discipline or formal discipline, is very old, but in the late nineteenth century, it had acquired a patina of scientific legitimacy by attaching itself to the notions of recapitulation theory and Lamarckism. Recapitulation theory, known in its sound-bite form as "ontogeny recapitulates phylogeny" suggested that every child was essentially repeating all of the stages of biological and cultural evolution in his or her own lifetime. Lamarckian mechanisms added on each new stage of evolution from the experiences of each generation. This doctrine of inheritance of acquired characteristics implied that you could pass your learning down to your children, improving their genetic lot while avoiding the dreaded consequences of hereditary degeneration. Conveniently, some educators also found a rationale for forcing children to memorize and recite Latin declensions because children of the age in which this was typically learned are reliving a primitive era of human development, when memorization of concrete details was supposedly done using repetition (Gould, 1977)!

Thorndike thought all this to be ludicrous. He never bought either Lamarckism or Recapitulation as evolutionary mechanisms, opting instead for Mendelism and natural selection early and throughout his career. As for formal discipline, he said it was a theory that likens ability to "amounts of something which can be stored on a bank, to be drawn on at leisure" (Thorndike, 1903, p. 85). If it were true, said Thorndike and his Columbia colleague Robert Woodworth, then learning of new tasks would be easy, and a learned skill would transfer easily to a new situation requiring that skill. Instead, in a series of simple but telling experiments (Thorndike & Woodworth, 1901a, 1901b, 1901c) they discovered that individuals trained on the task of estimating areas of a range of shapes and sizes would become near perfect after several trials; when the subjects were expected to use the same rule of cognitive judgments (e.g., "I tend to judge this with a minus error") on a new range of shapes and sizes, their accuracy would drop to about 50%. Thus, reasoned Thorndike and Woodworth, the skills learned in one setting do not expand the mind's raw capability; instead, only the "identical elements" of thought between the two tasks should transfer. Once again, Thorndike focused on adaptability to local conditions as the hallmark of his educational philosophy.

Dewey: The Reflex Arc in a Social System of Meaning

The similarities between the views of Thorndike and Dewey at the beginnings of their careers are often overlooked, possibly because they arrived at these views in different ways. Dewey also came to psychology and to his later philosophy through James, but Dewey was already in his 30s when James' *The Principles of Psychology* was published; in order to make the shift, Dewey would have to first dump G. W. F Hegel—the Idealists' Idealist. Simultaneously, in order to deal with the Darwinian paradigm shift and modern physiology, he would have to dump the Classical doctrine of "ideas" as well. As early as 1884, Dewey was claiming that the notion of simple ideas that combine into complex ideas as mental chemistry, which had run from Locke to John Stuart Mill, was dead. He understood that the "New Psychology" of laboratory introspection *a la* Wundt was in the ascendency, but he himself never subscribed to it (Dewey, 1884). As late as 1890, he was still arguing for an Idealist Hegelian sense of self as a sub-process of a larger consciousness that subsumes everything, the notion of the Absolute (Dewey, 1890/1977). By 1896, though, he had made the switch, and had converted fully to James' parallelism. In his famous article "The reflex arc concept in Psychology" (Dewey, 1896), he argues that reflex response cannot be divided into segments of stimulus-idea-response or peripheral stimulation followed by central nervous system idea followed by muscular response. Rather, there is no need for physiological processes to change into ideas and back again, because according to parallelism, the electrical activity of the nervous system and the flow of experience are two views of the same process. In fact, Dewey goes further. First, he notes that stimuli and responses are not separate from one another, but part of a continuous, moment by moment, ongoing spiraling process of coordination: Stimuli and responses were functions, not things. To separate them is to misunderstand the process of adaptation. Second, the process is one of transformation of *meaning*: When a girl responds to a hot candle flame by withdrawing her hand, the flame now has a connotation of pain and danger that it did not have before. Although James is barely mentioned in the article, he had clearly gained a convert.

Dewey opened the Laboratory School at University of Chicago in the very same year, and simultaneously began publishing on education virtually. Right away, in "My Pedagogical Creed" (1897), Dewey sets out the central tenets of the theory of education that he would elaborate richly in his masterwork *Democracy and Education* (Dewey, 1916) and for the rest of his life. He claims that education is simultaneously and indivisibly both psychological and social. The child's instincts, powers, habits, tastes, preferences, and importantly, current level of growth all form together the starting point. Education is not preparation for the future, but connected and motivated by tasks for their own sake, and useful at the moment they are learned: That education is literally and all the time its own reward means that no alleged study or discipline is educative unless it is worthwhile in its own immediate having (Dewey, 1916, p. 61).

One reason for this emphasis on the present is that if children are educated to a future purpose, the choice of that future purpose is likely to be wrong. This does not mean that the future should not be considered. On the contrary, educational choices should always be made to further "continuity of growth": Instead of assuming that a static set of lessons in a particular subject will stand the child in good stead, the educator must choose lessons that set the pupil up for "deeper and more expansive learning" later. Such tasks protect the desire to go on learning (Dewey, 1938, p. 48). The "vice of imposed ends" (Dewey, 1916, p. 61) is pernicious.

But at the same time, all of these things must be continually interpreted and translated into terms of their social equivalents. For a school is first and foremost a community whose purpose is to confer the social heredity of an entire culture. The method of doing so is to embed that heredity in countless everyday tasks starting at the youngest age, from home. Knowing how to do those tasks in and for a community forms the ongoing motivation for learning, and the occasions for embedding more abstract lessons. The social community of the school, like the community of the society, will provide the very structure of meaning of the acts of learning, a structure of meaning that the child is fully embedded in, taking from and contributing to, for life.

Dewey criticized the Formal Discipline theory of education for its thoroughgoing reliance on the external imposition—upon a child—of a body of knowledge that has been thoroughly abstracted from context and meticulously categorized and rationalized (See Dewey, 1900/1956, 1916, 1929/1996). In a classical education, for the upper classes, this body of knowledge started from Platonic ideals and worked forward—in other words, it consisted of the study of sublime thought over practical activity. Then this body of knowledge was imposed upon a child by practice in order to strengthen the innate faculties of observation, perception, memory or judgment, and so on (Dewey, 1929/1996). Interestingly, Dewey agrees with Thorndike on a significant point: He believes that extended rote practice is only useful for learning specific skills, not for increasing general abilities (Dewey, 1916).

Evolution

A final area of agreement between Dewey and Thorndike, and one which would foster implicit serious divergences later (neither man seemed to criticize the other by name in public), is the theory of evolution. As was noted above, both men chose Darwin over Lamarck and Haeckel; Lamarckian mechanisms had been used to support modern Formal Discipline Theory. Neither man believed in innate *racial* differences, although as I argue below, Thorndike's hereditarian views tended to support the racial status quo. Race is largely missing in Dewey's educational work,[1] but he was a political liberal all of his life (Westbrook, 1991).

One way to discuss their differences is to recognize that each took different things from Darwin. Thorndike was mindful that Natural Selection over generations led to "divergence of character and extinction of the less-improved forms" (Darwin, 1859). A great number of characteristics vary from small to large, from long to short, and from intelligent to less intelligent. The environment selects adaptive traits from these variables. Thorndike had learned about Galtonian correlations when he moved from Harvard to Columbia to study with Galton's student, James McKeen Cattell. He became a staunch advocate of the virtues of quantitative measurement of human characteristics. He became famous for a statement, repeated in various formulations from 1903 for the rest of his life, for example, "Whatever exists at all, exists in some amount. To know it thoroughly involves knowing its quantity as well as its quality" (Thorndike, 1918, cited in Joncich, 1968, p. 283, n). His preferred method of measurement was the correlation. Individual differences were pervasive, real, and measurable. The question for psychologists was *how much* of those differences were innate.

Although Thorndike was a moderate hereditarian, and although most of the parametric statistics used in social sciences were originated by those associated with the "Galton Chair of Eugenics" at University College, London (see Kevles, 1995), to peg Thorndike as a simple eugenicist would be to miss much subtlety in his thought. As the man who required the first statistics course of graduate students in Education (in 1902), he was to become fairly sophisticated about statistics and genetics. Yes, there is evidence for heritability in psychological characteristics. But he disagreed with Charles Spearman's notion of "general intelligence": Intelligence is not unitary, but composed of many possible skills (as his identical elements research showed), and perhaps not neatly matched up with genes: "The genes do not come out of a dictionary!" he would say (Deary, Lawn, & Bartholomew, 2008; Thorndike, 1940/1969, p. 138). The intercorrelations among abilities do exist, but he noted they are lower than eugenicists would like. And he scathingly denounced the idea that the races have distinctly separate distributions of intelligence as "sheer nonsense" (Thorndike, 1940/1969, p. 148). He made the same point for gender differences: The degree of overlap of a characteristic in the two gender distributions generally outweighs the mean differences, if any. If eugenics is possible, he had theoretically calculated that breeding would take much longer to have an effect than generally supposed. But, inheritance is significant, and in some cases, great.

> Philanthropists and reformers have suffered from extreme ignorance of human inheritance. Some of their proposals seem valid only if traits acquired by a person are perpetuated in his genes and offspring (Lamarckism); but they are not. Some are valid only if the original unborn individual differences among men are very slight [environmentalism]; but they are very great. Some of the hopes of devotees of eugenics also seem to assume a simplicity of the gene determination of important human qualities which is quite out of harmony with the evidence. (Thorndike, 1940/1969, pp. 191–192, bracketed information added)

He then goes on to explain the phenomenon of regression toward the mean would mean that many high-value persons who produced offspring would produce children with more average abilities, and that many children with outlier abilities are from parents' average in that ability. Finally, he says: "Not a single case of the causation of some highly desirable human trait by one gene has been found" (Thorndike, 1940/1969, pp. 192–193n).

Thorndike did not reject the possibility of eugenic change: He was a progressive after all, and a strong proponent of the value of the scientific method for the betterment of humankind. Some of his statements on the desirability of manipulating the relative likelihood of "good" versus "bad" genes are chilling from our current point of view. He noted that the "estimable" welfare work of reformers ignores the role of genes because to do otherwise would not "gratify the natural impulse to relieve, comfort and console" (Thorndike, 1943, p. 176). And he also deplores a "bigoted antagonism towards any efforts to select better genes for survival" (pp. 176–177). If we could eliminate the possibility of those with hereditary diseases, or very low ability, why would we not do so?

Finally, he noted that everyone at every level has biological determinants in their makeup; that is no excuse for not teaching them. He suggested that teachers be evaluated on the distance that they can move a student from where they started, but not solely so. Biological determination provides an upper limit. But he did not believe that inherited capabilities are good because they are original. "The original tendencies of man … have never been right … only one thing in [man's nature] is unreservedly good, the power to make it better" (Thorndike, 1913a, pp. 281–282).

And yet, even though Thorndike was not an explicitly racist hereditarian, he seems not to have seriously considered that there might be serious defects in a society that needs scientific answers alone. His faith in psychological science as an instrument of human progress had turned social justice into an empirical question. Bad science or bad inferences may have led to the "sheer nonsense" of attributing racial differences in intelligence to innate causes, but the differences remain; besides, good science will fix it. Anything else was not his concern. The educational reformer as a young man had become an old man in 1939 who now saw that the world could only change slowly, and beyond believing that intelligence and morality are positively correlated, he did not seem interested in questioning values. His penchant for measuring everything concretely tended to make things that should be moral questions empirical ones. More to the point for educational methods, his love of measuring everything also required things that can be counted and ranked. Data requires discreteness. Discrete things are fixed. Knowing becomes knowledge. Countable knowledge is static.

Finally, Thorndike was a believer in tests: He created dozens of them and profited by them; he helped found The Psychological Corporation, which to this day publishes the Weschler series of intelligence tests. His graduate student, Fredrick J. Kelly, created the first multiple-choice test for reading in 1914 (Sokal, 1987). By creating the empire of testing, he simultaneously created almost the entire profession of the modern Educational Psychologist, whose métier involves the design and evaluation of sophisticated psychometrics in the service of modern urban school districts. Such tests are deployed by School Psychologists and Special Education teachers as well as administrators everywhere. But it is important to remember that Thorndike's initial impulse for his life's work was scientific progressivism: He wanted to overturn the status quo in education and replace it with an unbiased and objective method of achieving an American Meritocracy[2] in a Darwinian world.

Thorndike's Progressivism became the conservative status quo by redefining a point of view as an objective lack of point of view, and redefining moral questions as scientific ones. Thorndike's source of authority is the impartiality of science in answering questions of "human nature": In his worldview, the job of the scientist is to bring the methodology of psychological science to bear on questions such as *how much* intelligence is determined by heredity, presumably avoiding ideology. By framing questions in this way, he did as much as anyone to professionalize Psychology and Education. But among the social sciences, Psychology is the discipline most invested in universalist objectivity, and psychometrics was the way this was achieved. Thorndike never seemed to question the very idea of meritocracy, the inequalities that thwart it, or the negative byproducts of scientific administration. The testing technology that Thorndike promoted was intended to be content neutral, or at the very least, the content would be either agreed upon by those educated technocrats who make the tests, or extracted by counting the frequency of material in existing texts and tests. In spite of Thorndike's early commitment to adaptive learning, the tests become about methodology of testing content, not evaluating the process of learning. Ellen Condliffe Lagemann (2000), in her institutional history of educational research, points out that Thorndike had constructed a theory of education without watching teachers teach. Is it any wonder that his tests, created for the use of a proliferating class of educational administrators, become used as measures of "accountability?"

Dewey, by contrast, often seemed to understand that educational methods had broader, sometimes hidden, societal consequences. Specifically, he worried that a biological eugenic's argument was being used by the upper classes to justify their own rule. Characteristically, instead of attacking this view directly, he built from the ground up an alternate view of how heredity works.

In contrast to the Galtonian view that individual differences in intelligence were heritable from the distant evolutionary past, for Dewey, intelligence is intelligent action *now*: adaptive activity in current circumstances. The notion of adaptation, to be sure, was taken from Darwin (and James) and Dewey was not above making extrapolations from primitive, or as he was wont (unfortunately) to say, "savage" man. But the savage is a metaphor, and always in Dewey, the savage, by surviving through the invention of tools, is not doing something primitive that we have outgrown, but doing exactly what *we* should be doing: solving current problems through ingenuity and continuous testing. He did not want to use scientific methodology to measure the results of education (and presumably hold teachers and administrators accountable); he wanted to infuse the modern progressive spirit of scientific inquiry into education itself. When children at the Dewey School were directed to imagine how primitive humans survived, it was to encourage a discussion (beginning at age seven) on how human ingenuity helped us survive in a hostile battle of man against nature (one of these ways was to know nature: its topography, its geography, the local flora, fauna, and water sources). The Dewey students, like prehistoric humans, also made their own tools (Mayhew & Edwards, 1936/1966). To Dewey, solving a problem—particularly one that you chose to solve, in the living context and moment that you need to solve it—is how real knowledge is gained. This is an epistemology of intelligent action.

"Heredity means nothing more nor less than the original endowment of the individual" (Dewey, 1916, p. 43). The child is not doomed to recapitulate his or her past evolution; education is about escaping the past, not repeating it. The curriculum of the Dewey School focused on the *social history* of humans from primitive societies, through village life, through modern times, and *not* a recapitulationist history (Mayhew & Edwards, 1936/1966). How a hereditary capability was used in the past does not determine its adaptive use today. Furthermore, "these original capacities are much more varied and potential, even in the case of the more stupid, than we as yet know properly how to utilize" (Dewey, 1916, p. 43). Dewey recognizes that heredity theoretically limits education, but it is difficult to determine each individual's limitations. Accordingly, the teacher's job is to educate the child in front of us, not to categorize and rank her prematurely on a dubious construct of ostensible innate intelligence.

Dewey realized that Rousseau's "natural man," alone and separate from human society, cannot exist. By the same token, spontaneous normal ontogenetic development is "pure mythology" (p. 64). Nature, he says, develops in accordance with the uses to which it is put. And, as we shall see, to Dewey, education is *guided growth*: "Guidance is not external imposition. *It is freeing the life process for its own most adequate fulfillment*" (Dewey, 1902, p. 17, italics in original). These views on heredity and development show him to be a true constructivist, because growth is determined neither by genetics nor learning, but is, to use a modern term, epigenetic in character. And, of course, the acquisition of knowledge comes as an impetus from the child, and is radically active rather than passive (see below).

Finally, those of us who actually read Darwin recognize that one of the great pleasures of *The Origin of Species* is the web-like interconnection of all life: The interdependence of birds, mistletoe, and trees; the way in which a fenced-in area of fir trees on a barren heath can develop an entire new ecosystem over time—these are aspects that balance "nature red in tooth and claw" (originally from Alfred Lord Tennyson, 1850) and "survival of the fittest" (originally from Herbert Spencer (1851) but co-opted by Darwin in later editions of the *Origin*) with countervailing pressures. Dewey, who began his adult life as a Hegelian scholar, is comfortable with the kind of systemic thinking, and the dynamic dialectic found in a Darwinian view of nature. Well before a child could be introduced to Darwin's proper theory, the Dewey school would embed the notion of the interdependence of humans in nature. To take one of many examples, children would be introduced to coal from their natural home appreciation of it—as fuel. Coal would be weighed, burnt, and weighed again; then they might be introduced to the concepts of fossil plants, coal beds, coal mines, miners, and mining procedures (Mayhew & Edwards, p. 43). Dewey also believed that Darwin "naturalized" philosophy—he made philosophy testable (Dewey, 1909). But I have been unable to find anything in Dewey's work on education that is a justification for ranking of pupils by ability. Given that Thorndike considered individual differences in ability to be a fact of nature guaranteed by Darwin, this is a radical position.

Education as Socially Centered Intelligent Action: Dewey's Constructivism

John Dewey was perhaps unique among the theorists of his day in having created a philosophy of education that begins with a constructivist epistemology rooted in pragmatism and works its way up to a critique of the structure of modern society. Although his practical experience in education was limited to approximately eight years (1896–1904), founding and supervising the famous "Laboratory School" (informally called the "Dewey School") affiliated with the University of Chicago, his publication history in the philosophy of education was life-long, beginning in 1890 and running through 1938. In fact, he said that his classic *Democracy and Education* (1916) was the best summary of his entire philosophy in a single book (Letter to Horace Kallen, July, 1, 1916, cited in Westbrook, 1991, p. 168). There have been many analyses of this work over the last century (e.g., Tomlinson, 1997), and it is not my purpose to discuss these efforts here. Still less is it my task to chronicle the vast influence Dewey has had on Education, broadly speaking. I want to confine my comments here to two large issues: First, I will address how an individual learns under Dewey's constructivist epistemology and then I will note the positive and negative influences of society on the child's processes of learning. It will soon become apparent that however much he may have agreed with Thorndike on the need to reform education away from Classicism and Formal Discipline toward current adaptation, the purpose of those reforms is not to find objective ways of measuring and promoting the *best* students to succeed, but to create *equal* citizens of Democracy devoted to free inquiry. He wanted educational systems to avoid the "vice of imposed ends" and to promote personal and cultural "growth." In the end, Dewey's critiques of the educational system and society are almost shockingly relevant to the current day, not to mention to "constructivism in an age of accountability."

Principles of Dewey's Constructivism: How Learning Happens

The impetus for learning is goal-directed and an ongoing construction of meaning. Stimulus-response learning, when it occurs, is unconscious and not intelligent action, which is conscious, provisional, adaptive and risky. All actions have objects. To act on an object is to have a goal (Dewey, 1916). The goal is adaptation, from disequilibrium to assimilation, eliminating extraneous movements and setting up for the next action (p. 17). Direction is simultaneous and successive (p. 18). "all direction is but redirection; it shifts what is already going on into another channel" (p. 31).

Although Dewey was aware of stimulus-response (or, following Thorndike, trial and error) psychology, he did not choose it. For Dewey (1896) a response is not *to* a stimulus but *into* a stimulus: Once one has responded, a stimulus' meaning has been changed by the consequences of the action. The same stimulus could mean different things depending on the goal of the action. Meaning and purpose drive action: Stimulus and response have no independent existence: "When I hear a noise and run and get water and put out a blaze, I act intelligently; the sound meant fire, and fire meant need of being extinguished" (p. 35).

But by 1902, in *The child and the curriculum*, he had elucidated the different ways in which the child sees his or her goals, and how that clashes with the adult-derived curriculum:

> But we have here sufficiently fundamental divergences: first, the narrow but personal world of the child against the impersonal but infinitely extended world of space and time; second, the unity, the single wholeheartedness of a child's life, and the specializations and divisions of the curriculum; third, an abstract principle of logical classification and arrangement, and the practical and emotional bonds of a child's life. (Dewey, 1902, p. 7)

As the child grows older, the process of knowing becomes a continuous feedback loop of experience that starts with an anticipation, prediction or hypothesis, and is followed by affirmation or contradiction, followed again by refining of hypotheses, gathering of more information, and forming a tentative conclusion. All thinking involves risk: "Where there is reflection there is suspense" (Dewey, 1916, p. 183). This of course is Pragmatism: It is based on the notion that knowledge results from what you do to test an idea, and therefore is bound up with methods. Fortunately, there are many methods of investigation: Their results either cohere with and converge on one another or a method, when applied, uncovers a contradiction (James, 1907). Reflection or thinking "makes it possible to act with an end in view. ... Thinking, in other words, is the intentional endeavor to discover specific connections between something that we do and the consequences which result" (p. 81). To be sure, the capacity for reflection increases with age: A young child acts "to see what happens"; with age, action is gradually brought into alignment with complex ends (Mayhew & Edwards, 1936/1966). But the end of all this, ultimately, is adaptation to ever-changing circumstance. Dewey's intelligent action requires conscious foresight: "To be conscious is to be aware of what we are about: conscious signifies the deliberate, observant, planning traits of activity" (p. 58).

The goals for knowledge come first and foremost from within the child, based on the child's current interest and state of knowledge. They could hardly come from anywhere else. But the questions a child will have will come from the culture the child is immersed in and concerned with becoming a member of. This is useful to the educator.

One of the defining aspects of constructivism is the active construction of knowledge from the child's point of view. Traditional education, even in Dewey's day, required only that a child acquiesce to the program of culture to be put into him. William Torrey Harris, the commissioner of education at the turn of the twentieth century, said that a child's role is "to receive, to accept. His part is fulfilled when he is 'ductile and docile'" (cited in Westbrook, 1991, p. 98); Dewey used these same words as the foil to contrast with his own view of an active child in 1902 (Dewey, 1902, p. 8). Piaget famously said that "to understand is to invent" (Piaget, 1948), recognizing that passive education is not only boring and coercive, but that for a child to copy the state of a teacher's mind is literally impossible. Dewey also knew that a child must act to learn, from his or her own standpoint. Therefore, an educational aim must be based on the intrinsic needs and habits of the one to be educated (Dewey, 1916). Each child, each parent, and each community vary in these needs and habits, so although it may seem a quixotic goal to start with a child's suggestions, they help to diagnose where to start with that child; such an approach has a practical as well as a doctrinal appeal. In the Dewey School, this was a general principle. Teaching involves suggestion and learning involves imitation, to be sure, but they are to aid, not initiate:

> Both must serve as added stimuli to bring forth more adequately what the child is already blindly striving to do. It was accordingly adopted as a general principle that *no activity should be originated by imitation. The start must come from the child through suggestion; help may then be supplied in order to assist him to realize more definitely what it is that he wants.* (Mayhew & Edwards, 1936/1966, p. 61, italics in original)

At the Dewey School, teachers carefully collaborated on what that curriculum should be in frequent meetings. Indeed, the principle of self-direction was extended to teachers: "Mr. Dewey had the greatest real faith of any educator I have known in the classroom teacher's judgment in what children can and should do" said George Myers, a Professor of Mathematics at University of Chicago and the School of Education (Mayhew & Edwards, 1936/1966, p. 366n). In other words, there is little need for the deadening hand of administrators to enforce *accountability* when teachers are fully *responsible*. As the school grew, some specialization into "departments" and more traditional subjects became necessary, but the same collaborative spirit held. Apparently only after Dewey left were formal tests introduced. Mayhew and Edwards' (1936/1966) memoir of the Dewey School does not mention tests once except in the negative. They called this change "reactionary." Charles Judd replaced Dewey at the University of Chicago and immediately took the school and the Department of Education in a Thorndikian direction, encouraging the use of laboratory research in Education (Lagemann, 2000).

Dewey noted: "The vice of externally-imposed ends has deep roots. Teachers receive them from superior authorities. ... As a first consequence, the intelligence of the teachers is not free. ... Too rarely is the teacher so free from the dictates of authoritative supervisor, textbook on methods, prescribed course of study, etc., that he can let his mind come into close quarters with the pupil's mind and the subject matter. This distrust of the teacher's experience is then reflected back in lack of confidence in the responses of the pupils" (Dewey, 1916/2016, p. 127).

The power to grow, intrinsic motivation—"cumulative movement toward a later action" (p. 49)*—is innate*: Growth is a central idea in Dewey's educational philosophy. The drive to grow is the central motor of all education: "We do not have to draw out or educe positive activities from a child, as some educational doctrines would have it. Where there is life there are already eager and impassioned activities. Growth is not something done to them; it is something they do" (p. 49). The notion of growth in *Democracy and Education* (1916/2016) is pervasive, yet vague. Perhaps the idea is more practically expressed by Mayhew and Edwards' (1936/1966, p. 60) thoughts on selecting activities for a curriculum: "Each activity, because of its intimate relation to the needs of life, calls for expansion and enlargement, creates a demand for further activity, reveals a further need, and suggests something to satisfy that need, brings in new controls, new materials, and more refined modes of activity. The little child's liking for novelty and variety, his need for renewed stimulus, are satisfied and supplied with no sacrifice of the unity of his experience." When Dewey realized that his educational philosophy had led too many progressive educators to confuse his approach with "child-centered learning" he came up with a more precise definition and set of examples. One must first ask the question: "Does this form of growth create conditions for further growth, or does it set up conditions that shut off the person who has grown in this particular direction from the occasions, stimuli, and opportunities for continuing growth in new directions?" (Dewey, 1938, p. 29). For example, learning to speak creates a motive to speak and provides a tool to gain wider experience. Learning to read does the same thing. This is similar to Piaget's notion of "the widening grasp of consciousness": Piaget (1976/2015) as a child, immersed in experience, is helped to see and grab hold of larger and larger pieces of experience. This is what Dewey (1916/2006) would call a freeing of activities, except that whereas Piaget focused on logico-mathematical thought, Dewey's domains are much wider, and contain ideas of nature, culture, social structure, and history. *All meaning is social, and therefore the curriculum should reflect and inculcate this culture, and reinforce the lesson that all learning is done in a community where each has a job to do and a contribution to make.*

So far, we have discussed that all actions have meaningful goals, that those goals should originate with the child's intrinsic interests, and that education is about freeing of activities for their "most adequate development." If we add to that that Dewey was against formally constructed curricula and tests, we arrive at the Dewey "progressive educator" caricature and cliché. If we had stopped there, a reader might conclude that the label "child-centered" in its most pejorative sense applies. To some degree, Dewey's own abstract, lofty, and idealistic writing style is to blame, but if we look at what was actually taught at the Dewey School, we find a more sophisticated view. If the teacher can find the crossover point between what is being taught and something that the child wants to know, then, as every good teacher knows, internal motivations replace external rewards. Children naturally want to be a part of the activities around them, and to identify with the older children and adults in their lives.

In the Dewey School, the mechanism for drawing children into the intrinsic reinforcements of meaningful life was the "occupation" (Palermo, 1992). The curriculum began at about age four with "household occupations" that a child saw in his or her daily life, such as (for both boys and girls) cooking, sewing, and carpentry. Dewey promoted these activities not because he was in favor of the so-called Manual Training Movement. He was highly skeptical of any limited form of industrial or occupational training for its own sake, or worse, for the sake of preparing the lower classes for a limited role in industrial work (Labaree, 2011). Neither are they merely meant to make book-learning more interesting and palatable to young students, although they clearly do provide an initial impetus to engage in reading, measuring and math in order to solve problems (Mayhew & Edwards, 1936/1966). Rather, they are the primary mechanism for the "freeing of activity" or furthering of growth that is central to his method, and they should be taught to everyone, regardless of class. They have an almost moral dimension (see DeFalco, 2010):

> For in schools, occupations are not carried on for pecuniary gain but for their own content. Freed from extraneous associations and from the pressure of wage-earning, they supply modes of experience which are intrinsically valuable; they are truly liberalizing in quality. Gardening, for example, need not be taught either for the sake of preparing future gardeners, or as an agreeable way of passing time. It affords an avenue of approach to knowledge of the place farming and horticulture have had in the history of the race and which they occupy in present social organization. (Dewey, 1916, p. 235)

For the young child, there was little difference between play and work, but there were innumerable positive byproducts of focusing on making of cultural artifacts for specific purposes. The most famous of these in the Dewey School era is the "clubhouse" for the debating club constructed by the 13-year-old group, with considerable collaborative help from younger children according to their abilities, but by the time this project was done, such creations were almost routine to the children. They had cooked their lunches (with measuring, weighing, and calculating) virtually every day. They had made "primitive" lean-to's in the forest like early humans, and learned the interdependence of humans with nature. They had furnished a Colonial Era room with furniture they had made themselves and pottery they had made themselves, fired in a kiln they had built themselves. They had experimented rigorously on various combinations of metals for alloys, determining why the mixture of metals for pewter was valued. Before the Colonial Era was studied, they had made maps and tracked explorations for the discovery of the New World. They did not so much study division of labor as they practiced it. Everyone had a "job to do," which provided an impulse to learn about occupations in the larger world, and gave the children the sense that all products, all technologies were the products of someone's labor. And they learned that to do big things required dividing up tasks, coordinating, and cooperating. Such practices also tended to cut down the need for external discipline, because not only is reward intrinsic to the work, but also everyone knows implicitly and explicitly that they are responsible to the community for the quality of their work. If all works well, all members of the community can be proud of their contributions to the whole.

> These occupations of both play and work become direct instrumentalities for the execution of meaning. They became magnets for gathering and retaining an indefinitely wide scope of intellectual considerations. They became avenues along which and by means of which the feeling, thinking, acting child grew into greater power, ability, and sympathetic understanding of himself in relation to the physical and social world; they led to the discovery of the spiritual quality of value that attaches itself to things that are of use and to relationships that are held dear. (Mayhew & Edwards, 1936/1966, pp. 266–267)

A curriculum that supports growth is one based on the interplay of social, technological, and political history, evaluated by a process of experimentation and hypothesis testing. Dewey understood, though, that dialectically opposing the impulses from a child are the forces of culture. Parents and teachers have an interest in continuing societal norms. As a social constructivist, Dewey believed that all meaning is social, all education is communication, and all communication is potentially educative (Dewey, 1916, 1917; see Brinkmann, 2013). As an erstwhile Hegelian, he clearly understood that a culture constructs a child's sense of self, and the actions of individuals constitute the culture. Thus, he never avoided questions of curriculum, and was as concerned with what should be taught as well as how it should be taught. The theory of occupations is the sociocultural mechanism to take a child from his own interests to the social meanings in community. What of the road after that? An examination of the curriculum of the Dewey School (Mayhew & Edwards, 1936/1966), and his other early writings (Dewey, 1902, 1915, 1916) suggests that three strands of knowing are integrated into a curriculum. As noted earlier, knowledge of nature is essential to Dewey's system. How might primitive individuals have survived in nature? What might they have known about the terrain, the plants and animals and the weather? What might they have known, and what do we need to know? Second, how did invention of technology out of nature promote human survival and advancement? And finally, how did human societies develop from a relatively primitive social structure to modern democracies? These three strands of nature, technology, and social progress are tied together. Technology, from lean-to shelters and bows and arrows, to farming, to the modern industrial implements of life wrests from nature what humans need, and provides distinctive occupations and social structures to bring about the changes and prosper from them.

The two essential areas of curriculum for Dewey were History and Science. As Fallace (2009) masterfully describes, Dewey fashioned his theory of History to avoid several of the pitfalls of his contemporaries. He rejected Hegel's metaphysical idealistic teleology, scientific positivism, recapitulation theory, sociological historicism, and elements of Herbart's cultural epoch theory. The dialectic of spirit does not guarantee the forward march of history; neither does the march of science in and of itself. There are no transcendent laws of change. Dewey realized that recapitulation was biologically incompatible with Darwinism (see above), so one cannot wait until certain "stages" appear in a child to teach certain topics: Culture is not in the genes. Finally, neither does sociological progress follow a certain path: That history has taken this route does not mean that it must have taken it, although Dewey recognizes that as with natural selection, later eras are more likely to incorporate the successes of earlier eras, and therefore, social organization tends toward more complexity.

Fallace (2009) calls Dewey's view of History "pragmatic historicism." History develops contextually, through successive adaptations. In order to understand the meaning of culture in the present, you must understand the history that led up to it, even if it was built contingently through time. The meaning of the present *is its history*. Because all knowledge is gained by "intelligent action," the child needs to find some way to experience history directly. Therefore Dewey and the teachers at the Laboratory School started with "savage" or "primitive" social organization and worked their way up, not because the sequence had been in any way foreordained, but because in order to truly understand the later more complex developments, a student needs to understand the earlier, simpler phases first, or at least what modern society takes to be simpler.

None of this means that one need postpone the modern world entirely. The scientific method of investigation can proceed in parallel with an exploration of cultural growth, even though science took epochs to develop. One could, for example, examine metallurgy in a scientific way while discussing the discovery of metals. The process of deciding how to test the principles of leverage can be explored in the context of the discovery of levers. Indeed, one of the more challenging aspects of teaching in the Laboratory School was how to elicit possible hypotheses for testing from the interests of the children themselves, come to agreement, set out a plan, test and evaluate, get results, and repeat if necessary. If teachers could find ways that the discovery was made historically, and do the original test in some form, so much the better. Finally, to consolidate their knowledge, children would share with others what they learned by creating a little stage play of the process, performed for the entire school assembly.

An initial read of the curriculum could lead someone to believe that the teachers were following a recapitulatory curriculum, but in the full context of Dewey's theory (largely developed in in the 1890s: Fallace, 2008, 2009), one sees that they were engaged in a much more challenging and sophisticated task. Any curriculum that becomes entirely set runs the risk of becoming the dead, codified, rationalized lesson plans of the past. Such plans could be taken by administrators and imposed from outside, which would run the risk of not matching the needs of teachers and their students in their moments of learning. This is just as much common practice today as it was in Dewey's time, of course. He was against education by "The Classics," and a rote method of teaching them as much as some are against "The Common Core" and the standardized way of testing it today.

For all this sophistication, Dewey appears to have largely avoided a truly radical approach for his day. There is very little explicit mention of race in any of his educational writings, even though Dewey is known to have been a progressive for his time on the issue (Westbrook, 1991). His approaches to child development, history, and science are all linear and progressive, and therefore, ethnocentric (Fallace, 2010). To avoid this charge, he would have had to develop a curriculum that views all cultures equally, and he did not. To Dewey, a "savage" who discovered fire was a genius in his day, but that does not mean that that culture has much to offer modern society currently. In spite of the fine contributions of diverse past cultures, some cultures are still behind others. It was to Dewey a simple fact of history that Native Americans, faced with the "superior" weaponry of the Western Colonialists, would be in dire trouble, even if neither group was biologically or culturally inferior to the other overall.

To some, such as Margonis (2009), Dewey's implicit progressivist view of history, that history marches forward from savage to democrat is enough to undermine his whole program. Margonis points out that, in spite of his position that manual training is and should not be classist in nature for the presumably white children in the Dewey School, he praised just such a curriculum for black children in *Schools for tomorrow* (Fallace & Fantozzi, 2015). To be sure, Dewey was concerned that these children learn a trade to help their families, and this trade would lead to increased self-confidence that would eventually help them rightfully take their place as equals to other races, but Dewey never seemed to suggest that they simply *demand* the right to better schools as equals.

Thorndike and Dewey on Democracy

E. L. Thorndike was a scientific progressive in education, not in politics, especially as his life wore on. He generally voted Republican, including for the opponents of F. D. R. (Joncich, 1968), but although he was always in demand for speaking engagements, he was careful not to support specific political causes in public. Instead, he preferred to present himself as an unbiased booster of science itself, advocating above all for the professionalism of educational and psychological researchers. His political positions were implied in his scientific statements about how human nature worked; therefore unearthing them requires some detective work.

The best source for his later beliefs is his final book, *Human Nature and the Social Order*, funded by the Carnegie Corporation and published in

1940 after a decade of planning and work. The original version was more than 1000 pages, with many tables and figures, and data ranging from rank ordering of human desires and wants, the relationship between intelligence and status in society, the pay of various managerial occupations and so on. An abridged version of about a third in length was issued in 1969, removing much of the outdated data, but leaving Thorndike's views intact (Thorndike, 1940/1969), including his views on values, philanthropy, welfare, economics, government, and law.

The overarching themes of Thorndike's life come through in this book. If, as he said, everything that exists, exists in some amount and can be measured, then "We have the possibility and desirability of a natural science of values" (Thorndike, 1940/1969, p. 158). He claims that if we knew the list of things valued and the weights of these for "all sentient beings" we could make a science of value as objective as of anything else. He then sets out to make such a list of the good life or "Desirable Provisions to be Made for Man," proposing such impractical dependent variables as, for example, "maintenance of the inner causes of joy of living at or above their present average" (Thorndike, 1940/1969, pp. 180–181).

Thorndike's project is clearly a universalist one; he was, in principle, proposing that science come up with a rational way for figuring out how to better the lot of humanity. He exhorts educated experts like himself to create the methodology for improving the lot of humanity, and as such can be seen as a liberal technocratic elitist, a common enough type of intellectual in the first Progressive Era, but a position that was explicitly rejected by Dewey, who disliked intellectual oligarchies as much as economic ones (Westbrook, 1991).

This is exemplified by the second theme of the book: That individual differences in capabilities, talents, and tastes are endemic and ineradicable among humans. Thorndike sees this as mere tough-minded practicality, consistent with Darwin and measured by Galtonian correlations. The belief allows him to suggest that though factory work may be repetitive and monotonous to him, many factory workers would nevertheless freely choose to do it, considering the alternatives.

Finally, Thorndike's opinions on larger economic issues are pro-capitalist and anti-socialist. He notes in a section on "Misleading attitudes towards capital" that humanitarians who "lament that capital receives more than its due and labor less than theirs" fail to note that the only ways to increase income is for workers to become more efficient, or for people to invest in capital goods: "Those who lament the high ratio of the wages of capital to the wages of labor seem unwilling to heed the fact that the cure for the evil that they attribute to capital is to have more of it" (p. 235). He did not claim that unions are bad; he seemed to think that working for oneself was the best circumstance, but that science could help unions improve working conditions; teachers' unions were good, but he did wish that they would set aside some of their dues for scientific investigations of pedagogy. Again and again, he emphasizes that the chief issue is finding out and matching people's talents to jobs, and that science is the cure to making jobs more enjoyable, governments more just, and life more fulfilling.

Thorndike's views were the received wisdom of their day among those of his class and generation, but were made to seem modern by the removal of religion and the addition of science. They were also highly meritocratic and individualistic, but universalistic, in the sense that sociological analysis of America's power imbalances by race or class was almost entirely absent. Not to put too fine a point on it, but Thorndike's analysis was also almost entirely white, as was Dewey's.

For a book entitled *Democracy and Education* (1916/2016), there is remarkably little discussion of democracy. This is in spite of the fact that Dewey was a committed public intellectual and activist from the time he arrived in Chicago, and continuing throughout his life. There are some early stories of Dewey as a distracted absent-minded professor, and in his personal demeanor he appears, both early and late, to be a mild-mannered New Englander. But his marriage to Alice Chipman Dewey in 1886 appears to have given him permission to move away from the abstractions of Hegel and quasi-religious moralism to a more concrete engagement with the world, even after Alice became somewhat embittered and sad following the death of two of their sons; she was also ousted from her position as Principal of the Laboratory School, which precipitated the Deweys' move from Chicago to New York. John Dewey was known to be a liberal at least from the time he arrived in Chicago: He immediately sympathized with labor on the famous Pullman strike, worked with Jane Addams to uplift the poor and the working class at Hull House, voted to the left (in the 1930s he voted to the left of F.D.R.), and lent his famous name to the founding of the NAACP (National Association for the Advancement of Colored People), the ACLU (American Civil Liberties Union), and the New School for Social Research (Ryan, 1995; Westbrook, 1991). He served as the first president of the professors' union, the AAUP (American Association of Universities Professors). Virtually all of this had happened before or around the publication of *Democracy and Education*, but none of it made it into the book. After its publication, he marched for the women's suffrage movement and wrote frequently for the liberal magazine

The New Republic, and occasionally for *The Nation*. *Democracy and Education* was meant to be a textbook; perhaps Dewey thought that expressing his political views would weaken the impact of his arguments. One of his biographers claims that in an era largely before academic tenure, he might have been cautious in the years before and during the First World War about expressing his opinions in his philosophical work; not a few professors at his own institution lost their jobs for it (Westbrook, 1991).

"The democratic conception in education" is the chapter of *Democracy and Education* that deals most directly with democracy. It is a short chapter mostly concerned with an historical review of philosophy of education, but the centrality of the chapter for the book, and for Dewey's life, activism and thought, cannot be denied. For Dewey, education and meaning are social, but people belong to many groups of which they are ideally freely associated members. We cannot choose our family or race, but freedom of association is one of the cornerstones of American Democracy. Dewey most famously said that democracy was more than a form of government: "it is primarily a mode of associated living, of conjoint communicated experience" (Dewey, 1916, p. 50). Participation in groups and our responsibilities to other people in them make us who we are, but if we communicate only to the fellow members in our interest groups or classes, our discourse becomes selfish, and our subculture becomes insular and sterile. Democracy can only become a "conjoint communicated experience" if we seek common ground with other groups outside of our habitual social haunts.

Dewey was firmly against class divisions. Although he recognized that city children must have different training than rural children, he approved of vocational education not because it provided "good workers" to employers, but because he wished to erase the divide in American education between practical education for the lower classes and Platonic academic education for the upper classes. He included manual tasks for kids of the upper-middle class (see above), precisely because such training required cooperation among all children of the community, and thus fostered the ability to work together required in a democracy. If we begin early enough, both the attitude of democrats, and the belief in the importance of individual action and responsibility will become second nature to a child. She will be eager to contribute her own individual talents to the community as a whole.

Freedom of association is also key to Dewey's long commitment to Democratic Socialism, albeit a Democratic Socialism of his own devising. He was clearly not a Marxist or an advocate of violent overthrow of the Capitalist system. Revolutionary force would devalue the independence required for "intelligent action." As time went on, he realized that the Soviet experiment had devolved into the brutality of Stalin's regime; it could hardly have ended up otherwise, since virtually all Russian social reform had been and continued to be authoritarian and top down. So he became a staunch anticommunist socialist. He was not much of a state socialist either. He was not a supporter of Franklin Delano Roosevelt, whom he thought was too concerned with saving capitalism from itself: He voted for Eugene Debs before, and the Socialist Party's Norman Thomas during the F.D.R. years. When he realized that the very term socialist was anathema to most Americans, and that the then current Socialist Party was itself mired in orthodoxy, he started, and failed miserably to continue, a socialist third party without the name.

His biographers (Ryan, 1995; Westbrook, 1991) have spilt much ink trying to determine just what sort of socialist Dewey was; he comes nearest to what has been called Guild Socialism. In Guild Socialism, people naturally and voluntarily associate into groups according to their individual diverse interests. The groups thus formed become work councils associated with various jobs and professions, and act as checks to the concentration of economic and social power that is endemic to capitalist "oligarchies"[3] Above these various lobbies would be the government itself, which is theoretically given a much broader mandate from the people at large. One form this takes, of course, is unions, and Dewey was an indefatigable champion of teachers' unions and professorial unions from the beginning of the movement. The guilds in this system, however, do not just negotiate better pay and working conditions, but overall more fulfilling, less alienated forms of work.

Dewey believed strongly in individual autonomy as the cornerstone of democracy, but he was not a follower of Locke or John Stuart Mill. Rather, because all meaning is social, each individual is constructed through cooperation with and in obligation to others. Individuality is not a starting point or a given. At the Dewey School, individual experimentation was balanced with social obligation.

Dewey had a faith in the individual action of *equal* individuals. Thus, he refused to put his faith in elites, even, or especially in a liberal technocratic elite (Westbrook, 1991). Because each of us may belong to many interest groups simultaneously, Guild Socialism means that we advocate for ourselves and against the concentrated powers of Capitalism from within the diverse solidarities that we choose. But it is neither a melting pot, nor a multicultural vision. There are not multiple democracies for Dewey; there is the one democracy that results from all of us having been educated to see that our diversities overlap. The NAACP, the AFT (American Federation of Teachers), the AAUP, the AFL-CIO (American Federation of Labor and Congress of Industrial Organizations), even the League of Nations or the Outlawry of War Movement are all groups of voluntary association. The wonder of John Dewey was that even though he was bitterly disappointed by the failure of some of these groups (the latter two among them) he never stopped joining them.

Conclusions: Thorndike and Dewey for a Diverse America?

What, then, can we say about the legacies of these two men, the most influential theorists of American Education in the twentieth century? In the first Progressive Era, both were influenced by evolution to replace the moribund codified classical system with an education defined as adaptation to current circumstances. I believe they were largely successful. But Thorndike was a psychologist, concerned with researching the nature of intelligence and with measuring the effectiveness of educational methods. He was concerned with raising the professionalism of psychologists and educators by promoting a new science, rather than with reforming society itself. As the fields of Psychology, Educational Administration, and even the teaching profession itself were professionalizing at the same time, it is perhaps understandable that Thorndike would focus his efforts for evaluation and change from above and outside the classroom. His love of measuring things led to standardized, marketable tests on arithmetic, reading, writing, geography, reasoning, and handwriting from 1908 to the end of his life, with a particular upsurge in the 1920s, by which time, educational companies were producing such tests in the millions, and continued to do so as the American high school population doubled each decade (Joncich, 1968; Lagemann, 2000). And yet, although the methods described in his many textbooks are often meticulous, the content that is eventually tested is not novel. Furthermore, the very professionalism and scientific objectivity that he promoted tended to downplay questions of value; as noted above, he believed values to be as subject to ranking and empirical validation as any other domain, and he states his lists forthrightly, without argument. Is it any wonder that if content is separated from method in modern testing, that there would be such debate over a "Common Core" today? Is it any wonder that a separation between administration and teaching would lead to an "accountability" regime?[4]

In contrast, the idealized version of the Dewey School seems like a utopia: A community of scholars is led by independent, inventive teachers who encourage experimentation in learning that fosters individual growth and intrinsic motivation in their pupils, without tests or ranking. This ideal community also fosters solidarity: It teaches children that everyone has a "job to do" that makes them responsible to the community and gives them a way to contribute their diverse talents to the whole. The construction of a meaningful self in a meaningful culture leads to a meaningful life with non-alienating work. The norms of value emerge seamlessly from the community itself.

Can this utopia work in an increasingly politically, racially, and economically segregated America? It would seem that one flaw that Dewey and Thorndike shared was the implicit belief that we all held, or potentially held the same values. Can we have a "conjoint communicated experience" of democracy if our freely chosen associations do not overlap? If every school is its own little intentional community built on its own norms, do we face a future of thousands of individual communities not evaluated against one another? Are we willing to continue to accept some utopias that profess creationism and others scientific method or some that accept nationalistic race pride versus others that promote interracial cosmopolitanism? Perhaps the desire to create something optimistically called the "Common Core" is an implicit attempt to force the kind of social agreement that Dewey hoped would rise from the grass roots up, and Thorndike hoped would filter from the highly educated down. But groups that are now, rightly, demanding their own voices are not likely to accept either the homogenization or the implicit advantages of dominant groups that such an approach implies.

Dewey offers a small ray of hope here. As he always hated dualisms, class divisions, and the evils of externally imposed ends on educators, he implied that the methods of other sciences, including Psychology, might not be appropriate for education. In *The Sources of a Science of Education* (Dewey, 1929), he would collapse evaluation into practice. There is a tendency, says Dewey, for administrators to want to use science to raise test scores immediately, and for new or unwise teachers to expect a recipe for teaching. The value of educational science is not in the result of an experiment *on teachers,* or *on students,* with a raise in test scores the immediate result, it is the use of a scientific result *in the minds of teachers imbued by their training with an attitude of engaged inquiry* to adapt that finding to the diverse students in their charge. Professionally responsible teachers, with control over their means of work, would, through "intelligent action" promote an evolution of practice informed by science, their culture, and the lives of their students:

> To suppose that scientific findings decide the value of educational undertakings is to reverse the real case. Actual activities in educating test the worth of the results of scientific results. They may be scientific in some other field, but not in education until they serve educational purposes, and whether they really serve or not can be found out only in practice. The latter comes first and last; it is the beginning and the close: The beginning, because it sets the problems which alone give to investigations educational point and quality; the close, because practice alone can test, verify, modify and develop the conclusions of these investigations. The position of scientific conclusions is intermediate and auxiliary. (Dewey, 1929, pp. 32–33)

Notes

1. Indeed in Mayhew and Edwards' memoir (Mayhew & Edwards, 1936/1966) of how the Dewey School operated, there is virtually no mention of the Civil War or slavery in the curriculum up through age 14.
2. Not that Thorndike himself used the word; the word "meritocracy" entered the language—in a pejorative sense—in 1956, according to the Oxford English Dictionary.
3. Yes, Dewey used this term, chiefly in *Conduct and Human Nature* (1922). His views remind one of the ideas of that other erstwhile Vermonter, Bernie Sanders.
4. And as Lagemann (2000) trenchantly points out, throughout the early twentieth century, the administrators and researchers were almost all men, and the teachers almost all women.

References

Brinkmann, S. (2013). *John Dewey: Science for a changing world.* New Brunswick, NJ: Transaction Publishers.

Coleridge, S. T. (1829/1873). In T. Fenby (Ed.), *Aids to refection in the formation of a manly character on the several grounds of prudence morality and religion.* Liverpool: Edward Howell. Original work published in 1829.

Cox, B. D. (1997). The rediscovery of the active learner in adaptive contexts: A developmental-historical analysis of transfer of training. *Educational Psychologist, 32*, 41–55.

Darwin, C. (1859). *On the origin of species. Or the preservation of favoured races in the struggle for life.* London: John Murray.

Deary, I. J., Lawn, M., & Bartholomew, J. (2008). A conversation between Charles Spearman, Godfrey Thompson, and Edward L. Thorndike: The internal examinations inquiry meetings, 1931–1938. *History of Psychology, 11*, 122–142.

DeFalco, A. (2010). An analysis of John Dewey's notion of occupations – Still pedagogically valuable? *Education and Culture, 26*(1), 82–99.
Dewey, J. (1884). The new psychology. *Andover Review, 2*, 278–289.
Dewey, J. (1887). *Psychology*. New York: Harper Brothers.
Dewey, J. (1890/1977). On some current conceptions of the term "self". *Mind, 15*, 58–74.
Dewey, J. (1896). The reflex arc concept in psychology. *Psychological Review, 3*(4), 357–370.
Dewey, J. (1897). *My pedagogic creed*. New York: E. L. Kellogg & Co.
Dewey, J. (1900/1956). *The school and society*. Chicago: University of Chicago Press.
Dewey, J. (1902). *The child and the curriculum*. Chicago: University of Chicago Press.
Dewey, J. (1909). Darwin's influence on philosophy. *Popular Science Monthly, 75*, 90–98.
Dewey, J. (1915). *The school and society* (revised ed.). Chicago: University of Chicago Press.
Dewey, J. (1916). *Democracy and education*. New York: Macmillan.
Dewey, J. (1917). The need for recovery of a philosophy. In J. Dewey et al. (Eds.), *Essays in a pragmatic attitude*. New York: Henry Holt.
Dewey, J. (1922). *Human nature and conduct: An introduction to social psychology*. New York: Henry Holt.
Dewey, J. (1929). *The sources of a science of education*. New York: Horace Liveright.
Dewey, J. (1929/1996). The quest for certainty. In J. A. Boydston & L. Hickman (Eds.). *The collected works of John Dewey 1882–1953* (Middle Works 9, pp. 200–215). Charlottesville, VA: InteLex.
Dewey, J. (1930). From absolutism to experimentalism. In G. P. Adams & W. P. Montague (Eds.), *Contemporary American philosophy: Personal statements*. New York: The Macmillan Company.
Dewey, J. (1938). *Experience and education*. New York: The Macmillan Company.
Fallace, T. (2008). John Dewey and the savage mind: Uniting anthropological, psychological and pedagogical thought, 1894–1902. *Journal of the History of the Behavioral Sciences, 44*, 335–349.
Fallace, T. (2009). Repeating the race experience: John Dewey and the History curriculum at the University of Chicago Laboratory School. *Curriculum Inquiry, 39*(3), 381–405.
Fallace, T. D. (2010). Was John Dewey ethnocentric? Reevaluating the philosopher's early views on culture and race. *Educational Researcher, 39*, 471–477.
Fallace, T., & Fantozzi, V. (2015). A century of John and Evelyn Dewey's "Schools of to-morrow": Rousseau, recorded knowledge, and race in the philosopher's most problematic text. *Educational Studies: Journal of The American Educational Studies Association, 51*(2), 129–152.

Gould, S. J. (1977). *Ontogeny and phylogeny*. Cambridge, MA: Belknap of Harvard Press.

James, W. (1890/1983). *Principles of psychology*. Cambridge, MA: Harvard University Press.

James, W. (1907). *Pragmatism: A new name for some old ways of thinking*. New York: Longmans, Green.

Joncich, G. (1968). *The sane positivist: A biography of Edward L. Thorndike*. Middletown, CT: Wesleyan University Press.

Kevles, D. J. (1995). *In the name of eugenics*. Cambridge, MA: Harvard University Press.

Labaree, D. F. (2011). How Dewey lost: The victory of David Snedden and social efficiency in the reform of American education. In D. Tröher, T. Schlag, & F. Ostervalder (Eds.), *Pragmatism and modernities*. Rotterdam: Sense Press.

Lagemann, E. C. (2000). *The elusive science: The troubling history of education research*. Chicago: University of Chicago Press.

Margonis, F. (2009). John Dewey's racialized visions of the student and classroom community. *Educational Theory, 59*, 17–39.

Mayhew, K. C., & Edwards, A. C. (1936/1966). *The Dewey School: The Laboratory School of the University of Chicago, 1896–1903*. New York: Atherton Press.

Menand, L. (2001). *The metaphysical club*. New York: Farrar, Straus, and Giroux.

Palermo, J. (1992). Dewey on the pedagogy of occupations: The social construction of the hyper-real. *Philosophy of Education: Proceedings of the Annual Meeting of the Philosophy of Education Society, 48*, 177–186.

Piaget, J. (1948). *To understand is to invent: The future of education*. New York: Grossman.

Piaget, J. (1976/2015). *The grasp of consciousness: Action and concept in the young child*. Hove, UK: Psychology Press.

Poggi, G. (1983). *Calvinism and the capitalist spirit: Max Weber's Protestant ethic*. London: Macmillan.

Richardson, M. J., & Slife, B. D. (2013). A 'narrowing of inquiry' in American moral psychology and education. *Journal of Moral Education, 42*, 193–208.

Russell, W. F. (1949). Edward L. Thorndike, 1874–1949. *Teachers College Record, 51*, 26–28.

Ryan, A. (1995). *John Dewey and the high tide of American liberalism*. New York: W. W. Norton.

Sokal, M. M. (1987). *Psychological testing and American society, 1890–1930*. New Brunswick, NJ: Rutgers University Press.

Spencer, H. (1851). *Social statics*. London: John Chapman.

Tennyson, A. (1850). *In Memoriam A. H. H.* London: Edward Moxon.

Thorndike, E. L. (1898). Animal intelligence: An experimental study of the associative processes in animals. *Psychological Review, Monograph Supplements, 2*, 1–109.

Thorndike, E. L. (1903). *Educational psychology*. New York: Science Press.
Thorndike, E. L. (1906). *The principles of teaching*. New York: A. G. Seiler.
Thorndike, E. L. (1911). *Animal intelligence*. New York: Macmillan (Reprinted Bristol: Thoemmes, 1999).
Thorndike, E. L. (1913a). *Educational psychology. Vol. 1. The original nature of man*. New York: Teachers College.
Thorndike, E. L. (1913b). *Educational psychology. Vol. 2. The psychology of learning*. New York: Teachers College, Columbia University.
Thorndike, E. L., & Murchison, C. (1936). Edward Lee Thorndike. In C. Murchison & C. Murchison (Eds.), *A history of psychology in autobiography volume III* (pp. 263–270). Worcester: Clark University Press. https://doi.org/10.1037/11247-011
Thorndike, E. L. (1940/1969). *Human nature and the social order*. Cambridge, MA: MIT Press.
Thorndike, E. L. (1943/1969). *Man and his works*. Port Washington, NY: Kennicat Press.
Thorndike, E. L., & Woodworth, R. (1901a). The influence of improvement in one mental function upon the efficiency of other functions. *Psychological Review, 8*, 247–261.
Thorndike, E. L., & Woodworth, R. (1901b). The influence of improvement in one mental function upon the efficiency of other functions. The estimation of magnitudes. *Psychological Review, 8*, 384–395.
Thorndike, E. L., & Woodworth, R. (1901c). The influence of improvement in one mental function upon the efficiency of other functions. Functions involving attention, observation, and discrimination. *Psychological Review, 8*, 553–564.
Tomlinson, S. (1997). Edward Lee Thorndike and John Dewey on the science of education. *Oxford Review of Education, 23*, 365–383.
Weber, M. (1905/2002). *The protestant ethic and the spirit of capitalism and other writings* (Trans. & Ed.: Baehr, P., & Wells, G. C.). New York: Penguin.
Westbrook, R. B. (1991). *John Dewey and American democracy*. Ithaca, NY: Cornell University Press.
Woodworth, R. S. (1952). Edward Lee Thorndike: A biographical memoir. *National Academy of Sciences Biographical Memoirs, 27*, 207–237.

CHAPTER 3

The Confucian Concept of Learning

Liqing Tao

This chapter focuses on the concept of learning in Confucianism, laying out the Confucian emphasis on learning as a process, and delineating relations between learning and thinking, learning and questioning, learning and practice, and learning and teaching. Drawing mainly from Confucius' *Analects* and partially from his later followers, Mencius' eponymous work *Mencius*, Xun Zi's eponymous work *Xun Zi*, and the chapter of *Xue Ji* (*On learning*) from the Classic *Li Ji* (*On Rites and Rituals*), this chapter will highlight the unique constructive nature of knowledge acquisition in Confucian educational thinking. In conclusion, the chapter addresses some implications of the Confucian concept of learning for current educational practice.

Background

Confucianism has been the greatest influence on Chinese education for more than 2000 years (Chen, 1993). Confucianism is broadly and briefly defined here as a school of thought that originates from and centers on Confucius' thinking, advocating a harmonious society through individuals' moral cultivation and humanistic ways of government (Yao, 2000).

L. Tao (✉)
School of Education, College of Staten Island/City University of New York, Staten Island, NY, USA

D.W. Kritt (ed.), *Constructivist Education in an Age of Accountability*, https://doi.org/10.1007/978-3-319-66050-9_3

Educational thoughts play a critical role in Confucianism as the premise for self-cultivation and social improvements.

Born into a war-torn society that saw rapid social changes and the crumbling of traditional social orders, Confucius was determined to devote his life to restoring the social harmony and political order through re-establishing the ancient rites and rituals. At the center of this restorative effort was education (Gardner, 2014; Ni, 2002). To Confucius, education was the means to cultivate talents who would adhere to the appropriate rituals and were morally upright as individuals and administratively capable as officials who would govern through humaneness (Qian, 2011). Both the internal development of personal traits and external knowledge acquisition for administrative abilities were predicated on the participation of individual learners in education.

It is clear that politically Confucius was a conservative who wanted to restore the old traditional social orders. It is also clear that the social order he yearned for and sought to restore had already collapsed by his time (Yao, 2000). Yet, as a serious scholar who used education and learning as the means to achieve his political goals, Confucius was quite an avant-garde path-maker in Chinese education. He was not only the first in record to make education available to all who were willing to learn in spite of their social status, but he also advanced significant educational thoughts and practices that have had long lasting influences on China's education and society (Lee, 2000).

What Is Learning?

To Confucius and Confucian scholars in the pre-Qin period (before 221 BC), learning was a complex process that involved the following essential relationships: those between learners and learning, between learning and thinking, between learning and questioning, between learning and practice, and between learners and teachers. In educational practice, these relationships have served continually as the foundation for education in later China and have influenced many Asian countries (Chung, 1995; Wang, 1990; Yun, 1996). These relationships, though, are not conceived as attributes separable from each other. Instead, they are best perceived as part of an interrelated whole.

Confucius (511 BC–479 BC?, 1980) believed that learning starts with the learner. The emphasis on learners is subtly played out in a pair of synonyms about the word learning in Chinese. Etymologically, the concept of learning and studying are represented in the same Chinese character Xue

学 (learning or studying). In practice, they are mostly interchangeable and almost inseparable in Chinese. To Confucian scholars of the pre-Qin period, the use of the same character Xue to capture these two slightly differentiated aspects of knowledge acquisition was only natural because for Confucius and his followers, learning entails studying by the learner. What this implies is that learning is effortful. Learners have to set their minds on the objectives of learning, be persistent through the process, be open to diverse perspectives, and immerse themselves in what they are studying without thinking of exterior gratification. One's learning starts with oneself (9.19)[1] and is for oneself (14.24). Confucius emphasized the importance of setting his mind on learning (2.4), seizing learning whenever appropriate (7.22; 19.22), and being a joyful learner (1.1). Yan Hui, one of Confucius' best students, showed these desirable characteristics and was described in *the Analects* as persisting in learning even when living in poverty (6.3; 6.7; 6.11).

It is worth pointing out now that Confucian scholars at that time were aware of the differences between these two concepts of learning and studying. In *the Analects*, Zi Xia, a close disciple of Confucius, made the point that "even if someone is known to have not studied, I would say he is learned if he is performing filial duties with elders, serving rulers with loyalty, and keeping promises with friends" (1.7). It is the learner that matters, and it is the ultimate purpose of learning that matters in defining what is learning. This point will be revisited later. For now, differences between learning and studying are noted; it is the ultimate goal of self-transformation that infuses these two aspects into one. Self-transformation is not easy. It requires effort and consciousness, whether in studying or in the practice and application of learning. Learning therefore has its roots in learners, who take initiatives, are committed to learning, and award themselves with the process of learning itself (8.17). Those who set their minds on learning have taken the first step toward self-transformational learning (2.4).

According to the Confucius, learning can only occur when studying goes hand in hand with thinking: "studying without thinking leads to confusion, and thinking without studying is dangerous" (2.15). I will consider only the first half of the statement here, and will leave the comment on the second half to the next paragraph. It should be pointed out that the word Wang 罔 (confusion) has several connotations in Chinese. Aside from "being confused" or "being perplexed," it can also mean "being gullible" or "being deceived." Confucius' statement can have all these connotations. Confucius highlights three relevant points here about the important role thinking plays in learning. First, it implies that learning is learner based. It can only occur when the learner is actively engaged through thinking, whether to adequately capture the essence of what one is learning or to integrate it into one's knowledge structure as Xun Zi (313 BC–238 BC?, 1974, p. 8) claimed that "one needs to think through one's readings for comprehensive and integrative understanding." Studying without thinking could also cause confusion when what has been studied is not integrated into a connected whole, leaving the learner unaware of the big picture. Second, learning also involves making a value judgment through careful thinking about the substance of what one is learning. While the learner should not have any preconceived bias when approaching learning something new (9.4), he/she should have a critical stance toward the subject matter. Mencius (372 BC–289 BC?, 2015, p. 285) made a similar but explicit claim that it is better not to have the book than to have one if one completely trusts it. Third, knowledge or what one can learn really does not all reside in books or any other material representations from which one is studying. Knowledge, as implied in the statement, resides between the learner and the books or other material representations of knowledge. In fact, learning only occurs when the learner can think through one's own thinking, "discern other three corners by knowing one corner" (7.8), or the ability to generalize one's learning to something new. Therefore, thinking is a constructive step in which progressive knowledge acquisition is achievable.

The latter half of the statement emphasizes the reciprocal nature of the relationships between learning and thinking. It is obvious that Confucius was emphasizing a necessary balance; the danger can come from empty thinking or baseless speculations that are not bolstered by studying, because such thinking can lead to erroneous decisions and wrong actions. Therefore, thinking all day and all night without serious study is useless to a learner (15.31). Purposeful studying provides the necessary content for thinking, requiring a learner to be continuously engaged in reflecting upon knowledge. Confucius noted the gradual nature of knowledge acquisition and the growth of our understanding when he said that we "learn new insight by reviewing the known" (2.11). By reviewing what we have learned, we are capable of deepening our understanding and therefore constructing new insight from it. It should be noted that the Confucian role of thinking is almost always learning related and reality based (16.10), focusing on specific contexts and showing a clear pragmatic tendency (Li, 2015) toward content-based and context-based thinking.

Community also has an important role to play in learning. *Xue Ji* explicitly lays out the importance of study with peers in a learning community: "If students study alone without the company of peers and friends, they become superficial in understanding and limited in their learning" (Xu, Yang, McEwan, & Ames, 2016, p. 13). The importance of community support for knowledge acquisition is realized in the third pair of relationship in the Confucian concept of learning, the one between learning and questioning. Questions arise when one is actively engaged in studying and thinking. Raising these questions to one's teachers, peers, and other knowledgeable participants in various learning contexts is a vital part of learning. The interactions that occur as a result of asking questions can expand one's views, help one to clarify confusions, and consequently contribute to a continuous process of deepening understanding. Therefore, questioning is practiced and encouraged by Confucian scholars as a crucial part of learning. Confucius is well-known for asking questions whenever he visited Duke Zhou's Temple, asking for information or for clarifications (3.15). He would even ask questions in earnest of those considered to have lesser knowledge than him (5.15; 8.5). Asking questions is, in fact, the main approach in Confucius' teaching, a distinctive format of his interactions with his students and visitors. Questions do not always have to have ready or known answers. They often serve as the means to lead discussions to obtain answers (9.8) or explore learning at a different level (1.15; 3.8). *Xue Ji* comments: "Those who are good at asking questions approach their task as if carving hard wood. First, they chip away at the soft parts and then set to work on the knots. If they keep at it, the difficulties are gradually resolved" (Xu et al., 2016, p. 15).

Interestingly, *Xue Ji*'s description also presents a unique image of Chinese belief about knowledge. It is an image of methodically chipping away the puzzles and doubts around the clouded body of knowledge, echoing the learner-centered mentality. It is an active image that highlights the significance of the internal nature of learning even when knowledge is constructed through a process of outward interactions. It is this inward–outward integration of Confucian concepts that informs the unique Chinese compound word for knowledge or scholarship: Xue Wen 学问 (learning and questioning),[2] leaving no doubt about the active integration of questioning as part of the knowledge acquisition process. Knowledge takes on an active identity in the Chinese compound word Xue Wen. The level of learning-related sophistication in asking appropriate but differentiated questions was used by Confucius as a way to assess and guide students' progress (1.15).

Students' questions were used as indicators of their learning progress and signaled to the Master whether to move on with the next stage of instruction.

Similar to the relationship between learning and questioning, the relationship between learning and practice and application also highlights the perception that practice and application are necessary for learning. To Confucian scholars, practice and application constitute a natural part of learning as well as a reflection of learning. While Xue 学 (learning) and Xi 习(practice/application) are two different Chinese characters for different concepts, they were promoted and perceived together for the first time in Confucius' *Analects*: "Is it not a pleasure to learn and practice the learning from time to time?" (1.1). Since self-transformation is the ultimate purpose of education and learning, it is natural to believe that the final assessment of learning is to find out how transformed one has been in the real world. This is exactly what Zi Xia, a prominent Confucian disciple, meant when he stated that one's practices of filialness with elders, loyalty to serving superiors, and trustworthiness with friends would make that person a learned man (1.7). While he might seem extreme in making this statement, Zi Xia was actually emphasizing the importance of using practice and application in real life as the yardstick for learning, making practices and applications an ultimate means of assessment. It should be pointed out that even in this statement, learning is not overlooked but is implied to have different possible forms, as elsewhere presented in the *Analects*, such as learning through observations (7.22) or emulating righteous behaviors (1.14). In fact, learning as a process involving both learning and practice and application has become a unified concept as reflected in the compound word in Chinese for study or learn: Xue Xi 学习 (study or learn), signifying the essential role of practices and applications in learning. The compound word of Xue Xi shows that practice and application of what one learns are not conceived as extensions of learning but themselves are part of learning and can feed back into one's learning, making them a natural touchstone for learning. Xun Zi in his *Exhortation to Learning* has an interesting description of how laudable learning and despicable learning are different from each other in real life:

> What a Jun Zi has learned would go into him through his ears, be understood by his heart, be distributed to his limbs, and eventually show up in his postures. … What a petty man has learned would go into his ears and come out through his mouth. There are only four inches between a man's ears and

> mouth, how can it transform and beautify his whole person? ... While a Jun Zi's learning transforms and beautifies his whole person, the petty man's learning is only used to please others through words. (Xun Zi, 1974, pp. 5–6)

While we do not precisely know how to measure personal qualities based on learning, it is quite clear that treating personal transformation as the outcome of learning was popular among Confucian scholars (Li, 2015). For example, Mencius (2015, p. 91) touched upon the educational outcome as understanding and sticking to the moral principles governing human relations. *Xue Ji* has a description of the annual assessments for students that accentuates moral growth and personal transformation as the most important outcomes of learning (Xu et al., 2016, p. 11). Xun Zi (1974, pp. 6–7) likewise insisted on moral cultivation as a measure of one's book learning. All this points toward the inseparable role practice and application have in learning.

Confucius believed that teachers are also learners. *Xue Ji* has famously summarized this reciprocal relationship:

> it is only in learning that we realize our inadequacies, and it is only in teaching that we realize our limitations and perplexity. It is only in realizing our inadequacies that we are able to become self-critical, and only in realizing our limitations that we are able to improve ourselves. Teaching and learning complement each other. This is what the "Command of Yue" means when it says: "teaching and learning are two halves of a whole that inform each other." (Xu et al., 2016, p. 10)

Making learning part of teaching and teaching part of learning has many ramifications. This statement highlights the parallel processes, challenges, and potentials that learning and teaching share. Learners and teachers alike are engaged in a process of studying, thinking, and reflection that leads them to ask questions about the adequacy of their own knowledge and discover their own limitations. In turn, such questions and discoveries provide motivation and directions for their further learning. Learning and teaching are contexts which engender further learning needs: the more one learns and teaches, the more one needs to learn. Teaching thus involves a tremendous amount of learning. As part of teaching, learning comes naturally as an outcome of an interactive as well as a reflective and self-discovery process. Learning is necessary not merely in response to learners' puzzles and questions, but is also necessitated by one's own need for deepening and broadening contextual understanding of issues at hand or as indicated by Confucius' insistence on a teacher's capacity of discovering new insight through reviewing old and familiar things (2.11). In this light, as a teacher Confucius would happily declare that he was never fed up with learning and never tired of teaching (7.2). The proposition that teachers are also learners shows that teachers are and should be practicing what they are teaching, engaged in doing what they are advocating—learning for self-transformation and self-cultivation. Confucius presented himself as an exemplary model of a life-long learner, continually engaging in the process of self-transformation (4.8). Such an approach is hailed by Confucian scholars as absolutely necessary (Xun Zi, 1974, p. 6). It implies how important it is for teachers to always have the mindset of a learner. It not merely sensitizes them to their own continual needs for knowledge, but also helps them empathize and put themselves in the position of learners, develop the capacity to view learning from a learner's perspective, and be responsive to their students' needs, questions, and challenges.

This relationship between learning and teaching brings us back to the Confucian concept of learning as an effortful, volitional, and learner-centered process. Teachers are not merely knowledge-givers, but more importantly, seekers of ever-deepening and expanding knowledge, engaged in thinking, reflection, questioning, interactions, self-discovery, and practicing what they are teaching through learning and self-cultivation. They are part of the learning community they help to build. It is perhaps this particular emphasis on teachers as learners that has brought a high esteem to teachers and a reverence for knowledge (with the teacher as the embodiment of it) in traditional Confucian societies.

These key elements of learning are inter-connected. Changes in one would generally affect the others. Central is the learner's mentality, which would impact learners' engagements in the learning process of studying, thinking, questioning, and practicing. Teachers as learners could and should provide motivational and exemplary models to naturally inculcate learners with appropriate values. While thinking and asking questions about learning-related issues are important, the concept also emphasizes the indispensable role of practice and application as part of learning, indicating the essentially active nature of learning as captured in personal practice and application. Effortful and conscious engagements in thinking, discussions, and practice are conceived as a gradual knowledge acquisition process, affecting not merely the learning but more importantly the learners and their self-transformation.

In short, it is a process of learner-centered, constructive, and continuous efforts that is directly connected to social practices and to learner growth. This Confucian concept of learning has set the tone for how knowledge has been perceived and acquired in China over two millennia, and in other Asian countries for hundreds of years.

Implications of Confucian Concept of Learning: What It Means for Us Today

While the Confucian concept of learning has morphed and changed through history with both positive and negative consequences, its main themes still generally hold in educational circles in China and many East Asian cultures. The Confucian concept of learning offers three implications for current Western educational practices.

First, the Confucian concept of learning can help us take another look at how knowledge acquisition occurs. Confucian scholars are not expressly interested in epistemology but demonstrate their pragmatic insight in their teaching and education practices. Knowledge acquisition has been treated as an effortful constructive process in which learners deepen their understanding, enrich their knowledge, and practice learning in real contexts, continually refreshing knowledge. In contrast to treating knowledge as a prescribed body of standards and curricular prescriptions external to learners, this focuses education on learners, individual growth, encouraging learner involvement rather than a rigid and presumptive format, and on developing inter-connections and reflective learning rather than superficial copying. Such classrooms would emphasize learners' engagements in the learning process, and learning situated in individual students' prior knowledge, learning needs, and learning paces. This conceptualization of learning emphasizes the continuous and connected nature of learning, integrating personal efforts with group interaction and discussions. In sum, this conceptualization tells us three things about knowledge acquisition: personal efforts are a necessary part of knowledge construction; acquired knowledge emerges as inter-connected rather than a group of discrete objects; and knowledge acquisition is a process that is generative of further learning needs.

Second, the Confucian concept of learning can help us re-conceive what can serve as the indicators of such knowledge acquisition. Reliance on standardized tests is not adequate because the summative, outside-learning process does not reflect the true nature of learning and account for the learning process. The Confucian concept of learning suggests possible points in the process where assessments can occur and what principles of assessment should be. In order to contribute to continued learning, assessments must reflect that learners are engaged in thinking and reflection, and developing questions. Assessments can take place when learners ask questions. Learner questions could be used to evaluate whether they have thought through what they have been learning and can move to the next stage of instruction. Levels of questions should reflect the gradual process of deepening and broadening understanding about a subject area. Another possible point of assessments is at the stage when learners are practicing what they have learned. Instead of treating practice and application as mere extensions and enhancements of learning, teachers need to recognize practice and application as authentically capturing the performance of learning, a naturally occurring assessment of the learning growth. More importantly, assessment based on practice and application should not be separated from the learning process. Instead, it should be used as feedback on what is being studied and provide formative rather than summative information about learning. In this sense, practice as assessment is not disruptive to the learning process but occurs naturally as part of learning. Formats of assessment could include teacher observations or student self-monitoring checks or both. While teacher observations may be used for summative purposes, learner self-monitoring checks would greatly contribute to learner-improvement as a whole person. Teachers can play an important role in assisting learners with self-monitoring checks, which are not merely a list of dos and don'ts; learners should come to evaluate their own learning practices.

Two principles of assessment are highlighted in the Confucian approach. Generalizing learning to new contexts focuses learners on the intricate relationship between in-depth understanding of the subject matter and a sensitivity to contextual requirements. Homeostasis between the knowledge level of the subject and the contexts means that changing one affects the other. In addition, discovering the new through reviewing the old and familiar shifts focus from connecting the studied subjects to new contexts to developing new insights into those subjects. Both principles can help educators conceive and design assessments that, as a non-intrusive part of the learning process, contribute to bringing about desired learning outcomes.

Considering the naturally occurring assessment possibilities, the Confucian concept of learning can provide some dearly needed counter-balance perspective to current accountability measures that are based on a-contextual universal standards and criteria. Accountability can be realized in a less rigid, non-intrusive, form in which learners who are engaged in the learning process at various stages are assessed to help them progress through the process. The focus is making sure that a non-intrusive form of assessment is used to account for and enhance the learning process.

An additional benefit is that the Confucian concept of learning may help us understand Chinese immigrant students and many East Asian students in our classrooms. As one of the fastest growing student populations in our school systems, these students warrant our educational attention to ensure they receive adequate educational services. The Confucian concept of learning, as a cultural mark for many East Asian countries, has become an important component of immigrant students' educational identity. The learning behaviors exhibited by these Confucian heritage students must be appropriately interpreted by Western teachers to facilitate their successful inclusion into learning communities in the West. There are several features that can usually be observed in these students. These students are usually pretty good at completing assigned work; they expect to expend such efforts. Accordingly, using preview and review assignments is one way to capitalize on their strengths. They are not shy about asking questions if the questions arise from effortful engagements with assignments, whether as a preparatory study for class or a practice exercise in the form of homework. These students are not inclined to ask questions as a result of quick associations without careful and adequate thinking time. But teachers need to provide guidance about asking questions in a Western classroom. The down side of students' efforts might also be seen when they use rote memorization, instead of questions, to respond to preparatory assignments.

Due to the heavy emphasis on learning and knowledge acquisition, Confucian heritage students tend to exhibit different personal choices in school subjects than their Western peers. For example, they tend to select and perform well in math and sciences classes, usually perceived as subjects that entail both gradual knowledge buildup and constant practice. But their participation in other subjects such as sports, arts, and the humanities tend to be more limited. There might be various reasons (in addition to language) for this. But one reason is the Confucian emphasis on the types of knowledge that can be pragmatically and visibly reflected in math and sciences, particularly when mediated through strong parental input, thus limiting their own personal choices. Such limitation of personal choices may be detrimental to them in Western contexts. School counselors and teachers can help them realize the value of personal choices in school and beyond.

Finally, these students usually respect teachers. This view of teachers could be used to interpret some observable student behaviors in classrooms. At times these students appear to be reticent, seldom challenge teachers or peers and are usually not confrontational, listen to teachers' words intently, sometimes literally, and appeal to teachers for conflict resolutions. Their silence in class, barring language difficulties, could simply be the result of respect. In addition, in their silence many of them engage actively in thinking through note-taking and give their full attention to listening during instructional times. Teachers should be sensitive to these psychological characteristics and avoid interpreting these behaviors exclusively from a Western cultural perspective. Teachers can also turn this respect into powerful learning opportunities for students by giving them sufficient time to reflect on learning, and ushering them into an educational culture that values active and brainstorming group discussions and dialogues. This should not, however, be interpreted as an absolute characterization of Confucian heritage students. After all, they are also immersed in the Western culture's social and historical contexts.

The Confucian concept of learning has undergone continuous changes since its inception, and has also left some worthwhile lessons for us to ponder. I will briefly mention two salient educational practices in Chinese history in which the Confucian concept of learning was misapplied. First, in the ancient Chinese school curriculum, particularly after Confucian classics were installed officially as orthodox texts for learners (Chaffee, 1995), memorization of texts became a primary means of learning; Confucius was opposed to this learning practice (13.5). To avoid such a trap, he emphasized the needed balance between learning and thinking, and between learning and practice. Second, overemphasizing superficial forms and formats in learning, a harmful practice, prevailed for many years. China used to have a special kind of essay format in the Ming and Qing times called Ba Gu Wen 八股文 (literally Eight-Legged Essay), a stereotyped writing with very limiting requirements for forms and content. Premised upon the idea that learned Confucian scholars were the most talented government officials, the essay was introduced to the civil service examinations to identify those who could articulate Confucian thoughts. However, the targeted Confucian content was actually stifled by the restrictive format. Many a test-taker resorted to learning that was removed from practice and application, and had nothing to do with self-transformation. Consequently, learners wasted many productive years in preparing for such examinations. The restrictive rules and format of these essays were eventually eliminated. Too many rules and restrictions in form, even though in the name of Confucian learning, thwarted the true purpose of learning. The key to averting such distortion is to keep education learner-centered, constructive, and transformational.

The Confucian concept of learning provides a perspective on knowledge and knowledge acquisition process that can enrich discussions of current educational practices. But without guarding against possible misinterpretations, the Confucian concept of learning, like any other theory of learning, can also be misused.

Notes

1. A reference to Confucius' *Analects* will be cited in parentheses with its book number followed by a period sign and a chapter number. To make the discussion concise and the chapter within the length limit, most of the quotations to the *Analects* are not directly cited but referenced.
2. The compound Chinese word Xue Wen (literary learning and questioning) as knowledge or scholarship, still in use today, appeared already in the Warring States Confucian scholars' works such as in *Mencius* and *Xun Zi*, indicating the long existing traditional acceptance of this active view of knowledge as underlined by learning and questioning.

References

Chaffee, J. W. (1995). *The thorny gates of learning in Sung China: A social history of examinations*. Albany, NY: State University of New York Press.

Chen, J. (1993). *Confucius as a teacher: Philosophy of Confucius with special reference to its educational implications*. Petaling Jaya, Malaysia: Delta Publishing.

Chung, E. Y. T. (1995). *The Korean Neo-Confucianism of Yi T'oegye and Yi Yulgok: A reappraisal of the 'Four-Seven thesis' and its practical implications for self-cultivation*. Albany, NY: State University of New York Press.

Confucius. (511 BC–479 BC?, 1980). 论语 [*The Analects*] with explanatory notes by Yang Bojun. Beijing, China: China Press.

Gardner, D. K. (2014). *Confucianism: A very short introduction*. New York: Oxford University Press.

Lee, T. H. C. (2000). *Education in traditional China: A history*. Boston: Brill.

Li, Z. (2015). 论语今读 [*A modern day annotated Analects*]. Beijing, China: China Book Press.

Mencius. (372 BC–289 BC?, 2015). 孟子 [*Mencius*] with translation and annotations by Fang Yong. Beijing, China: China Press.

Ni, P. (2002). *On Confucius*. Belmont, CA: Wadsworth.

Qian, M. (2011). 孔子与论语 [*Confucius and his Analects*]. Beijing, China: Jiu Zhou Press.

Wang, J. (1990). 儒家思想与日本文化 [*Confucianism and Japanese culture*]. Hangzhou, China: Zhejiang People's Press.

Xu, D., Yang, L., McEwan, H., & Ames, R. T. (Trans.). (2016). 学记 [*On Learning*]. In D. Xu & H. McEwan (Eds.), *Chinese philosophy of teaching and learning: Xueji (学记) in the twenty-first century*. Albany, NY: State University of New York Press.

Xun Zi. (313 BC–238 BC?, 1974). 荀子简注 [*A briefly annotated Xun Zi*] with annotations by Zhang Shitong. Shanghai, China: Shanghai People's Press.

Yao, X. (2000). *An introduction to Confucianism*. Cambridge, UK: Cambridge University Press.

Yun, S. (1996). Confucian thought and Korean culture. *Korean Cultural Heritage, 2*, 108–113.

PART II

Engaged Learning for Understanding

CHAPTER 4

Pedagogic Doublethink: Scientific Enquiry and the Construction of Personal Knowledge Under the English National Curriculum for Science

Keith S. Taber

As a curriculum area, science would seem to be particularly suited to constructivist approaches to education. There are at least three distinct lines of thought that might lead to this conclusion. For one thing, much of the work that was part of the explosion of interest in science education as a research area (around the 1970s and 1980s) was undertaken from a constructivist stance on student learning and thinking. Secondly, scholarship into such areas as the history, philosophy, and psychology, of science suggests that the way in which science itself proceeds needs to be understood from a constructivist perspective. Finally, there has in recent decades been a strong international impetus to increase engagement with authentic enquiry—that is in terms of engaging students in the process of constructing understanding through the interplay of empirical work and the personal and social building of conceptualisations of the natural world.

Yet in practice more traditional notions of the science curriculum—as a body of pre-processed knowledge to be communicated through teaching and assessed in high-stakes tests—can often be firmly established in the

K.S. Taber (✉)
Faculty of Education, University of Cambridge, Cambridge, UK

D.W. Kritt (ed.), *Constructivist Education in an Age of Accountability*,
https://doi.org/10.1007/978-3-319-66050-9_4

minds of key stakeholders, such that even when lip-service is paid to, for example, the importance of teaching about the nature of science or the need for enquiry-based science teaching, there is considerable systemic resistance to real changes in the nature of science teaching and learning.

This chapter explores these issues—the drivers for a more constructivist approach to science education and the sources of inertia retarding change. The chapter draws upon the situation in England where the relationship between official guidance to teachers and teacher educators on the one hand and curriculum and assessment policy on the other sends out mixed messages, such that it is not fanciful to suggest teachers need to adopt a kind of doublethink in order to cope with the contrary expectations they are subject to. That is, teachers are pressured to adopt and act on a range of expectations that in practice are mutually inconsistent. The English context has been particularly rich in government-sponsored advice to teachers on how to undertake their professional work, but issues raised here are reflected to varying degrees in many other contexts: not least in the debates about the merits of what are seen as progressive and traditional approaches to teaching in the United States.

Constructivism and Research in Science Education

The strength of constructivist thinking on science education as a research field from the 1970s onwards was such that it became seen as a dominant perspective—or even the equivalent of a paradigm of the kind Kuhn (1970) posited in "normal" periods of science (Fensham, 2004; Taber, 2009). Researchers informed by the constructivist aspects of Piaget's (1970/1972) programme exploring the development of thinking in children and adolescents (e.g., Driver & Easley, 1978), and by Kelly's (1963) personal construct theory (e.g., Gilbert & Watts, 1983), were highly influential in shifting the dominant focus of research away from the general patterns of thought that students of particular ages were capable of demonstrating (i.e., the core focus of Piaget's own work) to exploring the specificity and variety in student thinking about particular science topics. Work exploring alternative conceptions or alternative frameworks, and later on conceptual change in science, became major foci of educational research activity, leading to a vast literature (Duit, 2009). Some of these studies clearly championed constructivist principles, some nominally name-checked constructivism as an assumed perspective, and much reported work that at least implicitly relied on assumptions about the educational significance of the personal and sometimes idiosyncratic nature of students' ideas (Taber, 2009). Indeed, one criticism raised was that at the height of its influence, constructivism was so dominant that it distorted the field of science education to the exclusion of other valuable complementary perspectives (Solomon, 1994).

The extent to which this research activity engaged with constructivist thinking in any depth was variable. One of the most influential theorists was Glasersfeld (1989), who developed a position labelled as radical constructivism, which adopted a strong epistemological position on the nature of human knowledge as necessarily due to personal construction. For Glasersfeld the external physical world constrains the sensory information available to make sense of experience (e.g., a person cannot walk through brick walls), but perception involves interpretation in making sense of sensory information—the human cognitive apparatus necessarily "re-codes" sensory input so what reaches consciousness is a much processed signal (Taber, 2013b). A person's only meaningful reality is that (necessarily channelled and interpreted) experience, as we can have no direct unmediated engagement with the external world. This theoretical perspective initiated much debate from those who engaged with the philosophical positions underpinning constructivist work (Matthews, 1998; Scerri, 2003, 2012; Taber, 2010c).

Most of the studies in science education, however, did not explicitly explore such issues, but relied more on a psychological grounding for constructivism that did not engage with arguments about epistemology in general (the origins and grounds of knowledge), but only with issues of how students developed their ideas.[1] This was based on the clear empirical evidence that (1) students attending science classes would commonly arrive with ideas about topics inconsistent with the curriculum content they were to be taught, and that, particularly in some topics, (2) they were almost as likely to demonstrate alternative conceptions after being taught the topic as before, albeit that their post-instruction thinking sometimes reflected an interaction between pre-instructional thinking and teaching (Gilbert, Osborne, & Fensham, 1982).

A key claim made by some researchers was that alternative conceptions explored in their work were highly stable and tenaciously retained, and so not readily changed by teaching. This claim was subject to some criticism (e.g., Claxton, 1993) but has—with an important qualification—been supported by much research since. Students' alternative conceptions vary across a range of dimensions (Taber, 2014), and some are quite labile and not particularly significant for learning. However, some common alternative conceptions have been shown to readily become well established in student thinking and then very difficult to modify (Gilbert & Zylbersztajn, 1985; Taber, 2013a).

Influences of Constructivist Research on Science Teaching Practice

Much of the research exploring how students (of various ages, in diverse national contexts) understand a wide range of science topics was justified as educational research in terms of being useful to inform curriculum design and classroom practice. The argument was that if science teachers had a better understanding of the ways in which students already understood topics and how they commonly interpreted teaching, then science teachers would be better prepared to spot such patterns of thinking and channel student thinking towards the target understandings in the curriculum. Teachers could challenge common alternative conceptions and develop specific pedagogy to persuade students towards desired conceptual change (Clement, 1993). This was an extensive research area that was not limited to science education researchers (although science concepts were common foci for work on conceptual change undertaken from within more general fields exploring learning such as general psychology/cognitive science/learning sciences).

The research into students' ideas therefore fed into work on pedagogy and curriculum development (Driver & Oldham, 1986; Russell & Osborne, 1993). Teachers were encouraged to begin a topic by eliciting student thinking, so as to make explicit students' existing conceptions. This allows teachers to take on those ideas and argue (preferably with suitable empirical demonstrations) for why the scientific models and concepts work better. This pedagogy could have the potential to encourage students to form new potentially unhelpful ideas during the elicitation activity (Claxton, 1993), and to then feel they should commit to and defend those ideas they have been asked to share (Claxton, 1986), and so may seem counter-productive. Yet research suggests that many of the most tenacious alternative conceptions have their origins in implicit knowledge that people develop from experience and which is automatically drawn upon during perception/cognition without conscious control or awareness (DiSessa, 1993; Smith, DiSessa, & Roschelle, 1993). Given that, allowing student thinking to continue to operate at a tacit level without being challenged is likely to allow it to continue to operate insidiously, often without the learner having any awareness that their way of making sense of teaching is quite different to that intended by the teacher.

Influences from Science Studies Scholarship

Another area of relevance relates to the various strands of science studies that have explored the processes by which science produces knowledge. This is a vast area of scholarship, which cannot be done justice here, but some examples can be offered. The work of Thomas Kuhn (1970), for example, emphasised the importance of being socialised into a particular way of thinking about the natural world for channelling how evidence is understood, and the substantial challenge of undergoing "paradigm-shifts" between scientific world views. Kuhn did not suggest science was irrational, but did argue that it was difficult for any scientists trained within a particular tradition to step outside that framework and look at evidence from a neutral standpoint—a point that applies to human experience, generally, given that to be fully human is to have been encultured within some worldview or another (Geertz, 1973). Other scholars have built upon this work to demonstrate how scientists' commitments to what now seem clearly inadequate ideas may have been perfectly logical at the time (Thagard, 1992).

Kuhn also highlighted the role of the creative, imaginative aspect of scientific work that has been critical in many scientific discoveries (Koestler, 1978/1979; Miller, 1986). This has been widely acknowledged by some scientists but tends to be underplayed in science education in relation to the logical aspects of scientific work (Kind & Kind, 2007; Taber, 2011b). Forming and testing ideas is only part of the scientific process, as science is a community-mediated activity and the scientist has to convince her or his peers that their ideas are valuable as descriptions of nature or as explanatory tools. Science therefore has a very strong rhetorical aspect (Gilbert & Mulkay, 1984), something that has been reflected in recent years by active research exploring the role of argumentation in science learning (Erduran, Simon, & Osborne, 2004).

Moreover, there has been a strong focus within some areas of science studies, and some work in science education, on a shift between seeing science as about the discovery of how nature is, to being about constructing representations that are necessarily human inventions. The idea that human beings, with their particular mental capacities and apparatus, are able to adequately understand the world (and the sometimes co-existing scientistic notion that if we do enough science we will one day understand everything) were sensible assumptions for early modern scientists who adopted a natural theology perspective of "reading the book of nature", as their religious worldview led them to expect that God wanted people to make sense of

His creation (Yeo, 1979). Even if some scientists still adopt such commitments privately today, such ideas are no longer admissible as part of scientific argumentation itself, and for many scientists an implicit commitment to the universe being comprehendible seems little more than an act of secular faith. Indeed in recent times the scientists seeking to persuade the public that science is a kind of epistemological panacea, have tended to be those most critical of religious beliefs (Cray, Dawkins, & Collins, 2006).

Yet analysis of science-in-the-making demonstrates just how indirect and reliant on boot-strapping the constructions of some scientific products are—the "discovery" of sub-atomic particles in physics being one high profile example (Knorr Cetina, 1999). It has been recognised that the work of the science teacher is parallel to this, with teachers using language and gestures and models and so forth as rhetorical tools to help learners construct the objects of science for themselves in their own imaginations (Lemke, 1990; Ogborn, Kress, Martins, & McGillicuddy, 1996).

The Drive for Enquiry-Based Science Teaching

A third important consideration is the international movement towards what has been described as enquiry-based (or inquiry-based) science education rather than simply learning science as a "rhetoric of conclusions" (Schwab, 1962). Science as an activity is about enquiry into the natural world, to develop further understanding through the interplay between, on the one hand, empirical observations and investigations and, on the other, the development of theory. An authentic science education therefore needs to give learners the experience of enquiry. Of course professional scientific enquiry relies upon scientists having an extensive specialised knowledge base, access to state-of-the-art apparatus and well-equipped laboratories, and being able to engage with scientific problems continuously over extended periods of weeks and months. School science cannot draw upon a comparable resource base, and it was recognised well over a century ago that transposing scientific enquiry into schools could not simply mean expecting students to undertake self-directed unguided enquiry (Jenkins, 1979).

Despite this, there has been a considerably influential movement arguing for teaching science as enquiry (Lawson, 2010). This can be considered as part of the broader impetus to shift the emphasis of science teaching away from teaching primarily about some of the findings of science ("content") to including more emphasis on the nature of science ("process") (Clough & Olson, 2008; Hodson, 2009; Lederman & Lederman, 2014; Matthews,

1994). Indeed influence from the "nature of science" lobby has allowed a richer understanding of scientific enquiry (as being much more nuanced than simply testing hypotheses through controlled experiments) to evolve within science education (Lederman & Lederman, 2012; Osborne, 2014).

Objections to Constructivist Science Education

Teaching through enquiry has also been a focus of the debates within the wider educational community that has seen what are viewed as constructivist approaches to pedagogy heavily criticised in some quarters (Berube, 2008; Taber, 2010a; Tobias & Duffy, 2009). This is a complex debate, but one key problem is how constructivist teaching is understood by some of its critics—especially when it is considered that constructivism, child-centred instruction, enquiry-based teaching, active learning, and progressive pedagogy, can be clumped together as synonymous (Kirschner, Sweller, & Clark, 2006). Critics have argued that constructivist science teaching is minimally guided and assumes students can rediscover major scientific ideas for themselves, whereas teaching will only be effective when there is direct instruction of difficult, abstract ideas. Some have even argued that enquiry teaching is favoured in some school systems because the teacher does not need any specialist scientific knowledge as they are teaching learners to find things out for themselves (Cromer, 1997). These criticisms ignore how a main driver for the constructivist movement in science education was the recognition that much minimally guided enquiry work would not be effective as students would develop their own alternative conceptions (Driver, 1983), which once formed were likely to be reinforced by (necessarily "theory laden") observations (Nickerson, 1998).

In one important sense, constructivist thinking *does* suggest that every learner has to rediscover every taught idea for themselves—no matter how directly they are instructed. But constructivist pedagogy is certainly not about open-ended enquiry with minimal guidance from the teacher. Constructivist pedagogy requires a dialogic approach that engages students' own ideas, and explores them critically and in relation to evidence, as a phase in a multifaceted process of presenting the case for why canonical scientific ideas have been developed and adopted (Mortimer & Scott, 2003). An authentic constructivist science education does not require that learners abandon their existing ideas and convert to believe scientific ideas, as science offers theoretical accounts to support understanding and is not about belief, but rather that students become convinced that scientific ideas represent useful and sensible ways of thinking about the natural world (Taber, 2017). Constructivist teaching requires learners to engage in actively thinking about things for themselves, but always supported by suitable scaffolding so that the intellectual challenge of understanding abstract scientific accounts is manageable. Constructivist ideas, when taken in the round (Scott, 1998), inform an optimally guided form of instruction (Taber, 2011a). A more detailed discussion of the criticisms of constructivist thought within science education can be found elsewhere (see Chapter 5 in Taber, 2009).

The English Context

The context of England[2] is of particular interest because the government has adopted educational policy that explicitly accepts some key constructivist ideas—as in some other countries (Bell, Jones, & Car, 1995)—yet this has happened within a wider policy context that severely undermines substantive attempts to adopt research-based constructivist approaches in the classroom on a regular basis. This presents teachers with a dilemma about how to proceed in planning schemes of work and instruction. This account focuses on the period since a major change in the education system in England that was proposed at the end of the 1980s (DES/WO, 1988) and implemented from the early 1990s. This was the point at which the considerable professional autonomy schools and teachers had enjoyed in matters of curriculum was considerably reduced by the first implementation of a prescribed National Curriculum (NC) that state funded schools were required to follow.

The NC has been modified in various ways since its first introduction, although the originally implemented version of the science curriculum was substantially retained until major revisions in 2007 (Qualifications and Curriculum Authority, 2007a, 2007b). Further substantial revisions have recently been produced (Department for Education, 2014). The chronology of different adjustments to curriculum, and related assessment regimes, is complex and the present account focuses on key themes which have been constant throughout the process:

- that the government specifies the science curriculum for students across ages 5–16;
- that the government controls the formal assessment framework within which schools and examination boards have to work;

- that the government offers copious advice to teachers on how to best organise and carry out classroom teaching.

Where the NC specified the prescribed topics to be taught for each phase of schooling in some detail, the guidance went well beyond this to include curriculum sequencing and pedagogy. At the lower secondary school level ("Key Stage 3", for 11–14 year olds) guidance included a model scheme of work for each topic setting out lessons and possible lesson activities (QCA, 2000), and a "framework" document showing how to build up a coherent course from the different topics (Key Stage 3 National Strategy, 2002a).

Where the curriculum and assessment strands of policy are largely backed by legal force (based on powers vested in the Secretary of State for Education by the UK Parliament), the guidance on pedagogy is, officially, purely advisory. This is however an issue where doublethink may operate: teachers are not *required* to follow non-statutory guidance, which only offers suggestions—yet teachers generally assume they are *expected* to follow the guidance. All schools are subject to regular inspection by the schools inspection service, which publishes reports and grades for individual schools, and an unsatisfactory grading can lead to a school being put into "special measures" where the school management may have to cede control of the school.

As an example, at one point it was suggested in government guidance that all effective lessons have three components—beginning with a starter activity, moving to a main learning activity, and concluding with a plenary session. This three-part lesson was never an officially required lesson structure, but as it was something school inspectors might look for and comment on, it was not unknown for school head teachers to instruct their staff that all lessons must have this structure (Shaw, 2012). Similarly, where research suggests that meaningful learning of complex or counter-intuitive material (like much that is taught in science) is a slow process that may show uneven development over periods of weeks and months, teachers are told that school inspectors would expect to see visible progress in learning during a single observed lesson. Teachers working with the author and colleagues on a curriculum development initiative were very resistant to the idea that any lesson might leave an idea "hanging" for students to reflect on between classes. Although that might sometimes be educationally sensible, it was seen as dangerous in case inspectors visiting a class expected to see a plenary session at the end of the lesson where students could (supposedly) demonstrate clear progression in learning during that session. Teacher colleagues were also very worried about teaching schemes where sequences of similar but incrementally more difficult tasks were used to scaffold learning about difficult concepts—inspectors expected to see learning had a good pace, and teachers would not be comfortable spending extended periods of time on what seemed much the same form of learning activity (as might be indicated in authentic enquiry) in case visited by inspectors.

Government Guidance on Effective Science Teaching

The English Government has been open to being informed by educational thinking in developing its educational policies. During recent decades the government has under a number of initiatives sought to encourage teachers to adopt pedagogy influenced by constructivist thinking and research. Two particular themes are that (a) teaching needs to take into account and respond to students' alternative conceptions and (b) science teaching needs to involve students in learning about scientific enquiry. Both of these features are to be welcome as reflecting international research and scholarship in the field of science education. Moreover, government seems to have been genuine and well-meaning in taking up these principles. However, as will be suggested below, the wider policy context has worked against effective adoption of the kinds of pedagogies research suggests are needed to meet these intentions.

Recommendations for Teaching Informed by Students' Ideas

The body of constructivist research suggests that learning science is a process of knowledge construction that is interpretative, incremental, and so iterative (Taber, 2014). That is, students inevitably make sense of teaching in terms of their existing conceptual resources (given the nature of human cognition), and build up their understanding piecemeal (given the limitations of working memory when handling unfamiliar material), and so are likely to build upon their existing understandings when they can make sense of teaching in these terms. To respond to this, teachers need to be able to perceive the material to be taught from the learner's perspective, and devise learning activities that are designed to channel student thinking from their existing conceptions towards scientific models, and that build up new conceptual understandings through manageable learning quanta. Once students are thinking about a science topic along inappropriate lines they are likely to develop those existing lines of thought, so the teacher needs to work dialogically (Mercer, 1995), seeking feedback on how teaching is being understood, and using this to make adjustments where indicated. This means that schemes of work have to be designed to fit the way students learn, and then teaching itself requires ongoing "online" modifications of the lesson plan during lessons (Taber, 2014).

The government department in England has through its various agencies[3] advised teachers that students commonly develop alternative conceptions about science and has recommended that effective science teaching involves eliciting and where appropriate challenging students' conceptions. This was one aspect highlighted in a short-lived prescriptive national curriculum for initial teacher education (Department for Education and Employment, 1998), and was a major theme of an extensive teacher development initiative (initially known as the "Key Stage 3 National Strategy", where this referred to the 11–14 age group, and later rebranded as the National Strategies) where a considerable amount of teacher development material was produced informing teachers about common student conceptions and suggesting activities for more effective teaching (e.g., Key Stage 3 National Strategy, 2002b).

This material was research-informed, and in some cases quite sophisticated (e.g., Millar, 2003). However, much of the guidance was written as though eliciting students' ideas could be a quick and unproblematic activity (fitting the role of lesson starter perhaps in the ubiquitous three-part lesson), and, similarly, the function of the teacher to challenge, modify, or develop, students' thinking was presented as straight-forward (Taber, 2010b). To adopt a truly constructivist pedagogy requires teachers to develop their teaching of a topic customised for each class (Brock, 2007), taking into account the development of students' thinking at all stages—and also requires having sufficient time to include bespoke demonstrations, thought experiments, and the like, designed to respond to specific ideas elicited from students. However, in practice the sheer amount of content prescribed for teaching in the NC severely limited the time a teacher could commit to any one topic. This undermined the kind of extended engagement with new ideas in a range of contexts, including customised activities to respond to specific student conceptions identified, likely to bring about substantive and long-lasting conceptual change.

Recommendations to Teach About Scientific Enquiry

The original plan to introduce a NC in schools included an "attainment target" (i.e., something which would be formally assessed) relating to the philosophy and history of science (Statutory Instrument, 1989). That this did not materialise was less a principled change of direction than a response to the reception of the original draft NC by the teaching profession. The initial plans for a NC prescription in one teaching subject (science) that would require all pupils to be formally assessed across about 20 (21 or 17 in different drafts) distinct assessment areas was recognised by those who would have to implement it as completely impracticable. The result was a statutory curriculum with four attainment targets, of which Sc1 was "Scientific Investigation" (with Sc2–4 being basically biology, chemistry, and physics, although these labels were not used). At the time these changes were planned, it was suggested that teachers would be able to develop practical activities for their classes, drawing from any aspects of the curriculum, to teach and assess students in that aspect of science.

The imposition of a NC on teachers was also the imposition of a new national assessment regime showing that from the beginning of the process the official policy closely linked curriculum and assessment. A danger in such an approach is that the reasonable notion that "if it is worth teaching, it is worth assessing" can readily become twisted to lead to assessment-led teaching where what gets assessed is what it is easy to assess reliably (and in particular, to quantify), so what gets taught is what is easy to assess, rather than what it is considered important to learn. This has certainly been seen in the English NC era. The NC required all students to be assessed in science before leaving primary school with the expectation that on starting secondary education at 11 years of age, students would arrive with an assigned "NC level" which should inform such matters as student grouping in secondary school. Further formal assessments would be carried out for all 14 year olds.

This is in a context where previously students had been not been subject to formal national assessments before external examinations at age 16, with schools selecting from a range of examination boards, each independent of government (generally having been set up by Universities), and offering their own syllabi. This was a system where there was flexibility in the subjects offered so it was possible for schools to choose courses leading to examinations from a wide range of options such as in general or integrated science; the core science subjects of biology, chemistry, and physics; and a range of other options such as rural studies, astronomy, geology, or automotive engineering science. Even under a single subject heading, such as biology, examination boards might offer examination specifications with different emphases or options. This allowed schools to reflect local circumstances and to meet the needs of diverse groups of students. As syllabi could vary considerably across different examination boards, it was possible for a teacher to choose a syllabus that reflected their interests or strengths within a subject. Some syllabi were actually designed by examination boards in partnership with, and to meet the needs of, particular groups of schools.

Under the new NC regime, however, all students had to follow the common curriculum and be assessed across Sc1–4 according to the prescribed criteria. (It was possible for schools to offer separate courses of biology, chemistry, and physics, but students had to then take all three subjects which collectively had to cover, and extend beyond, the NC "science" curriculum.) The number of English examination boards was limited to three (requiring mergers of existing boards), and each was only allowed to offer two alternative examination specifications per subject. At the end of secondary school, when students were 16, the teachers would be responsible for assessing students' skills in Sc1, while the students would take formally invigilated, externally marked, examinations to test their knowledge and understanding in Sc2–4.

The decision to use teacher-assessment of students' attainment in scientific investigation was in principle a progressive move. Investigative skills could be tested during authentic school laboratory work rather than in the more artificial context of formal examinations. Teachers were also encouraged to be creative and explore different contexts to assess students, and it was even acceptable to repeat the assessment process at different times to allow students to develop their skills and achieve at higher levels.

However, although teachers were to be entrusted with making the assessments, which counted as 20% of the final science marks in the high stakes school leaving examinations, they were not trusted to do so without due scrutiny. Teachers had to send students' reports of their practical work, annotated to show how marks were awarded according to the set criteria, as evidence of the investigative work undertaken, for moderation by staff employed by the examination boards. Where the moderators could not find sufficient evidence to unambiguously support marks awarded, these were reduced. This undermined the logic of asking teachers to assess during normal school practical work across a wide range of investigative activities. Very quickly teachers came to use fairly standard activities that had been proven to produce the evidence required. Moreover, rather than sampling appropriate activity from diverse laboratory work, there was a tendency to prioritise practical work suitable for the kinds of assessment needed. In some cases this had repercussions for lower secondary teaching, as practical work during the early years of secondary science sometimes came to be seen as preparation for the particular kinds of "investigations" found suitable for scoring and demonstrating evidence of good marks later in the school.

There was a tendency for prioritising controlled experiments where variables could be measured, and plotted on a line graph—as this most readily fitted the assessment criteria—so distorting students' experience of the range of forms of scientific enquiry. More often than not, these investigations "enquired" into science that students should already know: how the radius of a conductor affected current flow; how concentration of acid influenced its rate of reaction with a carbonate; how the distance of a lamp from some pondweed influenced the rate at which it released bubbles of gas. Moreover, teachers found that higher marks were achieved if they assessed different assessment criteria in different activities—when students were asked at any one time to focus on planning an investigation, or collecting data, or analysing data, or evaluating a procedure. That is, students were commonly taught and assessed in scientific enquiry by disjointed activities such as analysing data they had not collected.

An innovation which had seemed to have potential to support enquiry work in schools had in effect largely curtailed any meaningful enquiry in school laboratories (Taber, 2008). Again teachers were encouraged to adopt a form of doublethink, knowing that they were free to (indeed, supposedly, encouraged to) carry out and assess whatever practical work they thought was educationally valuable, but also knowing that they were judged by how well students achieved in relation to criteria best met by undertaking discrete activities in familiar contexts (that did not require genuine enquiry) within a specific narrow model of experimental method that they had been coached in applying. Official policy had, counter to intention, effectively curtailed enquiry teaching in many schools. Recognising problems, the government changed Sc1 from just being about scientific investigations to being more widely about scientific enquiry. Initiatives were supported to develop teaching about the relationship between ideas and evidence in secondary school science (Braund, Erduran, Simon, Taber, & Tweats, 2004). However, there was much criticism of the students' experience of the science curriculum and the impression of science it offered (Cerini, Murray, & Reiss, 2003; Osborne & Collins, 2000)—including the excessive carousel of topics to be taught and the lack of opportunities to make science appear more relevant to many learners.

The government did take into account these criticisms and the advice of science education experts (Millar & Osborne, 1998), and this led to a complete overhaul of the school science curriculum. The outcome was a prescribed NC for science with much reduced compulsory content and structured so as to balance consideration of specific science topics with broader aims relating to the nature of science processes (Qualifications and Curriculum Authority, 2007a, 2007b). Ongoing criticism of the over-prescriptive, one-size-fits-all, NC had after a decade and a half led to a completely re-thought approach to the science curriculum which offered considerable more flexibility and room to focus much more on enquiry and other aspects of the nature of science. This included the adoption by one of the examination boards of a novel "specification" (the term which had replaced "syllabus" in the NC era) which offered opportunities for much more context-based teaching, with the intention to regularly change the specific topics included to reflect current issues of socio-scientific relevance. Including exploration of socio-scientific issues in school science (Sadler, 2011) was seen as important to prepare young people for full citizenship in modern societies where policy discourse incorporates scientific arguments about environmental issues, medical technology, and so forth. There is also a strong case that socio-scientific issues offer particular contexts to support cognitive development and challenge gifted learners of science (Taber, 2016).

Responses to a Progressive Curriculum

The reaction to the 2007 version of the NC for science was interesting. Some teachers did not seem to believe it was to be taken seriously. Some teaching colleagues suggested that although many of the topics previously prescribed were no longer actually mentioned in the new curriculum, they would surely still be expected to teach them all; after all, they had been part of the recommended framework and scheme of work. Teachers expected that parents, head teachers, and inspectors would still expect topics previously prescribed to be taught. Many younger teachers had only worked under the NC regime and seemed to readily adopt the doublethink that although they knew that the 2007 NC specified what must now be taught, they were really nonetheless still expected to teach what was no longer specified.

The new examination courses designed for the more liberal curriculum were subject to extensive criticism in the press and other public media. This is unusual in England where each year's external examinations are subject to scrutiny—errors in question papers are widely reported, and most years the newspapers run reports that higher pass rates or lower pass rates must mean educational standards are dropping[4]—but the curriculum content is usually largely ignored. Commentators who normally took little interest in school science and had no expertise in education were quick to criticise the idea of science lessons that might include discussion of socio-scientific issues as being only suitable for the public house (i.e., a place for informal chat over drinks). In particular the senior minister, the Secretary of State for Education, decided that science teaching that exlpored how diverse values, interests, and perspectives, impinged upon the application and social uptake of science (i.e., classroom activity requiring much more than just understanding the science concepts) was not rigorous enough (Beck, 2012), and despite offering rhetoric of "empowering teachers" and wanting "a National Curriculum that acts as a foundation of core knowledge – not a detailed blueprint for lesson plans" (Gove, 2011), demanded a return to science teaching that involved learning of a great deal of traditional science content. That is, a return to an approach out of keeping with international trends, and which had stymied the teaching of authentic enquiry skills, as well as teacher creativity, and—as far as many school students were concerned—personal relevance. The result was a further revision of the NC and a return to a content-packed list of prescribed topics (Department for Education, 2014). The teachers adopting doublethink were proved correct—they were still expected to teach the relentless carousel of science topics whatever the more stripped back NC documents may have officially prescribed. The opportunity for teachers to have more freedom and follow their professional judgement had, in the opinion of powerful reactionary voices, led to too many making the wrong choices.

Coda

At the time the author of this chapter entered science teaching, school teachers were trusted to make substantive decisions about curriculum and were left to take professional responsibility for determining pedagogy. Over two decades into the NC era teachers now expect to have curriculum prescribed, and to be accountable not only for examination results in high stake tests, but also for being seen to follow "approved" pedagogy in the classroom.

Teachers have also become widely adept at taking up and implementing successive waves of government-sponsored initiatives (on literacy in the classroom, on the use of educational technology, on providing for the gifted, etc.) knowing that any strong interest and funding support from the government will normally be short-lived and that scrutiny will often be at a surface level. It is in this context that science teachers in England were asked to adopt constructivist inspired teaching techniques, and to teach and assess enquiry in the form of "scientific investigations". The common response was in many regards the sensible one: to incorporate these expectations within their work in a way that was clearly obvious (to any observing members of the school leadership team or any visiting inspector) without fundamentally changing their professional practice. Eliciting students' ideas could make a suitable starter in a three-part lesson, and investigations could be developed to allow students to convert routine practical exercises into line graphs, based on averages of repeated measurements to ensure reliability, and preferably including a circled outlying point to demonstrate that a questionable datum had been noticed, and giving a credit-worthy opportunity to suggest a standard improvement to the method.

It was suggested earlier that there is a sense of Orwellian doublethink in operation here. Teachers have to believe in constructivist educational principles, while believing that they can teach effectively in a context which does not support substantive constructivist teaching. Teachers have to believe that enquiry is at the heart of science, while also believing that good science teaching means covering copious content and offering algorithmic practical work that never moves away from what is clearly already known (so that outcomes can be expected and fitted to the appropriate assessment formalism). Many science teachers in England can show considerable ingenuity in producing lessons offering the expected indicators of constructivist pedagogy and enquiry learning while meeting all the myriad other expectations of the content-heavy curriculum, nominal enrichment for diverse groups, recommended pedagogical devices, and, in particular, teaching targeted on what they know is likely to be included in high stakes examinations. Just what these skilful, creative, science teachers could achieve if ever they were allowed to take full professional responsibility by prioritising their own aims for their students' learning, and then teaching accordingly, is sadly, for the foreseeable future at least, likely to remain a matter for speculation.

Notes

1. It could be suggested there is a sleight of hand here, as such a distinction could be considered to presume some fundamental difference between how individual people develop beliefs about the world and how science comes to knowledge. If the difference between how a schoolchild comes to adopt a particular conception of some aspect of nature (e.g., there is no gravity in space because there is no air), and how a scientist comes to adopt a particular conception of some aspect of nature (e.g., that the observed speed of light is invariant for all observers) is a matter of degree (e.g., levels of skills and expertise) rather than due to the operation of different cognitive processes then there is no in principle difference between the fallibility of a child and that of the community of science. The adoption of a constructivist perspective requires the abandonment of traditional notions of (scientific) knowledge as true, justified belief (Taber, 2013b).
2. England is one constituent country of the United Kingdom of Great Britain and Northern Ireland (UK). However, there are differences in the education systems in England, Scotland, Wales and Northern Ireland (although the Welsh system is largely closely aligned with that in England). Scotland in particular has major differences compared to the English situation. The present chapter therefore limits its scope to considering the situation in England, and some parts (but not all) of what is discussed here also apply elsewhere in the UK.
3. A characteristic of government in the UK in recent decades has been the establishment of quasi-independent agencies or non-ministerial departments to follow through on government policy, and which are from time-to-time rebranded, abolished, merged, and so on. These have included a Teacher Training Agency which became the Training and Development Agency for Schools, and a Qualification and Curriculum Agency, the Office for Standards in Education, the Office of Qualifications and Examinations Regulation, and a General Teaching Council for England. The latter was supposed to be a professional body for teachers, but was both established, and then later wound-up, by government decree.
4. National examinations in the UK adopt an odd mix of criteria referencing (with grade boundaries expected to reflect published grade descriptions) and norm referencing (with some critical grade boundaries shifted to better match distributions of grades awarded in previous years). The popular press commonly interpret increases in pass rates as a sign of decreased rigour in the examination system with questions getting easier or more generous marking; they have also interpreted decreases in pass rate as a sign that teaching quality is falling and schools are not as good as they used to be.

References

Beck, J. (2012). Reinstating knowledge: Diagnoses and prescriptions for England's curriculum ills. *International Studies in Sociology of Education, 22*(1), 1–18. https://doi.org/10.1080/09620214.2012.680322

Bell, B., Jones, A., & Car, M. (1995). The development of the recent National New Zealand Science Curriculum. *Studies in Science Education, 26*, 73–105.

Berube, C. T. (2008). *The Unfinished Quest: The plight of progressive science education in the age of standards.* Charlotte, NC: Information Age Publishing.

Braund, M., Erduran, S., Simon, S., Taber, K. S., & Tweats, R. (2004). Teaching ideas and evidence in science at key stage 3. *Science Teacher Education, 41*, 12–13.

Brock, R. (2007). Differentiation by alternative conception: Tailoring teaching to students' thinking – A review of an attempt to target teaching according to the alternative conceptions of electricity held by year 7 students. *School Science Review, 88*(325), 97–104.

Cerini, B., Murray, I., & Reiss, M. (2003). *Student review of the science curriculum: Major findings.* London: Planet Science/Institute of Education/Science Museum.

Claxton, G. (1986). The alternative conceivers' conceptions. *Studies in Science Education, 13*, 123–130. https://doi.org/10.1080/03057268608559934

Claxton, G. (1993). Minitheories: A preliminary model for learning science. In P. J. Black & A. M. Lucas (Eds.), *Children's informal ideas in science* (pp. 45–61). London: Routledge.

Clement, J. (1993). Using bridging analogies and anchoring intuitions to deal with students' preconceptions in physics. *Journal of Research in Science Teaching, 30* (10), 1241–1257. https://doi.org/10.1002/tea.3660301007

Clough, M. P., & Olson, J. K. (2008). Teaching and assessing the nature of science: An introduction. *Science & Education, 17*(2–3), 143–145.

Cray, D., Dawkins, R., & Collins, F. (2006, November 5). God vs. science. *Time.* Retrieved from http://www.time.com/time/printout/0,8816,1555132,00.html

Cromer, A. (1997). *Connected knowledge: Science, philosophy and education.* Oxford, UK: Oxford University Press.

Department for Education. (2014). *Combined science: GCSE subject content.* London: Department for Education.

Department for Education and Employment. (1998). *Requirements for courses of initial teacher education: Annexe H – Initial teacher training National Curriculum for Secondary Science.* London: Department for Education and Employment / Qualifications and Curriculum Authority.

DES/WO. (1988). *Science for ages 5 to 16.* London/Cardiff, UK: Department for Education and Science/Welsh Office.

DiSessa, A. A. (1993). Towards an epistemology of physics. *Cognition and Instruction, 10*(2&3), 105–225.
Driver, R. (1983). *The pupil as scientist?* Milton Keynes, UK: Open University Press.
Driver, R., & Easley, J. (1978). Pupils and paradigms: A review of literature related to concept development in adolescent science students. *Studies in Science Education, 5*, 61–84.
Driver, R., & Oldham, V. (1986). A constructivist approach to curriculum development in science. *Studies in Science Education, 13*, 105–122.
Duit, R. (2009). *Bibliography – Students' and teachers' conceptions and science education*. Kiel, Germany: IPN – Leibniz Institute for Science and Mathematics Education.
Erduran, S., Simon, S., & Osborne, J. (2004). TAPping into argumentation: Developments in the application of Toulmin's argument pattern for studying science discourse. *Science Education, 88*(6), 915–933.
Fensham, P. J. (2004). *Defining an identity: The evolution of science education as a field of research*. Dordrecht, The Netherlands: Kluwer Academic Publishers.
Geertz, C. (1973). Thick description: Toward an interpretive theory of culture. In C. Geetz (Ed.), *The interpretation of cultures: Selected essays* (pp. 3–30). New York: Basic Books.
Gilbert, G. N., & Mulkay, M. (1984). *Opening Pandora's box: A sociological analysis of scientists' discourse*. Cambridge, UK: Cambridge University Press.
Gilbert, J. K., Osborne, R. J., & Fensham, P. J. (1982). Children's science and its consequences for teaching. *Science Education, 66*(4), 623–633.
Gilbert, J. K., & Watts, D. M. (1983). Concepts, misconceptions and alternative conceptions: Changing perspectives in science education. *Studies in Science Education, 10*(1), 61–98.
Gilbert, J. K., & Zylbersztajn, A. (1985). A conceptual framework for science education: The case study of force and movement. *European Journal of Science Education, 7*(2), 107–120.
Glasersfeld, E. V. (1989). Cognition, construction of knowledge, and teaching. *Synthese, 80*(1), 121–140.
Gove, M. (2011). *Michael Gove speaks to the Royal Society on Maths and Science*. London: Department for Education and Employment / Qualifications and Curriculum Authority.
Hodson, D. (2009). *Teaching and learning about science: Language, theories, methods, history, traditions and values*. Rotterdam, The Netherlands: Sense Publishers.
Jenkins, E. W. (1979). *From Armstrong to Nuffield: Studies in twentieth-century science education in England and Wales*. London: John Murray.
Kelly, G. (1963). *A theory of personality: The psychology of personal constructs*. New York: W W Norton & Company.

Key Stage 3 National Strategy. (2002a). *Framework for teaching science: Years 7, 8 and 9.* London: Department for Education and Skills.

Key Stage 3 National Strategy. (2002b). *Misconceptions in Key Stage 3 science.* London: Department for Education and Skills.

Kind, P. M., & Kind, V. (2007). Creativity in science education: Perspectives and challenges for developing school science. *Studies in Science Education, 43*(1), 1–37. https://doi.org/10.1080/03057260708560225

Kirschner, P. A., Sweller, J., & Clark, R. E. (2006). Why minimal guidance during instruction does not work: An analysis of the failure of constructivist, discovery, problem-based, experiential, and inquiry-based teaching. *Educational Psychologist, 41*(2), 75–86.

Knorr, C. K. (1999). *Epistemic cultures: How the sciences make knowledge.* Cambridge, MA: Harvard University Press.

Koestler, A. (1978/1979). *Janus: A summing up.* London: Pan Books.

Kuhn, T. S. (1970). *The structure of scientific revolutions* (2nd ed.). Chicago: University of Chicago.

Lawson, A. E. (2010). *Teaching inquiry science in middle and secondary schools.* Thousand Oaks, CA: Sage.

Lederman, N. G., & Lederman, J. S. (2012). Nature of scientific knowledge and scientific inquiry: Building instructional capacity through professional development. In B. J. Fraser, K. G. Tobin, & C. J. McRobbie (Eds.), *Second international handbook of science education* (pp. 335–359). Dordrecht, The Netherlands: Springer.

Lederman, N. G., & Lederman, J. S. (2014). Research on teaching and learning of nature of science. In N. G. Lederman & S. K. Abell (Eds.), *Handbook of research on science education* (Vol. 2, pp. 600–620). New York: Routledge.

Lemke, J. L. (1990). *Talking science: Language, learning, and values.* Norwood, NJ: Ablex Publishing Corporation.

Matthews, M. R. (1994). *Science teaching: The role of history and philosophy of science.* London: Routledge.

Matthews, M. R. (Ed.). (1998). *Constructivism in science education: A philosophical examination.* Dordrecht, The Netherlands: Kluwer Academic Publishers.

Mercer, N. (1995). *The guided construction of knowledge: Talk amongst teachers and learners.* Clevedon, UK: Multilingual Matters.

Millar, R. (2003). Teaching about energy. In Key Stage 3 National Strategy (Ed.), *Strengthening teaching and learning of energy in Key Stage 3 science: Notes for tutors* (pp. 161–179). No place of publication given: Department for Education and Skills.

Millar, R., & Osborne, J. (1998). *Beyond 2000: Science education for the future.* London: King's College.

Miller, A. I. (1986). *Imagery in scientific thought.* Cambridge, MA: MIT Press.

Mortimer, E. F., & Scott, P. H. (2003). *Meaning making in secondary science classrooms.* Maidenhead, UK: Open University Press.

Nickerson, R. S. (1998). Confirmation bias: A ubiquitous phenomenon in many guises. *Review of General Psychology, 2*(2), 175–220.

Ogborn, J., Kress, G., Martins, I., & McGillicuddy, K. (1996). *Explaining science in the classroom.* Buckingham, UK: Open University Press.

Osborne, J. (2014). Scientific practices and inquiry in the science classroom. In N. G. Lederman & S. K. Abell (Eds.), *Handbook of research on science education* (Vol. 2, pp. 579–599). New York: Routledge.

Osborne, J., & Collins, S. (2000). Pupils' and parents' views of the school science curriculum. *School Science Review, 82*(298), 23–31.

Piaget, J. (1970/1972). *The principles of genetic epistemology* (trans: Mays, W.). London: Routledge & Kegan Paul.

QCA. (2000). *Key stage 3 schemes of work.* No place of publication given: Qualification and Curriculum Authority.

Qualifications and Curriculum Authority. (2007a). *Science: Programme of study for key stage 3 and attainment targets.* London: Qualifications and Curriculum Authority.

Qualifications and Curriculum Authority. (2007b). *Science: Programme of study for key stage 4.* London: Qualifications and Curriculum Authority.

Russell, T., & Osborne, J. (1993). *Constructivist research, curriculum development and practice in primary classrooms: Reflections on five years of activity in the Science Processes and Concept Exploration (SPACE) project.* Paper presented at the third international seminar on Misconceptions in the Learning of Science and Mathematics, Cornell University, Ithaca.

Sadler, T. D. (Ed.). (2011). *Socio-scientific issues in the classroom: Teaching, learning and research.* Dordrecht, The Netherlands: Springer.

Scerri, E. R. (2003). Philosophical confusion in chemical education research. *Journal of Chemical Education, 80*(20), 468–474.

Scerri, E. R. (2012). Some comments arising from a recent proposal concerning instrumentalism and chemical education. *Journal of Chemical Education, 89*(11), 1481–1481. https://doi.org/10.1021/ed101025f

Schwab, J. J. (1962). The teaching of science as enquiry (The Inglis Lecture, 1961). In J. J. Schwab & P. F. Brandwein (Eds.), *The teaching of science.* Cambridge, MA: Harvard University Press.

Scott, P. H. (1998). Teacher talk and meaning making in science classrooms: A review of studies from a Vygotskian perspective. *Studies in Science Education, 32*, 45–80.

Shaw, M. (2012). Here endeth the three-part lesson. *TES.* Retrieved from http://www.tes.co.uk/article.aspx?storyCode=6219960

Smith, J. P., DiSessa, A. A., & Roschelle, J. (1993). Misconceptions reconceived: A constructivist analysis of knowledge in transition. *The Journal of the Learning Sciences, 3*(2), 115–163.

Solomon, J. (1994). The rise and fall of constructivism. *Studies in Science Education, 23*, 1–19.

Statutory Instrument. (1989). *The Education (National Curriculum) (Attainment Targets and Programmes of Study in Science) Order 1989*. London: HMSO.

Taber, K. S. (2008). Towards a curricular model of the nature of science. *Science & Education, 17*(2–3), 179–218. https://doi.org/10.1007/s11191-006-9056-4

Taber, K. S. (2009). *Progressing science education: Constructing the scientific research programme into the contingent nature of learning science*. Dordrecht, The Netherlands: Springer.

Taber, K. S. (2010a). Constructivism and direct instruction as competing instructional paradigms: An essay review of Tobias and Duffy's constructivist instruction: Success or failure? *Education Review, 13*(8), 1–44. Retrieved from http://www.edrev.info/essays/v13n8index.html

Taber, K. S. (2010b). Paying lip-service to research?: The adoption of a constructivist perspective to inform science teaching in the English curriculum context. *The Curriculum Journal, 21*(1), 25–45.

Taber, K. S. (2010c). Straw men and false dichotomies: Overcoming philosophical confusion in chemical education. *Journal of Chemical Education, 87*(5), 552–558. https://doi.org/10.1021/ed8001623

Taber, K. S. (2011a). Constructivism as educational theory: Contingency in learning, and optimally guided instruction. In J. Hassaskhah (Ed.), *Educational theory* (pp. 39–61). New York: Nova. Retrieved from https://camtools.cam.ac.uk/wiki/eclipse/Constructivism.html

Taber, K. S. (2011b). The natures of scientific thinking: Creativity as the handmaiden to logic in the development of public and personal knowledge. In M. S. Khine (Ed.), *Advances in the nature of science research – Concepts and methodologies* (pp. 51–74). Dordrecht, The Netherlands: Springer.

Taber, K. S. (2013a). A common core to chemical conceptions: Learners' conceptions of chemical stability, change and bonding. In G. Tsaparlis & H. Sevian (Eds.), *Concepts of matter in science education* (pp. 391–418). Dordrecht, The Netherlands: Springer.

Taber, K. S. (2013b). *Modelling learners and learning in science education: Developing representations of concepts, conceptual structure and conceptual change to inform teaching and research*. Dordrecht, The Netherlands: Springer.

Taber, K. S. (2014). *Student thinking and learning in science: Perspectives on the nature and development of learners' ideas*. New York: Routledge.

Taber, K. S. (2016). The nature of science and the teaching of gifted learners. In K. S. Taber & M. Sumida (Eds.), *International perspectives on science education for the gifted: Key issues and challenges* (pp. 94–105). Abingdon, UK: Routledge.

Taber, K. S. (2017). Knowledge, beliefs and pedagogy: How the nature of science should inform the aims of science education (And not just when teaching evolution). *Cultural Studies of Science Education, 12*(1), 81–91. https://doi.org/10.1007/s11422-016-9750-8

Thagard, P. (1992). *Conceptual revolutions.* Oxford, UK: Princeton University Press.

Tobias, S., & Duffy, T. M. (2009). The success or failure of constructivist instruction: An introduction. In S. Tobias & T. M. Duffy (Eds.), *Constructivist instruction: Success or failure?* (pp. 3–10). New York: Routledge.

Yeo, R. (1979). William Whewell, natural theology and the philosophy of science in mid nineteenth century Britain. *Annals of Science, 36*(5), 493–516. https://doi.org/10.1080/00033797900200341

CHAPTER 5

The Practice Turn in Learning Theory and Science Education

Ellice A. Forman

Unlike many other post-industrial countries such as Great Britain (Taber, this volume), the United States does not have a national curriculum for science or other disciplines. Instead, in the late 1980s, the National Council of Teachers of Mathematics (NCTM) released standards for mathematics education, which was soon followed by the science education standards (National Research Council [NRC], 1996). Before the first revision of the NCTM Standards in 2000, several learning theorists were asked to contribute chapters to a volume that reviewed the research behind the standards (Kilpatrick, Martin, & Schifter, 2003). These chapters focused on learning in areas such as cognitive science, situative learning, and sociocultural theory. In this way, NCTM clarified the influence of current learning theories and research on the standards in mathematics. More recently, the NRC has published a series of books that show how research and theory in psychology, sociology, anthropology, and linguistics apply to instruction, learning, and assessment in mathematics and science (e.g., NRC, 2007).

Although each political entity creates its own policy documents and curriculum materials to inform its educational practices, an international perspective has emerged on the importance of changing our traditional ways of teaching school science (e.g., Forman, Engle, Venturini, & Ford, 2014;

E.A. Forman (✉)
Department of Instruction and Learning, University of Pittsburgh, Pittsburgh, PA, USA

D.W. Kritt (ed.), *Constructivist Education in an Age of Accountability*,
https://doi.org/10.1007/978-3-319-66050-9_5

Mody, 2015). There are several reasons for this. First, teacher-centered approaches to instruction are now viewed as less engaging than more student-centered classrooms (Engle & Conant, 2002). Second, traditional school science gives the misleading impression that factual knowledge and rote laboratory procedures are the major characteristics of scientific practice (Mody, 2015; Windschitl, Thompson, & Braaten, 2008). To correct this mistaken view of science as tedious and routine, the most recent version of the science standards (NRC, 2012) emphasizes the importance of asking students to engage in authentic scientific practices such as employing models, conducting empirical investigations, using evidence-based arguments to reconcile disagreements, and drawing conclusions. Thus, teachers are being asked to radically change the content of their lessons and the nature of authority structures and accountability requirements in their classrooms (Forman & Ford, 2014). In a nutshell, the aim of these policy documents is to transform classrooms into settings where activities more closely resemble those of professional scientists: this is often called the "practice turn" (Ford & Forman, 2006; Passmore, Gouvea, Giere, 2014).

This chapter explains the nature of the practice turn in science education by showing how it is grounded in current learning theories as well as in the field of science studies. Science studies has helped us identify and define some key features of scientific practice such as modeling, representation, and argumentation. Recently, these practices have been successfully employed in a few elementary through high school classrooms. Research based on those settings allows us to better understand the implications of the practice turn for teacher education and future classroom-based research.

What Is the Practice Turn in Learning Theory?

In the past 30 years, educational psychologists have begun to recognize the multiple paradigms that now inform our understanding of cognition and learning. For example, Sfard proposed a distinction between two metaphors for learning: acquisition versus participation (1998). The acquisition metaphor is the oldest and most prominent theory of learning in psychology. Much of cognitive science and cognitive developmental research portrays learning as the acquisition of skills, concepts, procedures, or schema in a hypothetical mental storage device. The learner is viewed as an owner of these mental entities and learning involves the accumulation, refinement, or re-organization of mental contents. Transfer is seen to occur when the owner applies skills or knowledge structures across contexts.

In contrast, Sfard's participation metaphor can be seen in the work of cultural psychologists (Cole, 1996; Rogoff, 2003) and anthropologists (Lave & Wenger, 1991). This metaphor views the learner as a member of a community of practice. As Lave and Wenger argue, learning involves a process of legitimate peripheral participation as newcomers enter the community and engage with old-timers. The communities that they reported on were not in formal educational settings. This metaphor of learning may be applied to a wide range of contexts, such as midwives and butchers, where groups of people work together toward common goals. In the participation metaphor, learning involves identity change. One salient example is the community of Alcoholic Anonymous (AA), where newcomers begin viewing themselves as social drinkers but cannot become old-timers until they change their identities to recovering alcoholics (Lave & Wenger, 1991). Each community described by Lave and Wenger has its own characteristics. In some communities, learning the practice of old-timers is accessible and easy; in other communities learning by newcomers is restricted by old-timers. In this way, the processes and products of learning are "shared" (sometimes unequally) by members of a community.[1]

What Is the Practice Turn in Science Studies?

For the past 40 years, the field of science studies has investigated what scientists do through laboratory studies, ethnographies of laboratories, and historical accounts (Lehrer & Schauble, 2006a, 2006b; Mody, 2015; Passmore et al., 2014). This work stands in contrast to the cleaner, more logical, but unrealistic view of the scientific method known as positivism (Ford & Forman, 2006; Windschitl et al., 2008). Future scientists and consumers of science need to understand that scientific practice is complex, messy, social, and political. It is also possible that this more realistic view of science may attract new groups of people who appreciate the creative, unpredictable, and human features of scientific practice (Mody, 2015).

Many of the summaries of the science studies literature focus on the interrelated features of modeling, investigation, representation, and argumentation (e.g., Passmore et al., 2014). Several prominent science educators have emphasized the centrality of modeling in science because it allows them to show how scientific practice is multi-faceted but holistic (e.g., Lehrer & Schauble, 2006a, 2015; Windschitl et al., 2008). In addition, modeling is how scientists make sense of the complexities and uncertainties of the physical world (Passmore et al., 2014).

The essence of scientific modeling is analogy (Lehrer & Schauble, 2006a, 2006b). The simplest version of the analogy is the mapping of correspondences between familiar objects (e.g., the solar system) and unfamiliar targets (e.g., the atom). Quite soon in their investigations, scientists find constraints in these mappings when the simple models fail to generate accurate predictions or explanations of natural phenomena. Thus, as Nersessian (2008) proposes, imaginary models based on hybrid representations must be created to address those constraints.

Passmore and her colleagues (2014, p. 1176) articulate three key features of models: "models are defined by the context of their use; models are partial renderings of phenomena; models are distinct from the representational forms they take." That is, they view models as processes (not mental structures) that are responsive to the demands of their use. Models must be similar to the phenomena they represent but, like maps that depict terrain features or political entities, they must leave out many details. Finally, representations may or may not be used as models: their status depends upon how they are used by agents.

An important voice in science studies is Nancy Nersession (2008), who studies scientists in current laboratories as well as in the historical record. In her review of experimental, ethnographic, and historical evidence, Nersession argues that mental models enable the kinds of reasoning that occur in scientific practice. These mental models depend upon material or symbolic representations (diagrams, mathematical equations, oral and written descriptions and explanations, and even physical gestures) that provide the supports for simulations of the physical world. Change in scientific concepts is based on a process of "bootstrapping, which consists of cycles of construction, simulation, evolution, and adaptation of models that serve as interim interpretations of the target problem" (p. 184). Although for Nersessian, the individual creates mental models, the process of modeling also occurs in social and cultural contexts that support and constrain scientific outcomes. For example, she argues that James Clerk Maxwell's discoveries about the electromagnetic field were affected by Scottish approaches to mathematical problem solving (based on geometry) in contrast to approaches by continental physicists such as Ampère.

The nature of scientific representations was the subject of Latour's (1990) ethnographic study of a laboratory. He observed that the material aspects of everyday science (e.g., raising colonies of rats, dissection of tissues) received little attention in professional conferences or publications. Instead, the representations on paper (called inscriptions) were the primary focus of oral and written arguments between and among groups of scientists. These inscriptions (graphs, two and three dimensional representations, metaphors, narratives, or mathematical equations), can become the source of scientific explanatory power if they were also "immutable, presentable, readable, and combinable" (Latour, 1990, p. 26). In other words, the messy realities of laboratory life do not travel well and are not the basis for scientific progress. Inscriptions not only travel, they can be discussed by people who weren't present at the laboratory and can be critiqued, elaborated, simplified, or embedded in revised versions.

One salient example of this is the inscription for DNA (the double helix). Earlier in its development, Linus Pauling, a well-known chemist at the time, proposed a three-chain helix. Watson and Crick, however, had previously rejected the three-chain model in favor of a two-chain representation (Latour, 1987). Because of the need to strengthen their argument with Pauling and others, Watson and Crick quickly began to explore additional aspects of the double helix that were consistent with known biochemical principles and x-ray data (taken by Franklin). Passmore and her colleagues (2014) suggest that the double helix inscription by itself was not a model of DNA; it became one when it afforded a better understanding of its function (to explain genetic inheritance). By inventing this powerful inscription and winning the competition with Pauling, Watson and Crick were credited with the discovery of the DNA model.

Drawing on other sources from science studies (e.g., Bazerman, 1988; Longino, 2002; Pera, 1994), Ford and Forman (2006) emphasized the nature of scientific argumentation in communities. They posited the necessity of dual roles (of construction and critique) to illustrate the social mechanism by which peer review creates communal authority. These two roles operate proactively and reactively: constructors of claims must ground their explanations in evidence and logic when they anticipate critique; the peer reviewers must respond to the constructors' claims using counter-evidence and logic. Later, the critiquers become the constructors so that the dual roles continue but with different actors assuming those roles. Through this social and discursive process, the reliability and validity of claims are warranted. In addition, nature "speaks" through the material practices of science in which tools and inscriptions serve to constrain the kinds of claims that can be made (Pickering, 1995).

In summary, modeling has shown us how scientific concepts emerge and get established through argumentation based on inscriptions and other material practices in the scientific fields (Latour, 1987; Nersessian, 2008).

Passmore et al. (2014) suggest that the studies of the sociocultural contexts of scientific sense making are valuable resources for educational applications. They draw from a range of studies of how scientific professionals interact daily with their colleagues and use material and symbolic resources to understand how nature works. For many science educators, models and modeling are a key focus in the practices of scientists and should be important in science instruction (Lehrer & Schauble, 2015; Passmore et al., 2014; Windschitl et al., 2008).

How Can the Practice Turn Be Applied to Science Education?

Windschitl and his colleagues (2008) propose that model-based inquiry (MBI) should replace the scientific method (TSM) as the dominant paradigm for school science inquiry activities. They argue that TSM has done more harm than good in science education due to its tendency to distort the nature of science by reducing the creative processes of the discipline to a lockstep set of procedures that do not make sense to students. These procedures consist of "observe, develop a question, develop a hypothesis, conduct an experiment, analyze data, state conclusions, generate new questions" (p. 942). Unfortunately, these procedures are confusing to students for several reasons: the questions are usually provided by the teachers, not the students. Because these questions are not model-based, they seem content-free (labs are often artificially divorced from content-focused instruction). In addition, TSM makes it seem as if all of science relies on experimentation, which is not the case for historical sciences such as evolutionary biology. Also, TSM rarely asks students to explain the patterns they observe in the laboratory, which is a fundamental aim of scientific investigations (Chinn & Malhotra, 2002). Finally, Windschitl and his colleagues argue TSM is too easy for teachers since it emphasizes procedures over explanations or concept development.

Instead, Windschitl et al. (2008) suggest that scientific inquiry should be oriented toward "reasoning with and about models" (MBI; p. 944). Model-based inquiry should become the organizing principle for science education. Since the core aim of science is to use models to represent our emerging concepts of the natural world, teaching in this way would make instruction much more authentic and engaging. They further propose that instruction be organized around five epistemic characteristics of scientific knowledge building: that knowledge be "testable, revisable, explanatory, conjectural, and generative" (p. 943).

Lehrer and Schauble (2006b, 2015) can help us connect the pedagogy of MBI with learning theory when they discuss the practice turn in the learning of science. They review the multiple images of learning science as reasoning, conceptual change, and practice. The first image, science-as-reasoning, is closely related to the domain-general skills of the scientific method ([TSM]; particularly those identified by Inhelder & Piaget, 1958). Since these skills are viewed as transferring across task contexts and disciplinary domains, TSM is like Sfard's (1998) metaphor of learning as acquisition. The second image, science-as-conceptual change is also part of Sfard's metaphor of learning as acquisition, since mental concepts such as "heavy" and "large" become refined and integrated into a new mental structure (i.e., density). This occurs when children recognize that sometimes large objects are light (Styrofoam) and small objects are heavy (steel), thereby requiring a new concept of density (the ratio of mass per unit volume). The third image, science-as-practice seems to be close to Sfard's (1998) second metaphor, learning as participation. Lehrer and Schauble (2015) cite evidence from science studies as demonstrating parallels between learning in scientific communities and in classrooms. They argue that learning science as practice differs from the other two images because skills and concepts are assumed to be individual possessions whereas practices are aspects of a scientific community that shares a common discourse, tools, and routines to create scientific knowledge. Windschitl and his colleagues admit that MBI is "ambitious pedagogy" (2008, p. 963). Versions of this new paradigm for instruction (and teacher education) appear in the classroom-based research literature, with children and adolescents (e.g., Lehrer & Schauble, 2012; Metz, 2004; Passmore & Stewart, 2002) and with beginning science teachers (Windschitl, Thompson, & Braaten, 2012).

Lehrer and Schauble (2015) devote most of their space to the practice of modeling, which they see as a central feature of science. They argue that models can be viewed as the products of science but they also figure in the production of new knowledge. Modeling as a practice should take different forms in classrooms than in professional communities due to the limited expertise of novice scientists. In their work with classroom teachers, they create instructional design experiments (Cobb, Confrey, diSessa, Lehrer, & Schauble, 2003) in which inscriptional supports for increasingly sophisticated model-based reasoning are introduced.

In one example (Lehrer & Schauble, 2006b), young children (approximately 6 years old) were given physical materials (Styrofoam, springs, wooden dowels, etc.) to build a representation of an elbow. Children's initial representations displayed physical similarities (bumps to indicate the joint; fingers made of Popsicle sticks) to the target (elbow) but not functional similarities (ability to bend in characteristic ways). These initial representations helped the children better understand the instructional goal (to make an analogy between one object and another). Nevertheless, the children became dissatisfied with these inadequate models once they carefully observed the constraints imposed on range of motion by their own elbows. Like scientists, the children saw the need to revise their initial representations to do a better job of embodying the functional features of elbows. "This shift from literal similarity to mapping relations is a hallmark of analogical reasoning…More powerful analogies are based not on surface similarity, but on interconnections and constraints among relations and systems of relations" (p. 373). Somewhat older children (approximately 8 years), however, could create models of "the arm as a third-class lever, with the elbow acting as the fulcrum" (p 373). Here the children's three-dimensional inscriptions served as models for understanding the mechanical advantage of the biological system.

Passmore and her colleagues (2014) remind us of the need to differentiate models from representations when evaluating their use in classrooms. They argue that an object (e.g., a boat) may be viewed as a simple representation if its purpose is to illustrate the physical features of objects that may float (i.e., limited cognitive challenge). If, however, it is used as a tool to reason about fluid displacement, then it could become a model for the sophisticated concept of buoyancy (i.e., higher cognitive challenge). They suggest that teachers focus on learning objectives that stress the use of representations to conceptualize and reason instead of objectives that merely ask students to create those inscriptions. Building upon the example of the elbow modeling activity, Passmore and her colleagues proposed that teachers focus on this question, "how is it that an elbow allows you to pick up something," instead of the confusing question about making an object that "works like an elbow" (Passmore et al., 2014, p. 1182).

Passmore et al. (2014) continue in their discussion of the value of model-based inquiry for education by reminding us that any natural system could be modeled in many ways. Each model provides different resources for reasoning about the natural world. Instead of focusing on the "correct" model, they suggest that we need to help students connect their underlying conceptions of phenomena with representations that are useful and meaningful for solving problems. This recommendation echoes Lehrer and Schauble's (2012) suggestion that having access to multiple kinds of inscriptions can support students' reasoning about their affordances and constraints. Lehrer and Schauble cite an historian of science, Pickering (1995), as helping us see that "modeling typically entails a struggle ... with the physical world to arrange the conditions for seeing" (p. 704). When we simplify students' investigations by eliminating the messy struggles with different forms of representation, we restrict their experiences with these key aspects of authentic scientific practice.

Another component of scientific practice is argumentation. The instructional goals of the dual role framework (construction and critique) proposed by Ford and Forman (2006) resemble those of Berland and Reiser: "sense-making, articulating, and persuading" (2009, p. 4). Articulating one's ideas to others is already part of traditional school science and making sense of evidence is also a frequent obligation. However, integrating persuasion with sense making and articulating is crucial to involving students in authentic disciplinary practices. Thus, the different components of engaging in argument need to be used in service of sense making for these activities to resemble the "grasp of practice" (Ford & Forman, 2006).

Like other science educators, Manz (2015) contrasts the practices of scientists and those of classroom teachers and students. After reviewing the science education literature on argumentation, Manz finds that students often have trouble supporting their claims with evidence, warrants, and backings, and with understanding the necessity of counter-argument. She concludes that these difficulties may be a result of teaching argumentation as a set of skills to master in isolation. This resembles concerns raised by Windschitl and his colleagues (2008) about instruction based on the scientific method. Drawing from the science studies literature, Manz (2015) outlines the components of scientific practice as an activity system, with argumentation as a valuable tool. She proposes that argumentation arises as a response to the uncertainty of modeling. Contested claims in arguments occur for many reasons in this literature: material practices, entire investigations, data representations, as well as models. Like Pera (1994), Manz argues that science is about three actors: the person who puts forth the claim, the phenomena from nature that "speaks" through its representations, and the community that contests the claim using disciplinary norms and practices. Manz views scientific practice as inherently dialogic (i.e., involves constructors and critiquers of claims that must be supported by theory and evidence).

To translate this to the classroom, Manz (2015) proposes that students must be introduced to a different activity system (not merely to a new set of skills or participant structures). She identifies which features of science practice could be developed and adapted to the classroom context. This activity system, which she calls an epistemic culture, has several components including new goals and new community norms. For example, these new goals would include making sense of phenomena, articulating that understanding, and persuading others by making argumentation a frequent classroom activity. It would also involve a stance toward the inherent uncertainty of scientific ideas and practices. This would require teacher scaffolding of new classroom community norms that fostered shared authority and included accountability to the discipline. These recommendations have features like those suggested by Berland and Reiser (2009), Engle and Conant (2002), and others.

Conclusions

Recent developments in learning theory have begun to influence education by asking teachers to incorporate authentic disciplinary practices into classroom instruction (Passmore et al., 2014). In the United States, these recommendations are embodied in the National Standards for mathematics and science education (NCTM, 2000; NRC, 2012). The practice turn in science education relies upon a theory of learning as participation (Sfard, 1998). These recommendations include three connected features in their instruction: "rhetoric, representation, and modeling" (Lehrer, Schauble, & Petrosino, 2001, p. 251).

Instead of relying on a set of disembodied laboratory procedures and teacher-centered didactic instruction, advocates of this ambitious pedagogy propose that teachers and students create a new activity system that supports an epistemic culture for authentic scientific inquiry (Manz, 2015; Windschitl et al., 2008). The aim of this alternative culture is to introduce students to the creative aspects of scientific practices and to engage them in activities that involve representing, explaining, persuading, testing models, and making sense of scientific inquiry.

Clearly this form of ambitious pedagogy has limitations. First, much of the research literature in science education is based on the older learning theory, using the acquisition metaphor (Sfard, 1998). Since this influential metaphor has helped guide the field for many years and has produced a wealth of findings about important topics such as conceptual change (diSessa, 2006), it would be premature to dismiss it as irrelevant to understanding classroom learning. Second, ambitious pedagogy requires more resources (time, energy, materials, deep disciplinary knowledge) in an already overwhelmed and underfunded educational system in the United States and elsewhere in the world (Forman et al., 2014).

Nevertheless, the participation metaphor (Sfard, 1998) and the science studies literature (Passmore et al., 2014) open new areas for meaningful investigation in the learning sciences and science education. One rich area of research is in teacher education, which was addressed by Windschitl et al. (2012). Another critical area of research is the need to highlight the importance of sense making in education in this age of accountability. As Chinn and Malhotra (2002) argue, classroom tasks typically fail the test of authentic inquiry in science. This echoes the message from Windschitl and his colleagues (2008) to reject the centrality of the so-called scientific method for model-based inquiry. Both groups of educators emphasize the importance of meaningful instruction.

Another implication for future research is the need to reimagine our notions of teaching science to children from non-dominant communities (Bang, Warren, Rosebery, & Medin, 2012). Bang and her colleagues explore recent work in fields such as marine microbiology and indigenous science to sketch out alternatives to our narrow views of the relationships between nature and culture. They argue that our settled notions about science and scientific inquiry need to be "desettled" for several reasons. First, the settled notions of what counts as science often result in devaluing the contributions of marginalized groups of students. "Deficit discourses operate to control the scope of what constitutes an acceptable explanation, argument or analysis, what 'it' looks and sounds like, whose narratives and experiences are valued and for what purposes" (p. 303).

Second, Bang et al. (2012) refer to the latest research in biological science to re-conceptualize the boundary between nature and culture. They summarize the work of an indigenous Canadian scientist, Michael Blackstock (2002), who uses his cultural background to help him view water as a crucial fluid connector between organisms in an ecosystem. His perspective helps Bang and her colleagues critique the "human-centered ontology" of science (2012, p. 307) that is becoming increasingly outdated as we deal with the new demands of fields like ecology and climate science. Bang et al., argue that this literature forces us to reflect on the comments of students that might challenge our notions of the sharp divisions between animate and inanimate beings. Instead of treating these kinds of conceptions as wrong, teachers and students need to view these ideas as useful conjectures to build upon when modeling complex natural systems.

Educational reformers have repeatedly warned us that students leave school without a firm grounding in the disciplines that they study (Shulman & Quinlan, 1996). In recent years, educators have promoted learning goals that foster productive disciplinary engagement (Engle & Conant, 2002; Forman et al., 2014). In the field of science education, there has been a recommendation that we try to embody the practices of scientists in classroom activities through modeling, representing, and arguing (Ford & Forman, 2006; Lehrer & Schauble, 2006a; Passmore et al., 2014). Nevertheless, teaching these practices as discrete skills, divorced from content, seems to be counter-productive. In the hope of making learning science meaningful and interesting, several science educators have proposed the need for viewing these practices as aspects of a model-based activity system (Manz, 2015; Windschilt et al., 2008). This kind of activity system should also offer equal access to learning for all, not just for those from privileged communities (Bang et al., 2012). In this way, the practice turn in science education has begun to help us desettle our notions of school science in ways that might improve teacher preparation and student learning in the future.

Note

1. A more extensive discussion of the historical roots and current applications of the participation metaphor can be found in Ford and Forman (2006).

References

Bang, M., Warren, B., Rosebery, A. S., & Medin, D. (2012). Desettling expectations in science education. *Human Development, 55*, 302–318.

Bazerman, C. (1988). *Shaping written knowledge: The genre and activity of the experimental article in science*. Madison, WI: University of Wisconsin Press.

Berland, L. K., & Reiser, B. J. (2009). Making sense of argumentation and explanation. *Science Education, 93*(1), 26–55.

Blackstock, M. D. (2002). Water-based ecology: A first nations' proposal to repair the definition of a forest ecosystem. *BC Journal of Ecosystems and Management, 2*, 1–6.

Chinn, C. A., & Malhotra, B. A. (2002). Epistemologically authentic inquiry in schools: A theoretical framework for evaluating inquiry tasks. *Science Education, 86*, 175–218.

Cobb, P., Confrey, J., diSessa, A. A., Lehrer, R., & Schauble, L. (2003). Design experiments in educational research. *Educational Researcher, 32*(1), 9–13.

Cole, M. (1996). *Cultural psychology: A once and future discipline*. Cambridge, MA: Belknap Press of Harvard University Press.

diSessa, A. (2006). A history of conceptual change research. In R. K. Sawyer (Ed.), *The Cambridge handbook of the learning sciences* (pp. 265–281). New York: Cambridge University Press.

Engle, R. A., & Conant, F. R. (2002). Guiding principles for fostering productive disciplinary engagement: Explaining an emergent argument in a community of learners classroom. *Cognition and Instruction, 20*, 399–483.

Ford, M. J., & Forman, E. A. (2006). Redefining disciplinary learning in classroom contexts. In J. Green & A. Luke (Eds.), *Review of educational research* (Vol. 30, pp. 1–32). Washington, DC: American Education Research Association.

Forman, E. A., Engle, R. A., Venturini, P., & Ford, M. (2014). International examinations and extensions of the productive disciplinary engagement framework. *International Journal of Educational Research, 64*, 149–155.

Forman, E. A., & Ford, M. (2014). Authority and accountability in light of disciplinary practices in science. *International Journal of Educational Research, 64*, 198–209.

Inhelder, B., & Piaget, J. (1958). *The growth of logical thinking from childhood to adolescence: An essay on the constructional of formal operational structures* (trans: Parsons, A. & Milgram, S.). New York: Basic Books.

Kilpatrick, J., Martin, W. G., & Schifter, D. (Eds.). (2003). *A research companion to the principles and standards for school mathematics*. Reston, VA: National Council of Teachers of Mathematics.

Latour, B. (1987). *Science in action*. Milton Keynes, UK: Open University Press.

Latour, B. (1990). Drawing things together. In M. Lynch & S. Woolgar (Eds.), *Representation in scientific practice* (pp. 19–68). Cambridge, MA: The M.I.T. Press.

Lave, J., & Wenger, E. (1991). *Situated learning: Legitimate peripheral participation*. New York: Cambridge University Press.

Lehrer, R., & Schauble, L. (2006a). Cultivating model-based reasoning in science education. In R. K. Sawyer (Ed.), *The Cambridge handbook of the learning sciences* (pp. 371–387). New York: Cambridge University Press.

Lehrer, R., & Schauble, L. (2006b). Scientific thinking and scientific literacy. In W. Damon, R. Lerner, K. A. Renninger, & E. Sigel (Eds.), *Handbook of child psychology* (Vol. 4, 6th ed., pp. 153–196). Hoboken, NJ: Wiley.

Lehrer, R., & Schauble, L. (2012). Seeding evolutionary thinking by engaging children in modeling its foundations. *Science Education, 96*, 701–724.

Lehrer, R., & Schauble, L. (2015). The development of scientific thinking. In R. M. Lerner (Ed.), *Handbook of child psychology and developmental science* (Vol. 2, 7th ed., pp. 671–715). New York: Wiley.

Lehrer, R., Schauble, L., & Petrosino, A. J. (2001). Reconsidering the role of experiment in science education. In K. Crowley, C. D. Schunn, & T. Okada (Eds.), *Designing for science: Implications from everyday, classroom, and professional settings* (pp. 251–278). Mahwah, NJ: Lawrence Erlbaum Associates.

Longino, H. (2002). *The fate of knowledge*. Princeton, NJ: Princeton University Press.

Manz, E. (2015). Representing student argumentation as functionally emergent from scientific activity. *Review of Educational Research, 85*(4), 553–590.

Metz, K. E. (2004). Children's understanding of scientific inquiry: Their conceptualization of uncertainty in investigations of their own design. *Cognition and Instruction, 22*(2), 219–290.

Mody, C. C. M. (2015). Scientific practice and science education. *Science Education, 99*(6), 1026–1032.

NCTM. (2000). *Principles and standards for school mathematics*. Reston, VA: The National Council of Teachers of Mathematics, Inc.

Nersessian, N. J. (2008). *Creating scientific concepts*. Cambridge, MA: MIT Press.

NRC. (1996). *National science education standards*. Washington, DC: National Academy Press.

NRC. (2007). *Taking science to school: Learning and teaching science in grades K-8*. Washington, DC: National Academy Press.

NRC. (2012). *A framework for K-12 science education: Practices, crosscutting concepts, and core ideas*. Washington, DC: National Academies Press.

Passmore, C. M., Gouvea, J., & Giere, R. (2014). Models in science and in learning science: Focusing scientific practice on sense-making. In M. Matthews (Ed.), *International handbook of research in history, philosophy and science teaching* (pp. 1171–1202). Dordrecht, The Netherlands: Springer.

Passmore, C. M., & Stewart, J. (2002). A modeling approach to teaching evolutionary biology in high schools. *Journal of Research in Science Teaching, 39*(3), 185–204.

Pera, M. (1994). *The discourses of science*. Chicago, IL: University of Chicago Press.

Pickering, A. (1995). *The mangle of practice: Time, agency, & science*. Chicago, IL: University of Chicago Press.

Rogoff, B. (2003). *The cultural nature of human development*. New York: Oxford University Press.

Sfard, A. (1998). On two metaphors for learning and the dangers of choosing just one. *Educational Researcher, 27*(2), 4–13.
Shulman, L. S., & Quinlan, K. M. (1996). The comparative psychology of school subjects. In D. C. Berliner & R. C. Calfee (Eds.), *Handbook of educational psychology* (pp. 399–422). New York: Simon & Schuster.
Windschitl, M., Thompson, J., & Braaten, M. (2008). Beyond the scientific method: Model-based inquiry as a new paradigm of preference for school science investigations. *Science Education, 92*, 941–967.
Windschitl, M., Thompson, J., & Braaten, M. (2012). Proposing a core set of instructional practices and tools for teachers of science. *Science Education, 96*, 878–903.

CHAPTER 6

How Constructivism Can Boost Success in STEM Fields for Women and Students of Color

Oscar E. Fernandez

According to a recent National Science Foundation (NSF) report (National Science Foundation, 2015), women have earned 57% of all bachelor's degrees in biosciences and social sciences since the late 1990s, but only about 20% of bachelor's degrees in engineering, computer science, and physics over the same time period. The same NSF report documents a similar profile of degree attainment for students of color. Roughly 50% of the bachelor's degrees they earned in 2012 were in psychology or the social sciences (about 25% and 23%, respectively), while engineering, the physical sciences, and mathematics/statistics each constituted just 12%. *Why is there such a stark contrast in degree attainment between Science, Technology, Engineering, and Mathematics (STEM) and the social sciences for both groups of students? And what makes the social sciences so popular among both groups?*

There are several contributing factors to these two issues. Many—including family resource disparities and differences in access to high-quality instruction—are beyond the average educator's control. However, there are at least two that are not: the content's *context*, and the content's *delivery*. This chapter draws on several sources to help understand how these two factors contribute to the "STEM degree attainment gap" for women and

O.E. Fernandez (✉)
Department of Mathematics, Wellesley College, Wellesley, MA, USA

D.W. Kritt (ed.), *Constructivist Education in an Age of Accountability*,
https://doi.org/10.1007/978-3-319-66050-9_6

students of color, and the simple tweaks an educator can employ to boost success in STEM for women and students of color. Given the central role of mathematics courses (and, more broadly, content) in the pathway to a STEM degree, the discussion is focused on women and students of color and their experiences with mathematics. Luckily, mathematics has a rich history of research-backed methods, approaches, and programs proven to broaden participation (and boost performance) in math for all students. Two particular programs profiled at the end of the chapter illustrate how including the components discussed in this chapter can dramatically boost success in STEM for women and students of color.

The Content's Context: Why It Matters, and What to Do About It

In its 2010 report entitled *Why so few? Women in science, technology, engineering, and mathematics* (Hill, Corbett, St. Rose, & AAUW, 2010), the American Association of University Women notes that "well-documented gender differences exist in the value that women and men place on doing work that contributes to society, with *women more likely than men to prefer work with a clear social purpose*" (emphasis added). The report continues:

> Regardless of the origin of the difference, most people do not view STEM occupations as directly benefiting society or individuals (Diekman, Brown, Johnston, & Clark, 2009; National Academy of Engineering, 2008). As a result, STEM careers often do not appeal to women (or men) who value making a societal contribution. (Eccles, 1994; Sax, 1994)

These findings suggest that fields with *intrinsic* or at least *discernable* societal relevance have particular appeal to women students. (Good examples of the "intrinsic" variety are the social sciences (e.g., psychology), while good examples of the "discernable" variety are the biological sciences).[1] The findings also hint at the first of a few tweaks to be presented in this chapter that educators can employ to increase women students' interest in STEM:

Tweak #1: Make the content more societally relevant.

This does not have to involve a complete overhaul of the curriculum. As a simple example, a teacher could replace some of the current in-class examples with ones that contain some degree of societal relevance. (For instance, when discussing real-world applications of trigonometry, use the percentage of the population getting a cold throughout the year rather than a Ferris wheel. Both applications illustrate sinusoidal functions well, but the former has much more societal relevance.) Chosen appropriately, these examples will illustrate the STEM concepts just as well as the original examples *and* have the added benefit of potentially increasing interest in the content for women students in the class.

Context is just as important for students of color. A 2010 study by the UCLA Higher Education Research Institute surveyed over 5000 minority and non-minority STEM majors and found that "the relevance of science course work to students' lives had a significant impact on academic and social adjustment for underrepresented minority students in the sciences, which *underscores the importance of experiential learning and understanding the application of knowledge*" (emphasis added) (Hurtado, Newman, Tran, & Chang, 2010). A possible explanation for why context is also important to students of color comes from the large body of research (c.f., Hurtado et al., 2010; Oakes, 1990; Rovai, Gallien, & Wighting, 2005; and references therein) suggesting that students of color are "field dependent" learners, defined as "learning that is highly influenced by the context in which knowledge and skills are imbedded" (Oakes, 1990). More specifically, field dependent learners prefer "learning [that] is related to the *life experiences* of the student" (emphasis added) (Rovai et al., 2005). Unfortunately, most STEM courses are not taught in this way:

> These [science and math] courses may be so abstract that students who do not have the (abstract) reasoning skills or high interest or external motivation (family expectations) find them dull and difficult. Consequently, many students conclude, perhaps incorrectly, that they are unable to succeed in or learn science. The result of the attempt to gear high school science courses toward college preparation is that courses are focused on abstract science and are largely devoid of practical applications, technology, *or the relevance of science to society and its problems.* (Johnston & Aldridge, 1984, emphasis added; also Oakes, 1990)

These finding suggest a second simple tweak to the curriculum:

Tweak #2: Personalize the content.

For example, an educator might give out a survey on the first day of class asking students for their hobbies and interests, and incorporate that information into their course in a meaningful way (e.g., change the context of portions of lessons to align with certain respondents' interests, or design homework assignments based on the feedback received).[2] When combined with increased societal relevance, these curricular changes could have particular appeal to students of color and women students alike.

The Content's Delivery: Why It Matters and What to Do About It

If women students prefer *work* with a clear social purpose, perhaps they also prefer a *learning* environment that is more social than the traditional lecture format. Indeed, there is ample evidence that collaborative learning environments help women students learn better than a competitive one:

> Girls prefer to learn as a part of a group, and the observation has been made that in same-sex groups in a coed science classroom, girls engage in collaborative and cooperative activities combined with lots of conversation about the activity (Guzzetti, 2001). In a male-dominated classroom, which is likely to be the case especially in physics and engineering, the atmosphere is apt to be competitive and the focus will be on individual success (Zohar & Sela, 2003). Girls want to see how everything is connected, and their way of achieving that is to discuss how each member in the group perceives the topic. Even if you try to get most girls to work by themselves, they will prefer to collaborate with another student (James, 2009).

This preference for cooperative/collaborative learning environments is also shared by students of color, given their likelihood of being "field dependent" learners:

> Ibarra (2001) suggests that the field dependent learner prefers student-centered [learning environments]. They. . .are negatively affected by criticism, and prefer the observational approach to learn concepts (i.e., they learn best by relying on examples). Such learners also prefer small group activities and thrive when allowed opportunities to exchange information with peers (Rovai et al., 2005).

The beneficial effects of small-group learning in STEM for women and students of color are well-documented. In a 1999 meta-analysis (Springer, Stanne, & Donovan, 1999), the authors remarked that "links between cooperative learning theory, research, and practice have been characterized as 'one of the greatest success stories in the history of educational research'" (Slavin, 1996, p. 43). They cite earlier meta analyses that "have consistently reported that cooperation has favorable effects on achievement and productivity, psychological health and self-esteem, inter-group attitudes, and attitudes toward learning." The particular findings in (Springer et al., 1999) themselves are telling: "the main effect of small-group learning on achievement, persistence, and attitudes among undergraduates in STEM was significant and positive," and "the 0.51 effect of small-group learning on achievement reported in this study would move a student from the 50th percentile to the 70th percentile on a standardized (norm-referenced) test. Similarly, the 0.46 effect on students' persistence is enough to reduce attrition from STEM courses and programs by 22%" (Springer et al., 1999).

Now, the study authors (Springer et al., 1999) found that *all students* experienced these beneficial effects, not just women or students of color. But those populations of students, they found, benefited even more: "the positive effects of small-group learning were significantly greater for members of underrepresented groups (African Americans and Latinas/os)," and likewise, "more favorable attitudes were especially evident in groups of women" (Springer et al., 1999).[3] These findings suggest the next tweak:

Tweak #3: Infuse the course with small-group learning opportunities.

The three tweaks presented thus far, along with the overarching principles they embody (i.e., personalized, societally relevant content learned in a small-group environment), provide an excellent foundation for boosting success in STEM courses for women and students of color. The first two tweaks are straightforward enough to implement. But that is not necessarily the case for small-group learning—one needs to wrestle with many questions about the implementation. For example, should students be given a worksheet that guides them step-by-step through the content, or should they merely be told what the end product must be and left to discuss among themselves how to proceed? These and other questions about implementing small-group learning are discussed in the next section.

Small Group Learning: How to Make It Work for You

Springer et al. (1999) note that small-group learning often comes in one of two flavors: cooperative learning "described as a 'structured, systematic instructional strategy in which small groups work together toward a common goal'"– and collaborative learning, which is "characterized by relatively unstructured processes through which participants negotiate goals, define problems, develop procedures, and produce socially constructed knowledge in small groups." There is some evidence to suggest that the specific type of small-group learning utilized does not matter (insofar as the beneficial outcomes of small-group learning are concerned),[4] which allows the educator some freedom in deciding how to incorporate small-group learning into the design of the course without jeopardizing its added benefits. But one particular structure—inquiry-based learning (IBL)—has been shown time and again to be especially effective.

Nilson (2003) summarizes the effects on various learning outcomes (e.g., comprehension, analysis, etc.) of the most common teaching methods. Only one method—IBL—is effective for *all* nine learning outcomes listed. Nilson (2003) points out that IBL "has several definitions in the literature that are not entirely consistent with each other." Nonetheless, nearly all of these definitions share one characteristic: "constructivist" or "inductive" teaching, where the learning process is launched "with a *realistic*, problematic situation and requires that students research and assemble facts, data, and concepts to resolve it" (IBID, emphasis added). When done in small groups, this is precisely the learning environment that seems to work best for women and students of color. This also leads to the first of a few tips for making small-group learning (in the style of IBL) work effectively:

Tip #1: Structure the small-group work around IBL activities that feature realistic situations and require inductive reasoning.

Recall that inductive reasoning is a "bottom up" process that *begins* with specific observations and moves to successively broader generalizations/ theories. Successfully implementing inductive reasoning as part of the IBL process is a delicate matter that, if not done correctly, can eliminate the benefits of small-group learning. In Nilson's (2003) words:

> [For IBL] to be effective, students must have sufficient guidance and scaffolding through the inquiry process – that is, explicit directions about what to do and how to do it, assuming they are dealing with new material...With a solid knowledge base, they can start thinking more like experts. They are better able to identify key characteristics of a problem as well as the procedures

> and algorithms to solve it, thereby drawing on "internal guidance" (Kirschner et al., 2006). Acquiring this knowledge base may require somewhat more conventional learning strategies.

These findings suggest a teaching style that mixes conventional interactive lectures (to increase students' background and knowledge base) with periods of inductive teaching.[5] This leads to our second tip:

> Tip #2: Make sure students working on the small-group IBL-based activities have the sufficient knowledge base required to understand those activities.

For instance, before leading students through an IBL activity in which they discover the Pythagorean Theorem, they should be comfortable with right triangles and the notation a^2 (i.e., the square of a number). These facts could be introduced to students through a mini lecture just before the IBL activity, for example. Students could then be given a carefully constructed worksheet that gently guides them (inductively) from facts about specific right triangles eventually to the Pythagorean Theorem (which is true for all right triangles).

Though there are a variety of ways to structure an IBL activity, worksheets are one of the most popular incarnations of IBL activities (at least in mathematics). A good worksheet will "lay out a proven sequence of problem-solving steps for students to follow, sometimes with hints and rules of thumb" (Nilson, 2003). Among the many benefits are that "students don't rush headlong into problems without first identifying the useful information they do and don't have, classifying the problem, visualizing it (in mathematics, the physical sciences, and engineering), and performing whatever other steps are prescribed for reasoning through the type of problem. As a result, students display improved task performance" (Nilson, 2003).

Now, crafting effective worksheets requires patience, skill, and trial-and-error. But luckily some fields—mathematics included—have networks of educators who have already carefully created these kinds of worksheets for certain courses (e.g., first-semester calculus). Many of these are freely available through sources like the online Journal of Inquiry-Based Learning in Mathematics (http://www.jiblm.org). This leads to the next tip:

Tip #3: Consider using carefully constructed worksheets that inductively guide students to the main results/theories, complete with suitable hints along the way.

The three tips discussed above form a solid foundation for implementing IBL activities in any mathematics course. (Many more resources can be found on websites such as that of the Academy of Inquiry-Based Learning, http://www.inquirybasedlearning.org). And as we have discussed, when structured appropriately and based on small-group work, these activities improve various learning outcomes for women and students of color. In mathematics, one program that has combined all of the features discussed thus far and has been *incredibly* successful in boosting learning outcomes for students of color is the Emerging Scholars Program (ESP).

Case Study: The Emerging Scholars Program

The Emerging Scholars Program "aims to increase the number of college freshmen excelling in calculus who come from groups historically underrepresented in mathematics based disciplines, in particular women, Latinos, African Americans and students from rural areas" (James, Jurich, Estes, & American Youth Policy Forum [AYPF], 2001). The program's structure implements the tweaks and tips we have discussed:

> At the heart of ESP are its discussion sections, which are linked to calculus lecture sections. ESP discussion sessions are longer than non-ESP discussion sections, and also have fewer students – usually a maximum of 24 as opposed to 40 in a non-ESP section. Students work individually or in small groups on specially crafted problems that are unusually challenging. ESP also provides a social support group among students with similar academic goals by planning activities that link social interests with scholarly ones. (IBID)

Note that ESP sections are attached to a course, and participants are given "unusually challenging" problems to work on. Thus, the ESP sections are *not* remedial or otherwise "supplemental instruction." The course furnishes students with the "knowledge base" needed and the ESP sections then layer on the inquiry-based learning activities. Moreover, the emphasis on small-group learning, focus on "specifically crafted problems," and *social* support all fit the strategies we have discussed for boosting success in STEM for women and students of color. These features likely contribute to the successful track record of ESP programs (which "have been replicated by more than 100 colleges and universities across the country" (IBID):

- At the University of Texas at Austin, evaluations indicated that "students who participated in ESP had odds of earning an A or B almost *five times higher* than non-participants" (emphasis added) (IBID). This is remarkable, especially since "about 46.5% of participants were Latino [and] 19.3% were African-American…[and] about 42.7% of the participants were women" (IBID).
- At the University of Wisconsin-Madison, "evaluators reported that ESP students were twice as likely to receive a B or better in calculus than their non-participating counterparts" (IBID). Moreover, "ESP students maintained higher success rates in second and third semester calculus than non-participants" (IBID). There, too, the participants were largely under-represented students ("50% from minority groups, and 50% white students, most from rural backgrounds").
- At California State Polytechnic University, Pomona, ESP participants "achieved a mean grade in calculus *more than six-tenths of a grade point above non-ESP students* (on a four-point grade point scale)" (emphasis added; IBID). Moreover, "within three years after entering the institution, 52% of non-ESP students had withdrawn from the institution or changed to a non-mathematics based major, compared with 15% of ESP students" (IBID).

See Acera (2001) for more information on the history, success, and details of the ESP program. It is worth mentioning that ESP-like programs have also been created for other fields— including chemistry and computer science—and recent research shows they are just as effective as the mathematics-based ESP programs (Adams & Lisy, 2007; Powell, Murphy, Cannon, Gordon, & Ramachandran, 2012).

Now, ESP programs, as successful as they are, do not address all of the obstacles faced by women and students of color in STEM courses. Several of the factors already mentioned—including family resource disparities—are known to affect persistence in STEM courses for women and students of color (and, therefore, ultimately contribute to the STEM degree attainment gap previously discussed) yet are not (explicitly) addressed by ESP programs. There are, however, existing programs that *do* take a comprehensive approach to addressing the challenges faced by women and students of color in STEM. In the next section, we discuss perhaps the most successful such program—the Meyerhoff Scholars Program.

Case Study: The Meyerhoff Scholars Program

In 1989 Freeman Hrabowski III—a mathematician and now president of the University of Maryland, Baltimore County (UMBC)—started the Meyerhoff Scholars Program (MSP) with the aim of increasing the numbers of students of color pursuing doctoral studies in STEM fields. He described the main components of the program in great detail in an article written for the *Notices of the American Mathematical Society* (Hrabowski III, 2001):

> (1) recruiting top minority students in mathematics and science ...; (2) providing a Summer Bridge program that includes mathematics, science, and humanities course work, training in analytic problem solving, group study, and social and cultural events; (3) offering comprehensive merit scholarship support ...; (4) actively involving faculty in recruiting, teaching, and mentoring (5) strong programmatic values, including outstanding academic achievement, study groups, collegiality, and preparation for graduate or professional school; (6) involving students in sustained, substantive summer research experiences; (7) encouraging students to take advantage of departmental and university tutoring resources; (8) ensuring the university administration's active involvement and support and soliciting strong public support; (9) providing academic advising and personal counseling; (10) linking [students] with mentors from professional and academic fields; (11) encouraging a strong sense of community among the students; and (12) involving students' parents and other relatives who can be supportive.

We can see many of the components discussed in this chapter present in the MSP program. (In particular, Dr. Hrabowski, 2001, notes that "we have found that group study is one of the most important for students in mathematics.") We also see extra layers of support shown to foster success in STEM for students of color (e.g., involving students in meaningful research experiences). Given the phenomenal success of ESP programs—where just a few of these components were present—how successful has this more comprehensive program been? The numbers speak for themselves: "More than 1200 students have participated in the undergraduate Meyerhoff Scholars Program since its inception in 1988. More than 90% of the participants who graduated received STEM degrees, with > 40% matriculating to top PhD or MD-PhD programs, 20% to STEM Masters programs, and 20% entered professional (mainly MD) programs" (Summers & Hrabowski, 2014).[6]

Conclusion

It is hard to make direct "cause-effect" links in education. But it is reasonable to expect that incorporating what is known about how women and students of color learn best into the design of the activities/courses/programs they are involved in is likely to improve the learning experience for those students. As discussed, there is ample research suggesting that a few tweaks to educators' course structure/design can boost success in STEM fields. Small-group learning, in particular, resonates well with these students' preference for social learning environments. As we saw in the previous two sections, when structured in a constructivist/inductive manner (e.g., IBL), and complemented with more conventional teaching methods, this combination has proven particularly effective at boosting learning outcomes for women and students of color. Implementing these changes in one's courses may require some finessing, however, especially when it comes to incorporating small-group learning (recall the intricacies discussed earlier).

We close with one interesting observation that emerges from reflecting on the research discussed herein: *what is best for women and students of color is often also best for all students (and even non-students)*. For example, in infusing a STEM course with societal relevance one not only makes STEM more appealing to one's women students, but also helps combat the fact that "most people do not view STEM occupations as directly benefiting society or individuals" (Hill et al., 2010). Similarly, by including more small-group learning activities in STEM courses one not only boosts success for students of color (given that they are more likely to be "field dependent" learners), one also boosts *all* students' success, given the beneficial effects of small-group learning discussed above. Rarely do we get such "win–win" scenarios in education. What's more, rarely are such changes reasonably simple to implement. All that is really required is a STEM educator's willingness to *try*—or, in scientist-speak, to *experiment*—with the tweaks and tips presented in this chapter. Sure, there are a host of other factors that will influence the success of such experiments—though again, there is ample research and existing literature that can help, like that associated with MSP—and it is reasonable to expect that the first few attempts will not go exactly as hoped. But as any good scientist knows, and as any good STEM educator constantly reiterates to their students: *if at first you do not succeed, try, try, try again.*

Notes

1. Biomedical engineering and environmental engineering are also examples of the "discernable" variety. Indeed, they "have succeeded in attracting higher percentages of women than have other [STEM] subdisciplines like mechanical or electrical engineering" (Gibbons, 2006; also Hill et al., 2010).
2. Yet another possibility is for the educator to identify specific real-world instances where his/her students might run into the content to be learned, and work backwards from that to develop lessons which teach the material in that context. The author successfully used this approach in his book, *Everyday Calculus: Discovering the Hidden Math All Around Us* (Fernandez, 2014).
3. The study also found that "students' achievement was significantly greater for groups composed primarily or exclusively of African Americans and Latinas/os" (Springer et al., 1999).
4. The study (Springer et al., 1999) reports that "no significantly different effects on achievement were apparent between cooperative, collaborative, and mixed forms of small-group learning." However, as they note: "We did not have sufficient data to evaluate the effects of different forms of small-group learning on students' attitudes."
5. There is a long history in mathematics of courses taught in a "pure IBL" style, where students do *all* of the work themselves, discovering for themselves what theorems are important without outside help (or even help from the instructor). This "Moore method" (named after the mathematician who pioneered it) has been shown to be incredibly successful at producing mathematicians (Coppin, Mahavier, & May, 2011), and modifications of it to include small-group learning have also been shown to boost learning outcomes (though to the author's knowledge, no studies have been done on the Moore method's effects on women or students of color).
6. Furthermore, "most of the Meyerhoff graduates (86%) earned science or engineering bachelor's degrees (students in good academic standing who leave S&E fields before graduation become supported by other UMBC scholarship programs)" (Summers & Hrabowski, 2014).

References

Acera, R. (2001). *Calculus and community: A history of the emerging scholars program*. New York: The College Board.

Adams, G. M., & Lisy, J. M. (2007). The Chemistry merit program: Reaching, teaching, and tetaining students in the chemical sciences. *Journal of Chemical Education, 84*(4), 721.

Coppin, C. A., Mahavier, W. T., & May, E. L. (2011). *The Moore method: A pathway to learner-centered instruction*. Cambridge, UK: Cambridge University Press.

Diekman, A. B., Brown, E. R., Johnston, A. M., & Clark, E. K. (2009, June). *Communal goals as inhibitors of STEM careers*. Poster presented at the National Science Foundation Joint Annual Meeting, Washington, DC.

Eccles, J. S. (1994). Understanding women's educational and occupational choices: Applying the Eccles et al. model of achievement-related choices. *Psychology of Women Quarterly, 18*(4), 585–609.

Fernandez, O. E. (2014). *Everyday calculus: Discovering the hidden math all around us*. Princeton, NJ: Princeton University Press.

Gibbons, M. T. (2006). Engineering by the numbers. In *Profiles of engineering and engineering technology colleges* (pp. 11–46). Washington, DC: American Society for Engineering Education.

Guzzetti, B. (2001). Texts and talk: The role of gender in learning physics. In E. B. Moje & D. G. O'Brien (Eds.), *Constructions of literacy: Studies of teaching and learning in and out of secondary schools* (pp. 125–146). Mahwah, NJ: Erlbaum.

Hill, C., Corbett, C., St. Rose, A., & American Association of University Women. (2010). *Why so few?: Women in science, technology, engineering, and mathematics*. Washington, DC: AAUW.

Hrabowski, F., III. (2001). The Meyerhoff scholars program: Producing high-achieving minority students in mathematics and science. *Notices of the AMS, 48*(1), 26–28.

Hurtado, S., Newman, C., Tran, M., & Chang, M. (2010). Improving the rate of success for underrepresented racial minorities in STEM fields: Insights from a national project. *New Directions for Institutional Research, 2010*(148), 5–15.

Ibarra, R. A. (2001). *Beyond affirmative action: Reframing the context of higher education*. Madison, WI: University of Wisconsin Press.

James, A. N. (2009). *Teaching the female brain: How girls learn math and science*. Thousand Oaks, CA: Corwin.

James, D. W., Jurich, S., Estes, S., & American Youth Policy Forum. (2001). *Raising minority academic achievement: A compendium of education programs and practices*. Washington, DC: American Youth Policy Forum.

Johnston, K. L., & Aldridge, B. G. (1984). The crisis in science education: What is it? How can we respond? *Journal of College Science Teaching, 14*(1), 20–28.

Kirschner, P. A., Sweller, J., & Clark, R. E. (2006). Why minimal guidance during instruction does not work: An analysis of the failure of constructivist, discovery, problem-based, experiential, and inquiry-based teaching. *Educational Psychologist, 41*(2), 75–86.

National Academy of Engineering. Committee on Public Understanding of Engineering Messages. (2008). *Changing the conversation: Messages for improving public understanding of engineering*. Washington, DC: National Academies Press.

National Science Foundation. (2015). *Women, minorities, and persons with disabilities in science and engineering*. Washington, DC: National Science Foundation.

Nilson, L. B. (2003). *Teaching at its best: A research-based resource for college instructors*. Bolton, MA: Anker Pub Co.

Oakes, J. (1990). Opportunities, achievement and choice: Women and minority students in science and mathematics. *Review of Research in Education, 16*, 153–222.

Powell, R. M., Murphy, C., Cannon, A., Gordon, J., & Ramachandran, A. (2012). *Emerging scholars program – A PLTL-CS program that increases recruitment and retention of women in the major*. Philadelphia, PA: University of Pennsylvania.

Rovai, A., Gallien, L., Jr., & Wighting, M. (2005). Cultural and interpersonal factors affecting African American academic performance in higher education: A review and synthesis of the research literature. *Journal of Negro Education, 74*(4), 359–370.

Sax, L. J. (1994). Retaining tomorrow's scientists: Exploring the factors that keep male and female college students interested in science careers. *Journal of Women and Minorities in Science and Engineering, 1*(1), 45–61.

Slavin, R. E. (1996). Research on cooperative learning and achievement: What we know, what we need to know. *Contemporary Educational Psychology, 21*(1), 43–69.

Springer, L., Stanne, M., & Donovan, S. (1999). Effects of small-group learning on undergraduates in science, mathematics, engineering, and technology: A meta-analysis. *Review of Educational Research, 69*(1), 21–51.

Summers, M., & Hrabowski, F. (2014). Preparing minority scientists and engineers. *The FASEB Journal, 28*(1).

Zohar, A., & Sela, D. (2003). Her physics, his physics: Gender issues in Israeli advanced placement physics classes. *International Journal of Science Education, 25*(2), 245–268.

CHAPTER 7

Reconceptualizing Accountability: The Ethical Importance of Expanding Understandings of Literacy and Assessment for Twenty-First-Century Learners

Kathryn Hibbert and Luigi Iannacci

The twenty-first century ushered in a renewed urgency to address the ways in which educators and policy makers alike conceptualize, value and measure knowledges and skills. In this chapter, we focus on literacies. We acknowledge that there are several debates in the literature surrounding the terminology. For the purposes of this chapter, we have elected to use the term "multiliteracies" as defined by Cope and Kalantzis (2009a, 2009b, 2013) to signal the plurality of literacies. We also acknowledge the debates around the use of the term "21st century skills" agreeing with Silva (2009) that they are "not new" but "newly important" (p. 631). Despite the great deal of attention assessment has received over the past few decades, recognizing its value *for* teaching and learning (Black, 2006; Black & William, 1998; Gipps, 1994; Torrance, 2007; Torrance & Pryor, 1998)— the richness and

K. Hibbert (✉)
Interdisciplinary Centre for Research in Curriculum as a Social Practice, Faculty of Education, Western University, London, ON, Canada

L. Iannacci
School of Education, Trent University, Otonabee College, Peterborough, ON, Canada

D.W. Kritt (ed.), *Constructivist Education in an Age of Accountability*, https://doi.org/10.1007/978-3-319-66050-9_7

complexity generated through plurality in assessment approaches is often lost in the data generated by the dominant metrics used to evaluate school effectiveness and student's levels of literacy.

It is this issue that we are most concerned with. While most scholars agree that *literacies* include multiple modes, texts and contexts (Cope & Kalantzis, 2009a, 2009b; Freebody & Luke, 2003; Jewitt, 2008; Kress, 2000), assessment practices remain rooted in regimes of measurement insensitive to the situatedness of learning and knowing. Rather, complex practices are reduced to metrics valued by governance regimes that are relatively easier to manage, compare and distribute. Attention to expanding collective capacities in assessment and evaluation has not kept pace with the expanding ways in which we have come to think about literacy and literacy pedagogies.

For example, Kereluik, Mishra, Fahnoe, and Terry's (2013) analysis of various frameworks of "21st century learning" indicates:

> ...a somewhat paradoxical state of affairs when we think about 21st century knowledge. First, [a] synthesis of these different frameworks suggests that nothing has changed, that this tripartite division between what we know, how we act on that knowledge, and what we value has always been important. That said, though these foundational ideas have always been key to learning, in some vital ways (particularly given advances in technology and globalization), everything has changed. (p. 128)

How is it possible, given our expanding understandings of what it means to be literate in a globalized world, that particular, discrete, easily measurable components of literacy continue to be heralded—and worse, accepted—as "evidence" of literacy success?

Social relations that occur outside of the school—and the nexus of power that informs these relations—have direct influence on the microdynamics of literacy curriculum. Pinar (2004) laments that "the 'invasion' of public schools is long over and 'corporatization' is triumphant" (p. 5) and as such, schools have become "a skill-and-knowledge factory" (p. 3). Within this context, educators have "lost control of the curriculum" (p. xi):

> ... right-wing reform has rendered the classroom a privatized or domestic sphere in which children and their teachers are, simply, to do what they are told. It is a feminized and racialized domestic sphere politicians – mostly

> (white) men – are determined to control, disguised by apparently common-sensical claims of "accountability". (p. xiii)

The discursive shift to corporatization dominates discussions about the purposes of education where references to "human capital", "adding value", and "meeting the needs of the economy" (Lipman, 2011, as cited in Au & Ferrare, 2015, p. 6) have usurped earlier references to building strong communities and critically thinking citizens. Accountability in this configuration is not about *learning*, but about *controlling* what educators teach; about *controlling* the curriculum. As Foucault (1977/1995) noted, the "constant policing" and "general forms of domination" create "subjected and practised bodies" or *docile* subjects (27–28). Educators in the corporatized view are not autonomous professionals, but are reduced to technicians, "managing" student productivity. The school in this arrangement is no longer a school, but a business (Pinar, 2004, pp. 26–27).

The increased marketization of schooling is maintained and furthered by an adherence to standardized approaches to curriculum and assessment that govern what and when knowledge must be learned and demonstrated in order to prepare students to become viable producers. These "quality control" mechanisms have meant that professionals responsible for educating children (often woman at the elementary level) are viewed as accountable to this form of preparation and in need of monitoring, thus resulting in de-professionalization, de-skilling and silencing (Apple, 1986, as cited in Easthope & Easthope, 2000; Smyth, Dow, Hattman, Reid, & Shacklock, 2000). Punitive aspects of the corporatization of schooling have been directly linked to the populations they house, and the non-fiscal purposes they serve. The "hegemonic potential of corporate culture lies in its ability to readily subsume and appropriate social justice and affirmative action strategies into its corporate planning under the guise of representation and participation" (Blackmore & Kenway, 1993, as cited in Easthope & Easthope, 2000, p. 48). McNeil (2000) adds, "standardization equates sameness with equality in ways that mask pervasive and continuing inequalities" (p. 10). What ultimately perpetuates this masking is a fear of not being able to compete globally and thus potentially having to do with less (a characteristic indicative of hyper-capitalism) which results in reforms that constrain and limit teachers while holding them accountable to measures that prepare students for the global labor market. Apple (2000) articulates these connections plainly, "behind the stress on higher standards, more rigorous testing, education for employment, and a much closer relationship between education and the economy in general, is the fear of losing in international competition and the loss of jobs and money…" (p. 58). Within this climate of fear other aims and goals of schooling (democracy, critical citizenship) become marginalized or disregarded altogether (Majhanovich, 2005; Smyth et al., 2000).

First world anxiety and fear of the feminization of schools is consistently present in the rhetoric and discourse emanating from endless taken-for-granted arguments about the importance of increasing the number of male elementary teachers. This grand narrative has become so strong and inextricably intertwined with the "saving of schools" that it is now assumed that faculties of education purposely make or should make more offers to male applicants. The misogyny such arguments are based in is never uncovered as we continue to fixate on 'saving the boys' and the economy. Boys' poorer results on standardized test scores as compared to girls are used to validate this fixation:

> Public schools especially are attacked most vigorously, not only for their perceived failings (and their associations with women and children who overall are without financial resources), but simply because they are public and therefore represent a huge contradiction to a world that is increasingly interpreted through a market lens. Schools themselves are being redefined by the logic of the global economy, becoming less and less concerned with teaching children and more and more preoccupied with the needs of "consumers". Within the past few years, business leaders and conservatives have managed to write the agenda, as schools have come to be viewed in terms of inputs and outputs, as being in the business of working with human capital, with teachers being the sellers of the product and the public school system being that ultimately deplorable entity-a monopoly. (Metcalf, 2002, as cited in Cannella & Viruru, 2004, p. 139)

The consequences of hypercapitalism have also perpetuated the ways in which learning and teaching have become commodified in other ways as well. As mentioned earlier, within market-driven educational contexts, capital is understood as the solution to human problems (Cannella & Viruru, 2004) and "the construction of 'child needs'" is used to legitimize market-driven "solutions" (Au, 2011; Books, 2002; Canella, 2002, p. 12). Dei and Karumanchry (2001) have documented the ways in which this increased emphasis on marketization in education has silenced equity, reinscribed meritocracy, and pathologized students and parents while holding them responsible for their pathologized status.

Researchers have noted the links between globalization and the reliance on market solutions to address the "increased pressures on school boards, administrators and teachers to adhere rigidly to the management and measurements of standardized curricula and testing" (McNeil, 2000; Smyth, 2001 as cited in Hibbert & Iannacci, 2005, p. 716). Within this educational context, the solution to preparing students for the global market is a print-centric purchasable commodity. The relationship reconfigures one of "supplier-client", "to the extent that teachers and students are now encouraged to think of their selves as a commodity, and to focus on the end product of achievement as a sole barometer of success" (Bailey, 2014, p. 664). Indeed, Rheingold (2012) argues that this "climate prevents rather than encourages democratic forms of exchanges within and across social worlds", as it "narrows recognition and assessment to an almost exclusive focus on the production of test scores as legitimate markers of student achievement" (p. 1). In an increasingly technical context, "many of the more complex skills associated with teaching (e.g., curriculum planning and knowledge of students and communities) are rendered less and less acceptable relative to ... standardized testing" (Au, 2011, p. 34). We contend that it is time to abandon the marketization of the educational relationship between teacher and student in favor of one that positions *teachers as human rights advocates working for children in need of advocacy.*

A multiliteracies perspective that sees accountability as an ethical imperative that is respectful of and responsive to the semiotic diversity that abounds within classrooms repositions accountability as responsibility to students, parents, and the communities they belong to first and foremost. The participatory culture acknowledged in a multiliteracies approach values and respects the diverse knowledges that both students and their teachers bring to the learning encounter. Responsibility is focused on ensuring that the various assets and communication and identity options students have and bring with them to school are accessed, valued, and developed Cummins (2001). Accountability in the context of twenty-first-century literacies requires a critical sociocultural curriculum that uses assessment and evaluation strategies and tools that allow for the assets and identities to be demonstrated and furthered by both students and educators. Dawson and Siemens (2014) contend that "contemporary assessment practice needs to reflect...community-centric learning models" (p. 289) in their argument for a learning analytics model with "capacity to provide deep and nuanced insight into the learning activities of students" (p. 298). What would it look like if educators actively resisted policy inscriptions and instead, adopted new, "counter" subjective positions? What if, as they participate fully in the twenty-first-century literacy activities themselves, their own identity options begin to shift and expand, opening up possibilities for them to rethink their critical participation in the educational enterprise?

New Literacies Should Lead to New Assessments

The potential for professional transitions to occur as educators themselves are increasingly participating in 'new literacies' is not insignificant. Fenwick (2013) has noted that life course studies have been helpful in tracing this phenomenon, as "people's learning and identities, as well as their social networks and knowledge" (p. 361) can prompt a reflexivity that reconnects educators to their own learning experiences. Reflecting upon their own 'becoming' and understanding how that was defined by a particular gaze situates their understanding differently: "professionals are often caught in transitions structured by conflicting responsibilities to various stakeholders: sometimes they must choose ... in order to fulfill core ethical codes for their profession" (Fenwick, 2013, p. 362).

Murphy (2015) also introduces "an alternative theoretical framing that positions individuals as agentive":

> By drawing on and highlighting values driven by principles of potentiality, plurality and openness to unpredictability and unconventionality, I believe that multimodal literacy assessment can become an example of an epistemically responsible (Code, 1987, 2006) assessment, one that offers the possibility for multimodal literacy educators to engage in ethical assessment driven by principles that recognize the scope of contemporary literacy practices in meaningful ways. (p. 26)

However, to achieve this agency, educators must come to understand "power" as the struggle "against subjection, against forms of subjectivity and submission" (Foucault, 1982, p. 781) as that which governs "*through* the freedom and aspirations of subjects rather than in spite of them" (Rose, 1998, p. 155). Educators must first come to see that their own assessment gaze has been configured to see some things and not others, or privilege certain ways of knowing over others. Considering multiple ways of understanding learners through collaborative and constructivist forms of assessment that "open the dialogue and encourage greater participation in the decisions and judgements made in and about our educational practices"

(Delandshere, 2002, p. 1481) has the potential to radically alter what educators for years have conducted alone, in isolation, with a fixed set of criteria. Shifting the assessment gaze from a diagnosis, deficit finding lens to one that is focused on enabling assets and identities to become visible, developed and understood as information that can empower educators to create curriculum that responds to students' challenges requires critical reflexivity that undoes the hegemonic professional traditions that have been systematically inherited and internalized for years.

Accountability as an Ethical Imperative

What might motivate such a dramatic change within systems that are steeped in accountability traditions? It may be helpful here to get a sense of what these traditions are. Drawing on historical and comparative research that examines schooling in the age of accountability, Hopmann (2008) articulated the following levels of accountability:

- A first-order accountability, that is, an accountability arising in face-to-face relations (as described by psychological models);
- A second-order accountability characterized by how well one follows the rules and standards set by a resource-giver (as described by public administration theories);
- A third-order accountability seen as 'managerial accountability', that is, the use of accountability by a principal as a means to achieve better service and effectiveness of the agent; and finally,
- A fourth-order accountability based on the assumption that the one held accountable internalizes the norms, values and expectations of the stakeholders, and which puts himself or herself into action (as pointed by, e.g., theories of governmentality or professionalism). (p. 422)

It is prescient to note what is missing in Hopmann's levels: what is absent is attention to *the learner* as one 'in relation'; the learner as one expected to follow rules, the learner as the receiver of managed resources and accountability systems and the learner as *the key stakeholder* in schools.

In his doctoral work investigating the experiences of culturally and linguistically diverse early years' learners, Iannacci (2005) wondered, "What would happen if legally we began to insist that schools abide by principles that protect children from the tyranny of what we have configured for them in the name of education? What would schools look like?" (p. 380). Disrupting and challenging the dominant and reductionistic assessment practices may be achievable if we conceptualize education within a child rights framework (Harcourt & Hagglund, 2013; Iannacci, 2015). The United Nations Convention on the Rights of the Child (UNCRC) United Nations (1989) offers a policy framework that re-orients the adults (policy makers, educators, parents, leaders) to think of accountability as a responsibility *first to the learners themselves*, and by extension, their families and their communities—in other words, the world we seek to educate them to become active critical citizens within.

A scan of the literature since the adoption of UNCRC (Reynaert, Bouverne-de-Bie, & Vandevelde, 2009) concludes that "children's rights discourse" has been "embedded within the evolution of professionalization, a blue print of the education process" (p. 529). While we acknowledge that children's rights discourses are often located in the context of adults who presume to know what is best for the "ignorant, innocent and needy" (Arce, 2012, p. 365), we see the UNCRC as a commitment that we, as a society make *to the child*, in ways that guide our professional practices within an otherwise market oriented context. An emancipatory discourse forwarded by Arce argues that *it is possible and imperative to rebuild:*

- a strong conception of the rights of children;
- a strong version of "participation"
- a conception of children's rights sensitive to cultural diversity;
- a conception of children's rights that recognizes that there is no citizenship without duties, because there is no right holder without responsibilities;
- a children's rights corpus that includes excluded childhoods, amplifying the oppressed voices of the children of those childhoods;
- a children's rights discourse that transcends their infantilization;
- a children's rights discourse aware of the fact that rights are conquered in a complex reality where race, gender and class issues are as influential as age issues;
- a discourse of children's rights that does not work as a disciplining mechanism but as a tool for emancipation (Excerpts from Arce, 2012, pp. 395–396).

The United Nations Convention on the Rights of the Child

According to the general principles of the UN convention, economic, social and cultural rights and civil and political rights are "all seen as necessary for the full and harmonious development of the child's personality and inherent to the dignity of the child" (2010, p. 2). The four general principles are:

- That all the rights guaranteed by the Convention must be available to all children without discrimination of any kind (Article 2);
- That the best interests of the child must be a primary consideration in all actions concerning children (Article 3);
- That every child has the right to life, survival and development (Article 6);
- That the child's views must be considered and taken into account in all matters affecting him or her (Article 13).

The "Aims of Education" articulated in Article 29 include that "the education of the child shall be directed to:

(a) The development of the child's personality, talents and mental and physical abilities to their fullest potential;
(b) The development of respect for human rights and fundamental freedoms; and for the principles enshrined in the Charter of the United Nations"; (p. 28).

In particular, in Article 13, entitled "Freedom of Expression":

> The child shall have the right to freedom of expression; this right shall include freedom to seek, receive and impart information and ideas of all kinds, regardless of frontiers, either orally, in writing or in print, in the form of art, or through any other media of the child's choice. (p. 15)

Even in this sampling of the language from the UNCRC document, the direction is clear. The time has come for educators to reject the corporatization of their bodies and minds (and those of their students), in favour of developing an epistemic responsibility (Murphy, 2015) first and foremost to the primary stakeholders in education – our learners.

The Socio-cultural Focused Curriculum: Taking Up the Challenge

Schools are masterful sorting mechanisms: students are explicitly sorted by age and grade, by gender, by language, and by ability—a logic that Kritt (2011) describes as passing "everyone through the same sieve" (p. 1). In less visible ways, students are also often sorted by race, by class, by motivation, and so on. In a curriculum that is critically socio-cultural in focus, diversity is embraced as the expected 'norm' and the starting point of curricular planning. Through a multiliteracies approach (Cope & Kalantzis, 2009a, 2009b) in particular, learners are purposefully and actively engaged in *designing their own futures.* They are explicitly taught how power operates within and across various kinds of texts, in order that they may draw on that knowledge when needed to advocate for their own needs and recognize when their needs or their rights are being oppressed or subverted.

The aims/perspectives of a critical, sociocultural curriculum and assessment/evaluation that informs its design are as follows:

- It rejects the idea that students are "appropriately" placed in educational contexts based on convenience and metanarratives of development and dis/ability. It does not hold students accountable to grade/age/course identified norms, expectations, targets, benchmarks, and outcomes but rather is responsive to their cultural, intellectual, historical, political and linguistic legacies (Delpit, 2003).
- Students are therefore understood as endowed with, able to use and demonstrate these assets as they engage with new knowledge. These assets are themselves knowledge that benefits others within educational contexts including educators who simultaneously learn who students are and how to design curriculum for them that taps into their formed and developing literacies.
- Educational contexts and students within them are therefore seen as texts that need constant critical reading and re-reading to ensure that taken for granted and deficit-oriented perspectives are rejected as new responses that actively engage students in their critical citizenry are forwarded (e.g., not conflating students who are poor as in need of impoverished pedagogy, Iannacci, 2016).
- Resources used to develop socio-cultural curriculum are also seen as texts that need to be critically read and re-read in ways that enable educators to build a learning environment that provides students

opportunities to see and develop themselves in ways that reflect, respond, and fully realize their assets and identities.

- Similarly, assessment and evaluation tools, processes, practices, and policies are also understood as texts that need constant critical reading and re-reading so that they remain focused on allowing students to demonstrate their assets, legacies and semiotic diversities and to provide educators with these demonstrations so that they come to understand their abilities and how to respond to their learning (e.g., Clarke-Midura & Dede, 2010). In short, the knowledge acquired from sociocultural-based assessment and evaluation addresses who the child is and what will engage them in further developing their critical citizenship.

The governing text that educators draw from, refer back to and keep in mind as they design is not a series of mandated expectations (Common Core standards in the U.S.), but rather *The United Nations Convention on the Rights of the Child*. This does not entail a prescriptive implementation of its principles, but rather a critical reading and re-reading of the positioning and power of the child within it and within educational contexts so that any and all adult-centric measures and conceptualizations of accountability remain ethically focused on being responsive to students.

As Rheingold (2012) demonstrates through her articulation of the case of "Michael", "When academic content is purposefully infused with social relationships and community practices, learning matters to students in substantially different ways that what more commonly occurs in a standards-based system" (p. 7). To achieve a commitment to a reconceptualized accountability demands adherence to an ethic: "a theory or system of moral values" (Merriam-Webster, n.d., np). Those values have been articulated in the UNCRC declaration. However, learners need the adults in their world to break free of marketized visions of schooling that have constructed them both as "perpetual consumers" intent on their "long-term goal of profitmaking" to become "agents engaged in relationships" that learners need us to be (Hibbert & Iannacci, 2005, p. 725).

At the time of writing this chapter, we were witness to a historic global pact to collectively cut climate change. Canada's Environment Minister tweeted: "History is made. For our children". While leaders were celebrating their achievement in agreeing upon a collection of words criticized for not being legally binding, our thoughts returned once again to UNCRC: *a legally binding international agreement* that we have all but ignored in schools (Mitchell, 2005). What will it take to operationalize our collective duty of care?

Stephen J. Ball, a renowned professor of sociology of education observes that "measurement and monitoring as techniques for reflection and representation play a particular role within the contemporary relationship between truth and power and the self... we are constantly incited to invest in ourselves, work on ourselves, and improve ourselves – drive up our numbers, our performance, our outputs" (2015, p. 299). What if, collectively, we set an example for our youth, rejecting the systematic *bullying* by market tactics. What if instead of being 'bystanders' within our own profession, we *stand up*, and actively participate in education as a moral, legal[1], and political practice, redirecting our energy and attention toward meeting our commitments to our learners? We are taking that stand, and we invite you to join us.

Note

1. According to Lundy, Kelly, and Byrne (2013), "effective implementation is not achieved by legislative measures alone" arguing for four core approaches: training and awareness, the role of independent human rights' institutions, data, and national action plans (p. 456).

References

Apple, M. (2000). Between neo-liberalism and neoconservatism: Education and conservatism in a global context. In N. C. Burbules & C. A. Torres (Eds.), *Globalization and education: Critical perspectives* (pp. 57–77). New York: Routledge.

Arce, M. C. (2012). Towards an emancipatory discourse of children's rights. *International Journal of Children's Rights, 20*, 365–421.

Au, W. (2011). Teaching under the new Taylorism: High-stakes testing and the standardization of the 21st century curriculum. *Journal of Curriculum Studies, 43*(1), 25–45.

Au, W., & Ferrare, J. (2015). Introduction: Neoliberalism, social networks, and the new governance of education. In W. Au & J. Ferrare (Eds.), *Mapping corporate education reform: Power and policy networks in the neoliberal state* (pp. 2–24). New York: Taylor & Francis.

Bailey, G. (2014). Accountability and the rise of 'play safe' pedagogical practices. *Education + Training, 56*(7), 662–674.

Ball, S. (2015). Education, governance and the tyranny of numbers. *Journal of Education Policy, 30*(3), 299–301.

Black, P. (2006). Assessment for learning: Where is it now? Where is it going? In C. Rust (Ed.), *Improving student learning through assessment* (pp. 9–20). Oxford, UK: Oxford Centre for Staff and Learning Development.

Black, P., & William, D. (1998). Assessment and classroom learning. *Assessment in Education, 5*(1), 7–74.

Books, S. (2002). Making poverty pay: Children and the 1996 welfare law. In G. S. Canella & J. L. Kincheloe (Eds.), *Kidworld: Childhood studies, global perspectives and education* (pp. 21–38). New York: Peter Lang.

Canella, G. S. (2002). Global perspectives, cultural studies, and the construction of a postmodern childhood studies. In G. S. Canella & J. L. Kincheloe (Eds.), *Kidworld: Childhood studies, global perspectives, and education* (pp. 3–20). New York: Peter Lang.

Cannella, G. S., & Viruru, R. (2004). *Childhood and post-colonization: Power, education and contemporary practice.* London: Falmer Press.

Clarke-Midura, J., & Dede, C. (2010). Assessment, technology and change. *Journal of Research on Technology in Education, 42*(3), 309–328.

Code, L. (1987). *Epistemic responsibility.* London: University Press of New England.

Code, L. (2006). *Ecological thinking. The politics of epsitemic location.* New York: Oxford University Press.

Cope, B., & Kalantzis, M. (2009a). "Multiliteracies": New literacies, new learning. *Pedagogies: An International Journal, 4*, 164–195.

Cope, B., & Kalantzis, M. (2009b). A grammar of multimodality. *International Journal of Learning, 16*(2).

Cope, B., & Kalantzis, M. (2013). Multiliteracies: New literacies, new learning. In R. M. Hawkings (Ed.), *Framing languages and literacies: Socially situated views and perspectives* (pp. 105–135). New York: Routledge.

Cummins, J. (2001). *Negotiating identities. Education for empowerment in a diverse society* (2nd ed.). Los Angeles: California Association for Bilingual Education.

Dawson, S., & Siemens, G. (2014). Analytics to literacies: The development of a learning analytics framework for multiliteracies assessment. *The International Review of Research in Open and Distance Learning, 15*(4), 285–305.

Dei, G. S., & Karumanchry, L. L. (2001). School reform in Ontario: The 'marketization of education' and the resulting silence on equity. In J. P. Portelli & R. P. Solomon (Eds.), *The erosion of democracy in education: Critique to possibilities* (pp. 189–215). Calgary, AB: Detselig Enterprises Ltd.

Delandshere, G. (2002). Assessment as inquiry. *Teachers College Record, 104*(7), 1461–1484.

Delpit, L. (2003). Educators as "Seed People" growing a new future. *Educational Researcher, 32*(7), 14–21.

Easthope, C., & Easthope, G. (2000). Intensification, extension, and complexity of teachers' workload. *British Journal of Sociology of Education, 21*(1), 43–59.

Fenwick, T. (2013). Understanding transitions in professional practice and learning: Towards new questions for research. *Journal of Workplace Learning, 25*(6), 352–367.

Foucault, M. (1977/1995). *Discipline and punish: The birth of the prison.* New York: Random House.

Foucault, M. (1982). The subject and power. *Critical Inquiry, 8*(4), 777–795.

Freebody, P., & Luke, A. (2003). Literacy as engaging with new forms of life: The 'four roles' model. In G. Bull & M. Anstey (Eds.), *The literacy lexicon* (2nd ed., pp. 51–66). Frenchs Forest, NSW: Prentice Hall.

Gipps, C. (1994). *Beyond testing. Towards a theory of educational assessment.* London: Falmer Press.

Harcourt, D., & Hagglund, S. (2013). Turning the UNCRC upside down: A bottom-up perspective on children's rights. *International Journal of Early Years Education, 21*(4), 286–289.

Hibbert, K., & Iannacci, L. (2005). From dissemination to discernment: The commodification of literacy instruction and the fostering of 'good teacher consumerism'. *The Reading Teacher, 58*(8), 716–727.

Hopmann, S. T. (2008). No child, no school, no state left behind: Schooling in the age of accountability. *Journal of Curriculum Studies, 40*(4), 417–456.

Iannacci, L. (2005). *Othered among others: A critical narrative of culturally and linguistically diverse (CLD) learners' literacy and identity in early childhood education.* Unpublished doctoral dissertation, University of Western Ontario, London.

Iannacci, L. (2015). Reconceptualizing assessment in early childhood education: Narrative documentation and asset-oriented ways of understanding culturally and linguistically diverse children's literacies. *The International Journal of Holistic Early Learning and Development, 2*, 17–33.

Iannacci, L. (2016). Impoverished pedagogy: A critical examination of assumptions about poverty, teaching and cultural and linguistic diversity. In S. Singer & M. J. Harkins (Eds.), *Voices from the margins: Conversations about schooling, social justice, and diversity.* Montreal, PQ: McGill-Queens University Press.

Jewitt, C. (2008). Multimodality and literacy in school classrooms. *Review of Research in Education, 32*(1), 241–267.

Kereluik, K., Mishra, P., Fahnoe, C., & Terry, L. (2013). What knowledge is of most worth: Teacher knowledge for 21st century learning. *Journal of Digital Learning in Teacher Education, 29*(4), 127–141.

Kress, G. (2000). Multimodality: Challenges to thinking about language. *TESOL Quarterly, 34*(2), 337–340.

Kritt, D. (2011). Accountability to whom? Testing and social justice. A response to 'imagining no child left behind freed from neoliberal hijackers'. *Democracy and Education, 19*(2), 1–5.

Lipman, P. (2011). *The new political economy of urban education: Neoliberalism, race and the right to the city*. New York: Routledge.

Lundy, L., Kilkelly, U., & Byrne, B. (2013). Incorporation of the United Nations convention of the rights of the child in law: A comparative review. *International Journal of Children's Rights, 21*, 442–463.

Majhanovich, S. (2005). Immigrant students and Canadian education. Compromised hopes. In S. Majhanovich (Ed.), *Comparative and global equity access and democracy in education: Globalization, comparative education and policy research*. Dordrecht, The Netherlands: Springer.

McNeil, L. (2000). *Contradictions of school reform: Educational cost of standardized testing*. New York: Routledge.

Merriam-Webster Dictionary. (n.d.). Available http://www.merriam-webster.com/dictionary/ethic

Mitchell, R. C. (2005). Postmodern reflections on the UNCRC: Towards utilising Article 42 as an international compliance indicator. *The International Journal of Children's Rights, 13*, 315–331.

Murphy, S. (2015). Beyond governmentality: The responsible exercise of freedom in pursuit of literacy assessment. In M. Hamilton, R. Heydon, K. Hibbert, & R. Stooke (Eds.), *Negotiating spaces for literacy learning* (pp. 25–42). London: Bloomsbury.

Pinar, W. (2004). *What is curriculum theory?* Mahwah, NJ: Lawrence Erlbaum Associates.

Reynaert, D., Bouverne-de-Bie, M., & Vandevelde, S. (2009). A review of children's rights literature since the adoption of the United Nations convention on the rights of the child. *Childhood, 16*(4), 518–534.

Rheingold, A. (2012). Unalienation recognition as a feature of democratic schooling. *Democracy and Education, 20*(2), 1–8.

Rose, N. (1998). *Inventing our selves: Psychology, power and personhood*. London: Cambridge University Press.

Silva, E. (2009). Measuring skills for 21st century learning. *Phi Delta Kappan, 90* (9), 630–634.

Smyth, J., Dow, A., Hattam, R., Reid, A., & Shacklock, G. (2000). *Teachers' work in a globalizing economy*. London: Falmer Press.

Torrance, H. (2007). Assessment as learning? How the use of explicit learning objectives, assessment criteria and feedback in post-secondary education and training can come to dominate learning. *Assessment in Education: Principles, Policy and Practice, 14*(3), 281–295.

Torrance, H., & Pryor, J. (1998). *Investigating formative assessment: Teaching, learning and assessment in the classroom*. London: Open University Press.
United Nations. (1989). Convention of the rights of the child. Available at: http://www.ohchr.org/Documents/ProfessionalInterest/crc.pdf
United Nations Convention on the Rights of the Child. (2010). *United Nations*. Dublin, Ireland: Children's Rights Alliance.

CHAPTER 8

Where DAP Is Due: Constructing Community Across Difference with the Dialogue Arts Project

Adam Falkner

It is a rainy Tuesday morning in Brooklyn. A thick, knee-high film of fog snakes down Bushwick Avenue so all that is visible are the top halves of floating black gypsy cabs, orange and yellow umbrellas atop halal carts, the backpacked upper bodies of sleepy teenagers as they trudge toward the building for first period. Everything, its own tiny island amidst a strange sea of gray. It is, by most accords, the exact type of morning the snooze button was built for. Despite that, I am greeted by 12 of my 18 first-period students nearly 20 minutes before the school day begins, all cyphered around my classroom door like a wagon circle.

"Is he here yet?" Anthony asks, half a breakfast sandwich hanging out of his mouth. "We're here early. Is he here?"

DAP is an allusion to the Dialogue Arts Project curriculum, the focus of this chapter, as well as to the term used to describe informal handshakes, fist bumps, or other greetings of respect that are commonplace in many youth cultures.

A. Falkner (✉)
Teachers College Columbia University, New York, NY, USA

D.W. Kritt (ed.), *Constructivist Education in an Age of Accountability*,
https://doi.org/10.1007/978-3-319-66050-9_8

Two weeks prior, after a month of pleading, I was gifted a very small stipend to bring in "guest artists" to perform for and engage with my students for the semester. "Get them excited or something," I recall my principal encouraging. "And make sure everyone behaves." By most New York City standards, $200 is enough for an Uber to the airport and a cup of coffee on the way. As a 22-year-old writer and artist myself, however—constantly a twig-snap away from leaping into the nearest MFA program and getting on with my life's dream of writing the next Great American Novel or ghostwriting songs for Justin Bieber—I was sharply aware of just how far $200 could go. How, for example, if put toward things like buying artists' breakfasts in exchange for two hours' worth of their time in my classroom, it just might last the entire year. This particular morning was our second installment of what would become our "Live Literature Series," and students were, well. . .excited.

In the beginning, the idea was simple: I wanted to teach a creative writing elective that inspired young people around the possibilities of writing. Like most new teachers freshly ejected from the safe, synthetic cockpit of a graduate program and into the fire of an *actual* classroom, I was at once scrambling to sculpt a teacher identity that matched what all the textbooks told me I should be—reluctant but capable disciplinarian, kind but critical, methodically organized, attentive to each and every student with knifepoint precision—while at the same time relying, as we all do, for better and for worse, on the selves and experiences that had driven me to the idea of education in the first place. Or, put differently, a kind of "fake it until you make it" approach, combining parts of Today's Teaching 101 into a homemade approach to pedagogy that utilizes everything but the kitchen sink in order to get the job done. For me, that meant structuring a contemporary creative writing course, with what "get them excited or something" freedom I had, that placed Walt Whitman beside Kendrick Lamar, Lucille Clifton beside Willie Perdomo, and Emily Dickson beside Justin Torres. It meant doing my best to create a course which students wanted to attend, one that validated experiences and voices often left outside the canon of the traditional English classroom, one that implored young people to take their writing seriously.

I patch-worked together a course loosely modeled after what Jeff Kass (2000), a former teacher and mentor of mine, refers to as the "Archeological Approach to Creative Writing"—a philosophy that emphasizes the importance of "slowing down the world" (Kass & Beal, 2000, p. 10) or, that is, the process of mining one's life for the personal stories that matter most, and writing about them in rich, vivid ways. Amidst the vibrant artistic backdrop of New York City, we instituted a "live literature" com ponent to the course, where, every two weeks, I asked an especially electric guest artist—"electric" in proportion, of course, to (1) their availability to me via one of several writing circles that I socialized and wrote in and (2) their interest in breakfast as compensation for their time—to come into my classroom for the day, meet with young people, and perform their work in honest, uncensored ways.

Over the course of my first year or two in the classroom, I began to observe a deeply provocative and unexpected pattern in students' responses to these visiting artists, and, in turn, to one another. Through small sound bites and gestures, I started to notice a shift in our "Live Literature Series" from basic performances and literary discussions to multi-directional interaction on the work, and sociological questions of race, gender, and identity. Students began asking questions and sharing personal stories that transcended the work; questions and stories that would not typically have made their way within 100 yards of room 750, even if we'd set out to build a curriculum *specifically* for that purpose:

> Just because you were raised in a racist home, do you think that means you have to be at least a little bit racist yourself?
>
> The moment I came out to my parents, I wished I could have taken it back – they weren't ready to hear it and I wasn't ready to have them be so unsupportive.
>
> Sometimes I feel like the only thing people see when they look at me is my gender; it's as though everything else about who I am is an accessory.

While I could not put my finger on precisely what was happening in these moments—I was, in all transparency, too green an educator at the time to structure my teaching around them in any meaningful way—my gut told me that *something* was indeed occurring, and further, that it might be worthy of investigation. On the surface, it appeared that students were excited about not only the presence of artists in the classroom (they showed up early to set up, stayed late to break down, and scoured the city for writing workshops and performance opportunities) but also the prospect of using that art as a vehicle to engage in dialogue about their lives and the social and political circumstances surrounding them. And while this small string of loosely curated curricular moments was hardly a thing to call revolutionary, they consistently stood, to me, in stark contrast to the sound bites we often hear and read about the political indifference of young people today, rampant conflict and bullying across lines of identity, and the general level of "nothing" that schools and teachers are doing to combat both (Furlong, 2009). In essence, I knew quite early on during my initial years in the classroom that it was these moments of dissonance and discord, these kinds of "ruptures" in the fabric of the everyday educational experience, that I wanted to push against as a student and teacher, an artist, and researcher—and that my students, perhaps more so than I, would be fundamental in helping us understand their larger significance in our current cultural landscape. Before hearing from those students themselves, however, and exploring the curriculum shaped in response to them, it will be useful to first consider some of the scholarship underpinning this discussion.

Providing a Lens

When stepping back a moment to consider this story from a distance, it may be easy to see this work as education-specific, or designed to address only those issues that plague the imperfect science of teaching and learning. I couldn't be clearer, however, in insisting on its applicability outside the classroom as well. As I am writing this very chapter, the President of the United States has signed no less than four executive orders in a span of a single week in an effort to ban specific ethnic and religious groups from entering the country, and in so doing fanned a divisive national rhetoric pitting rich against poor, black against white, gay against straight, Muslims against Christians, and immigrants against everyone. Schools are a reflection of the world we live in, and represent a kind of ground zero for interactions between and around cultures and ideas, and thus ripe to engage the world in constructive ways. By focusing specifically on one experiment at one classroom in one city, I want to underscore the political urgency of this story, which to me is more broadly the work of humanizing all people, and empathizing across differences.

In an increasingly pluralistic and politically divided society, the need for self-awareness, tolerance, and communication across difference has never been more critical—and nowhere are the stakes higher than in the arena of public education. Many high school communities across the United States grapple with issues of bullying, harassment, and other forms of student conflict that are often the result of intolerance and misunderstandings across social identities (Griffin, Brown, & Warren, 2012). In an effort to rebuild tone and tolerance, however, schools have focused predominantly on addressing antagonistic student behavior, while struggling to address many of the underlying issues responsible for intergroup and interpersonal conflict, and the deterioration of community in schools (Dessel, 2010; Poteat & DiGiovanni, 2010). Advocates of critical multicultural education (Banks & Banks, 2010) have long argued that young people need to experience education in ways that push them to think critically about their own identities and the identities of their peers, and to use that reflection to cultivate safer, more tolerant classrooms.

In the past decade, many pedagogical approaches have emerged in an effort to engage young people in this type of critical education. Two of the more promising among those include (1) the use of autoethnographic writing (Carey-Webb, 2001) and performance poetry (Fisher, 2005) as methods for centering students' experiences in the curriculum and fostering classroom community and (2) the integration of intergroup dialogue (IGD) and the teaching of dialogue skills as a way to explore issues related to social justice in school (Gurin, Nada, & Zuniga, 2013; Stock, 1995). Separately, autoethnographies and IGD are becoming increasingly well-documented approaches within the realms of social justice and humanizing education (Freire, 2006). Few researchers, however, have explored their combined impact. This chapter examines an attempt to integrate the structured practices of both approaches into the secondary English classroom as a means of engaging young people in critical education.

To this end, I provide a brief exploration of the several critical areas of research from which this research emerges, and define and discuss several critical terms and their deeply rooted presence in the approach of the "Dialogue Arts Project" (DAP) curriculum—the curriculum at the centerpiece of the elective I taught. I contextualize my research by describing the high school context of the Kass Academy South (KAS) and the DAP curriculum itself. I discuss student outcomes in two particular areas, as identified through the Center for Studies in Educational Innovation's "Achievement, Innovation and Measurement (AIM) Matrix," (cited in Villanueva, 2013). I feature students' own voices as captured through interviews, archival documents/assignments, and survey responses, and discuss the potential for this work to inform practice and research.

The Foundation

Since the influential Dartmouth Seminar of 1966, many have identified and defended English and literacy instruction classrooms as particularly unique spaces in education through which to endorse explorations of identity, social justice, and civic engagement (Morrell, 2005). Just as Theodor Adorno's "Education After Auschwitz" (1959) reminds us of the vital role that education must play in being explicit about social injustice in the world, Ernest Morrell (2005) and others posit that the English classroom is the one discipline truly up to that task; to inviting into the learning process the sociological theories about inequities, and even the role that schools themselves play in reproducing them (MacLeod, 1987). Morrell's "Critical English Education" is one that insists on the political potential of the English classroom for its innate centering of language and literacy—tools that enable us to "construct ourselves" (p. 2) and speak back to the social circumstances around us.

As a pedagogical embodiment of critical English education, Patrick Camangian's (2009) work advocates for the use of autoethnographies (Alexander, 2005; Carey-Webb, 2001)—cultural narratives that build toward social analysis—to help young people develop critical self-reflection around social identity and build compassionate relationships with their peers (2010). Storytelling plays a critical role in enabling students to bring themselves and their lived experiences into the classroom (Dyson & Genishi, 1994). Carey-Webb (2001) and Camangian (2009) advance that work by encouraging the teaching of autoethnographies in schools to help students describe, explore, and speak back to their memberships to specific cultural groups, such as those rooted in race, gender, class, or sexual orientation, as a way to build more culturally competent and compassionate school environments (Alexander, 2005).

Maisha Fisher (2005) and Karina Jocson (2011) reported that many young people find spoken word and performance poetry to be important creative outlets for articulating their social realities. They propose the use of those approaches as effective pedagogical tools for helping students to develop critical literacy and self-reflection around political and social identity. In this context, in much the same way that performance poetry can be defined simply as "poetry that is written to be read aloud," the prelude "creative" refers to *any* writing—not merely poetry or spoken word—created with the intent of being shared audibly with others (Camangian, 2008). Creative autoethnographies, then, are individual cultural narratives written to be shared aloud for the purpose of celebrating and investigating social identity and difference in the classroom.

A separate, less literary approach to engaging young people in a critical English education is that of drawing students into verbal dialogue around the myriad issues of culture and identity that impact their lives (Stock, 1995). Building on a range of existing philosophies and definitions (Bakhtin, 1981; Bohm, Nichol, & Incebrary, 1996), the Program on Intergroup Relations (IGR) defines dialogue as a form of communication designed not for the purpose of reaching conclusions but rather understanding multiple perspectives and building authentic relationships with others (Zuniga, Nagda, & Sevig, 2001). They define IGD as "the process of dialogue during which two or more groups of individuals engage in face-to-face conversation in an effort to explore, challenge, and overcome the biases they hold about members of their own and other groups" (Adams, 2010). Despite its promising outcomes and widespread influence, however, IGD has largely existed only in college and university settings (Gurin, et al., 2013). The DAP curriculum was designed to combine some of the innovative pedagogical approaches outlined above, and to extend IGR's dialogue-based practices from college and university settings to secondary education.

Another White Teacher

In an effort to sidestep the familiar pitfall wherein academic research conveniently ignores the identity of the researcher, the core stories and biases that fuel them toward that work, and the ways in which both of those factors may impact a study, I'd like to offer a few truths. First, I identify not only as an educator and researcher but as a writer and artist as well. I am deeply motivated by art and story, and a desire to believe in their ability to transform lives and thus the world. While I am not blind to realities that data may convey, my efforts as a teacher-researcher are situated amidst an effort to support that intuition. I moved to New York City to accept a high school English placement as a New York City Teaching Fellow (NYCTF). At the time, the placement represented a comfortable salary, a free Masters degree, and an opportunity to work with teenagers in a remarkable city. Teaching fellowships like NYCTF and Teach for America, among dozens across the nation, incentivize academically capable college graduates to pursue the teaching profession in a way that prepares them for the grind of lesson planning. However, there is a demographic gap between the teachers hired (overwhelmingly white and from upper-middle-class backgrounds), and the schools and students they are serving (overwhelmingly non-white, often living at or below the poverty line). By their calculation, the former outweighs the latter—and admittedly, it may—but it does not account for the troublesome dynamic that persists in many classrooms in cities like New York, where each day thousands of over-privileged white teachers stand in front of classrooms populated by systematically oppressed black and brown youth. Over the course of my first five years in the classroom, my development as a teacher and my cultivation of curriculum were tied to an effort to minimize that problematic dynamic—to at once embrace my voice as instructor, while striving to highlight my students' voices, stories, and opinions more than my own. In some ways, such a feat is impossible.

I am a white man from an upper-middle-class family in the Midwest. I attended an overcrowded public high school and took advantage of the many extracurricular opportunities offered therein. Many of those extracurricular activities forced me to be very different and disparate versions of myself, and challenged me, as we all do, to "try on" a number of identities in an effort to find myself as a maturing young adult. My many conflicting identities as a youngster included: three-sport varsity athlete, musical theater nerd, hip hop artist, camp counselor and outdoor adventurer, a cappella choir soloist, school government secretary, experimental drug user, habitat for humanity organizer—the list goes on. While indeed a privileged scenario to find oneself in, my participation in so many different spaces was a way to defend myself from what I now recognize, some 20 years later, as a distinct effort to avoid the shame and discomfort I experienced around my own identity development as a gay man.

This "splitting" (Downs, 2012) of selves, while an effort toward protecting myself from both psychological and emotional (and physical) violence added to the isolation and secrecy I felt around my gayness. It was only through poetry (and later, drama and music) that I was able to bring those many selves together, to give myself permission to embrace all of who I was, and to authentically exist in the world. The DAP curriculum is deeply tied to my own experience with art as a young, queer man, and its healing presence in my own life as I struggled to navigate a number of fractured identities—a process I continued to explore and write about alongside my students during the time this research was conducted in the form of two separate books of poetry.

In addition to the importance of storytelling, and performance as a way to decenter and combat the unsettling demographic differences between teachers and students in urban schools, I believe that many young people today experience the pressure to "split" themselves along lines of identity, and suffer tremendously (and often quietly) as a result. Perhaps it can go without saying that this individual torment often results in the type of student conflict that the DAP curriculum aims to address. Any effort toward enabling young people to claim all of their identities at one time, to courageously stand in the light, and name their celebration and their shame, their desires and their fears—even if there is tension in that process—is a useful and even revolutionary practice.

The School and the Students

Kass Academy South (pseudonym) is a small high-performing public high school in East New York, Brooklyn. While the school does celebrate creative writing, its name derives from the belief that a command over all forms of written and spoken language is essential to becoming better educated and more expressive. The school consists of approximately 400 students, grades 9 through 12, nearly 72% of whom qualify for free or reduced lunch. KAS' student population is approximately 62% Black, 30% Hispanic, 4% White, and 1% Asian. Varying drastically in terms of their backgrounds, abilities, and interests in school, six high school sophomores—Mason, Kai H., Tia, Fancy, Solice, and Colby (pseudonyms)—were selected from a larger pool of participants.

Some of these young people were deeply connected to school and saw themselves as particularly capable learners—such as Kai H., an African-American female from a middle-class, two-parent household, who self-described as "intelligent" and "driven," and boasted one of the highest grade-point averages in the class. Others, such as Mason, a Puerto Rican-American young man who lived with his grandmother in the South Bronx, were considerably less connected to the grade-driven culture of school and struggled academically. Some students self-described as middle class, others as "poor" or living at or below the poverty line. Some identified as "writers," such as Fancy and Solice, two young women (one white, one black, respectively) from single-parent households in Brooklyn, while Colby—who described herself as "hating school" altogether—hesitated to do so as willingly. Some of these young people, such as Solice, were popular among the student body and had deep-reaching relationships with students and teachers from across the school, while others, such as Colby and Kai H., were more isolated and tended to stick to themselves or a very small group of friends. Some of these students self-described as having bullied others, while others self-describe as having been judged, made fun of, "pushed to the side," or made to feel isolated because of "who they are or where they come from." All of these students demonstrated significant interpersonal skills and were capable of articulating their experiences in the course through language, and were enthusiastic about doing so.

I viewed my students as the principal knowledge-holders regarding their own lives and experiences (Freire, 2006), and present my findings from their viewpoint. While the methodology and intricacies of the DAP curriculum should be saved for a subsequent paper, it is worth noting that its hybrid approach centering both autoethnographic writing and the teaching of dialogue-based skills calls for a careful triangulation of data—both stories and statistics. Chiefly interested in students' abilities to "perspectivize" with others, and "take risks" as writers and communicators, I collected student writing samples, transcripts of interviews conducted at the culmination of each four-week unit, and conducted a year-end exit survey. Based on those initial observations, I used critical teacher inquiry (Duncan-Andrade & Morrell, 2008) to guide my investigation and engaged in a practice of continual problem posing, data gathering and analysis while simultaneously teaching. Suffice to say, there is great deal of data that exists to help tell the story of how these six students experienced the program—only a portion of which is included in this discussion. It is my hope, however, that the data highlighted here around the specific themes of perspectivizing and risk-taking is illuminating in its insight into the inner lives of my students, and how constructivist practices like those at the heart of this program may be worthy of experimentation in other courageous educational spaces.

Perspectivizing and Risk-Taking Toward Connectedness

While students' reactions to the program were many, a significant portion of their self-reflections revolved around two interrelated themes: perspectivizing and risk-taking toward connectedness.

Perspectivizing

The Center for Studies in Educational Innovation defines "perspectivizing" as the ability to engage in original empathetic responses informed through examining an issue from multiple perspectives (Villanueva, 2013). In other words, perspectivizing is the ability to consider and empathize with experiences different from one's own. The DAP elective pushed students to examine and reconsider assumptions they held about each other and various social groups—including their own. Students were given consistent opportunities—through sharing and listening to another person's creative autoethnography, as well as through structured dialogue group activities—to encounter cultural perspectives and narratives quite distinct from their own. Two central themes emerged: perspectivizing *in school*, and reconsidering the layered lives, identities and experiences of their peers, and perspectivizing *out of school* as well as reconsidering the experiences and opinions of their own families. It is important to note that the act of perspectivizing does not require (and often did not result in) agreement or changes in opinions, but the debriefing dialogues that students engaged in about their work within the unit often helped lead them toward recognizing shared experiences.

Colby, who self-identified as "hating school," reported that hearing the autoethnographies of her peers prompted her to not only consider new and different perspectives, but to *want* to come to class:

> When I come to this class, and it's a free write day or a dialogue day or a poetry day – I really wanna hear what people are saying I wanna hear what they are feeling. And I'm not usually like that. . .At first I didn't want to be here. But it became really cool, because I'm a really introverted person, and I don't like people that much. But it's really interesting to find out how other people see the world, and how different it is from the way I see it.

In this way, Colby's ability to consider the stories and perspectives of her peers enabled her to reconsider her own tendency to judge other students. In a personal essay, Colby also reported that her experience made her want to get to know people better.

In much the same way that Colby felt her involvement in the program enabled her to see her peers differently, Mason—likewise self-defined as a "judgmental person"—reflected on how he was challenged to carry that perspectivizing outside of school. Throughout his time in the course, Mason wrote extensively about his complicated relationship with his father, and how his father influences his sense of self as a man. In an interview, Mason told me about how the program's activities helped him to consider his father's inconsistent presence in his life in different, more humanizing ways:

> I end up writing a lot about my father. It's like – I don't wanna talk about him all the time. I might be talking about a love poem or something and I then all of a sudden I just end up using a damn quote from (him). And it's like, ugggh, you're still in my head dad. And you know, it's crazy cause I just talked to him the other day. … he changed so much. And it was like… I mean, it was annoying, like "Why didn't you change when I was with you?" And *now* you change? But it was still dope to talk to him, and I was proud of him that he changed…

Similarly, Solice thought the writing process deeply impacted her ability to reexamine and empathize with her mother. Solice and her mother were not, in Solice's words, "that close." She described her mother as being overly present in her life, and over-involved in ways that were "frustrating and really aggravating." Despite that strained relationship, Solice was well aware of how central a role her mother plays in her life, and how influential she has been in her socialization as a young female. "Whatever I do," she says, "it goes back to my mother. Sometimes in positive ways, and sometimes in negative ways." Solice wrote a poem in the voice of her mother, in which she offered a set of instructions for how to be a young lady. In it, she demonstrates many of the things that complicate their ability to see "eye to eye" on many issues. Below is an excerpt from that piece:

> When you go out on the
> street, you are representing me.
> If your hair looked fucked
> The first thing they say is "Why her
> mother let her outside like that?"
> You are a reflection of me
> Even when I'm not there.

Ultimately, the development of the larger poem—though it is in her mother's voices—captures Solice's own feelings toward motherhood, female sexuality, and socialization. At the end of this unit, Solice shared that she felt the opportunity to write in her mother's voice helped her wrestle with her mother's perspective and to consider why she "pushes her" around what it means to be a young woman of color.

In some cases, students not only reported being able to better understand and empathize with people in their life outside of school, but they shared their creative autoethnographies with their families and friends as a way to better explain themselves. Fancy, who also described her relationship to her mother as "difficult," said she was able to hold more meaningful conversations with her family by sharing the autoethnographies she produced: "I show my mom my writing, and then sometimes it kind of changes her opinion and makes her feel more open to me, and more accepting of me and we can have a dialogue with each other..."

Tia also reported that the work she produced helped her communicate more meaningfully with her mother outside of school—particularly around issues connected to her body image and weight. "This really helped me," she reported, "to get (things) off my chest. Now, I don't really jump at (my mother) when we talk about (my body image) at home."

Risk-Taking Toward Connectedness

It is also critical to look at the other side of the dialogue—where students' own perspectives and experiences are the ones being empathized *with*. Connection, or the ability to forge meaningful, authentic relationships with others, is the essence of the human experience (Brown, 2015). Vulnerability and the willingness to take risks in showing ourselves to others are fundamental in hurdling many of the divisive feelings of shame, guilt, and fear that result in interpersonal conflict in schools. The DAP program asked students to step into some of their own vulnerabilities around social identity and share about their lives as pathways toward building bridges with others. Their responses fell largely into two basic themes: risk and vulnerability through the writing and sharing of autoethnographies, and risk and vulnerability through dialogue.

Tia wrote extensively about both her body size and her sexuality throughout the course of the year, both of which represented difficult and "hard-to-talk-about" topics for her. Self-described as "thick" and sometimes "really emotional" about the way others perceive her because of her physical weight, Tia reported that the course gave her the opportunity and the structure to write about those themes in ways that were ultimately healing, and quite empowering. Early in the year, Tia developed a poem called "Thick" in which she wrote about a series of isolated moments from her life when her body size deeply impacted her sense of self, or how she thought others perceived her. She wrote about early experiences in school, where she was bullied and treated poorly because of her weight, titling each chapter according to specific "triggers" connected to those experiences: The stairs, The halls, TV, Mason, Summer, and Now. Below are two excerpts from some of those initial drafts of "Thick," after Jon Sands (2011):

> ...I walk through the halls, carrying
> books upon books upon books.
> I try to shut out the stereotypical
> thinking but I cant...
>
> ...Mason makes me feel like nothing.
> Mason would say things like "You fat.
> You are really fat." He'd say,
> "No one will love you like me."
> And you know what? I believed him.

Tia took risks more and more as the semester went on. In a follow-up interview about her experience in the course, she reflected on producing "Thick" and why she felt it necessary to take those risks in her writing:

> The identity that I chose – being "thick" – like, it was a touchy subject, because I don't talk about it...it hits a part that I don't wanna touch. And when I do, I either get upset or I get really emotional, or I'll just be like it's whatever, it's gonna be like that sometimes when you gonna hit a part that you don't wanna touch – but you might as well take a risk, because it's writing and writing take risks. So I just wanted to take that risk, because I never talk about it.

Tia speaks to the ways in which the writing and sharing enabled her to take risks in talking about herself. Ultimately, she also reported that by sharing about herself and "digging deep" into the vulnerable parts of her own identity as a young, "thick" woman of color, she was able to push her classmates into doing the same. Students' risk-taking approaches to the process of building and sharing their creative autoethnographies fostered an environment that enabled students to push themselves to develop compassion for one another.

Though difficult to discern the point at which the sharing of autoethnographies and the exchange of personal stories around identity officially becomes "dialogue," students experienced and discussed "risk in conversation" with one another a bit differently. Kai H. wrote a formal evaluation essay in which she explicitly named the types of risks she felt she observed in dialogue with her classmates:

> Beyond just writing about our lives in very intimate ways, we also told the stories behind our pieces and how they made us feel, and shared about how those stories impact how we see each other at school. Those risks caused some of us to feel uneasy, and in certain cases, vulnerable, but when we opened up to our groups, we…let out the truth, told our stories, and felt more connected to each other as a result.

Kai H.'s candid reflection captures the degree to which the dialogue process, in particular, enabled students to engage deeply with one another about difficult personal subject matter. Similarly, Mason reported that engaging in this work enabled him to "just go for it" when talking about issues of identity that might otherwise make him feel unsafe or vulnerable. Those risky conversations enabled students to feel "more connected to one another" as a result.

New Ways of Seeing

This chapter provides a glimpse into just some of the ways that a group of young people experienced and benefited from a high school elective course combining the structured practices of creative autoethnography production and dialogue skills. In doing so, it demonstrates the positive potential to combat what is increasingly being referred to as a "bullying crisis" in high schools across the United States (Klein, 2013). As opposed to looking critically at how to quell "bullying behavior," a number of critical practices might build opportunities for empathy and community in the classroom as a way of addressing deeper issues of school culture, intolerance, and conflict. Talking with Mason, Colby, Solice, Fancy, Tia, and Kai H. about their experiences in the "DAP class" led me to consider the potential for this work to influence how educational communities *beyond* the traditional realms of classrooms and schools grapple with their own cultural climate issues related to intolerance and conflict across lines of identity.

Performance (and perhaps the arts more generally) can be an incredibly effective and disarming tool for bringing, as Tia put it, "hard to talk about topics" into the classroom. Research has shown that many people hesitate to engage in difficult dialogue around identity, culture, and diversity because they feel they do not know how to engage appropriately, or that they are not informed enough to do so in the "right" ways (Singleton & Linton, 2007). This fear of "getting it wrong"—and the subsequent unwillingness to engage—has contributed, in no small way, to the counterproductive narrative of tolerance that is prevalent in many school communities across the country. It is certainly easier to tolerate than it is to engage deeply with one another in ways that challenge our discordant selves to come in contact. A shared experience pushes us to ignore the mantra that suggests there is a "right" vocabulary with which to engage around these issues, and it enables us to give credit to (and find connection through) our emotional responses.

Students' general success (and self-reported enjoyment) with the autoethnographic approach as an entry point into larger issues of culture and identity suggests the importance of prioritizing individual stories and testimonies over buzz words and terminology. Many current trends in critical multicultural research stress the importance of social justice terminology, such as power, privilege, discrimination, racism, homophobia, and so on (Gorski, 2013; Ravitch, 2007). While there is little skepticism that each and every one of those terms are *vital* to an eventual understanding of the foundation of this work, and the difficult task that is building bridges across differences, introducing those terms as a starting point can in fact be more divisive, more detrimental, and more boring than beneficial. When students were able to explore and share their own individual *stories* and cultural narratives through the creative autoethnographic approach, they were able to truly become invested in the larger dialogue around identity and school culture. Stories, after all, are a universal currency.

Teaching and exploring self and social identity as a polycentric idea increases the potential of individuals to see themselves as reflected in relevant discourses of culture and diversity (Vinz, 2000). Asking students to consider themselves not only in terms of race and gender but also in terms of socioeconomic status, sexual orientation, language and nation of origin, body size, and spirituality or religion, to name a few, pushed students to examine the ways in which people can be at once privileged and not privileged, seen and not seen, and in so doing, helped them work toward generating empathy for groups and individuals. When given the opportunity to see our identities as a collection of diverse, malleable, and sometimes contradictory group memberships, we are able to see beyond the black/white-gay/straight-rich/poor binaries that often keep us exhausted by, fearful of, and resistant to conversations around cultural conflict. As

Tatum (2003) proclaims, it is when we are able to see "who we are in our full humanity, embracing all of our identities, that we are able to create the possibility of building alliances that may ultimately free us all" (p. 21).

Final Thoughts

A critical education is one where, as Morrell (2005) and others indicate, students are pushed to consider their own lives in relationship to the world around them. One where, moreover, they are drawn into dialogue around the social and political factors that shape their lives, and encouraged to promote engagement with one another in ways that are reflective of those factors. In other words, a critical education is one where real-world problems are not kept at bay from instruction but rather invited into it, starting, chiefly, with the real worlds of students' lives. It is one where tolerance is not preached but rather interrogated. The English classroom, like few other places in schools, represents a nexus at which issues of language, culture, identity, and power inevitably intersect. As such, it is up to teachers themselves to create curricula that not only addresses these issues but places them squarely at the center of instruction—curricula that is proactive in the process of learning about students' lives, concerns, and fears around engaging with one another and society.

In much the same way that English teachers must lead the charge in using their classrooms to reimagine the world as one where perspectivizing and connectedness are fundamental, young people themselves must also recognize their own power to drive those difficult dialogues in ways that most adults in their lives cannot. High school students are infinitely more open and engaged across differences than most adults (certainly the adults currently leading this country), and need to be supported in their efforts to locate that autonomy to speak back to the world as it exists both within and beyond their schools. "The arts," Maxine Greene (2000) famously said, "cannot change the world, but they may change human beings who might change the world." They may challenge and enable us to see more in our day-to-day experiences, hear more on normally unheard frequencies, and to become awake to what the mundane of routine has kept hidden. This chapter is written with the hope that other educators will respond to the call to construct and execute courageous, arts-based curricula where students can speak back to the realities defining their lives, learn to search for agreement with others, and to perceive and value difference, especially when the world around them seems to be calling for the opposite.

References

Adams, M. (2010). *Readings for diversity and social justice.* New York: Routledge.

Adorno, T. (1959). *Education after Auschwitz.* No publisher.

Alexander, B. K. (2005). Performance ethnography: The reenacting and inciting of culture. In N. Denzin & Y. Lincoln (Eds.), *The sage handbook of qualitative research* (3rd ed., pp. 411–441). Thousand Oaks, CA: Sage.

Bakhtin, M. M. (1981). *The dialogic imagination: Four essays.* Austin, TX: University of Texas Press.

Banks, J. A., & Banks, C. A. M. (2010). *Multicultural education: Issues and perspectives.* Hoboken, NJ: Wiley.

Bohm, D., Nichol, L., & Incebrary. (1996). *On dialogue.* London: Routledge.

Brown, B. (2015). *Daring greatly: How the courage to be vulnerable transforms the way we live, love, parent, and lead.* New York: Avery Publishing Group.

Camangian, P. (2008). Untempered tongues: Teaching performance poetry for social justice. *English Teaching: Practice and Critique, 7*(2), 35–55.

Camangian, P. (2009). Real talk: Transformative English teaching and urban youth. In W. Ayers, T. Quinn, & D. Stovall (Eds.), *Handbook of social justice in education.* Mahwah, NJ: Erlbaum.

Carey-Webb, A. (2001). *Literature and lives: A response-based, cultural studies approach to teaching English.* Urbana, IL: National Council of Teachers of English.

Dessel, A. (2010). Prejudice in schools: Promotion of an inclusive culture and climate. *Education and Urban Society, 42*(4), 407–429.

Downs, A. (2012). *The velvet rage: Overcoming the pain of growing up gay in a straight mans world.* New York: Da Capo Lifelong.

Duncan-Andrade, J. M. R., & Morrell, E. (2008). *The art of critical pedagogy: Possibilities for moving from theory to practice in urban schools.* New York: Peter Lang.

Dyson, A. H., & Genishi, C. (Eds.). (1994). *The need for story: Cultural diversity in classroom and community.* Urbana, IL: National Council of Teachers of English. Web. 6 Nov. 2013.

Fisher, M. (2005). From the coffee house to the school house: The promise and potential of spoken word poetry in school contexts. *English Education, 37*(2), 115–131.

Freire, P. (2006). *Teachers as cultural workers: Letters to those who dare to teach.* Boulder, CO: Westview.

Furlong, A. (2009). *Handbook of youth and young adulthood: New perspectives and agendas.* London: Routledge.

Gorski, P. (2013, February). *Social justice: Not just another term for diversity.* Commission for Social Justice.

Greene, M. (2000). *Releasing the imagination: Essays on education, the arts, and social change* [Electronic version]. San Francisco: Jossey-Bass.

Griffin, S. R., Brown, M., & Warren, N. M. (2012). Critical education in high schools: The promise and challenges of intergroup dialogue. *Equity & Excellence in Education, 45*(1), 159–180.

Gurin, P., Nagda, B. A., & Zunega, Z. (2013). *Dialogue across difference: Practice, theory, and research on intergroup dialogue.* New York: Russell Sage Foundation.

Jocson, K. (2011). Poetry in a new race era. *Daedalus, 140*(1), 154–162. Web. 15 Dec. 2013.

Kass, J., & Beal, S. (2000). *Underneath: The archeological approach to creative writing.* Ann Arbor, MI: Red Beard Press.

Klein, J. (2013). *The bully society: School shootings and the crisis of bullying in Americas schools.* New York: New York University Press.

MacLeod, J. (1987). *Ain't no makin' it.* Boulder, CO: Westview.

Morrell, E. (2005). Toward a critical English education: Reflections on and projections for the discipline. *English Education, 37*(4), 312–322.

Poteat, V. P., & DiGiovanni, C. D. (2010). When biased language use is associated with bullying and dominance behavior: The moderating effects of prejudice. *Journal of Youth and Adolescence, 39*(10), 1123–1133.

Ravitch, D. (2007). *EdSpeak: A glossary of education terms, phrases, buzzwords, and jargon.* Alexandria, VA: Association for Supervision & Curriculum Development (ASCD).

Sands, J. (2011). *The new clean.* Austin, TX: Write Bloody Publishing.

Singleton, G. E., & Linton, C. (2007). *Facilitator's guide, courageous conversations about race: A field guide for achieving equity in schools.* Thousand Oaks, CA: Corwin Press.

Stock, P. L. (1995). *The dialogic curriculum: Teaching and learning in a multicultural society.* Portsmouth, NH: Boynton/Cook Publishers.

Tatum, B. D. (2003). *Why are all the black kids sitting together in the cafeteria?: And other conversations about race.* New York: Basic Books.

Villanueva, A. (2013). *Implementing a district-wide professional development initiative: What it means to educate for the 21st century.* Unpublished doctoral dissertation, Columbia University, New York.

Vinz, R. (2000). *Becoming (other)wise: Enhancing critical reading perspectives.* Portland, ME: Calendar Islands Publishers.

Zuniga, X., Nagda, B. A., & Sevig, T. D. (2001). Intergroup dialogues: An educational model for cultivating engagement across differences. *Equity and Excellence in Education, 35*(1), 7–17.

CHAPTER 9

A Constructivist Perspective on Games in Education

Linda G. Polin

Play is considered a leading activity for development in children, in part, because it provides opportunity for players to construct meaning and reach beyond the known and real into the possible and imagined (Vygotsky, 1978). Games provide a particular kind of playscape, one in which possible action is shaped by not only players but also goals and rules and contingencies. This developmental potential of games has been leveraged in learning settings since well before the computer age (e.g., De Vries & Slavin, 1978).

The rise of collaborative video game spaces in popular culture is pushing school-based gaming away from solo-play puzzles or drill and practice games of the past, and into virtual worlds of multiplayer engagement in which the setting, objects, and activities are interdependent, requiring coordination and collaboration to solve complex curricular problems (Barab, Thomas, Dodge, Carteaux, & Tuzun, 2005; Dede, Clarke, Ketelhut, Nelson, & Bowman, 2005). Like textbooks and computers, games do not exert an objective impact on students in school. Classrooms

Special thanks to Rolin Moe, Seattle Pacific University, Institute for Academic Innovation, for insightful critique of the manuscript.

L.G. Polin (✉)
Davidson Professor of Education and Technology, Graduate School of Education and Psychology, Pepperdine University, W. Los Angeles, CA, USA

D.W. Kritt (ed.), *Constructivist Education in an Age of Accountability*,
https://doi.org/10.1007/978-3-319-66050-9_9

are complex sociocultural spaces in which materials, personal and institutional histories, and local actions interact. Sometimes, these interactions are in concert, while sometimes they are in conflict.

It makes little sense to examine or discuss the impact of games on learning without thoughtful consideration of the ways in which their use and meaning is mediated by the elements of the pedagogical context in which they might be used. Despite substantial learning theory on the topic, gameplay in school is rarely described as mediated by the instructional moves of the teacher, nor the social and cultural milieu of the students, school, and community. Thus, in consideration of school learning, it may be more useful to examine games in terms of their support or compatibility with tenets or characteristics of a particular pedagogy.

Most studies of games and learning regard games as places where learning occurs, focusing on the mechanisms and type of learning that can be found in various types of games. Researchers have looked most often at games outside the boundaries of the classroom, for example, in after-school clubs, at home or in lab settings (Kafai, 2010; Squire, 2011; Steinkuehler, 2007). For the most part, studies have revealed significant and sophisticated development in game-players as they reason, debate, and construct solutions to game problems, activities, and contingencies (Steinkuehler & Duncan, 2008). This work has clearly established the value of games as learning spaces and thus the potential value of games in formal schooling. As a result, specially funded research and development projects have applied game-based learning in schools, particularly in STEM (science, technology, engineering, and mathematics) subjects (Barab et al., 2005; Dede et al., 2005).

This chapter expands the games conversation in terms of pedagogy, examining the role and potential of games in the classroom from a sociocultural or social constructivist approach to school learning to consider pedagogical moves those designs afford the teacher: what they lead toward or away from, and what participation structures they make possible for students.

Theorizing About Learning with Games

Theories of learning have evolved over the past 30 years as researchers have sought to understand the failure of cognitive transfer, a basic premise of schooling, to deliver on its promise (Brown, Collins, & Duguid, 1989; Resnick, 1991). From studies of learning in informal settings (Gonzales,

Moll, & Amanti, 2005), learning on the job (Hutchins & Klausen, 1996), and in practitioner communities (Lave & Wenger, 1991; Suchman & Trigg, 1996), and in everyday life (Rogoff, Murtaugh, & de la Rocha, 1984), researchers from anthropology, sociology, sociolinguistics, psychology, and communication have identified *social engagement around shared work* as a powerful mechanism for supporting learning. Their research, together with Russian psychology, forms a family of social learning theories. These are known variously as *situated learning, cognitive apprenticeship, cognitive constructivism, distributed cognition, social constructivism, communities of practice, sociocultural historical theory*, and *activity theory*. The first four emphasize the scaffolding value of situativity, of experiencing learning in the context of its use. However, while these recognize the interaction between and influence of the individual and the social, they describe them as distinct, separate, and immediate. The last four cohere around two critical tenets. First, they do not demarcate individuals from the various contexts in which those individuals find themselves. Rather, they acknowledge that each participates in the co-construction of the other, that they are mutually constituted. Second, they are mindful of the ontology of the individual and the cultural milieu. Schooling, for instance, is both a construction of its history as a sociopolitical institution and a construction of the individuals occupying it at a particular moment. Available artifacts, peers, and near-peers contribute to and shape the learning process. Activity theory, socio-cultural historical theory, and the communities of practice model move beyond the notion of context to consideration of cultural and historical influences as critical mediators of the learning process.

Though these theories describe how people learn and develop understanding, neither cognitive constructivism nor social learning theory offers an explicit pedagogical model (Baviskar, Hartle, & Whitney, 2009; Richardson, 2003; Windschitl, 2002). This is partly a function of the theories themselves, which privilege direct experience over direct instruction as the mechanism for learning. The two differ in pedagogical implication, in part, because of their different focus. Where constructivism focuses on the student, social learning theory focuses on the student-in-activity, consisting of actions, artifacts, people, motive, history, and context. From this perspective, the key to learning is in the features of the task or activity, what meaning it offers learners, how they come to engage with it and each other, and where it leads them.

In a classroom, the teacher is partly responsible for giving meaning to the materials and activities by invoking them in particular activity contexts (e.g., take out your math books because we are going to do math now). It is also carried in the learning objects and routines in the classroom, most of which have historical trajectories (e.g., textbooks, desks, tests, teacher-led questioning and presentation). Students also bear responsibility in the construction of meaning in the classroom, bringing with them their own perspectives and understandings, both academic and personal. For example, math is about answers, or I calculate remaining hit points in my Pokémon game.

A major point to consider is that a game is a material object—its meaning and its use are subject to negotiation and interpretation by users. To illustrate the malleable meaning of a classroom game, consider the case of the mathematic game DragonBox.

The Case of DragonBox

DragonBox intends to introduce players to procedures used in solving linear algebra equations. It is a drill and practice program, but cleverly disguised as a game in which successful solutions of problems power up a dragon egg, with the ultimate goal to hatch it. Game tasks require players to isolate the box containing the egg (i.e., the x or unknown quantity, on one side of the screen) by manipulating objects on the screen. For instance, by using a white card to cancel out a black card, while remembering to add the same card to both sides of the screen, and so on. As the game progresses, the icons fade away and standard mathematical symbols and notation take their place while the same successful procedures continue to be invoked to isolate x. The game is designed to be played solo, but there are suggestions and guides for teachers to introduce key ideas and support transfer of those ideas from the game to 'real math'. The product includes an online community of support for players, teachers, and parents (dragonbox.com).

Two recent research studies (Long & Aleven, 2014; Solarz, 2014) focused on the efficacy of DragonBox to support learning algebraic concepts. Though the outcome sought is the same, the two studies illustrate how different perspectives on teaching with a game result in radically different deployment of the same educational game.

In the Long and Aleven study, the game is the teacher. The researchers are interested in comparing DragonBox with a program designed by the researchers. Their research focuses on determining to what extent replaying levels that have already been successfully completed (replay) can increase achievement on a post-test measure of linear algebra knowledge. This is an experimental design, with classes randomly assigned to conditions. The interesting part of the study is the intervention, the experience itself, which they describe as students 'worked for five 42-minutes class periods on consecutive school days' (Long & Aleven, 2014). That is, they solo played for five sessions in a row. They were then tested, and those results compared to the pretest. Students were also asked about their 'enjoyment'. The teacher, or any pedagogical agent other than the game, is absent from the research (and classroom) framework. In this case, learning is a consequence of playing the game.

The second study of DragonBox proceeds quite differently. In this instance, the researcher is the teacher. She describes a very different implementation of the very same game. Working with a class of 20 twelve-year-olds, she first introduces them to the game, which they then play together on tablets and on the interactive whiteboard in the class. While students are engaged in the gameplay, the teacher takes a pedagogical stance that positions or frames the game as a collaborative and speculative venture for students:

> I acted rather like an observer – sometimes I helped students to understand English commands. I didn't interrupt, didn't make suggestions. I listened to my students and watched what they discovered…Students made a lot of mistakes and moved back many times. I can say – they learned by their mistakes. Sometimes they solved the problems together or they worked in pairs so there was opportunity to dispute a lot. I didn't interfere. (Solarz, 2014, p. 68)

In the Long and Aleven study, DragonBox is carrying the curriculum, and learning depends on scaffolding and fading of scaffolds in the game to pull students toward understanding. In the Solarz study, DragonBox is an occasion or opportunity for co-construction as students propose, debate, test, and revise actions together in open discussion. This teacher has reclaimed the game as a shared object-to-think-with, and she goes even further. She asks the students to step back from the computer game to recreate it with paper and pencil. To replicate the DragonBox equations, students need to construct a representational system for the math operations:

> I encouraged them to compare what they did before with the rules of DragonBox. ... Very slowly, students started to use the specific algebraic language in place of the language of the game. (pp. 69–70)

The teacher's mediating influence on the meaning, value, and use of the game in math class even extends beyond the actual boundaries of gameplay. And so, a game that seems to exactly fit the definition of gamified algebra practice becomes a powerful tool for learning when the teacher intervenes to build upon the possibilities she sees for students to discuss, debate, construct, revise, reflect, and self-monitor. It is the teacher's move that turns DragonBox into a social constructionist experience for her class.

As seen in this DragonBox example, it is not enough to describe features of games without regarding how they might function in the classroom, operating under a particular pedagogical approach framing their use, and without consideration of students' own experiences with games and school. However, this is complicated by the fact that learning theories are not pedagogical models. Teachers attempting to operate on sociocultural notions of learning must first translate ideas about learning into a pedagogical stance.

From Social Learning Theory to Classroom Teaching Practice

Development, that is, learning that is in process, arises in challenging activities that a learner is not yet able to carry out alone, lacking sufficient skill or knowledge, but can manage with help (Vygotsky, 1978). In this assisted performance situation, a more knowledgeable other assists the learner. Development results, in part, from interaction with those who can help, but that help must arise from mutual understanding. The more knowledgeable other is often the teacher in a classroom, but must also include peers who are by definition closer to the experience and knowledge of their fellow learner. This is teaching that leads to development. In classrooms, it falls on the teacher to create problem spaces 'in the zone' with participation structures that accommodate learners with partial understanding and that support collaboration across levels of competence.

All learning is mediated by people and things, and by the meaning they carry socially, personally, and historically (Cole & Engestrom, 1993). That meaning is available to the learner to frame and support understanding. Because language is a primary representation tool for conceptual thinking, classroom talk is an important resource for understanding what sense students are making of the activities and procedures they are engaged in, and what meaning they have ascribed to terms and concepts. Good dialogue is a back-and-forth between speakers, testing, contesting, and building on ideas. Yet, conversation in classrooms is often dominated by the teacher, and falls into the Initiate-Response-Evaluate (I-R-E) pattern of teacher inquiry, followed by student response, and teacher evaluation (Mehan, 1979). Rarely do students direct their speech to peers, and rarely do conceptual disagreements get worked through together.

The diversity among students in experience and knowledge inherent in every classroom is, in fact, a useful resource (González, Moll, & Amanti, 2005). Students can expand beyond the preconceptions of their own experience, and voiced misconceptions become opportunities for learning. When learning relies exclusively on nonresponsive materials, texts, or presentations rather than interaction, there is no opportunity for negotiation to ensure comprehension. Thus, even a stellar text product or multimedia presentation cannot be responsive to each learner developing those concepts.

Learning arises in and from activity that is challenging and personally meaningful. Challenging activities become a source of learning conversations when they are meaningful to the learner and the content to be learned is authentic. School offers a specialized kind of knowledge that differs from what is learned in everyday experience outside of school. Academic concepts are abstract, general, and formal; everyday experience is personal, immediate, and improvisational. The use of knowledge outside of school is immediate and instrumental. Knowing is useful because of what it results in, what it enables, or what value it yields. In school, the end goal of learning is typically having knowledge, not using it.

> Tasks that are designed to situate content are only useful in classrooms that allow such meanings to be explored. Likewise, classroom practices that emphasize making connections can only lead to robust learning when they are supported by tasks that create opportunities for students to grapple with the meaning and utility of content. (Gresalfi & Barab, 2011, p. 301)

For social constructionists, learning is dynamic, and assessment is most useful when it is used to understand emergent growth. Initially, understanding is co-constructed and external, but through experience the learner is able to internalize and later reproduce knowledge-in-action alone.

Assessment of learning can be taken from the unassisted or solo performance, especially in the production or construction of objects that make use of and represent learned concepts.

From the social constructionist perspective described above, teaching is a creative, if complicated endeavor. Teachers are tasked with connecting school curriculum and students' out-of-school life by locating and developing meaningful contexts for students to engage with disciplinary concepts and tools, by providing responsive assistance as students tackle challenging activities, supporting collaboration and dialogue, and making use of student constructions and performance for assessment. (Table 9.1 presents practical efforts to move from the *why* of learning theory to the *how* of pedagogy.) This is quite a set of demands. However, well-designed game spaces can support teachers' efforts. In particular, virtual game worlds are especially well matched to a social constructionist classroom.

Features of virtual worlds are analogous to life in 'the real world' outside the game. To begin with, the player inhabits a role and takes a position with regard to other people and activities in the game world. Time passes; actions matter. A varied landscape offers a wide range to explore activities in different locations and situationally useful objects, tools, and properties. In multiplayer games, the space is inhabited by other people with whom the player can engage, even team up. There is meaning for immediate small action but also building toward a larger world narrative, typically of a world-level problem or threat that all players are working to resolve.

Such 'thickly authentic' play spaces situate disciplinary learning in a 'real world'. As elaborate worlds, they can support complex academic concepts in

Table 9.1 From learning theory to pedagogy

Social learning principles Learning is...	*Pedagogic moves* Teaching should...
Different in school and out of school	Link school concepts to students' lives with personally meaningful/authentic activity
Results from assisted performance	Create participation structures for collaboration
Assisted by tools/artifacts that are themselves meaningful, language being the most powerful	Foreground the meaning of tools and materials used in context Provide space for dialogue around ideas and tasks
Arises in doing, in activity	Situate concepts in practices that use them
A dynamic state	Assess understanding in students' constructions and performances

practical 'worldly' activities to make school learning more real (Shaffer, 2006; Shaffer & Resnick, 1999). Though connections between school ideas and life outside school may not be easy to locate in typical arrangements for learning in the classroom, games that present an entire world for the game-player offer a middle ground, between school and out-of-school. A well-designed virtual world can embody complexity in relationships and systems; it can pose problems relevant to the world that require players to learn new information or procedures to resolve, and it typically provides in-game resources relevant to the solving. This bridging effect is even stronger for video games, especially complex, multiplayer, virtual game worlds that contain problems, resources, operate as rule-based systems, and support participation and player agency.

When players are learning to play a game, they jump right in and learn from participating in a scaffolded structure, usually something like a 'starting zone' that is a sequestered safe space with low cost for mistakes. Game manuals and shared player information on forums and blogs become reference material that the player turns to when stuck. In school, students get the information up front, they 'read the manual', but never actually get to play the game, that is, to apply the knowledge (Gee, 2007). Games reposition the text materials and the teacher-expert as secondary resources, and the actionable setting as the primary or foregrounded source of motive, ideas, and action.

In games, gameplay provides tangible, immediate results from actions and consequences from an episode of activity. These are subject to discussion, debate, comparison, reflection, and suggestion. Replaying based on new understanding is assumed, supported, and built into games. Yet in schooling, efforts tend to be binary: success or failure. Reflecting with data on failures or mistakes, and chances to retry are rare. Time and opportunity to discuss ideas and to handle the language of representation are also rare. Opportunities to iterate based on new understanding are practically nonexistent; yet these are the very elements of games that allow players to progress.

It is no surprise to find educational researchers studying learning in virtual worlds and harnessing many of their features in the development of specifically educational worlds in which curricular topics supply the backstory, the challenges, the roles, objects, and activities. The following sections discuss a variety of virtual world games in a progression from highly focused curricular games to the ultimate challenge of having students create games. This movement entails increasing the burden on the teacher to support out-of-game activities and interaction that will achieve pedagogical goals.

Teaching with Games

Though the in-game narrative, roles, and actions of a virtual world provide student-players an accessible view of academic content in use in a complex, ongoing world, it does not necessarily lead to the construction of formal academic concepts, even though they may be in use in solving in-game problems and completing in-game tasks. As seen in the DragonBox example, the understanding that appears in gameplay may not be completely or accurately appropriated by the student-player, especially if the scaffolds for acting with knowledge are very directive and narrow. When the student-player steps outside the game space to discuss, share, elaborate, and debate in-game experiences, the tool of language, and the mediating effects of peers and teacher are available to develop learning. It may be that only in participation in the collaborative space beyond the game, where ideas can be handled, checked, and refined, that learning truly happens.

Successful commercial games already expand beyond game boundaries, as players seek and offer help and opinions on gameplay. Researchers have documented the nature of information created and shared and debated about gameplay outside of the games and found evidence of logic, scientific reasoning, mathematics, argumentation, and other kinds of sophisticated engagement around seeking knowledge in order to master games (Steinkuehler, 2007; Steinkuehler & Duncan, 2008). For players, objects, actions, and game data become things to think with, tangible representations of ideas and procedures.

In games, as in real life, actions are subject to contingencies, anticipated and unanticipated. In games, contingencies are part of the challenge that makes play fun. No one way to do things or one right answer works all the time. It can seem that school is just about right answers and not about exploring curricular ideas, but the identity of the game-player includes expecting failure, iteration, and progression. It includes looking past finding a solution to weighing a range of responses in a variety of situations. The ambiguities and contingencies in gameplay are both part of the appeal and a source of problems that generate learning.

In a game-playing classroom, the teacher sets the frame for discussions. In the social constructionist classroom, that frame encourages student-players to verbalize, share, explore representations of ideas in practical application rather than simply acquire static, untested concepts. These discussions should take advantage of the game world as the applied space for thinking and tinkering with concepts. Discussions should be grounded in the game narrative as a source of making work meaningful and trying on disciplinary identity, for example, thinking about science concepts as a scientist solving a pressing problem in a community. Immersive worlds support this because they are:

> narratively rich, personally motivating, conceptually rich and situationally consequential. What's more these technologies provide important supports for teachers in their attempts to support students' engagement with content in ways that go beyond mere mastery of tools. By using immersive and iterative narratives that help students think differently with and about content, teachers can support students in being engaged with content procedurally, conceptually, consequentially, and critically. (Gresalfi & Barab, 2011, pp. 308–9)

Immersive virtual worlds provide reasonable, content-related context for subject matter ideas, tools, and artifacts to acquire relevance, for students to experience agency with them, and for problems and insights to arise for discussion (see Table 9.2). To the extent that the game narrative engages the student-player, that connection can become the way for the formal, abstract generalizations in disciplinary knowledge to connect with

Table 9.2 How games can help

Pedagogic moves Teaching should...	*Game features* A game can...
Link school concepts to students' lives with personally meaningful/authentic activity	Give academic form to student narratives
Situate concepts in practices that use them Provide conceptual knowledge with situated experience	Give applied relevance to curricular concepts by locating them within a living world
Foreground the meaning of tools and materials used in context of their use	Imbue tools with practical use and disciplinary meaning
Place students in a shared experience with interesting problems/issues that require assistance to solve Provide space for dialogue around ideas, problems, and tasks	Create participation structures for collaborative effort
Make failure and iteration an acceptable and useful part of developing competence	Make failure and iteration an inevitable but not terminal experience in gameplay
Assess understanding in students' constructions and performances	Require production of objects, tools, or actions that demonstrate knowledge

improvisational, immediate, everyday actions of student-players, to become useable ideas for student-players.

Virtual Worlds Built for Education

Educational games that embody immersive virtual worlds provide reasonable, content-related context for subject matter ideas, tools, and artifacts to come to life, to show dynamism and impact. Quest Atlantis (QA), Whyville, and River City are three examples of the variation in educational game worlds.

QA was developed as an online 3D graphical world, accessible to players through school classes. At its height, QA supported thousands of student-players around the world engaged in investigating and responding to in-world problems and challenges, most of which focused on environmental science. Pitched at upper elementary and middle school grades, QA was designed to be played at school, with teacher mediation, and to connect with the science curriculum. The Indiana University project staff provided professional development and support for teachers.

This educational multiplayer game included a backstory that gave the world, its people, objects, and activities meaning and purpose. The backstory of the overarching narrative for the world was represented in an introductory video story and printed novel form but is also enacted in dialogue with programmed characters in the game. QA arrayed adventure tasks or quests across seven categories of 'social commitments', including creative expression, diversity affirmation, personal agency, social responsibility, environmental awareness, healthy communities, and compassionate wisdom. QA tasks might begin in science but often ended with the requirement to write reports or narratives, which also made gameplay relevant to the literacy curriculum.

Despite its clear curricular linkage, QA did not sacrifice the agency or constructive opportunities to be compatible with schooling. Like commercial multiplayer virtual worlds, QA let players select and modify an avatar to represent themselves, and move freely around in the world, interacting with other players and with programmed characters in the world. In explaining the design decisions around QA, Barab and his colleagues (2007) expressed the desire to connect school learning to authentic contexts for its use, and at the same time help students formalize their personal, local, and relevant experiences outside of school. The world of QA offered problems that could be worked on and resolved by student-players, that is, students' actions had a clear impact on the world. Furthermore, these problems and issues had real-world analogs, for example, water quality. The problems in QA are solvable with curricular content that is embedded in authentic ways, in people who must be interviewed, in data that must be gathered from in-world collection procedures, and with in-world tools that are appropriate to the task.

In Quest Atlantis, players file written reports on actions and their impact, initially reviewed by their teachers, and are able to acquire the privilege of offering feedback about the reports filed by other players. The reporting is not additive nor presented as a post hoc assignment but rather is described and culturally supported in the game as part of the activity. That is, the reporting is essential to completing the quest. While this kind of task closure clearly functions as an assessment opportunity for the teacher, asking players to write up their experience or 'findings' leads players to reflect on what they've done and put words to their understanding of it. In this way, the reporting tasks, which function as assessments for the teacher, extend the learning process for the student-players.

Whyville, explicitly designed to support science inquiry in an informal, multiplayer, virtual world (http://www.whyville.net), is first and foremost a social space with a variety of discrete STEM-based games to play solo or with others. However, beyond a chat room, it includes a landscape made up of regions, a mail system and an economy, and players who can sport customizable avatars. Though it was not developed for use in schools, most activities in-world focus on STEM concepts. As a browser-based, free-to-join space on the web, it claims a registered user base in the millions and thousands of self-contained science activities. Like Quest Atlantis, it targets upper elementary/middle school classrooms. The 2D graphics world of Whyville is not a game itself, but it contains mini-games that encourage players to tinker with concepts and procedures in physics and biology, for example, to make a race car go faster by altering car parts or move a hot air balloon in order to make a timely drop onto a target on the ground. The games are mostly replayable simulations, allowing players to test and iterate to succeed. Occasionally, worldwide events are launched to provoke problems that can best be solved or understood in collaboration using science concepts and data analysis, for instance, an in-game epidemic of Whypox.

Whypox (Kafai, Feldon, Fields, Giange, & Quintero, 2007) is a regularly occurring event in the game world, during which time players are very likely to acquire Whypox, which manifests as spots on the avatar and the word 'achoo' randomly inserted amidst words in chat from infected players. Support for determining causes and remedies for Whypox exist in-world, mediated by a world location, the vCDC (virtual Center for Disease Control). Here, players can run simulations, discuss ideas and information in forums, and examine 'archives' from prior outbreaks. This establishes conditions and motives for engaging in a quasi-scientific investigation.

In an interesting investigation of players actively engaged with the event, researchers found that the game context overwhelmed the science. Players worked to perfect the model to improve accuracy of predictions by changing predictions based on feedback, not by varying the conditions in the model. There was little effort to ferret out or understand causal relations by varying elements in the simulator model, something a teacher could greatly enhance within the context of a classroom.

To be fair, Whyville is located in a landscape of an open and optional play space, albeit focused on activities that illuminate STEM topics, whereas Quest Atlantis is explicitly designed to support curricular goals, even referencing curriculum standards, and with the expectation of a teacher mediating students' experiences. The main critical difference between Quest Atlantis and Whyville is the lack of a binding narrative in Whyville that would pull together and make sense of the variety of topics, materials, activities, and events that arise or can arise there. In addition, though Whyville was not built for classrooms, its serious educational objectives are clear.

River City and EcoMUVE are more compact examples of virtual worlds that function as complex, closed simulations. Both Harvard projects are examples of what Dede refers to as a MUVE, multi-user virtual environment (Metcalf, Clarke, & Dede, 2009). As the term 'environment' implies, River City is a much more constrained world than Quest Atlantis, but likewise built with the intention of situating science activity in an authentic context, with an overarching narrative, supporting collaborative investigation into 'locally' meaningful problems. Like Quest Atlantis, River City players are represented by avatars, interact with other students in-game, and with programmed characters or agents who serve as mentors or provide, when asked, relevant anecdotes or data. Set in the nineteenth century, River City includes neighborhoods, industry, a hospital, and university. The river and the elements of the city play a role in the tale of water-, air-, and insect-borne illnesses that must be understood and eradicated.

When the first MUVE, River City, sunsetted at the end of funding, the Harvard group took lessons learned in the creation of EcoMUVE, a similar science environment supporting problem-based inquiry, in which problems are built into the world, as are the clues, tools, and solutions. Like Quest Atlantis, both River City and EcoMUVE (now offline) are driven by narratives and intend to weave together seemingly inert and isolated school knowledge and their players' experience solving problems embedded in a world narrative. EcoMUVE focused all activity on a pond and forest ecosystem. While River City did support some features typically associated with games, including a storyline and characters, the later development of EcoMUVE cannot be considered a game, but rather an immersive simulation in which students observe and gather data to discover the cause of a fish kill-off.

Immersive worlds attuned to school curricula, such as those listed above, are few and far between. They exist largely as the outcome of specially funded projects and, as funded inquiry, their focus is specific and limited. When funds are gone and research is completed, they disappear. But, they have and will continue to reveal a great deal about learning in and with games.

Commercial Games Appropriated for Learning

Given the popularity of the topic of games in education and the limited availability of robust educational games to support curricular imperatives, it's not surprising to find enterprising educators looking to existing commercial game worlds to repurpose them for the classroom. This, of course, shifts the burden of educational development onto the teacher, though in every instance described below, teacher collectives have cohered online to collaborate, problem-solve, and share focused activities for students. In comparing so-called serious games and entertainment games, Gee finds little difference at the design level, with one critical distinction: serious games demand the player demonstrate explicit knowledge, that is, show learning, while games for entertainment make no such demand on the player, relying instead on the built-in need for the player to carry learning forward to new game contexts, tasks, or engagements (Gee, 2008). This does not mean important learning experiences aren't or can't happen in entertainment games. It means that aspect has to occur outside the game space (e.g., in a classroom).

In the desirable category of virtual worlds, there are two kinds of play worlds. One is simply a sandbox space with no inherent purpose, but a lot of possibilities for driving activity, for instance, constructing buildings, making tools, cultivating, and shaping the landscape. In these multiplayer spaces, players set their own goals and roles. These landscapes do not rely on a narrative and there is no call to action beyond what the players decide they are doing. Such a space is not a game space per se, although of course players are free to assign goals and create or reframe aspects of the world as problems to be solved. A second kind of virtual world is explicitly a game, with narrative that describes the values and direction of actions in the game, with goals and quests for players to accomplish, 'win' conditions, and an end state. Typically, such worlds have limits on player construction, but actions players take in pursuit of game quests or in solving game problems have an impact on the world they see.

Both kinds of virtual worlds exist as commercially available software. As such, they typically offer high-quality graphics and interface, and support sophisticated player actions. Commercially successful multiplayer virtual world games, such as World of Warcraft (WOW), Minecraft, Elder Scrolls, and Star Wars: The Old Republic, have pushed gaming into family living rooms and out of the basement, in part, because the rich narrative, diversity of player roles, range of actions, and sheer scope of landscapes offer something for almost everyone. Additionally, as massively multiplayer game spaces, these game worlds support social interaction that can be casual chatter, role-playing dialogue, and strategic engagement to tackle a problem. Successful commercial games must teach their players how to play in order for the game to keep its player base and its revenue. It's not surprising then to see how remarkably good they are at onboarding and supporting new players, encouraging and sustaining a sense of player community. It is important to remember that these games are primarily commercial ventures, regularly updated and refreshed with new content and tweaks to gameplay that hold players' interest.

The WoW is not the first but clearly the most successful and long-running massive multiplayer online (MMO) virtual world game. The company still sports between nine to ten million subscribers globally. Players can play for free up to level 20 of 110 levels of character development, which is sufficient to get well immersed in the world. Like most MMOs, WoW is complex, diverse, challenging, and social. Teachers who turn to commercial games such as WoW must develop adjunctive activities and materials to foreground curricular content. This means seeing the opening for concepts in writing, geometry, or history, and being able to flesh them out with goal-directed activities.

> In Math – Damager Per Second (DPS) Analysis: Acquire two different weapons in world used by your character's class. Using the targeting dummies

in a capital city, find the average damage over time of each weapon and plot the data on a graph. Try the same experiment again, this time with gear that changes your character's agility, strength, attack power, or other melee-related statistic. Graph the new data. What is the relationship between the statistic you tested and the DPS output? (Gillespie, 2009)

One recent WoW project in the curriculum found students using the game as a basis for their English class work and reading assignments for *The Hobbit*. Students read the book on their own time, and then look for parallels between hero Bilbo Baggins and their own WoW characters. Sheehy also has students write short stories based on their characters to explore topics like empathy and failure. (Schwartz, 2013)

Teachers collaborated across distance to seed and support a wiki devoted to sharing lessons, assessments, and insights from the use of WoW with their school curricula. The WoW in Schools wiki is still available online, though considerably less active than it was initially (wowinschool.pbworks.com). Nevertheless, the game still runs commercially, and teachers still find it relevant to their revisions of classroom pedagogy (Carmichael, 2017).

WoW is not the only commercial game that has found its way into classrooms. The *Civilization* game franchise has evolved over versions from a single player to a multiplayer game that engages players in building a civilization as the decision-making ruler. The game requires exploration, conflict, and diplomacy through decision-making. It includes choice of historical eras and provides tools that influence the trajectory of development of city nations. These are conceptual tools, including culture, religion, technology, philosopher, and more. Recognizing the potential for schools, the company is partnering with an educational non-profit to build out data capture for teachers' use.

"For the past 25 years, we've found that one of the fun secrets of Civilization is learning while you play," Sid Meier, founder and director of creative development at Firaxis Games, said. "We've always focused on entertainment first, but we believe that our players—young and old—enjoy learning, even if they don't always enjoy education." (IGN, 2017)

Teachers will have access to an online component that provides reports on student progress, developer diaries, gameplay tutorials, instructional resources, and lesson plans. (IGN, 2017)

Portal2 is another commercial game adapting to classroom use. Portal2 is basically a long and difficult puzzle game that requires players to use strategy and physics to move through the space by blasting open and chaining together portals to move through walls, using counterweights to hold down buttons. It operates as a virtual world largely due to its narrative arc about an artificial intelligence gone rogue that gives partial explanations and directs player action. It can easily be viewed as a logic and physics simulator. Its connection to school was so obvious that the company launched a specifically educational community to assist teachers with connecting Portals2 gameplay to school topics (http://www.teachwithportals.com).

Minecraft is a special case of a multiplayer virtual world, in that it is not truly a game. It is a modifiable environment in which players can engage with each other, the programmed agent characters in the game (people, monsters, animals), and the landscape itself. It can fairly accurately represent biomes from desert to jungle and mountains to ocean. The land can be mined, moved, and used to build structures, forests, roads, farms, and so on. Players can access worlds hosted on public or private servers, or a server can be set up on a closed local network, for instance, for a school or classroom.

Minecraft is malleable, like clay, and many varied thematic servers exist, where player-managers have set up problems, obstacle courses, challenges, or just overarching world themes, for example, medieval or pirate worlds, Tolkein's middle earth, and even homage servers reenacting other video game titles such as Pokémon or FallOut. Minecraft is not just a children's game. College students and adults are deeply involved in building complex structures, including working computers. A quick search through YouTube will yield thousands of Minecraft tutorials, some of which have been created by eight year olds.

Minecraft is a fully built program, with a robust support community of teachers online, and a goodly number of useful add-ons that extend or vary playability. It first appeared in 2011, free to play, and became wildly popular. It is now owned by Microsoft. Early adopter educators created and continue to support a rich online space to share curricular ideas (including references to the current Common Core State Standards), raise instructional and technical problems, and share solutions (https://education.minecraft.net). Thus, Minecraft offers the attraction of a virtual world without being tied to typical video game tropes or limited by particular science concepts built into the activities. It is a blank page for the teacher and students to draw on together.

Making Games for Learning

Some have proposed that any use of games in school, short of having students build their own games, is 'instructionist' or didactic (Hayes & Games, 2008), based on the assumption that no construction is happening in games like Quest Atlantis or in adaptations of games like Warcraft. Early in this chapter, a tutorial algebra program appeared in two different deployments, one quite clearly instructionist and the other constructionist; same game but different experiences, based on how it was used in the classroom. Clearly, this is true of all materials and activities in classrooms. Any game can become a resource for learning depending upon what role it assumes in the classroom. So too, construction of material objects does not, in and of itself, guarantee learning. This caveat extends to the *do it yourself* (DIY)/ Makerspace movement (Halverson & Sheridan, 2014), which emphasizes the physical construction of shareable objects, and potentially creates an opening for social constructionism but does not guarantee it.

A step beyond Minecraft is the game development software program Gamestar Mechanic, aimed at the elementary and high school classroom. Programming a game from scratch requires some understanding of the development software first. And not surprisingly, game development programs appear in educational literature where the focus is predominantly on programming as part of new media literacies for students (Hayes & Games, 2008) or the value of computational thinking through activities such as game making (Repenning, Webb, & Ioannidou, 2010).

However, 'making' is actually a complex activity that begins with motive and design, and it is in unpacking the design piece that the value of making games shines through what is otherwise a largely computational experience. Because games are, essentially, workable testable models of some system of activity, they are potentially useful ways to model curricular knowledge that is likewise complex and systemic. Making models is definitely a way to demonstrate understanding of multivariate concepts in action, but when the designer's knowledge is still evolving, or in the zone described earlier in this chapter, making, testing, debugging, and remaking models are a great way to learn. Constructing a gameful model offloads some of the critical pedagogical practices of constructivism on the game-making software.

Gamestar Mechanic is a web-based platform for making and sharing 2D games. It supports fairly sophisticated game making without learning a programming language. It is intentionally designed for use with students in school, including lesson plan support for designs. The web hub (gamesta rmechanic.com/teachers) is a wealth of teaching resources and teacher forums.

Most available lessons pose challenging problems, but those problems are focused on strategic thinking, game features, and elements of design, for instance, the 'time travel through history' about mapping the historical era you are studying to the five elements of game design: rules, goals, mechanics, components, and space. It clearly depends on the teacher to make the game elements into curricular tools (e.g., for goals, what were the goals of westward explorers following the Louisiana Purchase).

Game making need not only be a digital experience. Board games and card games have enjoyed a reasonably successful and long-lived past in schooling. Both teachers and students know what they are, how they typically work, and what parts and pieces they include. Even young children can participate in the construction of a board game that can express their understanding of school concepts. Unfortunately, many tabletop games in school have taken the form of drill and practice on information, such as math facts or spelling drill.

Role-playing games are less widely known, and include 'live action' role-playing in which players dress up and act out narratives, digital role-playing in immerse games like the commercial ones mentioned previously, and tabletop games, the most famous of which is probably Dungeons and Dragons (D&D; dnd.wizards.com). In D&D, as it is widely known, players work as a team to move through a tabletop map of adventures, with guidance and interference from a player in the role of dungeon master. This player controls the narrative, creating problems and constraints for the other players to deal with as a team. D&D has existed for decades and is credited as the grandfather of multiplayer questing video games like WoW. The game's narrative structure and team play are what matters here, and they have actually been used successfully in college (Hergenrader, 2011) and high school English classes, following the initial reading of novels (Glazer, 2015, 2016).

The D&D game structure supports the construction of a story, a journey, and a grand quest. In addition, it identifies component roles that would be occupied by player classes such as a mage or a rogue. In Glazer's English classes, students developed character portrayals, maps, problems, and destinations for characters extending the plotline of *The Importance of Being Earnest*, *Beowulf*, and *Fahrenheit 451*. Just like students engaged in computer game creation, these role-playing students, working in teams, experienced planning, keeping and referring to discussion notes, designing, constructing scenery, maps and game pieces, rules for gameplay, dialogue for characters, quality testing, and debugging their assumptions and kinks in the gameplay. The critical element in all these activities was, of course, the teacher.

World Within a World

Games have a potentially powerful role in student learning in school by offering a world of experiences within a world of academia. However, that potential relies on the teacher to bring it to fruition. This chapter has examined the teacher's role in school gameplay from a social constructionist perspective that emphasizes these critical features: (1) linking school concepts with personal experience; (2) establishing collaborative problem-solving dialogue among peers and with the teacher; (3) locating the disciplinary ideas, language, and tools in challenging and applied contexts; (4) supporting mistakes and failures as sources of information for retrying; (5) helping students formalize personal experiences that illustrate or represent or link to academic concepts; and (6) seeing learning as dynamic and emergent through activities that are within reach but not doable solo (see Table 9.3).

Table 9.3 How virtual worlds support learners

Game features A game can...	*Learning* Students learn to...
Give academic form to student narrative experience	Acquire the language of the discipline
Give applied relevance to curricular concepts by locating them within a living world	Connect specific experiences with specific curricular content
Imbue tools with practical use and disciplinary meaning	Use material and conceptual tools associated with discipline/subject to get things done
Create participation structures for collaborative effort	Find assistance with challenging tasks from peers as well as teacher
Make failure and iteration an inevitable but not terminal experience in gameplay	Seek and use performance information to test and improve understanding
Require production of objects, tools, or actions that demonstrate knowledge	Construct objects, tools, or behaviors that are relevant to tasks/activities and that display current understanding

Conclusions

This chapter has suggested that virtual game worlds can support teachers attempting to realize a social constructivist approach to classroom pedagogy. Unfortunately, specifically, educational virtual worlds are few and far between. Some teachers have embraced the possibilities in commercial virtual worlds. Repurposing commercial virtual worlds is appealing, partly because of their quality and reliability. The most popular games tend to attract teacher collectives that construct and share ideas in online communities. But, not surprisingly, there are limits to the curricular coverage of teacher-made materials that have been shared. Furthermore, there are limits to what can reasonably be connected to school subject matter. Yes, players demonstrate strategic thinking, generate fan-fiction, research historical people, and calculate damage for different shot rotations, and these are wonderful things (Choontanom & Nardi, 2012; Gee 2007; Squire, 2005, 2011; Steinkuehler, 2007, 2008; Steinkuehler & Oh, 2012). They probably are not, however, sufficiently broad or differentiated targets to balance the effort required by a teacher to adopt and formalize them for the classroom. Game construction by and with students is another option with the advantage of leaving the subject matter up to the game creators, but requires deep subject matter knowledge on the teacher's part and a significant time commitment to in-class construction activities and discussion, though this becomes easier over time and with experience.

The value of virtual worlds in education—fully realized multiplayer spaces with backstory, quests, artifacts, and tools—is too great to abandon the concept. Indeed, the use of games in formal learning has expanded to higher education (Aguilar, Holman, & Fishman, 2015; Decker & Lawley, 2013; Sheldon, 2011) where it is appearing as a mechanism to restructure course activity and grant students informed agency. Funded research and development focused on gameplay, and specifically learning with games, will continue. However, in concert with research and development, work is needed in at least three areas.

First, educational virtual worlds, such as Quest Atlantis, need to be taken up and nurtured by commercial enterprises, without losing their explicit teacher support functions. Academic research and development efforts take seriously the preparation and support of implementing teachers. Often, this extra effort and expense is abandoned by commercial uptake of games developed in academia.

Second, professional development must help teachers realize the compatibility of social constructionist pedagogy and gameplay and game construction. The implementation of 'constructivism' is problematic for new and veteran teachers (Windschitl, 2002); therefore, it is imperative that professional development conveys the mutually mediating influence that pedagogy, curricular content, and gaming have on each other, and how to leverage that in the service of learning (Mishra & Koehler, 2007; Moe & Polin, 2016).

Finally, preservice programs for teaching should integrate gameplay, especially virtual world gameplay, into subject matter methods. Too often, topics arising out of technology are marginalized and sequestered in courses on 'technology'.

Virtual worlds as engaging, authentic, complex, and collaborative learning spaces for students and teachers are worth the investment. Research and development will continue to deepen our understanding of how virtual worlds 'teach' their players. New virtual worlds will appear in mainstream culture, potentially useful for education as well as entertainment. Regardless of the methods of delivery, the design of the game, or the structure or curricular contents in the social constructivist classroom, the teacher is the fulcrum for game use in schools.

References

Aguilar, S. J., Holman, C., & Fishman, B. J. (2015). Game-inspired design empirical evidence in support of gameful learning environments. *Games and Culture.* https://doi.org/10.1177/1555412015600305

Barab, S., Dodge, T., Tuzun, H., Job-Sluder, K., Jackson, C., Arici, A., et al. (2007). The Quest Atlantis Project: A socially-responsive play space for learning. In B. E. Shelton & D. Wiley (Eds.), *The educational design and use of simulation computer games* (pp. 159–186). Rotterdam, The Netherlands: Sense Publishers.

Barab, S., Thomas, M., Dodge, T., Carteaux, R., & Tuzun, H. (2005). Making learning fun: Quest Atlantis, a game without guns. *Educational Technology Research and Development, 53*(1), 86–107.

Baviskar, S. N., Hartle, R. T., & Whitney, T. (2009). Essential criteria to characterize constructivist teaching: Derived from a review of the literature and applied to five constructivist-teaching method articles. *International Journal of Science Education, 31*(4), 541–550.

Brown, J. S., Collins, A., & Duguid, P. (1989). Situated cognition and the culture of learning. *Educational Researcher, 18*(1), 32–42.

Carmichael, S. (2017). *A teacher's perspective on World of Warcraft in school.* Retrieved March 15, 2017, from https://www.classcraft.com/blog/features/teacher-world-of-warcraft/

Choontanom, T., & Nardi, B. (2012). Theorycrafting: The art and science of using numbers to interpret the world. In C. Steinkuehler & K. Squire (Eds.), *Games, learning, and society: Learning and meaning in the digital age* (pp. 185–210). London: Cambridge University Press.

Cole, M., & Engestrom, Y. (1993). A cultural-historical approach to distributed cognition. In G. Salomon (Ed.), *Distributed cognitions: Psychological and educational considerations* (pp. 1–46). London: Cambridge University Press.

De Vries, D. L., & Slavin, R. E. (1978). Teams-Games-Tournaments (TGT): Review of ten classroom experiments. *Journal of Research and Development in Education, 12*(1), 28–38.

Decker, A., & Lawley, E. L. (2013). Life's a game and the game of life: How making a game out of it can change student behavior. In *Proceeding of the 44th ACM technical symposium on computer science education* (pp. 233–238). New York: Association for Computing Machinery.

Dede, C., Clarke, J., Ketelhut, D. J., Nelson, B., & Bowman, C. (2005). *Students' motivation and learning of science in a multi-user virtual environment.* Paper presented at the annual meeting of the American Educational Research Association, Montréal, Quebec, Canada.

Gee, J. P. (2007). *Good video games + good learning: Collected essays on video games, learning, and literacy.* New York: Peter Lang Publisher.

Gee, J. P. (2008). Learning and games. In K. Salen (Ed.), *The ecology of games: Connecting youth, games, and learning.* Cambridge, MA: MIT Press.

Gillespie, L. (2009). *A new project – World of Warcraft in school.* Retrieved March 15, 2017, from http://edurealms.com/a-new-project-world-of-warcraft-in-school/

Glazer, K. (2015). *Imagining a constructionist game-based pedagogical model: Using tabletop role-playing game creation to enhance literature education in high school English classes* (Order No. 3731117). Available from Dissertations & Theses @ Pepperdine University – SCELC; ProQuest Dissertations & Theses Global. (1727755027). Retrieved at https://lib.pepperdine.edu/login?url=http://search.proquest.com.lib.pepperdine.edu/docview/1727755027?accountid=13159

Glazer, K. (2016). Beyond gameplay – Using role-playing game creation to teach Beowulf in a high school English class. In C. Williams (Ed.), *Teacher pioneers: Visions from the edge of the map.* Pittsburgh, PA: ETC Press.

González, N., Moll, L. C., & Amanti, C. (Eds.). (2005). *Funds of knowledge: Theorizing practices in households, communities, and classrooms.* Mahwah, NJ: Lawrence Erlbaum Associates.

Gresalfi, M., & Barab, S. (2011). Learning for a reason: Supporting forms of engagement by designing tasks and orchestrating environments. *Theory into Practice, 50*(4), 300–310.

Halverson, E. R., & Sheridan, K. (2014). The maker movement in education. *Harvard Educational Review, 84*(4), 495–504.

Hayes, B., & Games, I. (2008). Making computer games and design thinking: A review of current software and strategies. *Games and Culture, 3*(3–4), 309–332.

Hergenrader, T. (2011). Gaming, world building, and narrative: Using role-playing games to teach fiction writing. In *Proceedings of the 7th international conference on Games+ Learning+ Society Conference* (pp. 103–108). Pittsburg, PA: ETC Press.

Hutchins, E., & Klausen, T. (1996). Distributed cognition in an airline cockpit. In Y. Engeström & D. Middleton (Eds.), *Cognition and communication at work.* London: Cambridge University Press.

IGN. (2017). *Education-focused civilization game heading to schools in 2017.* Retrieved March 15, 2017, from http://www.ign.com/articles/2016/06/24/education-focused-civilization-game-heading-to-schools-in-2017

Kafai, Y. B. (2010). World of Whyville: An introduction to tween virtual life. *Games and Culture, 5*(1), 3–22.

Kafai, Y. B., Feldon, D., Fields, D., Giang, M., & Quintero, M. (2007). Life in the times of Whypox: A virtual epidemic as a community event. In *Communities and technologies 2007* (pp. 171–190). London: Springer.

Lave, J., & Wenger, E. (1991). *Situated learning: Legitimate peripheral participation.* New York: Cambridge University Press.

Long, Y., & Aleven, V. (2014). Gamification of joint student/system control over problem selection in a linear equation tutor. In S. Trausan-Matu, K. E. Boyer, M. Crosby, & K. Panourgia (Eds.), *Proceedings of the 12th international conference on Intelligent Tutoring Systems, ITS 2014* (pp. 378–387). New York: Springer.

Mehan, H. (1979). "What time is it, Denise?": Asking known information questions in classroom discourse. *Theory into Practice, 18*(4), 285–294.

Metcalf, S. J., Clarke, J., & Dede, C. (2009). *Virtual worlds for education: River City and EcoMUVE.* Paper presented at the MiT6 International Conference. Retrieved at http://citeseerx.ist.psu.edu/viewdoc/download?doi=10.1.1.504.7534&rep=rep1&type=pdf

Mishra, P., & Koehler, M. J. (2007). Technological pedagogical content knowledge (TPCK): Confronting the wicked problems of teaching with technology. *Technology and Teacher Education Annual, 18*(4), 2214.

Moe, R., & Polin, L. (2016). Locating TPACK in mediated practice. In K. Graziano & S. Bryans-Bongey (Eds.), *Online teaching in K-12: Models, methods, and best practices for teachers and administrators.* Medford, NJ: Information Today.

Repenning, A., Webb, D., & Ioannidou, A. (2010, March). Scalable game design and the development of a checklist for getting computational thinking into public schools. In *Proceedings of the 41st ACM technical symposium on computer science education* (pp. 265–269). New York: Association for Computing Machinery.

Resnick, L. (1991). Shared cognition: Thinking as social practice. In L. Resnick, J. Levine, & S. Teasley (Eds.), *Perspectives on socially shared cognition* (pp. 1–22). Washington, DC: American Psychological Association.

Richardson, V. (2003). Constructivist pedagogy. *Teachers College Record, 105*(9), 1623–1640.

Rogoff, B., Murtaugh, M., & de la Rocha, O. (1984). The dialectic of arithmetic in grocery shopping. In B. Rogoff & J. Lave (Eds.), *Everyday cognition: Its development in social context* (pp. 67–94). Boston: Harvard University Press.

Schwartz, K. (2013). World of Warcraft finds its way into class. *Mind/Shift KQED*. Retrieved March 15, 2017, from https://ww2.kqed.org/mindshift/2013/03/05/world-of-warcraft-finds-its-way-into-class/

Shaffer, D. W. (2006). Epistemic frames for epistemic games. *Computers & Education, 46*(3), 223–234.

Shaffer, D. W., & Resnick, M. (1999). "Thick" authenticity: New media and authentic learning. *Journal of Interactive Learning Research, 10*(2), 195.

Sheldon, L. (2011). *The multiplayer classroom: Designing coursework as a game*. Boston: Cengage Learning.

Solarz, I. (2014). A modern tool for a modern student. Video games in the exploration and learning of mathematics. *Didactics of Mathematics, 11*(15), 65–74.

Squire, K. (2005). Changing the game: What happens when video games enter the classroom. *Innovate: Journal of Online Education, 1*(6), 5. Retrieved at http://www.innovateonline.info/index.php?view=article&id=82

Squire, K. (2011). *Video games and learning: Teaching and participatory culture in the digital age*. New York: Teachers College Press.

Steinkuehler, C. A. (2007). Massively multiplayer online gaming as a constellation of literacy practices. *E-learning and Digital Media, 4*(3), 297–318.

Steinkuehler, C. A. (2008). Cognition and literacy in massively multiplayer online games. In J. Coiro, M. Knobel, C. Lankshear, & D. J. Leu (Eds.), *Handbook of research on new literacies* (pp. 611–634). New York: Routledge.

Steinkuehler, C. A., & Duncan, S. (2008). Scientific habits of mind in virtual worlds. *Journal of Science Education and Technology, 17*(6), 530–543.

Steinkuehler, C. A., & Oh, Y. (2012). Apprenticeship in massively multiplayer online games. In C. Steinkuehler & K. Squire (Eds.), *Games, learning, and society: Learning and meaning in the digital age* (pp. 154–184). London: Cambridge University Press.

Suchman, L., & Trigg, R. (1996). Artificial intelligence as craftwork. In S. Chaiklin & J. Lave (Eds.), *Understanding practice: Perspectives on activity and context* (pp. 144–178). New York: Cambridge University Press.

Vygotsky, L. S. (1978). *Mind in society: The development of higher psychological processes*. Cambridge, MA: Harvard University Press.

Windschitl, M. (2002). Framing constructivism in practice as the negotiation of dilemmas: An analysis of the conceptual, pedagogical, cultural, and political challenges facing teachers. *Review of Educational Research, 72*(2), 131–175.

CHAPTER 10

Social Studies, Common Core, and the Threat to Constructivist Education

Alan Singer, Eustace Thompson, and Catherine DiMartino

In an essay, "Public Goods, Private Goods: the American Struggle Over Educational Goals," published in the *American Educational Research Journal*, David Labaree (1997) argued that three conflicting goals were at the root of much of the educational debate in the United States. He identified the conflicting goals as democratic equality, social efficiency, and social mobility. According to Labaree, those who see the purpose of education as promoting democratic equality believe schools should focus on preparing citizens to function in democratic communities and a democratic society. Advocates of social efficiency tend to view education from the perspective of taxpayers and want schools to focus on preparing a skilled workforce. The social mobility, or what he calls a consumer perspective, emphasizes preparation of students to compete for higher status and higher earning positions in schools that mirror a hierarchical society that produces winners and losers (pp. 41–42).

A. Singer (✉) • E. Thompson
Department of Teaching, Learning and Technology, Hofstra University, Hempstead, NY, USA

C. DiMartino
Department of Administrative and Instructional Leadership, School of Education, St. John's University, Queens, NY, USA

D.W. Kritt (ed.), *Constructivist Education in an Age of Accountability*,
https://doi.org/10.1007/978-3-319-66050-9_10

What is interesting about the efficiency and mobility perspectives is that while they focus on individual student performance, advocates can claim to support social justice goals because they offer students from disadvantaged groups the opportunity to acquire marketplace skills and achieve economic advancement. In fact, this has been a major part of the push for Common Core Standards, high-stakes assessments aligned with the standards, the charter school movement, and calls for twenty-first-century college and career readiness. It has been a particularly potent argument for garnering support in poorer, minority communities for "educational reform" and has been used to dismiss opposition to testing and charter schools as protests led by teacher unions and privileged White families (Quinlan, 2016; Ravitch, 2010, 2014).

Both the efficiency and mobility perspectives lend themselves to what Paulo Friere (2000, 2004) calls the "banking method" where teachers, as Gramscian agents of corporate and state authority (Hoare & Smith, 1971), convey previously determined knowledge and workplace skills to willing, and unwilling, audiences. In addition, these hegemonic perspectives become excuses for social injustice deeply imbedded in a capitalist economy that has a strong history of racism. Students who fail to take advantage of supposed opportunities can be dismissed, and social policy can be absolved, because these students are judged as essentially having failed because of their own poor choices. What pretends to be a commitment to social justice is in effect a conservative justification for continuing social and educational inequality in American society. The extreme focus of the efficiency and mobility perspectives on skills acquisition tied to a high-stakes testing regime as manifested in the national Common Core Standards, and their appeal to minority parents who are gravely and legitimately concerned about the future of their children, makes these perspectives and Common Core serious threats to constructivist education and social studies as a vehicle for educating for active citizenship in a democratic society.

One reason Common Core is so connected to the "banking" or transmission model for education is its connection with entrepreneurs trying to profit by selling technology, computer software, online and print texts, and assessments aligned with their software and texts to larger integrated school markets. Joanne Weiss (2011), Chief of Staff to former US Secretary of Education Arne Duncan, who led the Obama administration's Race to the Top (RTTT) initiative, explained the advantages of Common Core for entrepreneurs in an online article published by the Harvard Business Review. According to Weiss (2011), "The development of common standards and shared assessments radically alters the market for innovation in curriculum development, professional development, and formative assessments. Previously, these markets operated on a state-by-state basis, and often on a district-by-district basis. But the adoption of common standards and shared assessments means that education entrepreneurs will enjoy national markets where the best products can be taken to scale" (n.p.).

The reason for the decontextualized skill focus of Common Core on reading, writing, and math is more closely related to the underlying political debate over education. When it comes to curriculum content, there is no general agreement in the United States over what should be taught, especially in social studies, but also in science where biology, geology (earth science), and physics challenge fundamentalist religious beliefs. Whatever claims are made by advocates of Common Core that the goal of American schools is to promote discovery and critical thinking, hallmarks of constructivism, they are actually deemed by many as too dangerous to be allowed into American schools because they encourage relativism (Jenkins, 2000) or as antithetical to a Christian perspective on education because they ignore biblical truths, which we suppose is another form of relativism (Rickert, 2009).

As social studies educators, we consider ourselves constructivists more as a matter of pragmatic practice than as advocates of an abstract educational principle. We reject relativism and identify with John Dewey's critique in *Experience and Education* (1938) of "dogmatic" constructivists and progressive educators who ignore the "meaning of subject-matter" and the importance of "organization within experience" and act as if teacher input into learning is an "invasion of individual freedom" (pp. 9 10).

For Dewey (1938/1954), and for us, educational principles become "concrete only in the consequences, which result from their application" (p. 20). We believe in structured classrooms and curriculum with structured student experiences to facilitate the learning of content and concepts and the mastery of academic skills. Along with Dewey (1916, 1938/1954), Greene (1993), and Freire (2000, 2004), we reject the banking approach to teaching and believe students make meaning from material as they grapple with organizing and understanding it, but also, along with Vygotsky (1934/1987), that teachers must develop and provide challenging material that extends student understanding to new levels. As classroom teachers, we continually engaged secondary school students in teacher-directed but project-based exploratory learning where they construct meaning as they test out ideas.

We view teachers as curriculum creators and classroom decision makers who continually play an active role in promoting student learning. As pragmatic social studies constructivists, one of our problems with Common Core is its rejection of contextual knowledge and insistence that students can make meaning of complex texts without prior understanding or experience, its preference for pre-packaged scripted lessons that remove teachers from the construction of meaningful curriculum, its regimentation of the classroom environment and focus on testing that takes away from the teacher's role as decision maker, its pretense of involving students in discovery and higher order thinking while narrowly channeling them down to only one available or acceptable path way, its focus on decontextualized skill acquisition that undermines both conceptual understanding and skill acquisition, and its reliance on published material aligned with high-stakes tests that turn classrooms into test prep academies. As opposed to a constructivist approach to social studies classroom practice, Common Core-aligned instruction at its best offers only a pretense of student involvement in knowledge construction.

Historical Background for Common Core

On January 8, 2002, President George W. Bush signed the No Child Left Behind (NCLB) Act at Hamilton High School in Ohio. In a speech at the signing ceremony, Bush laid out the basis for what would become the Common Core State Standards Initiative. He also made clear the connection between his goals for education in the United States and the continual assessment of students. According to Bush (2004), the "first principle" of NCLB was "accountability," and he defined accountability as testing. "In return for federal dollars," NCLB required states "design accountability systems to show parents and teachers whether or not children can read and write and add and subtract in grades three through eight" (p. 25). Bush explained to students in the audience that this meant testing. "The first way to solve a problem is to diagnose it. And so, what this bill says, it says every child can learn. And we want to know early, before it's too late, whether or not a child has a problem in learning. I understand taking tests aren't fun. Too bad. We need to know in America. We need to know whether or not children have got the basic education" (p. 25).

Seven years later, as he was preparing to leave office, Bush (2009) restated this same position on education, NCLB, and high-stakes testing in remarks delivered at the General Philip Kearny School in Philadelphia,

Pennsylvania. For Bush, the key to higher expectations remained increased testing. "How can you possibly determine whether a child can read at grade level if you don't test? And for those who claim we're teaching the test, uh-uh. We're teaching a child to read so he or she can pass the test ... Measurement is essential to success ... Measurement is the gateway to true reform, and measurement is the best way to ensure parental involvement."

Part of the problem with NCLB is that it was an ill-considered law. Passed in 2002, NCLB mandates were not scheduled to go into full effect until 2014, which meant politicians could take credit for championing educational reform, but there was plenty of time for the public to forget about who was responsible for the mandates or for a new administration and Congress to modify it when it became necessary (Spring, 2008).

NCLB requires the impossible that every child reach proficiency level by the 2013–2014 school year, or else states, districts, and schools would be in violation of the law. The federal government directed States to design the measurement tools that would show they were achieving measurable objectives. Penalties were set for states that did not comply. However, because of conservative opposition to federal intervention in state authority, the law permitted state education departments to set their standards very low and to make tests very easy.

In a very powerful opinion essay in the *New York Times*, Diane Ravitch (2016, SR 8), former Under Secretary of Education in the 1989–1993 Bush administration, at one time a member of a number of conservative think tanks, and once a major proponent of national education standards, explained why she reversed her position on Common Core and high-stakes standardized assessments. According to Ravitch, instead of supporting schools where teachers had the "autonomy to tailor instruction to meet the needs of the children sitting in front of them," the federal Department of Education mandated a standardized testing regime where the "tests became the be-all and end-all of education, and states spent billions on them. Social scientists have long known that the best predictor of test scores is family income. Yet policy makers encouraged the firing of thousands of teachers and the closing of thousands of low-scoring public schools, mostly in poor black and Hispanic neighborhoods." Curriculum is altered to boost test scores and in addition students spend hours taking the tests and weeks in intensive test preparation. Ravitch concluded that there is nothing to show for the billions of dollars spent to design and implement a fundamentally flawed approach to teaching and learning.

Education Without Content

As states lowered their individual standards to avoid the implications of NCLB, Common Core was born. Its proponents argued that if tests were going to have meaning, they would have to be based on a universal national standard. A major problem, however, was sharp disagreement over what is important to know and why. In 1995, when US and world history content standards were released by the National Center for History in Schools, they were widely denounced in the popular media and overwhelmingly rejected by the US Senate (Singer, 2015). In 2013, state legislators in five states—Missouri, Montana, Colorado, Oklahoma, and Indiana—considered bills to require the teaching of the biblical explanation of the origin of the universe as science (Brown, 2013). In Georgia, the superintendent of schools demanded that the word "evolution" be removed from the science curriculum to avoid offending religious and conservative parents (Daily Mail, n.d.; Singer, 2014a, 2014b).

Instead of openly airing debates over what is important to know and why, Common Core State Standards avoided the problem of conflicting curricular requirements in "red states" such as Texas and Alabama and "blue states" like New York and California by simply ignoring content and focusing on English-Language Arts and math skills and obscure measurements such as text complexity.

Private Funding Influences Government Policy

In an excellent article on *Huffington Post*, Joy Resmovits (2014) dissected the origins of Common Core. In 2006, a new bi-partisan group set out to create Common Core. It was funded by the Bill and Melinda Gates Foundation and supported by textbook publishers and test developers.

Because it was developed through the National Governors Association and the Council of Chief State School Officers, Common Core supporters thought they could claim it was a state-led initiative, not the work of the federal government or the publishing industry. The advisory board included representatives from the College Board testing company and a group called ACT, which is also involved in creating and marketing high-stakes assessments (Toch & Tyre, 2010). Mercedes Schneider (2013), who carefully tracked the development of Common Core on her EduBlog, deutsch29, showed how Gates' money was then spread around widely to influence universities, foundations, and state education departments to sign up in support of the initiative. Gates Foundation CEO Sue Desmond-Hellman later admitted that the foundation shared responsibility for poorly implementing the Common Core Standards and systematic change in public education (Desmond-Hellmann, 2016).

In 2009, the Obama administration joined the effort to impose Common Core Standards and tests with its RTTT initiative (Obama, 2010). The view of education promoted in Common Core was endorsed by President Barack Obama at a meeting with US governors in 2010 and is at the heart of the federal RTTT program. Originally, RTTT consisted of a voluntary competition by states for billions of dollars in federal Department of Education grants, but it evolved into a stick federal authorities could use to force states to accept Common Core and Common Core-aligned, high-stakes tests, teacher assessment based on student test scores, as well as charter schools in order to receive waivers from the impossible to achieve Bush era NCLB mandates.

Common Core Versus Constructivist Teaching

At their best, the Common Core Standards draw the attention of teachers to the need for conscious decision making, systematic planning, and coordinated instruction as they work to develop student academic skills, but this is basically teacher-centered instruction using commercial pre-packaged published or online material designed to boost test scores. However, as Carol Burris, a retired high school principal and a leading critic of Common Core, argues, the fundamental problem with Common Core is that it is conceptually backward (Strauss, 2014). Instead of motivating students to learn by presenting them with challenging questions and interesting content rooted in their interests and experiences, it removes substance from learning. According to engageNY, a website that encourages New York State teachers and schools to incorporate Common Core in their curricula, content-area teachers outside of English-Language Arts (ELA) are supposed to emphasize literacy experiences instead of the subjects they are supposed to be teaching. Skill acquisition is at the forefront of instruction and assessment. As a result, the tendency is for skills to be decontextualized, which means they are taught and practiced, divorced from meaning. When this happens, Common Core offers students no reason to learn (Singer, 2013).

In a constructivist classroom, literacy is not simply a technical skill. According to Freire, critical literacy requires reading and understanding both the world and the word so that people have the ability to use words to change the world. In this view, literacy is a necessary action for individual and societal freedom. Freire argues, and we agree, that interest in and the ability to "read the world" naturally precedes the ability to "read the word" (Freire & Macedo, 1987). When students are motivated to learn and want to discover new things about the world around them, skill acquisition comes easily. Children learn to read the same way they learn to walk and talk. But when students are turned off by learning and boring classroom practices, they will never acquire more than rudimentary skills. Just think how many young people practice musical scales on the piano before developing any enjoyment of performing and how this approach to learning completely turned them off to music.

Missing: Social Studies Content

The most common activity in a secondary school social studies classroom should be document analysis, document defined broadly to include edited and unedited primary sources, written statements, transcribed speeches, photographs, pictures, charts, graphs, cartoons, and even material objects. To promote student literacy, a well-organized curriculum should have students read and write about primary source documents in their ELA classes while they are analyzing them and discussing their historical context in social studies. In other words, Common Core can only make a significant difference in student performance when it recognizes the importance of motivating students to learn by engaging them in solving real problems where they can see the relationship to their lives. If it just pushes skills, it will not work.

An example of the content/skills misalignment is the way the New York State ELA and social studies curriculum address the European Holocaust. The reading list for the New York State Common Core English-Language Arts curriculum assigns books to grades based on text complexity, which is defined on the Common Core website as a combination of "levels of meaning, structure, language conventionality and clarity, and knowledge demands"; "readability measures and other scores of text complexity"; and "reader variables (such as motivation, knowledge, and experiences) and task variables (such as purpose and the complexity generated by the task assigned and the questions posed)" (engageNY, n.d.). However, assigning students books and articles to read based on text complexity makes for really bad content choices. Because the focus in English-Language Arts classrooms is on plot, character, theme, and vocabulary rather than history, and because the books are selected based on text complexity, students are introduced to the European Holocaust without historical background, often by teachers who never studied about the Holocaust themselves.

In New York State, for example, students first learn about the history of the European Holocaust and the systematic extermination of European Jews by Nazi Germany in the second semester of 10th grade. However, before that they are briefly introduced to the Holocaust through literature, but not as history. *The Diary of Anne Frank: A Play* by Frances Goodrich and Albert Hackett is recommended for 6–8th grade; *The Book Thief* by Markus Zusak and the speech, "Hope, Despair and Memory," by Elie Wiesel are recommended for study in the 9th and 10th grades. *The Book Thief* is assigned as reading before students have learned about the European Holocaust. Janet Maslin (2006), in a *New York Times* book review, described it as "Harry Potter and the Holocaust." The book is narrated by "Death" who apparently is unhappy with what he is assigned to do and confides to readers "To me, war is like the new boss who expects the impossible." Death, the narrator, claims "that I picked up each soul that day as if they were newly born. I even kissed a few weary, poisoned cheeks. I listened to their last, gasping cries. Their vanishing words. I watched their love and freed them from their fear." But the reality is that death did not cradle their souls, kiss their checks, or calm their fears. At another point, Death tells readers "Even death has a heart." But Death does not have a heart, there is no way to make the European Holocaust less horrible, and genocide, which continues into the twenty-first century, should not be made less horrible (Singer, 2014a, 2014b). Decontextualizing readers not only confuses students but also does not allow them to connect their education to current events.

The Core of Common Core

Another serious flaw in the national Common Core English-Language Arts reading standards is the result of the ideological point of view about literacy and learning of those who developed it. We are not sure if it was done intentionally or if they are actually unaware of it. The flaw is uncertainty about how we know what a document really means. Proponents of the national Common Core Standards claim deep meaning is inherent in a text. For constructivists, meaning is created through the interaction of the reader with the text because we can never really know exactly what an author from a different time period or who lived under different circumstances intended (Rosenblatt, 1969). This debate goes back at least as far as Socrates and Plato in the ancient Greek world and is a major point of contention when the US Supreme Court tries to interpret the Constitution. Yet the authors of the Common Core Standards seemed to have missed it.

At the core of Common Core is the idea that students must be engaged in close reading of texts (Common Core, n.d. a). According to the Common Core State Standards for English-Language Arts Reading standard number 1, students should "Read closely to determine what the text says explicitly and to make logical inferences from it; cite specific textual evidence when writing or speaking to support conclusions drawn from the text." Reading standard number 2 calls on students to "Determine central ideas or themes of a text and analyze their development; summarize the key supporting details and ideas." Reading standard number 3 calls on students to "Analyze how and why individuals, events, or ideas develop and interact over the course of a text." In each case, meaning is exclusively embedded in the text, reading passage, or primary source document.

The claim is that "close reading," which "stresses engaging with a text of sufficient complexity directly and examining meaning thoroughly and methodically" is the key to "college and career readiness" (Boyles, 2012/2013). That is because "Directing student attention on the text itself empowers students to understand the central ideas and key supporting details." In addition, it supposedly "enables students to reflect on the meanings of individual words and sentences" and "the development of ideas over the course of the text, which ultimately leads students to arrive at an understanding of the text as a whole."

David Coleman (2012), one of the lead authors and promoters of the national Common Core Standards, illustrated the "close reading of text" approach to reading and understanding in a 15-minute video in which he modeled a middle school lesson based on a close reading of Martin Luther King's "Letter from Birmingham Jail." At the start, Coleman systematically rejected teachers providing students with background information either orally or through a secondary source pre-reading assignment or providing guidance through questions. Coleman argued that through a cold reading of the text without instruction that scaffolded on previous knowledge, individual students would be able to figure out what is important to know by themselves about King and Birmingham. He recommended spending six to eight days close reading just this one text, which would be exceedingly difficult in the social studies curriculum but might be possible in an English class.

The Ideology of "Textualism"

This idea of a cold close reading of the text corresponds with the rationale for very conservative and restrictive Supreme Court decisions championed by Associate Justice Anton Scalia. In 1996, Scalia argued: "I am first of all a textualist ... If you are a textualist, you don't care about the intent, and I don't care if the framers of the Constitution had some secret meaning in mind when they adopted its words. I take the words as they were promulgated to the people of the United States, and what is the fairly understood meaning of those words" (Bissette & Pitney, 2014, p. 460).

While Scalia claimed to apply no context, just an unbiased view of the text, his record tells a very different story and challenges the idea that we can interpret text divorced from context. Somehow, Scalia consistently read the text to support the most reactionary interpretations of the US Constitution. In his time on the Supreme Court, its leading textualist argued for restrictions on abortion rights, removing voting protections, against federal health-care initiatives, in opposition to gun control, and that wealthy corporations are really "people" and are entitled to spend unlimited sums of money to influence elections because they have "freedom of speech" (Singer, 2006).

But there are other ways to read the Constitution and other texts. In 1985, Associate Justice William Brennan argued for the importance of understanding historical context. Brennan wrote:

> We current Justices read the Constitution in the only way that we can: as Twentieth Century Americans. We look to the history of the time of framing and to the intervening history of interpretation. But the ultimate question must be, what do the words of the text mean in our time. For the genius of the Constitution rests not in any static meaning it might have had in a world that is dead and gone, but in the adaptability of its great principles to cope with current problems and current needs. What the constitutional fundamentals meant to the wisdom of other times cannot be their measure to the vision of our time. Similarly, what those fundamentals mean for us, our descendants will learn, cannot be the measure to the vision of their time. (Bissette & Pitney, 2014, pp. 460–461)

We agree with Brennan, "the genius of the Constitution rests not in any static meaning it might have had in a world that is dead and gone, but in the adaptability of its great principles to cope with current problems and current needs" (Singh, 2002, p. 38). A cold close reading of text is never sufficient to discover meaning unless we also take into account the "context" or history of the document, and its implications for the present and future. This is a major reason that Common Core is seriously flawed and counter to constructivist best practice.

Misinterpreting the "Gettysburg Address"

Valerie Strauss (2013), an education reporter for *The Washington Post*, posted an excellent and very critical blog on the inadequacies of the Common Core's decontextualized approach to teaching primary source documents. She focused on a sample of a high school social studies and English unit called "A Close Reading of Lincoln's Gettysburg Address." Strauss was outraged, calling on her readers to "Imagine learning about the Gettysburg Address without a mention of the Civil War, the Battle of Gettysburg, or why President Abraham Lincoln had traveled to Pennsylvania to make the speech. That's the way a Common Core State Standards 'exemplar for instruction'—from a company founded by three main Core authors—says it should be taught to ninth and 10th graders."

Common Core's treatment of the Gettysburg Address highlights both some strengths and major weaknesses in its approach to teaching and learning. As reported by Strauss, key questions all focus on the writing process and vocabulary acquisition. Teachers are instructed not to ask "erroneous guiding questions" that require knowledge of historical context and research that takes students beyond the words in the text and gives actual meaning to the words. Specifically, teachers are told not to say, "Lincoln says that the nation is dedicated to the proposition that 'all men are created equal.' Why is equality an important value to promote?" They also must not ask students to draw inferences from the text through questions such as "Why did the North fight the Civil War?" or "Did Lincoln think that the North was going to 'pass the test' that the Civil War posed?" These are precisely the questions that interest students in the meaning of the document and its historical significance.

A close reading of text without historical context promotes reading without understanding. Students read the Gettysburg Address, recite the address, and rewrite the address, but learn nothing about what it meant for the formerly enslaved freedmen and the ongoing debate over racial equality in the United States that has been continuing the past 150 years.

This decontextualized Common Core approach to instruction is not just limited to this lesson on the Gettysburg Address; it is the core of Common Core. In the introduction to the "Revised Publishers' Criteria for the Common Core State Standards in English-Language Arts and Literacy, Grades 3–12," Coleman and co-author Susan Pimental (2012) make it clear that "The standards focus on students reading closely to draw evidence and knowledge from the text" and "developing students' prowess at drawing knowledge from the text itself is the point of reading" (p. 1). The "key criteria," really the only criteria in this document for text selection is "text complexity" because the purpose of the Common Core State Standards is solely to "require students to read increasingly complex texts with growing independence as they progress toward career and college readiness" (p. 3). Publishers are informed "The standards strongly focus on students gathering evidence, knowledge, and insight from what they read and therefore require that a majority of the questions and tasks that students ask and respond to be based on the text under consideration ... Text-dependent questions do not require information or evidence from outside the text or texts; they establish what follows and what does not follow from the text itself. Eighty to ninety percent of the Reading Standards in each grade require text-dependent analysis; accordingly, aligned curriculum materials should have a similar percentage of text-dependent questions. When examining a complex text in depth, tasks should require careful scrutiny of the text and specific references to evidence from the text itself to support responses" (p. 6).

Pragmatic Constructivist Response

As pragmatic constructivists, we argue the Common Core-teaching approach actually undermines student learning. Children learn to read the way they learn to talk. Reading, like speaking, is a social activity best taught by communities and through relationships. Children learn by watching older people, especially older children, read. They learn to read by discovering that important things they want to know are in the symbols. They learn to read because of the pleasure of discovery and praise from parents, teachers, siblings, and friends for their achievements. They learn to read both because it makes them part of a broader community and because they become independent of others, more grown up. Children learn to read because it gives them a private place to visit and, in the end, they learn to love to read because it opens their imaginations to unseen worlds.

But in Common Core-based instruction, reading is a mechanical activity that ignores student interest and the primary motivation to learn is your test score. To raise student scores, Common Core breaks reading down into a plethora of component skill parts (Common Core, n.d. b). In the 4th grade, Common Core has nine reading literature standards, ten reading informational text standards, two foundational reading skills standards, six language acquisition standards, six speaking and listening standards, as well as "Range, Quality, and Complexity" standards. Lost, if not missing, in the barrage of standards are qualities like imagination, sharing, creating, thinking, or more importantly, enjoying. Asking questions and having conversations are listed in the Common Core Standards as activities, but they are not emphasized as the core of understanding.

The Common Core approach to reading is like breaking a molecule down into individual elements. But as any science teacher can explain, once you break the molecular bonds that tie the atoms together, you lose all the properties of the original chemical. You now have hydrogen and oxygen, but you no longer have water. In Common Core, students may learn skills, but they do not learn to love reading or to really understand sophisticated written material.

Missing in Common Core's single-minded focus on skill acquisition is education for citizenship in a democratic society, a key goal of education identified by Labaree (1997) and a fundamental tenet of constructivism. According to its mission statement, "The Common Core State Standards provide a consistent, clear understanding of what students are expected to learn, so teachers and parents know what they need to do to help them. The standards are designed to be robust and relevant to the real world, reflecting the knowledge and skills that our young people need for success in college and careers. With American students fully prepared for the future, our communities will be best positioned to compete successfully in the global economy" (Common Core, n.d. c).

According to its mission statement, Common Core Standards are supposed to "provide a consistent, clear understanding of what students are expected to learn" and be "relevant to the real world." But "real world" expectations are defined as preparing students for "success in college and careers" and "to compete successfully in the global economy," not as participation in a democratic community. As best as we can ascertain, in the entire document, there is no real discussion of life in a democratic society and the role of education in promoting democratic processes and democratic values.

In our pedagogy, social action projects are a major part of constructive social studies education. We provide three projects—one in elementary school, another in middle school, and a third in high school—that illustrate pragmatic constructivism and how it can be used to engage student understanding of democratic citizenship. Each of these social action projects responded to student questions, required teacher guidance, and involved students in learning-by-doing. They also included an important literacy component.

Trick-or-Treat for UNICEF

The Morris L. Eisenstein (MLE) Learning Center in Brooklyn, New York, annually involves pre-school and elementary school-aged children in Trick-or-Treat for UNICEF to promote a love for reading and books as well as develop feelings of empathy for a diversity of others and a commitment to fairness. As part of the project, children learn about the importance of speaking out for others and themselves when they see or experience unfairness (Singer, 2011, p. 9).

UNICEF allows children to choose activities and locales they want to assist which helps families in this largely immigrant community respond to natural disasters such as the earthquake that devastated Haiti in 2010 and deadly floods in Guatemala in 2015. This creates an opportunity to involve the children along with parents and teachers to learn about different areas of the world and decide where they want to contribute. Trick-or-Treat for UNICEF at the MLE Learning Center allowed classes to redefine a holiday associated with individual greed into an opportunity for children to consider the question, "What is our responsibility to other people?"

The story of "Goldilocks and the Three Bears" helps the youngest children connect to the idea that children feel bad when they are hungry. Feeling sad about Little Bear helps them identify with other children whom they will never meet. They imagine how they would feel if their bowls were empty when it is time for lunch, "just like Little Bear."

To dramatize the problems of hunger and scarcity in other parts of the world, older children read and discuss stories about hunger or food shortages including *Bringing the Rain to Kapiti Plain* (Aardema, 1981) and *Legend of the Bluebonnet* (De Paolo, 1973).

In an age when many children are often victimized by war, Trick-or-Treat for UNICEF is a way to provide support for refugee populations. Sometimes, children at the MLE Learning Center read and discuss picture books about the nuclear bombing of Hiroshima as part of their decision-making process. Three excellent books are *Hiroshima no pika* (Maruki, 1980), *Sadako* (Coerr, 1997), and *Peace crane* (Hamanaka, 1995). Some years the children make chains of origami paper peace cranes to send to the Hiroshima peace memorial (Singer, 2011, p. 16).

Middle School Freedom Walkers

Nassau County, in the New York metropolitan area, is one of the most racially and ethnically segregated areas in the United States, which was puzzling to students at Alberta B. Grey Schultz Middle School (Resnick & Stamm, 2015) when they were learning about the Brown v. Topeka, Kanas school desegregation case. Their community, Hempstead, is 92% Black and Latino, and every student who attends their school is a member of a minority group. Yet neighboring Garden City is 88% Whites and its schools are 93% White. In 2011, students in Ms. LaMothe and Ms. Sumner's 8th grade classes asked if anything could be done about this. When they read about sit-ins and freedom marchers during the African American Civil Rights Movement, they knew what they wanted to do—have a freedom walk to Garden City and picnic in a park set aside for Garden City residents only (Singer, 2014a, 2014b, pp. 18–20). To organize their freedom walk, students learned about civil disobedience and designed and made their own t-shirts and posters. They also discussed the importance of organizational discipline so they could better present their demand for desegregating Long Island communities and schools.

Forty strong, the 8th graders marched out of the middle school cafeteria singing, "Ain't gonna let nobody turn me around, turn me around, turn me around, turn me around, ain't gonna let nobody turn me around, turn me around, turn me around, turn me around, gonna keep on walking, keep on talking, marching to the freedom land." The temperature on June 9, 2011, was in the mid-90s, but it did not weaken their spirits.

It was a one-mile walk from their school to the Hempstead-Garden City border and another mile to Grove Street Park. Each time they came to a "Stop" sign they chanted: "The sign says stop but we're not stopping." They gathered at a sign demarking the border between Hempstead and Garden City and sang "Ain't gonna let nobody turn me around" again.

The sign at the entrance to Grove Street Park says: "town residents and guests only." However, the Garden City Recreation Department graciously gave the students permission to enter the park and have a picnic. When the Freedom Walkers gathered at the entrance to the park, they discussed, "Why can't all the people of Long Island share their parks? If people can play in parks together, maybe we can go to school together. If we can go to school together, maybe we can live together. If we can live together, maybe the world will change."

High School Students Challenge the School-to-Prison Pipeline

Alfred E. Smith High School is a vocational school located in the South Bronx, part of the poorest Congressional District in the United States. Its student population is 98% Black and Latino, 88% of the students are eligible for free lunch, and almost one-third receive special support for learning disabilities. Teacher Pablo Muriel constantly seeks ways to engage his students, who enrolled in Smith for vocational training, and in academic subjects. Muriel, a conscious Deweyan and Freirian, uses social action to promote literacy. He recognizes that to truly engage students, action must flow from their concerns about themselves and their world. The purpose of education, according to both Dewey and Muriel, "is not mere preparation for later life," but the "full meaning of life" itself (Dewey, 1893, p. 660), and its role in the development of "self" is a process of "continuous formation" shaped through "choice of action" (Dewey, 1916, p. 408).

A major issue for Smith students is the way their school and community are perceived by the rest of the city, especially police who they feel target them. What constantly grates on them are the metal detectors at the entrance to the building that they pass through every day to enter. They studied about the school-to-prison pipeline (Alexander, 2010) and believe the metal detectors are part of the criminalization of Black and Latino youth in the United States. Students wanted to get the city to remove the metal detectors, so Muriel worked with them in their Participation in Government class to organize a citywide campaign to demand that the Mayor and the Education Department establish criteria for placing metal detectors in and removing them from public schools (Singer, 2015). Their campaign included research, blogging, petitioning, meeting with students in other schools, meeting with local public officials and school administrators, and a protest where all students lined up to enter the school passing through the metal detectors just at the start of the school day.

Conclusion

David Labaree (1997), in "Public Goods, Private Goods: the American Struggle Over Educational Goals," concluded that the "central problems with American education are not pedagogical or organizational or social or cultural in nature but are fundamentally political. That is, the problem is not that we do not know how to make schools better but that we are fighting among ourselves about what goals schools should pursue." While, as social studies educators and pragmatic constructivists, we basically agree with Labaree, we would modify this statement. The pedagogical, organizational, social, and cultural disagreements about education in the United States are fundamentally political. We do not know how to make schools better because we do not agree about what goals schools should pursue and what type of society schools should prepare young people to create.

We believe a pragmatic constructive approach to social studies education, infused with social action as preparation for life in a democratic society, would be an important step. With Dewey, we know the importance of giving students "something to do, not something to learn; and the doing is of such a nature as to demand thinking, or the intentional noting of connections; learning naturally results" (Dewey, 1916, p. 181).

Postscript: The Trump/DeVos Education Agenda

At the time of writing this chapter, President Donald Trump and Educational Secretary Betsy DeVos have primarily concentrated on promoting the privatization of education in the United States, with little attention to what or how things are taught. Trump has always sent his own children to elite, expensive private schools. DeVos is a major proponent of Christian education that uses the banking method to indoctrinate religious dogma (Rizga, 2017). Their agenda includes increasing the number of charter schools, both those operated by non-profit networks and schools owned or administered by for-profit corporations; expanding homeschooling; voucher programs that make it possible for more students to attend private and religious schools, and tax breaks to encourage "donations" to non-public schools. Each part of the program would have the effect of draining resources and political support from public education, and would probably draw off higher performing students and students from better structured families. Overall, their program will most likely increase racial, ethnic, religious, and class segregation in both schools and society. Arizona, which quickly endorsed the Trump/DeVos agenda, is a prime example of all of these problems (Goldstein, 2017).

Major charter networks and companies, religious schools, and online homeschool curriculum providers seem to universally offer teacher- or computer-directed content and skill instruction with little room for student initiative or teacher creativity, which will directly, and negatively, impact on possibilities for advancing constructivist pedagogy.

Trump and DeVos have both pledged to eliminate national Common Core Standards to supposedly re-empower states, localities, and parents (Ujifusa, 2017). Unfortunately, the states most likely to eliminate Common Core requirements and Common Core-aligned testing are also states in the South and Southwest with the worst records for public school funding, educating minority children, or promoting progressive curriculum and pedagogy.

References

Aardema, V. (1981). *Bringing the rain to Kapiti Plain*. New York: Dial Books.

Alexander, M. (2010). *The new Jim Crow: Mass incarceration in the age of colorblindness*. New York: New Press.

Bissette, J., & Pitney, J. (2014). *American government and politics: Deliberation, democracy and citizenship*. Boston: Wadsworth Cengage.

Boyles, N. (2012/2013). Closing in on close reading. *Educational Leadership, 70* (4), 36–41.

Brown, S. (2013). Creationism commotion: Five states have anti-evolution bills in play. *Americans United for Separation of Church and State*. Retrieved November 21, 2015, from https://www.au.org/blogs/wall-of-separation/creationism-commotion-five-states-have-anti-evolution-bills-in-play

Bush, G. W. (2004). Remarks on signing the No Child Left Behind Act of 2001 in Hamilton, Ohio, January 8, 2002. *Public papers of the Presidents of the United States George W. Bush 2002 Book 1* (pp. 23–26). Washington, DC: United States Government Printing Office.

Bush, G. W. (2009). President Bush discusses No Child Left Behind. *The White House*. Retrieved November 20, 2015, from http://georgewbush-whitehouse.archives.gov/news/releases/2009/01/20090108-2.html

Coerr, E. (1997). *Sadako*. New York: Puffin.

Coleman, D. (2012). Middle school ELA curriculum video: Close reading of a text: MLK "Letter from Birmingham jail". *engageNY*. Retrieved November 21, 2015, from http://www.engageny.org/resource/middle-school-ela-curriculum-video-close-reading-of-a-text-mlk-letter-from-birmingham-jail

Coleman, D., & Pimental, S. (2012). Revised publishers' criteria for the Common Core State Standards in English Language Arts and Literacy, Grades 3 – 12. *National Governors Association*. Retrieved November 21, 2015, from http://www.corestandards.org/assets/Publishers_Criteria_for_3-12.pdf

Common Core. (n.d.-a). *English Language Arts Standards – Anchor Standards – College and career readiness anchor standards for reading*. Common Core State Standards Initiative. Retrieved November 21, 2015, from http://www.corestandards.org/ELA-Literacy/CCRA/R/

Common Core. (n.d.-b). *English Language Arts – Reading Literature – Grade 4*. Common Core State Standards Initiative. Retrieved November 21, 2015, from http://www.corestandards.org/ELA-Literacy/RL/4/

Common Core. (n.d.-c). *Common Core Standards mission statement*. Retrieved November 21, 2015, from http://www.uwosh.edu/coehs/cmagproject/common_core/documents/CC_Standards_Myths.pdf

Daily Mail. (n.d.). Evolution may be banned in US schools. *Daily Mail.com*. Retrieved November 20, 2015, from http://www.dailymail.co.uk/news/article-207079/Evolution-banned-US-schools.html

De Paolo, T. (1973). *Legend of the bluebonnet*. New York: Putnam.

Desmond-Hellmann, S. (2016, May). *What if… A letter from the CEO of the Bill & Melinda Gates Foundation*. Retrieved July 24, 2016, from http://www.gatesfoundation.org/2016/ceo-letter

Dewey, J. (1893, November). Self-realization as the moral ideal. *The Philosophical Review, 2*(6), 652–664.

Dewey, J. (1916). *Democracy and education*. New York: Macmillan.

Dewey, J. (1938/1954). *Experience and education*. New York: Collier/Macmillan.

engageNY. (n.d.). Text list for P-12 ELA. *engageNY*. Retrieved November 21, 2015, from http://www.engageny.org/resource/text-list-for-p-12-ela

Freire, P. (2000). *Pedagogy of the oppressed*. New York: Continuum.

Freire, P. (2004). *Pedagogy of hope*. New York: Continuum.

Freire, P., & Macedo, D. (1987). *Literacy, reading the word and world*. South Hadley, MA: Bergin & Garvey.

Goldstein, D. (2017, April 7). Arizona frees money for private schools, buoyed by Trump's voucher push. *New York Times*. Retrieved April 14, 2017, from https://www.nytimes.com/2017/04/07/us/school-vouchers-arizona.html?_r=0

Greene, M. (1993). Diversity and inclusion: Towards a curriculum for human beings. *Teachers College Record, 95*(2), 211–221.

Hamanaka, S. (1995). *Peace crane*. New York: Morrow Junior Books.

Hoare, Q., & Smith, G. (Eds.). (1971). *Selections from the prison notebooks of Antonio Gramsci*. New York: International.

Jenkins, E. W. (2000). Constructivism in school science education: Powerful model or the most dangerous intellectual tendency? *Science & Education, 9*, 599–610.

Labaree, D. (1997). Public goods, private goods: The American struggle over educational goals. *American Educational Research Journal, 34*(1), 39–81.

Maruki, T. (1980). *Hiroshima no pika*. New York: Lothrop, Lee & Shepard.

Maslin, J. (2006, March 27). Stealing to settle a score with life. *The New York Times*. Retrieved November 21, 2015, from http://www.nytimes.com/2006/03/27/books/27masl.html

Obama, B. (2010, February 2). President Obama calls for new steps to prepare America's children for success in college and careers. *The White House*. Retrieved November 21, 2015, from https://www.whitehouse.gov/the-press-office/president-obama-calls-new-steps-prepare-america-s-children-success-college-and-care

Quinlan, C. (2016, April 11). The whitewashing of the opt-out movement. *ThinkProgress*. Retrieved June 22, 2016, from http://thinkprogress.org/education/2016/04/11/3767723/forgotten-activists-opt-out/

Ravitch, D. (2010). *The death and life of the great American school system: How testing and choice are undermining education*. New York: Basic Books.

Ravitch, D. (2014). *Reign of error: The hoax of the privatization movement and the danger to America's public schools*. New York: Vintage.

Ravitch, D. (2016, July 24). The common core costs billions and hurts students. *The New York Times*, SR 8.

Resmovits, J. (2014, January 10). How the common core became education's biggest bogeyman. *Huffington Post*. Retrieved November 21, 2015, from http://www.huffingtonpost.com/2014/01/10/common-core_n_4537284.html

Resnick, B., & Stamm, S. (2015). The state of segregation in the suburbs. *The Atlantic*. Retrieved June 22, 2016, from http://www.theatlantic.com/politics/archive/2015/01/the-state-of-segregation-in-the-suburbs/453987/

Rickert, P. (2009). A presuppositional critique of constructivism. *Christian Perspectives in Education, 3*(1). Retrieved November 21, 2015, from http://digitalcommons.liberty.edu/cgi/viewcontent.cgi?article=1035&context=cpe

Rizga, K. (2017, March/April). Betsy DeVos wants to use America's schools to build 'God's Kingdom'. *Mother Jones*. Retrieved April 14, 2017, from http://www.motherjones.com/politics/2017/01/betsy-devos-christian-schools-vouchers-charter-education-secretary

Rosenblatt, L. (1969). Towards a transactional theory of reading. *Journal of Reading Behavior, 1*(1), 31–51.

Schneider, M. (2013, August 23). A brief audit of Bill Gates' Common Core spending. *deutsch29*. Retrieved November 21, 2015, from https://deutsch29.wordpress.com/2013/08/27/a-brief-audit-of-bill-gates-common-core-spending/

Singer, A. (2006). Original in[compe]tents: Rightwing ideologues and the Supreme Court. *Social Science Docket, 6*(2), 2–9.

Singer, A. (2013). Turning Common Core on its head. *Social Science Docket, 13*(2), 2–6.

Singer, A. (2014a, March 14). Common Core and the holocaust. *Huffington Post.* Retrieved November 21, 2015, from http://www.huffingtonpost.com/alan-singer/common-core-holocaust_b_4964319.html

Singer, A. (2014b). *Education flashpoints, fighting for America's Schools.* New York: Routledge.

Singer, A. (2015, April 25). Students tell Mayor de Blasio turn off the metal detectors. *Huffington Post.* Retrieved June 22, 2016, from http://www.huffingtonpost.com/alan-singer/students-tell-mayor-de-bl_b_6735290.html

Singer, J. (2011). Trick-or-treat for UNICEF. In J. Singer (Ed.), *Using children's literature to teach about important Social Studies issues, Social Science Docket, Special Issue.* Albany, NY: NYSCSS.

Singh, R. (2002). *American government and politics: A concise introduction.* Thousand Oaks, CA: Sage.

Spring, J. (2008). *The American school: From the puritans to no child left behind.* New York: McGraw-Hill.

Strauss, V. (2013, November 19). The answer sheet, Common Core's odd approach to teaching the Gettysburg Address. *The Washington Post.* Retrieved November 21, 2015, from https://www.washingtonpost.com/news/answer-sheet/wp/2013/11/19/common-cores-odd-approach-to-teaching-gettysburg-address/

Strauss, V. (2014, September 14). The answer sheet, Common Core: Yes or no? A debate. *The Washington Post.* Retrieved November 21, 2015, from https://www.washingtonpost.com/news/answer-sheet/wp/2014/09/14/common-core-yes-or-no-a-debate/

Toch, T., & Tyre, P. (2010, June). How will the Common Core initiative impact the testing industry? *Thomas B. Fordham Institute.* Retrieved July 24, 2016, from http://www.edexcellencemedia.net/publications/2010/201006_CommonEdStandards/201006_EducationGovernance_TochTyre.pdf

Ujifusa, A. (2017, February 8). Trump will repeal Common Core, says Kellyanne Conway. *Education Week.* Retrieved April 14, 2017, from http://blogs.edweek.org/edweek/campaign-k-12/2017/02/trump_will_repeal_common_core_kellyanne_conway.html

Vygotsky, L. S. (1934/1987). Problems of general psychology. In R. Reiber & A. Carton (Eds.), *The collected works of L. S. Vygotsky* (Vol. 1). New York: Plenum.

Weiss, J. (2011, March 31). The innovation mismatch: "Smart Capital" and education innovation. *Harvard Business Review.* Retrieved at https://hbr.org/2011/03/the-innovation-mismatch-smart.html

CHAPTER 11

Toward a Resolution for Teacher-Student Conflict: Crafting Spaces of Rigorous Freedom with Classroom Debate

Dmitri Seals

Under the regimes of accountability that circulate in American public education, teachers truly have it rough. Squeezed between the needs of students and the demands of bureaucracy, their actions under public scrutiny and their profession under fire, teachers soldier on with low status, low pay, and high stress. This stress affects the health of teachers (Greenberg, Brown, & Abenavoli, 2016), the learning outcomes of their students (Arens & Morin, 2016), and their decisions to leave the profession (Sass, Seal, & Martin, 2011). A host of factors contribute to high rates of burnout among teachers, but among those I worked with over the past two decades, one theme stands out: the grinding tension between the values of humanizing, holistic education that brought them to teaching and the ever-changing bureaucratic achievement standards required by their districts and schools.

Resolving this tension will take tools and approaches that help teachers create humanizing educational experiences for their students without compromising their careers. This chapter explores one way forward, tracking recent efforts to develop academic debate as a versatile classroom tool simultaneously rooted in liberatory constructivism, well-developed by teachers for large diverse classrooms, and compatible with academic

D. Seals (✉)
University of California, Berkeley, Berkeley, CA, USA

D.W. Kritt (ed.), *Constructivist Education in an Age of Accountability*,
https://doi.org/10.1007/978-3-319-66050-9_11

standards. Debate has a track record of advancing literacy skill development and bringing content knowledge to life, but that is only half the battle. For students who don't connect well with traditional high school classrooms, debate can be a resource to grapple with the achievement standards required by their schools and districts, enabling them to critique, understand, and ultimately exceed those standards on their own terms as independent intellectuals.

The image of debate as an exclusive activity for privileged overachievers casts a long shadow, and it has taken hundreds of teachers working nationwide to challenge the old exclusive model. A movement of Urban Debate Leagues (UDLs) has created independent nonprofits in 22 US cities, each working with teachers in different ways to expand the circle of debate beyond the wealthy, white students who historically dominated the activity. Some offer only after school programming, but many have recently turned to classroom education (Belanger & Stein, 2012), and all are striving for their own perfect mix of engagement and rigor. In success and failure, these UDLs function as laboratories of pedagogy, churning out curriculum materials, course outlines, and teacher trainings that offer a wide range of approaches field-tested by a national community of teachers.

In the UDL network and in dozens of other classrooms, a new form of debate is emerging as a peer-driven forum where youth develop high-level intellectual and academic skills, and can serve as a power tool for teachers and a subversive resource for schools and districts. At its best, debate offers a chance to resolve what seems like an inherent contradiction between liberatory commitments and achievement standards into a productive dialectic. Still, the devil is in the details, and teachers have often resisted incorporating debate for reasons that resonate with the complicated history of the activity. This chapter will lead a tour from the competitive intensity of the national debate circuit through the community-oriented engagement of the urban debate network, taking the best of each influence to develop practical tools for teachers. First, as many debaters do, I will situate arguments in personal experience.

Classroom Debate from a Teacher's Perspective

My own work in urban debate began with an ambush. The day I interviewed for a teaching job at Maya Angelou High happened to be the same day the brand-new District of Columbia Urban Debate League made its pitch to the school. The principal asked me to sit in on the meeting, and by the end of the day—on top of my teaching load of four separate preps—I was the newly minted coach of the school's first debate team. I had no prior experience in debate, so I learned the ropes of the activity and the teaching profession all at once.

Debate practice quickly became the most rewarding and challenging part of my day. Maya Angelou was founded by public defenders to serve primarily court-involved youth, and most of our students had a distrust of authority well founded in years of hard experience. With its emphasis on student voice, debate was a sometimes-shocking departure from the educational environments these young people had encountered. Like many constructivist models, debate challenged expectations about the roles of student and teacher in ways that were frequently uncomfortable for both. Sometimes when the call to speak worked, it worked too well, and it took time to work out an approach that enabled students to take leadership in shaping debates without causing a cacophony.

As a new teacher still finding my way, I wasn't immediately convinced by the value of debate. The nascent UDL struggled to offer high-quality trainings and teacher support. The national circuit of debate was dominated by wealthy private schools, a hotbed of competitive hunger and unrecognized privilege. Still, once we learned how to run a decent debate practice—I had vital help from co-coach Colin Bane and student leaders, particularly early team captains Matthew Stevenson and Aisha Richburg—we were able to fashion both courses and afterschool practices that worked.

At their best, our practices were spaces of open inquiry where no idea was off-limits, with a high level of rigor driven by peer accountability. This allowed our students to make gains in academic skill in a daily experience of collective consciousness raising, wrapped in the exciting framework of team sport. The student relationships possible in debate, where young people could follow their passions to research, create, and advocate cases for social action, had me hooked. And the balance of spirit and rigor felt so right that it eventually transformed all my teaching, particularly in my math courses.

The feeling inspired me to help start the Bay Area Urban Debate League in Oakland, California. In my first year of graduate school I took a call from a debater friend, and before I knew it, I was giving 20–30 hours per week as a teacher and board member for this new nonprofit. When its executive director had to step down in the middle of our third year, I took over the position, learning fundraising and administration on the fly. When an opportunity came to found another UDL in Silicon Valley, it was too good to refuse, and all of a sudden I had spent 14 years working on debate, both in and out of the classroom.

Neither organization has the perfect answer to helping students thrive through debate; no teacher worth their salt believes that silver-bullet solutions can magically solve the problems of public education. Still, collectively the two organizations now serve over 20 schools, with about 600 students directly participating and about 100 teachers implementing debate in their courses. These teachers and their colleagues at their schools and across the country constitute a small army of educators working to sharpen classroom debate into a tool adequate to the challenge of diverse classrooms. In their quest to reclaim debate from its roots in exclusivity and privilege, they are digging out of a hole decades in the making.

The National Circuit: Achievement at All Costs

Through the 1980s, the national circuit of debate had little to offer teachers looking to bring their diverse classrooms to life. It had become a site in which elites, predominantly white and male, could build the rhetorical skills and high-powered networks to enter positions of authority (Cridland-Hughes, 2016; Fine, 2001).[1] The high level of challenge in debate, where accountability for excellence is immediately felt in the clash of arguments, made this activity perfectly suited to exclusivity: all too often, schools and students without the resources for private coaches and national travel schedules were laughed out of the room (Asad & Bell, 2014).

The rigors of debate are also a primary ingredient of effective classroom debate, a useful tool for constructivist teachers looking to navigate bureaucratic requirements of academic achievement. Anyone can get into an argument, but there is virtually no limit to the rigor of a full-fledged debate based in the deployment and critique of evidence. To capture this intellectual challenge, UDLs have chosen policy debate as their format. Also known as cross-examination debate, this is a mental sport where winning and losing depends on research and deliberation over highly charged political issues. Teams alternate between affirmative and negative sides: the affirmative supports a plan of action and the negative leverages evidence and arguments to tear this plan down.

With trophies, glory, and even college scholarships on the line, debaters on the national circuit can work incredibly hard, researching hundreds of pages of original evidence to support their arguments. Major tournaments regularly pack in over 12 rounds of debate over 3–4 days; with each round lasting roughly an hour and a half, debaters often grind through 18 or more hours of competition in a weekend. Debate rounds run into the wee hours of the night and preparation lasts even longer, and debaters often pull all-nighters to make sure they are ready for tournament day.

Young people see their hard work come to life in debate as they test their research and arguments against the best efforts of their peers. Students regularly present evidence from serious scholars—debaters are no strangers to Fanon, Foucault, and Spivak—along with newspaper evidence, policy briefs, personal stories, and even song lyrics. Before the digital age, teams were known to carry multiple huge rubber tubs of evidence to support their points. Now they carry laptops, share speeches by email and flash drive, and even occasionally fact-check and research new evidence during the debate round.

Even the basic terms and rules are open to debate: in the many variations on the old saying that "the only rules in debate are the speech times," the common thread is an invitation to challenge assumptions and expectations. In the last speeches of varsity debates, students cannot rely on established guidelines, a grading sheet, or even a stable set of conversational norms. Before any judge can decide, advanced debaters must make the case for the framework the judge should use to cast her ballot, advancing arguments for which factors are relevant, and how each factor should be weighed. The national circuit is a breeding ground for novel approaches to political argument, where prestigious tournaments serve as the perfect opportunity to "break" new cases and negative strategies drawing on hundreds of pages of original writing and research.

In a contradictory way, the competitive pressures of the national debate circuit can sometimes reduce the intellectual challenge for students. Coaches can sacrifice student-led creativity in the quest for victory, feeding arguments and case files to their debaters rather than supporting their original research. Adult judges determine the winning team, and debaters can go overboard in trying to please the judge rather than advocating coherent positions. Young people themselves can make debate exclusive, raising their speed, volume, or complexity to disadvantage their opponents at the cost of communication, engagement, and ultimately learning. Still, young people debating under the rigors of big-tournament competition tend to make impressive academic gains. Interestingly, the best evidence for these gains has come not from the national circuit of debate but from the movement that aims to reform it.

Urban Debate: Balancing Rigor with Engagement

Seizing on mainstream achievement metrics to build their movement, UDLs have invested in a string of peer-reviewed studies on the academic impacts of debate, particularly for low-income students of color. These studies have shown statistically significant advantages for college readiness among African-American debaters (Mezuk, 2009), high school graduation among low-income students (Anderson & Mezuk, 2012), and academic achievement gains across the board (Anderson & Mezuk, 2012; Mezuk, Bondarenko, Smith, & Tucker, 2011). Further studies have explored impacts on soft skills like self-confidence (Winkler, Fortner, & Baugh-Harris, 2013) and a broader range of outcomes in youth development (Anderson & Mezuk, 2015).

Every UDL models a different pedagogical and programmatic approach, but all rely on leadership from public school teachers and all share a mandate of engaging young people who would not otherwise flock to debate or academics. Like most youth-serving nonprofits, they judge themselves partly on how many young people they reach.[2] As a result, UDLs have become laboratories of pedagogy. Each one relies on a community of teachers working to make debate more approachable and engaging. Leagues exchange resources and ideas in bilateral partnerships and occasional national conferences and tournaments. At these gatherings, arguments burn bright in the UDL network about which program models and curriculum tools will best strike a balance between rigor and engagement.

The question they pursue is a classic: how to engage students who don't connect with school into an intensive intellectual activity like debate? UDLs have sought answers to this question with varying levels of success. In my experience, the ones where diverse teams have flourished tend to match the constructivist character of debate with the organizational infrastructure of big-team sports. In this model, teachers are facilitators of students' self-guided work, serving mainly to inspire exploration, promote internal student leadership, and ensure a positive team culture. In many of the largest teams, the most experienced and motivated students are responsible for the lion's share of direct instruction, recruitment and retention, and team management.

Some teachers have extended this constructivist trend by positioning debate as an empowering intervention in the politics of knowledge. Though this strategy is contested in the UDL network, it has been responsible for some of its largest competitive successes and attracted significant media attention (Miller, 2006; Thompson, 2014; Whiteley, 2007). Advocates of the strategy point out how the national circuit's norms of argument, topics of conversation, and reliance on traditional expert knowledge contribute to its exclusion of low-income students of color (Warner & Bruschke, 2001). To level the playing field, debaters and coaches have developed new forms of political argument: for instance, the three-tiered process developed at the University of Louisville incorporates "traditional academic sources, coupled with organic intellectuals and validated with our own personal experiences" (Warner, 2003).

Asserting the central value of personal experience as political knowledge—especially the experience of those who have lived through the harshest social problems—opens an opportunity to help students who have become disenchanted with school to realize the importance of their own perspective and take on identities as producers of knowledge. Sometimes in spite of their teachers or administrators, these students craft ways of representing themselves in the sphere of their local league that affirm the styles and identities they employ at home and with their friends. For instance, one young woman told me that after three years of policy debate she could "talk to anybody now. I can go home and be like 'What's up?' and then go to debate and be like, 'Your case don't have no solvency.' And I'm still me the whole time." She and other debaters stock cultural toolkits from mainstream debate and from more familiar sources (Swidler, 1986), developing strategies of action that bridge between their home life and the world of mainstream politics (Carter, 2003).

The early success of these more inclusive approaches to debate have inspired a new wave of deep school partnerships aimed at infusing debate into classroom practice and school culture. The idea of using debate "across the curriculum" as a pedagogical tool is of course not new (Bellon, 2000; Snider, Schnurer, & Snider, 2002), but UDLs have created a new groundswell in recent years (Belanger & Stein, 2012). The Boston Debate League first made Evidence-Based Argumentation into a core project of Boston schools and then passed it to the National Speech & Debate Association for replication at dozens more schools. Our Debate Pedagogy Initiative at the Bay Area UDL brought teachers together to create curriculum now in use by several districts and dozens of teachers, and new leagues like the Silicon Valley UDL have built "deep school partnerships" into their core models. The momentum of this effort makes this a particularly important moment to assess whether and how debate can help to resolve some core problems faced by public school teachers.

Constructivism and Accountability: Crafting Debate as a Tool for Teachers

For teachers buffeted by the changing winds of education reform priorities, any new pedagogical strategy faces a heavy burden of proof. Generally, new classroom tools fall into one of two troubling categories: (A) I love this, but my principal will hate me; (B) my principal will love me and I'll hate myself. Through the efforts of dozens of UDL teachers, debate is now well equipped to thread the needle between these categories, increasing teacher impact and quality of life while producing enough gains in skill and knowledge to bring a smile to the face of even the most stressed administrator.

The potential benefit to teachers and students comes largely from the constructivist spirit of debate pedagogy. By conducting their own research to support original arguments, students not only individually construct their own knowledge (Piaget, 1936/1952)but also validate and strengthen that knowledge through social interaction in a community of peers (Vygostsky, 1962). They learn to question everything, making their beliefs more robust by challenging assumptions (Von Glasersfeld 2001). Especially in math and science, but also across the curriculum, reintroducing debate makes learning more authentic to the lived experience of experts, who of course debate results constantly (Kuhn, 2010). Teachers do not fade into the background as in the worst misinterpretations of constructivism (Gordon, 2009); instead, they actively coach and guide, increasing the quality of debates and fueling research with content knowledge.

In appropriate balance, the rigor and intensity of debate can channel constructivist strategies too often dismissed as wishy-washy into measurable gains in skill and knowledge. Teachers working with UDLs have labored long and hard to spread the general academic benefits of debate more broadly in their classrooms. Outside the world of urban debate, scholars have noted the way that classroom debates raise the level of critical thinking (Hanna, 2014; Kuhn, 2010); perhaps even more importantly, in the right context they can raise the level of engagement and involvement for all students (Doody & Condon, 2012).

Plus, for teachers working in public schools, it matters that the activity is eerily well-matched to the Common Core State Standards,[3] which explicitly "put particular emphasis on students' ability to write sound arguments on substantive topics and issues" (Woodard & Kline, 2016). The standards have their flaws, but they are full to the brim with debate (and real-life) skills like "evaluate a speaker's point of view, reasoning, and use of evidence and rhetoric," "plan and present an argument that supports a claim," "delineate and evaluate the argument and specific claims in a text," and "Draw evidence from literary or informational texts to support analysis, reflection, and research" (Common Core State Standards Initiative, 2010). Advocates have made the point that the Common Core affords an opportunity to advance civic education through debate (McIntosh & Milam, 2016). The ability of debate to bridge academic achievement and liberatory education, between accountability and constructivism, is promising enough to demand exploration.

Critics have rightly noted several dangers that appear when traditional debate is imported into the classroom. Without a strong team culture, debate can promote unhealthy competition and hostility in the classroom (Goodwin, 2003) and privilege forms of argumentative speech at the cost of a broader lens (DeStigter, 2015). Students can resist the call to debate particularly in disciplines like science where they expect a more lecture-heavy form of pedagogy (Kuhn, Wang, & Li, 2010). Most frequent is the critique that classroom debate repeats the exclusion of the national circuit on a smaller scale: debate can elevate those who already have strong confidence and academic skill at the expense of struggling students, heightening existing inequalities (Bickmore & Parker, 2014; Hemmings, 2000). These concerns have often led educators to replace debate with more community-minded strategies like fishbowl discussions and structured dialogues (Jacobs, 2010).

Bringing any new strategy to life among the stresses of public school teaching presents a serious challenge, particularly in the context of an initiative as ambitious and all-consuming as the Common Core State Standards. Teachers and students are under constant external pressure; one teacher in San Jose told us she has to "go to all these trainings, and then department meetings, they are trying just to get everyone on the same page. All the teachers are boxed in on what they can teach, and it's more about keeping the boat afloat." For every teacher ready and willing to experiment with something new, there are several more who are locked into their current pattern because change takes time or simply because it works for them. The most common obstacle we hear from teachers is more practical than principled. The issue is not well-covered in literature on debate but is a common concern for constructivist teacher trainers (Hills, 2007): it is the concern that inviting student voice into the classroom will create a series of challenges in classroom management, logistics, and assessment that make debate more trouble than it's worth.

In my view, the adaptations made by teachers in the urban debate network have done much to rescue debate from these weaknesses and significantly lowered the bar of implementation challenge. Teachers still have to take a significant leap to invite students as leaders in knowledge production, and there is no escaping the fact that a high-functioning debate activity generally makes for a loud classroom. Still, the leap now comes with a safety net of materials and approaches crafted by public school teachers with equity and engagement in mind. For the teachers I've worked with, the balance between accountability and constructivism in debate works as long as students learn constructive criticism as an explicit skill with specific practices, and as long as teachers and students can temper competition with a spirit of supportive community.

Principles and Tools for Debate in the Classroom

Along with activities designed to channel the power of student voice, classrooms infused with debate can introduce new roles that bring a new spirit of youth-adult collaboration. The class is a team, in which individual achievement takes second seat to collective uplift. The teacher is a coach, responsible for the inputs, guidance, and encouragement by which the team as a whole can flourish. Students are debaters, producers of important knowledge who act as curriculum leaders and warm-hearted evaluators of each other's work. Debaters can rotate through team leadership positions that empower them to help the coach as they elicit the opinions and facilitate the work of their team. Team leaders can set agendas for topic research (e.g., what evidence should we look for to figure out the primary causes of the American Civil War?), contribute to rubrics used in judging debates, help the teacher develop and maintain debate evidence, lead trainings, or support team morale.[4]

These roles best take root in the presence of a few core community values that help embed the competitive rigor of debate in a supportive learning community. Though each teacher has their own version of core values, and many co-design them with their students, these tend to recur:

1. The twin right to speak and be heard: debaters learn to listen hard, validating the importance of their own speech by affirming the speech of others.

2. Harmony as collective responsibility: because debate carries a unique invitation to speak out loud, each debater has a responsibility to maintain harmony as voices start to ring out.
3. Responsible critique: anything is up for question, but all critiques must happen in the context of a good-faith effort to build each other's capacities.
4. Situated learning: teams consider decisions in the context of the long-term goals that students have for themselves and their communities.

Activities and Tools

The most powerful tools in the hands of debate teachers are activities designed to engage all students simultaneously in rigorous and joyful inquiry. Teachers working with UDLs have produced a menagerie of interesting activities, but we collect a few here that demonstrate that elusive balance between peer-driven accountability and inclusive engagement. The cornerstone of effective debate is the one used most often to anchor summative assessment at the end of units—the group role debate. Here, all students debate simultaneously in groups, rotating through roles of affirmative, negative, and judge. At the end of the debate, they turn in a variety of written materials, often including speech outlines, judge ballots, a set of structured notes known as the flow, and sometimes a companion essay evaluating arguments and evidence from the perspective of the judge.

As a technique that engages the whole classroom at once, the group role debate directly addresses the common critique that classroom debates tend to feature a few students at the front of the classroom while their peers sit as passive observers, often bored to tears. Debaters and judges need guidance in their roles: in addition to written role guides, often the first debate requires a full period devoted to performing and analyzing a sample debate. After this, debaters can guide each other to make debates more intensely focused and enjoyable as well. The sense of peer accountability kicks in as those who prepare well get the most out of the activity and those who don't put in the work have to face up to their peers. Teachers have given the group role debate a dizzying array of variations, with lengthy pre-written speeches or impromptu debates, standard affirmative versus negative or multiple sides, large teams or one-on-ones.

Once a few core tools are in place, these group role debates become relatively easy to put in action on nearly any topic. The first core tool is the evidence pack, the primary anchor of content knowledge in the debate classroom. Similar to the packet of information that fuels the document-based questions on high school Advanced Placement tests, the evidence packet can feature excerpts from primary and secondary sources gathered by teachers or by students to support the arguments of a debate. When using paper rather than a computer, debaters tend to heavily mark up their evidence and file it in the pockets of expanding file folders for easy retrieval in the heat of competition. Debate teachers learn to frame evidence packs as the sword and shield of debaters. A favorite classroom activity known as Evidence Scavenger Hunt challenges students to track down evidence to answer key arguments, and another called Evidence Racer builds the skill of rapidly identifying the perfect evidence to secure the win in a given debate scenario.

The second core tool is a form of structured note-taking unique to debate commonly known as flowing. When debaters take notes on speeches, they produce "the flow," which serves as the written anchor used by every speaker and every judge during all debates. Flows track the arguments of each speech in order, separating each thread of a speaker's argument into a horizontal chunk. Importantly, after the first speech of the round, flowing does not follow a linear pattern: debaters match new arguments visually against the old argument threads to which they respond. For instance, in a debate on the most important sources of climate change in a science course, points on the warming impact of methane would flow in a separate row from evidence on carbon dioxide even if one appeared at the start of the speech and the other at the end.

The flow is a great example of balancing rigor and engagement. On the engagement side, the active placement of arguments is much more fun than the rote mechanics of note-taking, and debaters under time-pressure often develop eclectic systems of abbreviation with the feel of a secret language. A selection from field notes shows how different the activity of note-taking can feel when infused with the energy of debate:

> After a teacher training in Oakland that featured a student speaking about how he flows in debate, his teacher approached him with wonder on her face. Shocked at the volume and quality of notes he was taking in debate, she asked, "Hey, if I called taking notes flowing in my class, do you think you'd do it?" His answer: "Hey, it's worth a try."

In telling this story, I am by no means suggesting that teachers merely re-label conventional tools like taking notes to make them seem more cool or exciting than they really are. The point is to bring academic skills to life in the context of making meaningful arguments, to integrate these skills into a framework that makes clear how useful, important, and thrilling they can be in the real world.

On the side of rigor, flowing can help train students to capture the salient features of speech. Dozens of UDL alumni have told us that this aspect of flowing helps them navigate in even the most boring lecture-based college course. Plus, the flow is a boon for teachers frustrated by how often the great ideas that come up in class discussion are lost in the writing process. With a little guidance from teachers, students can easily use a flow as the basis of an essay that weighs the best arguments from class discussion against each other. This sample flow shows the way arguments tend to be tracked horizontally across the speeches of a typical policy debate, with most arguments directly citing academic and journalistic evidence (Fig. 11.1).

A final set of tools attempts to build literacy skill by giving students power over texts, activities often grouped under the label "bringing text to life." Students often perceive required texts in school as agents of adult control. Debate fights this sensation by opening up more opportunities for student leadership in topic selection and research, and even when this is not possible, by recovering the original energy of texts. Debate teachers insist that in the real world, writing is fighting (Bourdieu, 2010; Reed, 1988); texts in almost any discipline carry real stakes and passions waiting to be released. An activity called Power Words starts with the comedy of a dull, monotone reading of a text, drawing a stark contrast to speeches that build drama and make stakes clear by emphasis on meaningful or "juicy" words. This activity pairs well with Act the Part, where students take on roles of famous speakers, bringing the text to life both through their performance and through their reflection on the lived context of the speech.

These activities are just the tip of a lively iceberg of materials, activities, and units that use debate and speech to explore the intersection of constructivism and accountability. Any pedagogical tool takes life through its adaptation and transformation in the daily work of teachers. A teacher in Oakland once told me that "when it comes to teacher training, most folks never practice what they preach." Co-curricular nonprofits like UDLs are at their best when they make sure to differentiate themselves clearly from scripted curriculum, instead delivering their tools in modular and editable form that invites teachers to make debate their own. Equipping teachers to lead the evolution of debate pedagogy is both right and effective, a perfect balance of practical efficacy and philosophical coherence.

First Affirmative Constructive	First Negative Constructive	Second Affirmative Constructive	Second Negative Constructive	First Negative Rebuttal	First Affirmative Rebuttal
PLAN: USFG incentives for solar desalination w/global modeling	Don't need the plan – desal already big and growing (Pappas 11)	Regulations and lack of funds stand in the way of desal – we need the plan! (Carter 2013)	Already a big push in the US for desal (Leven 2013) – we need to stop it, not make it worse!		Even if there are plants already, there aren't enough to address the crisis.
Megadroughts coming – worst in 500 years (Ross 2014)					
***Advantage 1:** Water crisis will kill US coastal economies - $5 billion lost in CA (Kiesel 2014)*	Turn! Plan misses the root of the problem, consumption, making all their impacts worse. (Wilder 2010)		Extend Wilder 2010. All the harms the Aff is talking about come from consumption, but the plan does nothing about it. (EarthTalk 2013)		Extend our evidence from Infrastructure News 2013. Our plan will save money and stop consumption over time.
Plan solves: Desal will save economy (Gleick & Wolff 2006)	Desal costs billions more than other ways of getting water (EarthTalk 2013) – will trade off with public schools	Costs will go down over time and save billions of dollars (Infrastructure News 2013) – no trade off with schools		Plan won't ever save $ - even if it did, we need school funding *now* – education is a human right, and comes before all their impacts	Extend our economy advantage – plan saves billions. With those billions we can build amazing schools.
***Advantage 2:** Water is key to life around the globe (Clark 2007)*		Desal creates thousands of jobs and adds to the economy (Whipple 12)		Without good schools, there won't be anyone to fill those jobs	Schools are good enough now – and they'll get better
Bad water kills millions every year – clean water is a basic human right! (Engqvist 2011)					
Plan solves: US leadership is key (King 2013)	Desal harms the environment and creates toxic waste (Francis 2014)	Solar desal is cleaner all the time – new tech makes everything possible (Peters 2014)	Desal causes global warming and kills animals (Danoun 07) – new tech won't change this		This is a trade-off between human lives saved by the plan and animals & plants harmed – humans win!
		They haven't touched our global advantage – plan saves millions of lives around the world!		Turn: If desal is bad for the US, it's bad for the whole globe. Globalizing it makes things worse for millions.	Other countries need water worse – and in different ways – than US. Neg wants to cheat them of clean water

Fig. 11.1 Sample flow tracking arguments and rebuttals across six speeches in a debate round

New Roles for Teachers, Schools, and Debaters

If we are to reclaim the status of teachers as intellectuals, we need to give teachers tools that empower them to explore creative pedagogical pathways without threatening their careers. From practical application to theoretical intervention, teachers and students have sculpted a version of classroom debate that can serve as an antidote to accountability dependent upon meaning-poor standardized tests. They have escaped standard critiques of progressive education by rooting constructivist impulses in the rigorous analysis of evidence. In the process, they have helped teachers escape their role as overseer of scripted curriculum and helped to resolve the culture war between schools and students, replacing punitive adult-driven forms of accountability with peer accountability in the context of a supportive team.[5]

In the schools where debate has taken off in the classroom, it has often come with a broader impact on the culture of the school. These schools tend to host afterschool debate programs for students who "catch the debate bug," and some have even gone so far as to host pep rallies for a team heading to a big tournament. Whether encouraged or not, leaders of the debate team tend to get involved in school policy debates, and debate programs have been known to re-inject serious issues into the popularity contest of student council elections. Melissa Wade, one of the founders of the UDL movement, shows that schools considering debate as a pedagogical strategy should take into account that awakening student voice and fostering critical thinking can come with a price:

> When we introduce an Urban Debate League program in a city, about half the principals usually show up in my office or at a tournament wondering what's going on with their students. They can' understand why all these students are suddenly in their office demanding computers and AP classes and money to go to tournaments. (Houppert, 2007)

Students inspired by debate can also pay a price for their awakening. Encouraged by debaters who seize academic achievement on their own terms and inhabit empowered roles as producers of knowledge, UDLs have often celebrated the capacity of debate to "make smart cool." What you hear less often are the stories of students who became so good at questioning assumptions that they lose faith in school altogether. Schools are sites where adults exercise power over youth, often in ways that are—or at least feel—arbitrary and unfair. These conditions can inspire young thinkers to take bold risks to challenge unjust authority. History is full of students who stood up to their teachers or their principal only to be shot down or kicked out. Brilliant young people like these need teachers not only to step up for them when the consequences come, but also to help them craft strategies that balance risk against reward and prepare them to be lifelong agents of change. Students emboldened by debate need support in constructing empowered intellectual identities that still take seriously the bureaucratic systems and power structures they will have to navigate in order to realize their dreams in the long term.

Teachers, particularly the idealists who hold dreams of liberating constructivist education, face the same challenges at school. They, too, experience arbitrary power and frustrated resistance, and they need the same kind of support. Classroom debate offers a way to help these teachers keep both their dreams and their careers alive in an age where accountability dominates in schools. It can also start to heal the long-standing conflict between students and teachers. By pushing beyond the zero-sum game between standards-based achievement and holistic, humanizing education, we can begin to reroute all the energy we spend in power struggles with students into pushing together for skill development in the service of authentic personal growth. Debate is only one way to resolve the conflict; we will need many connected interventions to equip students and teachers to achieve, redefine, and ultimately transform the standards of academic success.

Notes

1. The exclusionary character of debate in the past century may be in stark contrast to the role it played in the early United States, where ambitious students and teachers from subaltern backgrounds used it as a tool of education reform linked to expanding notions of citizenship (Bartanen & Littlefield, 2015).
2. Since the first league was founded in 1997, just over 12,000 young people from more than 290 communities have participated in UDLs. These loosely affiliated nonprofits operate in 22 cities, and generally at least one new league joins the network each year.
3. By a twist of historical fate, the lead architect of these standards, David Coleman of the College Board, was a very active debater who credits debate as a deep influence on his life, and keynote speaker for the annual dinner of the National Association for UDLs in 2016. As *The New York Times* notes:

"When Coleman attended Stuyvesant High in Manhattan, he was a member of the championship debate team, and the urge to overpower with evidence—and his unwillingness to suffer fools—is right there on the surface when you talk with him" (Balf, 2014).

4. The structure of student leadership in a debate-infused classroom is one of many points of constructive disagreement among teachers. Some make a point to build strongly structured roles with contracts, and others prefer loose roles that require students to flesh out details. Some build students' performance in leadership roles into the grading system for the course, and others explicitly craft leadership as a part of classroom culture that falls outside the scope of grading.
5. One of the most interesting findings in recent research on classroom debate is that it can increase capacities of critical thinking not only for students but also for teachers (Yang & Rusli, 2012).

References

Anderson, S., & Mezuk, B. (2012). Participating in a policy debate program and academic achievement among at-risk adolescents in an urban public school district: 1997–2007. *Journal of Adolescence, 35*(5), 1225–1235. https://doi.org/10.1016/j.adolescence.2012.04.005

Anderson, S., & Mezuk, B. (2015). Positive youth development and participation in an urban debate league: Results from Chicago Public Schools, 1997–2007. *The Journal of Negro Education, 84*(3), 362–378.

Arens, A. K., & Morin, A. J. (2016). Relations between teachers' emotional exhaustion and students' educational outcomes. *Journal of Educational Psychology, 108*, 800–813.

Asad, A. L., & Bell, M. C. (2014). Winning to learn, learning to win: Evaluative frames and practices in urban debate. *Qualitative Sociology, 37*(1), 1–26. https://doi.org/10.1007/s11133-013-9269-1

Balf, T. (2014, March 6). The story behind the SAT overhaul. *The New York Times*. Retrieved from https://www.nytimes.com/2014/03/09/magazine/the-story-behind-the-sat-overhaul.html

Bartanen, M. D., & Littlefield, R. S. (2015). Competitive speech and debate: How play influenced American educational practice. *American Journal of Play, 7*(2), 155–173.

Belanger, A., & Stein, S. (2012). *Closing the academic divide through debate*. Federal Reserve Bank of Boston. Retrieved December 16, 2016, from https://www.bostonfed.org/publications/communities-and-banking/2013/spring/closing-the-academic-divide-through-debate.aspx

Bellon, J. (2000). A research-based justification for debate across the curriculum. *Argumentation and Advocacy, 36*(3), 161–175.

Bickmore, K., & Parker, C. (2014). Constructive conflict talk in classrooms: Divergent approaches to addressing divergent perspectives. *Theory & Research in Social Education, 42*(3), 291–335. https://doi.org/10.1080/00933104.2014.901199

Bourdieu, P. (2010). *Sociology is a martial art: Political writings by Pierre Bourdieu* (G. Sapiro, Ed.). New York: The New Press.

Carter, P. L. (2003). "Black" cultural capital, status positioning, and schooling conflicts for low-income African American youth. *Social Problems, 50*(1), 136–155. https://doi.org/10.1525/sp.2003.50.1.136

Common Core State Standards Initiative. (2010). *English language arts standards.* Retrieved April 11, 2017, from http://www.corestandards.org/ELA-Literacy/

Cridland-Hughes, S. (2016). The Atlanta Urban Debate League: Exploring the making of a critical literacy space. *American Educational History Journal, 43* (1/2), 41–57.

DeStigter, T. (2015). On the ascendance of argument: A critique of the assumptions of academe's dominant form. *Research in the Teaching of English, 50*(1), 11–34.

Doody, O., & Condon, M. (2012). Increasing student involvement and learning through using debate as an assessment. *Nurse Education in Practice, 12*(4), 232–237. https://doi.org/10.1016/j.nepr.2012.03.002

Fine, G. A. (2001). *Gifted tongues: High school debate and adolescent culture.* Princeton, NJ: Princeton University Press.

Goodwin, J. (2003). Students' perspectives on debate exercises in content area classes. *Communication Education, 52*(2), 157–163. https://doi.org/10.1080/03634520302466

Gordon, M. (2009). The misuses and effective uses of constructivist teaching. *Teachers and Teaching, 15*(6), 737–746. https://doi.org/10.1080/13540600903357058

Greenberg, M., Brown, J., & Abenavoli, R. (2016). *Teacher stress and health.* Robert Wood Johnson Foundation. Retrieved from http://www.rwjf.org/en/library/research/2016/07/teacher-stress-and-health.html

Hanna, D. R. (2014). Using guided debates to teach current issues. *Journal of Nursing Education, 53*(6), 352–355. https://doi.org/10.3928/01484834-20140512-04

Hemmings, A. (2000). High school democratic dialogues: Possibilities for praxis. *American Educational Research Journal, 37*(1), 67–91. https://doi.org/10.2307/1163472

Hills, T. (2007). Is constructivism risky? Social anxiety, classroom participation, competitive game play and constructivist preferences in teacher development. *Teacher Development, 11*(3), 335–352. https://doi.org/10.1080/13664530701644615

Houppert, K. (2007, August 26). Finding their voices. *The Washington Post.* Retrieved from http://www.washingtonpost.com/wp-dyn/content/article/2007/08/21/AR2007082101715.html

Jacobs, G. (2010). Academic controversy: A cooperative way to debate. *Intercultural Education, 21*(3), 291–296. https://doi.org/10.1080/14675981003771033

Kuhn, D. (2010). Teaching and learning science as argument. *Science Education, 94* (5), 810–824. https://doi.org/10.1002/sce.20395

Kuhn, D., Wang, Y., & Li, H. (2010). Why argue? Developing understanding of the purposes and values of argumentive discourse. *Discourse Processes, 48*(1), 26–49. https://doi.org/10.1080/01638531003653344

McIntosh, J., & Milam, M. (2016). Competitive debate as competency-based learning: Civic engagement and next-generation assessment in the era of the common core learning standards. *Communication Education, 65*(4), 420–433. https://doi.org/10.1080/03634523.2016.1203007

Mezuk, B. (2009). Urban debate and high school educational outcomes for African American males: The case of the Chicago Debate League. *The Journal of Negro Education, 78*(3), 290–304.

Mezuk, B., Bondarenko, I., Smith, S., & Tucker, E. (2011). Impact of participating in a policy debate program on academic achievement: Evidence from the Chicago Urban Debate League. *Educational Research and Reviews, 6*(9), 622–635.

Miller, J. (2006). *Cross-X: The amazing true story of how the most unlikely team from the most unlikely of places overcame staggering obstacles at home and at school to ... community on race, power, and education.* New York: Farrar, Straus and Giroux.

Piaget, J. (1936/1952). *The origins of intelligence in children.* New York: W W Norton.

Reed, I. (1988). *Writin' is fightin': Thirty-seven years of boxing on paper.* New York/ Toronto, ON: Atheneum/Collier Macmillan Canada.

Sass, D. A., Seal, A. K., & Martin, N. K. (2011). Predicting teacher retention using stress and support variables. *Journal of Educational Administration, 49*(2), 200–215. https://doi.org/10.1108/09578231111116734

Snider, A., Schnurer, M., & Snider, A. (2002). *Many sides: Debate across the curriculum.* New York: International Debate Education Association.

Swidler, A. (1986). Culture in action: Symbols and strategies. *American Sociological Review, 51*(2), 273–286. https://doi.org/10.2307/2095521

Thompson, K. (2014). *Team's strategy using the n-word unsettles some in the collegiate debate community.* Retrieved January 8, 2017, from http://www.washingtonpost.com/sf/national/2014/11/09/teams-strategy-unsettles-some-in-the-collegiate-debate-community/

Von Glasersfeld, E. (2001). Radical constructivism and teaching. *Prospects, 31*(2), 161–173. https://doi.org/10.1007/BF03220058

Vygostsky, L. S. (1962). *Thought and language.* Cambridge, MA: MIT Press.

Warner, E. (2003). Go homers, makeovers or takeovers? A privilege analysis of debate as a gaming simulation. *Contemporary Argumentation and Debate, 24*, 65–80.

Warner, E., & Bruschke, J. (2001). Gone on debating. *Competitive Academic Debate as a Tool of Empowerment. Contemporary Argumentation and Debate, 22*, 1–21.

Whiteley, G. (2007). *Resolved*. Los Angeles, CA: One Potato Productions.

Winkler, C. K., Fortner, C. K., & Baugh-Harris, S. (2013). Overcoming educational challenges to women living in at-risk communities through urban debate. *Forum on Public Policy Online, 2013*(1).

Woodard, R., & Kline, S. (2016). Lessons from sociocultural writing research for implementing the Common Core State Standards. *The Reading Teacher, 70*(2), 207–216. https://doi.org/10.1002/trtr.1505

Yang, C.-H., & Rusli, E. (2012). Using debate as a pedagogical tool in enhancing pre-service teachers' learning and critical thinking. *Journal of International Education Research, 8*(2), 135.

CHAPTER 12

Activity Settings as Contexts for Motivation: Reframing Classroom Motivation as Dilemmas Within and Between Activities

Michael Middleton, Alison Rheingold, and Jayson Seaman

This chapter examines classroom motivation evolving from goal structures (Ames, 1992) through an activity-theoretical framework and illustrated by the ways middle-school students leveraged different sociocultural activities as they engaged in an extended, "real world," project-based curriculum unit. One small group's progress throughout the unit illustrates the way participation and learning were motivated by dilemmas within and between activities. These dilemmas were not solely related to academic issues but also stemmed from the social roles and identities children and adults occupy within different activities. Despite the putatively nonacademic nature of many of these dilemmas, they were central in shaping children's pursuit of school-related goals and their engagement with academic content over the course of the unit. In light of these findings, we use the concept of

M. Middleton (✉)
Hunter College/CUNY, New York, NY, USA

A. Rheingold
Holyoke Public Schools, Holyoke, MA, USA

J. Seaman
Department of Kinesiology – Outdoor Education, University of New Hampshire, Durham, NH, USA

D.W. Kritt (ed.), *Constructivist Education in an Age of Accountability*,
https://doi.org/10.1007/978-3-319-66050-9_12

multi-motivated learning activity to argue that "goal structures" are not only defined by surface features of the local classroom environment but also constituted by activity elements that are leveraged by members to generate, understand, and resolve problems at hand, a process which involves the coordination of motives across activities. We discuss recent developments in motivational research that urge greater attention to social and relational factors in shaping children's pursuit of school-related goals.

Conceptions of Classroom Motivation

Motivation is a topic of central concern to child developmentalists, educational psychologists, curriculum theorists, and, perhaps most of all, teachers. Children who do not display acceptable dispositions toward schooling have been characterized in the classroom motivation literature as "unmotivated" or "apathetic" toward learning (Thorkildsen & Nicholls, 1991). Perspectives on the nature and sources of this problem vary; in social cognitive traditions, it is understood to be a maladaptive personal orientation toward learning perpetuated by the existence of negative environmental cues (Ames & Archer, 1988; Pintrich, Marx, & Boyle, 1993). Implicit here is the view that the "motivation to learn" is a natural and desirable state and that being "unmotivated" in school is both undesirable and unnatural. Persistent problems with student motivation can therefore be ameliorated by altering teaching strategies and by sending positive messages about the value of "mastery" over "performance" at both the classroom and the school levels. In contrast, neo-Vygotskian cultural-historical traditions view motivation as a feature of participation in all social activities. Motivation to learn among school-age youth is a function of alignment with social practices of schooling and appropriation of associated near-term goals. Activity theorists view being "unmotivated" as also a natural and even predictable product of those same social practices.

There are several differences between social cognitive and cultural-historical perspectives on classroom motivation. The first essential difference lies in what is taken to be the evidence of motivation. For social cognitive frameworks such as achievement goal theory, demonstrating resistance or failing to take up school-related goals signals the absence of motivation or an improper orientation to learning. Willing, skillful participation in schooling practices, especially the desire and ability to independently adopt acceptable learning goals, provides evidence of motivation. In Vygotskian-inspired frameworks, such as cultural-historical activity theory, "unmotivated behavior" signals participation in social practices that arise naturally as a function of schooling, forming "interstitial communities of practice" (Lave & Wenger, 1991) that are, by definition, constituted by motivation. It does not signal absence of motivation but rather subjective alignment with objects and motives that undermine the dominant activity of schooling and are often self-defeating (Paradise, 1998). The classic ethnographies *Learning to Labor* (Willis, 1977) and *Jocks and Burnouts* (Eckert, 1989) essentially document this phenomenon. Independent adoption of acceptable learning goals signals subjective alignment with the objects and motives of schooling and also the likely existence of patterns of successful participation in other compatible social practices (Fleer, 2011; Hedegaard, 2011; Ochs & Taylor, 1992; Rogoff, 1990). The considerable methodological issues that stem from these differences have been the focus of much recent scholarship but are far from resolved.

Another crucial difference among these frameworks is the timescales that are considered relevant to the analysis. Motivation to learn among children and youth in cultural-historical theories reflects evolutionary processes concerning the organization of major life activities, in particular the rise of mass schooling (Dewey, 1899; Elkonin, 1972; Vygotsky, 1963). In other words, cultural-historical theories recognize motivation to learn as a cultural phenomenon arising alongside modern schooling that becomes a psychological condition of personhood in modern societies as children approach the school age and through increasing participation in schooling practices.

The recognition that motivation poses practical problems for educators and curriculum designers is not new, and, although even some cultural-historical scholars have recently suggested so (Wardekker, Boersma, Ten Dam, & Volman, 2011), it is questionable as to whether student motivation has gotten worse over time. By 1938, Dewey had already long recognized schooling as "a kind of institution sharply marked off from any other form of social organization" (p. 18) and one that was uniquely defined by the problem of motivating children to learn. Like contemporary activity theorists, Dewey saw motivation to learn not as an individual psychological problem but a phenomenon that is cultural and historical in nature and situated as a function of modern schooling practices. "The weakness of ordinary lessons in observation, calculated to train the senses, is that they have no outlet beyond themselves, and hence *no necessary motive*" (Dewey, 1915/1990, p. 134. emphasis added). He understood that interest in school learning would therefore be generated artificially, through "devices of art" on the one hand (1938, p. 19) and threats and coercion on the other hand. He sharply criticized both: "I frequently hear dulling devices and empty exercises defended and extolled because 'the children take such an interest in them'" (Dewey, 1912/1990, p. 206). These were the good teachers; bad teachers relied on other methods:

> the material of the lesson is rendered interesting, if not in itself, at least in contrast with some alternative experience. To learn the lesson is more interesting than to take a scolding, to be held up to general ridicule, stay after school, receive degradingly low marks, or fail to be promoted. (Dewey, 1912/1990, p. 207)

The subsequent century of psychological research on motivational problems can, in Wardekker et al.'s formulation, be summed as two key resolutions:

1. that adequate teaching procedures will take care of the motivation problems (see, e.g., Thorndike, 1913; Oelkers, 1998)
2. that motivation is part of the meta-cognitive skills a student needs to develop in order to be able to study properly (see, e.g., Boekaerts & Cascallar, 2006, p. 153).

Thinking aligned with Dewey rejects these on the grounds that they do not adequately account for the institution of schooling—that is, what kind of activity "schooling" is. His distinctive proposal—aside from radically reimagining education (see Dewey, 1934)—was informed by historical and anthropological analysis (Fallace, 2008; Seaman & Nelsen, 2011). He sought to engage children in *occupations* as a mode of organizing learning, which he defined as follows:

> By occupation is not meant any kind of 'busy work' or exercises that may be given to a child in order to keep him out of mischief or idleness when seated at his desk. By occupation I mean a mode of activity on the part of the child which reproduces, or runs parallel to, some form of work carried on in social life. (p. 132)

Among Dewey's several reasons for promoting occupations as a main curricular vehicle, chief among them was their plausibility at solving the problem of motivation. They would, at least in a mimetic way, link individual impulses with the motives of social activity, which would in turn alter the nature of the educational enterprise. "The difference that appears when occupations are made the articulating centers of school life are not easy to describe in words," he wrote. "It is a difference in motive, of spirit and atmosphere" (Dewey, 1899, p. 459). Dewey's ongoing effort to solve the problem of "motivation to learn" through curriculum designed around collaborative, socially consequential work signals the longevity of the problem (and not necessarily the emergence of a new educational crisis) as well as the problem's cultural-historical nature and institutional foundations. That the problem has not yet been widely solved further indicates the way institutionalized schooling continues to dominate conceptions of learning and the persistent limitations of the theories and methods still widely used to understand *motivation* in relation to school achievement, learning, ontogenetic development, and societal activity.

To identify ways youth relate domains of societal activity in classrooms to adopt school-related goals and engage with academic content, we use excerpts from small group interactions of middle-school children during a semester-long, interdisciplinary curriculum unit that sought to leverage "real world" activities to engage children in learning. Our interest stems from recent trends among educational psychologists studying achievement goals (Hickey & Zuiker, 2006; Nolen, Ward, & Horn, 2011; Turner & Patrick, 2008) and related interest among activity theorists in school motivation (Fleer, 2011; Miettinen, 2005; Roth, 2011).

A central concern of this chapter is the use of "real world" activities in school as pretexts for extended, shared inquiry and to encourage children's long-term adoption of school-related goals—particularly children who otherwise would be likely to demonstrate "lack of motivation" to learn. Like Wolff-Michael Roth's (2011), our own experience as former grade-school educators is that such children show increased interest when working together on "authentic" problems (see also Blumenfeld et al., 1991).

In our estimation, several complications within this line of curricular advocacy have not been adequately acknowledged, however, particularly concerning motivation. First is the argument that children are increasingly motivated by the more "authentic" tasks. Wardekker et al. (2011) maintain that schooling practices should connect as much as possible to activities children are engaged with outside of school. They write: "Our argument is that to engage young people's motivation, schools should make the relation of the curriculum to the students' experiences of practices outside the school explicit" (p. 156. cf. Ciani, Ferguson, Bergin, & Hilpert, 2010; Tharp & Gallmore, 1988). Wardekker and colleagues' position is that motivation will be generated if students discover the use-value of school practices or concepts within their existing nonschool activity. But, Säljö and Wyndhamm's (1993) insight that schooling shapes any task it incorporates confounds the claim that outside activities remain at all the same when they are leveraged by teachers; there is an issue, in other words, assuming commensurability of conceptual and material artifacts across various activities—a problem captured persuasively by Jean Lave's classic computational studies (Lave, 1988). "Authentic" activities may also refer to projects that are specially designed by a teacher on an ad hoc basis, perhaps in collaboration with a community organization. In contrast to the design Wardekker and colleagues propose, use-value as a "motivator" cannot be assumed within this approach but instead may be an emergent property of participation in a project. It is therefore doubtful that motivational dynamics are equivalent between these two design alternatives; this is a matter for future research.

Second, especially in ad hoc project-based designs involving "real world" initiatives, it is easy to overstate the authenticity of the resulting work while also underestimating both the transformation and the maintenance of schooling practices. Ironically, the rising acceptance of situated theories of learning might be contributing to this, where the design impulse is to stage apprenticeships in the cognitive and social practices of different disciplinary communities. As Hickey and Zuiker (2006) write:

> one should look to the knowledge practices [of disciplinary communities] themselves for the goals and values that motivated knowledge communities to construct and continually refine that knowledge. Ultimately, these goals and values concern the fundamental desire to participate more meaningfully in the knowledge practices of those communities. (p. 285)

The small group interactions presented as illustrations in this chapter suggest that group members might indeed participate in practices of different disciplinary communities during ad hoc projects designed for this purpose, but their participation cannot be understood as equivalent to workers engaged in the same practices (Popkewitz, 2007). We therefore believe strong claims of the authenticity of apprenticeship designs should be adopted cautiously. This complex tension has been expressed by Martin Packer (2001): "attempts to bring 'real-world' problems into the school classroom will founder on the fact that the tasks cannot remain the same. Because the social relations and cultural resources of the classroom are inevitably different from those in the real world, the tasks are always transformed" (p. 500). Our working hypothesis was that one of the likely ways tasks are mutually transformed is through the co-emergence and coordination of motives across activities. The main aim of our research was therefore to understand how the motives of different social activities are leveraged to facilitate children's adoption of culturally valued, school-related goals, particularly "learning *as such*" (Dewey, 1899, p. 466, emphasis added) or *learning activity* (Hedegaard & Lompscher, 1999).

Achievement Goal Theory: Moving Research Around the Sociocultural Turn

The issue of children's adoption of learning goals has been prominently approached using achievement goal theory. Achievement goals are defined as a comprehensive psychological "program" with "cognitive, affective, and behavioral consequences" (Elliot & Dweck, 1988, p. 11) that involves "ways of thinking about oneself, one's task and task outcomes" (Ames, 1992, p. 262). Researchers have concluded that the purposes for engaging in achievement behavior can meaningfully be categorized into two types of goals: *performance goals* and *mastery goals*. Performance goals involve engaging in achievement behaviors for the purpose of demonstrating one's competence. Mastery goals, on the other hand, involve engaging in achievement behaviors in order to develop one's competence. In general, mastery goals have been shown to relate to a host of beneficial educational beliefs and behaviors, whereas performance goals have been related to a mix of beneficial and maladaptive beliefs and behaviors. Implicit in achievement goal theory is a normative valuation of mastery over performance goals; however, it is increasingly believed that students can adopt multiple goals (e.g., Pintrich, 2000) and that some degree of performance orientation can contribute productively to achievement outcomes.

There is a general consensus that goal orientations can shift over time and across contexts. In educational environments, goal orientation may be prompted by perceptions of classroom features such as overt and tacit messages from the teacher, routine practices such as feedback methods, and collaborative versus competitive classroom arrangements (Ames, 1992; Meece, Anderman, & Anderman, 2006; Patrick, Anderman, Ryan, Edelin, & Midgley, 2001). These elements of the classroom and school environment have come to be known as "goal structures." Our argument is that goal structures are better conceived as constitutive features of social activities that are directed by objects/motives and shared or not shared by members, of which surface features of the classroom or school are only one aspect.

Over the last decade, some achievement goal theorists have begun to acknowledge the deeper structures of classroom arrangements and have been explicitly working to conceptualize motivation in increasingly social terms. Researchers have begun paying closer attention to the affective domain and to "context." This has resulted in an expanded view of motivational affordances and a more complex view of goals, yet scholars criticize achievement goal theorists for still tacitly maintaining a separation between the affective and the cognitive, the individual and the environment (Hickey, 2003; Hickey & Zuiker, 2006; Nolen et al., 2011). These criticisms have as their targets the tacitly maintained assumptions regarding what constitutes "social influences." For example, psychologists who have found relationships among children's successful social adjustment to school and a mastery orientation to learning still often approach the domains as independent and needing to be linked through statistical correlation (see, e.g., Ryan & Shim, 2008). Such projects are concerned that antagonism between the social/emotional and intellectual domains will shape motivation and intellectual development in potentially negative ways. These domains and outcomes are approached as mutually reinforcing but nonetheless separate. An argument against this approach to studying affective and psychological processes was made by Elkonin (1972):

> Such an approach, first of all, views the child as an isolated individual for whom society is merely 'an environing habitat' sui generis. Second, mental development is viewed merely as the process of adaptation to the conditions of life in society. Third, society is seen as the union of two mutually disjoint elements, a 'world of things' and a 'world of people,' both of which are primordial elements of the given in this 'environing habitat.' Fourth, it is the development of two fundamentally distinct sets of adaptive mechanisms – for adaptation to the 'world of things' and to the 'world of people' – that constitutes mental development. (p. 234)

Elkonin's challenge was to form an integrated framework for understanding social, emotional, and cognitive aspects of learning and development. Many motivation scholars, however, still maintain the dualistic assumptions Elkonin described. For example, Poortvliet and Darnon

(2010) studied the usual relationship in its inverse direction—how achievement goals influence social interaction and observed at the outset "that achievement situations are *often* embedded in social contexts and that individuals are *often* interdependent with their peers and coworkers" (p. 327, emphasis added). This suggests the existence of times when achievement situations are not embedded in social contexts. Likewise, Järvelä, Volet, and Järvenoja (2010) argued, "although motivation is an essential component of successful collaborative learning, students' motivation is continually challenged" (p. 17), requiring special effort for individuals to "restore their motivation and engagement" (p. 20). The implication is that thoughts, actions, and emotions that pull individuals "off task" have nothing to do with motivation per se besides interrupting it. In both of these studies, motivation is not seen as a naturally occurring element of human activity but a special property of individuals that fluctuates along a singular pathway—school activity—depending on a right set of environmental conditions.

The dualism between social and intellectual domains may also be perpetuated in subtle and unintended ways even in recent studies operating under "situated" assumptions. Gresalfi (2009) critiqued traditional achievement goal theory for reasons cited previously and conceived of focal classrooms as "a system of social practice that includes patterns of interaction, understandings, assumptions, attitudes, norms that serve to organize activity" (p. 330). She proposed that motivation and cognition are integrated as *dispositions* toward academic practices and are therefore shared among members in a classroom rather than individual properties. Gresalfi's study usefully illustrated how, in collaborative workgroups, children can collectively generate and take up dispositions toward mathematical practices. This facilitates a conception of mathematics as a fundamentally social practice and of students as participants in a classroom system of which motivation is a part. In this sense, Gresalfi's work represents an advance over studies that approach the need-motivational or affective sphere and intellectual development as correlated but ultimately separate. However, the study categorically excluded "off-task behavior" and coded social interactions only as they related to prescribed academic tasks. These methodological choices were, no doubt, limited by the scope of the study, but they also may continue to tacitly align motivation itself with being "on task" and thus overlook other regions of classroom and social practices that are implicated in learning and development and to which even seemingly on-task behaviors might be subordinated.

Finally, a subtle bias is also detectable in one other methodological element that appears in much of the recent research seeking to view motivation socially, including the work we present. The favored loci of these studies are highly collaborative, inquiry-based classroom settings (e.g., Järvelä et al., 2010; Morrone, Harkness, D'Ambrosio, & Caulfield, 2004; Turner & Patrick, 2008). There is good reason to make this sampling choice; since in situ research approaches largely depend on discourse-based rather than self-report survey data, it is necessary to capture situations where a lot of student talk can be recorded.

In a cultural-historical framework, however, a high degree of student involvement does not make learning through groupwork any more fundamentally social than a classroom organized around didactic instruction. In our own data, for instance, whole-class teaching often followed the initiate-respond-evaluate (I-R-E) format, a practice that achievement goal theorists have argued inadequately scaffolds learning (Turner, 2001). The teacher's use of this practice did not inhibit children's skilled participation either as classroom members or on meaningful tasks throughout the unit we studied. In fact, it appears that skilled participation in I-R-E lessons was prized even among some reluctant students in the class. If motivation and learning are fundamentally social, they are social at all times under all circumstances, not just when classrooms are organized around groupwork; learning to respond skillfully to teacher questions is as much a social activity as learning by working in groups (Matusov, Bell, & Rogoff, 2002). The favoring of collaborative arrangements in classroom research suggests that normative preferences for particular instructional approaches—which often do anecdotally appear to generate student interest more than didactic lessons—could be obscuring broader understanding of how schooling functions as a socially motivated activity at its core.

Cultural-Historical Conceptions of the Motive

A. N. Leont'ev (1978) developed what has become a canonical model and unit of analysis of human activity, particularly concerning *motive*: "in society a man finds not simply external conditions to which he must accommodate his activity, but that these same social conditions carry in themselves motives and goals of activity, his means and methods; in a word, society produces the activity of the individuals forming it" (p. 51). Leont'ev defines *need* as a directionless condition that finds its direction in practical human activity. "Only as a result of its 'meeting' with an object that answers it does [need] first become capable of directing and regulating activity" (p. 54). This position further holds that basic needs are not merely biological but arc culturally evolved; Miettinen (2005), for example, has argued that "need for recognition" within social practices and communities is foundational to psychological and social functioning in work organizations. Leont'ev's formulation, he argues, "is an argument against the long- standing tradition in psychology that sees the organic needs of the individual as the foundation of human motivation" (p. 54). The need for recognition becomes "functionally autonomous from biological needs" upon the emergence of a societal division of labor. At this point, needs become disconnected from biological needs and are culturally mediated. Hedegaard (2011) juxtaposes this conception with humanistic and social cognitive theories, which locate various levels of biological and social needs within the individual and posit that the individual is innately growth oriented and pursues need satisfaction through the formation of conscious goals.

Leont'ev developed his triadic conception of *activity* to understand how needs are objectified socially and materially, directing not only the actions of the subject but also the coordination with other individuals. Central to his model is the notion of *object. Object of activity* is historically formed through processes of socialization into work, which then becomes reflected in individual consciousness through participation in respective social practices—forming the basis for evolution of *needs.* (Arguably, a similar conception was the basis of Dewey's educational philosophy of *experience,* especially the principle of *interest*—see Miettinen, 2003, 2005.) *Object,* Leont'ev writes, is activity's "true motive."

One more point bears mentioning regarding how the concept of motive has evolved in activity theory: the practical inseparability of activity, learning, and identity in studies of motivation (Hickey, 2003; Nolen et al., 2011). While it is possible to foreground one of these aspects in analyses of school situations, one cannot, within what Hedegaard (2011) calls "wholeness" approaches, fully bracket other aspects of social life without distorting the focal phenomenon. Packer (2001) puts it the following way:

> schools engage in the practical and political matter of transforming the kind of person a child becomes ... Schools do not simply prepare 'problem solvers' of a particular kind, they help transform children into the workers and citizens who will reproduce our society, or who will transform it. (pp. 501–502)

Demonstrating "motivation to learn," in other words, inherently makes someone a particular kind of person in school; schools are not just promoters of learning but "sites for the production of persons" (Packer & Greco-Brooks, 1999). Being "unmotivated" therefore also makes someone a particular kind of person with respect to school practices, especially if this orientation leads to offending actions that recur over time. Polivanova's (2006) discussion of leading activity in adolescence is instructive here. She writes: "leading activity [is] (a) an *activity for the reproduction of human culture* and (b) a mechanism, specific to a given age, for the development of subjecthood" (p. 79); studies of motivation are therefore necessarily also studies of subjecthood. We return to this point later in order to express the developmental significance of children's adoption of learning goals in the broader context of "school-going" and other content-related activities.

Based on the issues raised about motivation-related goals in the context of a project-based collaborative unit, we now explore the ways students jointly engage in learning as a multi-motivated activity—in other words, how their actions shape possibilities for learning during activities with embedded goals.

Illustrating Multi-motivated Activities in the Classroom

We have chosen to illustrate our exploration of students' joint engagement in learning as a multi-motivated activity in a specific context: one seventh grade social studies class conducting an interdisciplinary curriculum unit that sought to integrate both academic and "real world" aims. This interdisciplinary unit was intended to teach children about civil rights from 1954 to 1964 through interviewing local citizens involved in the movement and then publishing biographies for distribution at a local library (see Sutter & Grensjo, 1988 for description of a project with similar aims). The examples presented here are from audio recordings of small groups of children as they worked together on tasks prescribed by the teacher and required by the evolution of project goals.

Children's collaborative efforts throughout the unit were structured to produce: bound biographies of local citizens engaged in the civil rights movement to be given to the African American special collection of a nearby University library and a stage performance in which students delivered short oral and photographic narratives about each interviewee, presented to a large audience consisting of parents, community leaders, and the interviewees themselves. Moreover, both products were explicitly intended to demonstrate children's conceptual development with respect to state curricular standards in History and Language Arts as well as development of research skills.

Children were assigned to groups of four by the teacher, and each group was assigned one community member to interview, write about, and profile in a presentation. We were particularly interested in motivational dynamics as they occurred during children's work together in their small groups, toward products that were meaningfully related to the goals of the overall unit. We conceived of these products of the children's work (e.g., interview protocols and interviews, biographical narratives) as objects of the children's activity and the periods of work throughout these phases as examples of "joint productive activity" (Tharp, 2005).

Specifically, we will use dialogue excerpts from the class to illustrate the tensions and resolutions of multiple motivations within activities and resolutions of those tensions toward learning. The illustrations included in this chapter come from one group that was assigned to interview and write about a leader from the community who was involved in national politics during the civil rights era.

In the larger study from which these excerpts are taken, we merged methods from Tharp (2005) and Barab and colleagues (Barab, Barnett, & Yamagata-Lynch, 2002; Barab, Hay, & Yamagata-Lynch, 2001). We began analysis with the Activity Setting Observation System (Tharp, 2005) to isolate episodes of joint productive activity where students worked in small groups to produce project-relevant artifacts. This resulted in focal episodes that were transcribed. We labeled these "episodes of work" and noted what the main tasks were in each episode. Lastly, we adapted from Gresalfi (2009) in inferring the forcefulness of dilemmas, to see which persisted and which were of little consequence.

Tension and Resolution Across Motivated Activities

Excerpts from transcribed group data are presented and described below to illustrate the emergence and resolution of dilemmas across three main activities: (1) "school-going," (2) "doing history," and (3) peer social relations.

"School-going" has been widely characterized in the cultural-historical literature as willing compliance with the normative demands of school without a corresponding personal investment in substantive learning.

Miettinen (2003) describes "school learning" as "characterized by memorization and reproduction of school texts. It is accompanied by an instrumental motivation of school success that tends to eliminate substantive interest in the phenomena and knowledge to be studied" (p. 325). For Engeström (1987), school-going predominates when children identify with school's *exchange value* over its *use-value* (see also Esmonde, Takeuchi, & Dradakovic, 2011; Lave, 1990; Lave & McDermott, 2002).

When we began the study, we anticipated and were sensitive to "pervasive tensions" that would exist between school-going and doing history. Barab et al. (2002) locate these tensions in the use/exchange value distinction, differentiating between "learning the material to receive a grade... and learning material because of its importance in addressing real-world problems" (p. 80). "Tensions are critical," they write, "to understanding what motivated particular actions and in understanding the evolution of a system more generally" (IBID). Substantial sections of our data, however, consisted of a more socially oriented talk especially between students Faith and Michael. Often this talk incorporated or related to academic content; we were therefore unwilling to disregard it as irrelevant to tasks at hand or accordingly to the adoption of school-related goals. We focus especially on Michael's participation in the unit since the three activity domains are negotiated most evidently in his case. Also, his participation changed most significantly in this unit as compared to previous ones "as if a spotlight was turned on behind him" as his teacher said; he was a vocal contributor during whole-class discussions, worked diligently on his written narrative, and developed a personal connection to his interviewee. In the discussion that follows, we argue for the importance of increased attention to this phenomenon with respect to motivation and activity, especially at the middle-school level.

Excerpts 1–3: Starting to Do Background Research for Interview Questions

The group had been instructed to conduct background research using classroom materials in order to prepare questions for an upcoming interview with George T, a prominent Black civic leader. Up until this point, children worked individually on this task. Students consulted a book about Black citizens in Maine, which George T authored. Here the use of the book was meant to generate a list of historical facts about their interviewee that would spur questions about his personal biography and experience, to be used in preparing their own narratives. They have been given template worksheets to use to take notes during their research.

Episode 1

Mrs. L: [to the whole class] If I am hearing conversation with your group I am

1. going to be confident that it's going to be on task. Maybe you could start by sharing
2. what you've learned so far since you haven't been working together.
3. Faith: I haven't learned very much. [said to her group]
4. Michael: *I have.*
5. Faith: Well, *you* can share Michael.
6. Mrs. L: There's some links out there... [said to the whole class]
7. Michael: *Yeah,* Faith.
8. Mrs. L: [said to Michael's group] When they're done with that book we might pass
9. that book around—that whole book was written by George T.
10. Faith: Oh, really.
11. Maddie: You all have George T?
12. Faith: Yeah, we don't have to go to the nursing home.
13. Michael: BTW, I'm left handed.
14. Faith: BTW, I'm right handed.
15. Michael: Well, left handers need their space.
16. Faith: Do you want to switch seats?
17. Michael: That would make sense.

In this excerpt, Mrs. L initiates the long period of groupwork that will follow, by expressing normative expectations for conduct—remaining on task—indicating that social banter is disallowed. She also indicates what on-task talk should consist of, taking turns sharing the results of independent research. Faith complies with Mrs. L's directive in line 3. In line 4, Michael also complies with the directive in a backhanded way—he still is within the parameters of acceptable behavior—but he jokes with Faith about his superior ability to have done research. Picking up on this, in line 5, Faith returns the joke by putting Michael in the position of needing to comply with Mrs. L's directive—it is debatable whether he can do this because it is unlikely he did the initial research. The joke is not finished; Mrs. L continues to frame the group's tasks, which Michael uses as an opportunity to validate the possibility that he did indeed complete the research. In lines 12–18, students carry on a previous conversation about another group's interviewee, and Faith and Michael engage in a more "pure" social activity, chatting informally a bit more before starting their work.

Michael and Faith's friendship and their identities as students are evident here. Mrs. L's directives are appropriated into their social activity by becoming the basis of a joke, which depends on shared knowledge of differences in their standings as "good students." They are in one sense doing school-going by complying with the directives, and they are in another sense doing exactly what Mrs. L has prohibited, since the interaction is really a series of friendly put-downs and not sincere compliance with the request to share research findings (which they do not get to for several more moments). Here, peer social relations is the dominant or "socially significant" activity (Elkonin, 1972; Polivanova, 2006), to which school-going is subordinated, helping in the moment to resolve an ongoing dilemma for Michael as someone who often comes to class disorganized and unprepared (despite his strong participation in the larger learning goals of the unit).

Episode 2

1. Michael: Which page?
2. Faith: Under "Small Acts of Courage" there's – No wait, under "civil rights" –
3. Michael: T.
4. Faith: No. Under civil rights research I would take "Local NAACP."
5. Michael: Or if you were smart like Michael, you'd do this.
6. Faith: Yeah but we don't need to know about him, we are going to learn about him.
7. Michael: Exactly. I just learned like a whole bunch of junk about him.
8. Faith: You don't want to learn about him. You want to learn about him when we
9. interview him. Not
10. Michael: Ohhh, I gotchu.
11. Faith: Yeah, that's the point of the interview.
12. Michael: Oh, yeah. So not about T. About T's part in the civil rights movement.
13. Ahh…

Here, Michael has approached the task at hand as one of directly researching biographical information on George T in order to complete a worksheet the teacher has given them; Faith has understood (correctly) the task to be researching George T's involvement in important events, completing the worksheet to use as a guide in later designing interview questions.

Michael makes their identities as students salient again in his joke "if you were smart like Michael" in line 5, but he clearly does not yet grasp the object they are working toward, shaping immediate task involvement as well as long-term project success. Faith helps him understand the difference between consulting a book for the purpose of completing a worksheet and doing research for the purpose of designing good questions that will produce substantive responses from their interviewee; progress is impeded without this understanding. This reveals a dilemma: Michael needs to grasp the object of an interview in order to contribute beyond rote performances of schoolwork, which would not serve the "real world" requirements of the project. This can be understood not merely as Michael "getting it" but the alignment between "'a generalized object of a historically evolving activity system' and a specific object as it appears to a particular subject at a given moment" (Engeström, Puonti, & Seppänen, 2003, in Miettinen, 2005, p. 57). This was a crucial step in Michael's appropriation of school-related goals in this unit, becoming a participant in the learning activity so that he can to contribute to the project.

Episode 3

1. Mrs. L: [comes over to this group] Alright, did everybody add to theirs [worksheet]?
2. Faith and Michael: [said concurrently] Yeah.
3. Mrs. L: Yeah? OK, is there something you still want to know?
4. Faith: Like, we found out information we just have like follow up questions.
5. Mrs. L: OK good, so somebody keep that.
6. Faith: Michael keep it.
7. Michael: I'm going to lose it.
8. Faith: Oh, Michael!
9. Michael: I lose everything.

In this episode, from much later in the class, after considerable productive time spent researching, Mrs. L comes around to check and see if students completed their worksheets. (Progress on the worksheets extended across multiple class sessions.) Faith indicates their progress, and Mrs. L instructs the group to keep track of the worksheet—which really is a crucial tool for progress in the first phase of the unit. Faith both initiates a joke and issues Michael a sincere directive as a groupmate in lines 6–9.

Faith and Michael's identities as students are again made salient. Given their other exchanges, it is likely that Faith knows that Michael is unreliable in precisely the way she is indicating, a fact that he willingly admits. She feigns exasperation, giving an indication of another feature of their friendship—that he sincerely relies on her to participate successfully in class (a point he also disclosed in an informal discussion when asked about relationships with others in the class). Here peer social relations are subordinated to school-going—complying with the teacher's directives to manage a worksheet—and marginally doing history, which has not emerged as a dominant activity yet at this point, except perhaps to Faith. The dilemma this resolves is that Michael has preemptively given himself an excuse if he loses the worksheet, as well as providing an opportunity to demonstrate responsibility if he successfully manages it for the group.

Excerpts 4–6: Continuing to Prepare Interview Questions
Groups have made slight progress on their research for the interview, which they continue to document on the worksheet.

Episode 4

1. Faith: I think we have enough questions, 'cause he's going to talk.
2. Sarah: Yeah.
3. Faith: Now we have to just get Juan caught up.
4. Michael: Ahhhh.
5. Faith: OK. Can I write? Oh, we each write.
6. Michael: We have our own, *Faith*. [emphasizes her name sarcastically]
7. Faith: Well, sorry. OK. So...
8. Mrs. L: Alright, so, a good first question. What do you think a good first question
9. would be?
10. Faith: What led you to be involved with the NAACP?
11. Mrs. L: Even—make it even broader.
12. Faith: Um, civil rights?
13. Mrs. L: So, "Can you tell us...can you share with us" what?

14. Faith: [unintelligible]
15. Mrs. L: "Your experiences in the Civil Rights Movement?"
16. Faith: Yeah.
17. Mrs. L: So, all of you write that down.
18. Michael: Under "questions?"
19. Mrs. L: Yup.

Several things are occurring in this excerpt. First, with Juan absent and the group starting to formulate questions, it is important that he "be brought up to speed" otherwise he will not know what to do in later phases of the interview preparation and possibly, the interview. In lines 5–7, Faith and Michael continue their running joke about their standing as students; Michael chides her for failing to follow the prescribed directions for completing the interview questions. Faith's misstep may be attributable to the fact that, in actuality, only one master sheet of interview questions is required for a successful interview, but for assessment and accountability purposes, each student has been directed to complete a question worksheet (completing school materials and doing what is really necessary to perform a successful interview is one ongoing aspect of the pervasive tension here between schooling and "real world" activity). In line 8, Mrs. L focuses students on the task at hand, which is to start to develop workable interview questions. At this point, the worksheet still figures prominently in their work, so compliance with it is important.

There are three dilemmas that arise in this episode, involving the structure of the overall unit as a collaborative learning exercise, the real-world demands of conducting an interview, and Faith, Michael, and now Juan's identities as students. The first dilemma emerges and is resolved in lines 3–4. Juan, a student who also often struggles in school, was absent on a critical day. The group structure (and the much-emphasized classroom/school culture of mutual support) is a resource here for maintaining Juan's ability to stay engaged in the unit. There is a deeper dilemma below the surface though, and this is spurred by the increasing realization of what the interview will entail. It has become clear to students that they will each have a role in the interview and therefore, that they each need to be prepared. If Juan came unprepared for whatever reason, it could cause embarrassment during the interview and reflect badly on the entire group. The final, related dilemma deals with the ongoing tension between conducting a "real world" interview and fulfilling school tasks in a way that evidences learning; completing the worksheet satisfies both. In this episode, doing history is starting to emerge as a socially significant activity. It is not yet clear if it has become dominant for any of the children yet.

Episode 5

1. Mrs. L: [comes over to this group and listens in to Faith reading] So, stop for a
2. second. Where did he, where did he experience discrimination? Can you guys have your
3. timelines out for me so I can give you – [referring to her going around and checking
4. people's timelines of the civil rights movement]
5. Faith: Mine's out.
6. Michael: I didn't finish my timeline. I didn't finish my timeline.
7. Mrs. L: OK. That isn't going in as a grade, so that needs to be a priority today. OK,
8. Michael? Can I see how much you've got done?
9. Michael: [going through stuff – for 5 seconds]
10. Mrs. L: It's really important that you don't fall behind. OK?
11. Michael: Hmm mmm.
12. Mrs. L: And, it would be much better if we were organized. What are you doing
13. during supervised study today?
14. Michael: Nothing.
15. Mrs. L: Can you come in my room?
16. Michael: Yeah.
17. Mrs. L: And maybe work on getting organized?

Throughout the unit, Mrs. L checked each group's progress as well as the independent assignments they were supposed to be completing. In this episode, she is checking on a timeline of major civil rights events; whole-class time was often spent reviewing the "background knowledge" and helping students put their interview subjects' biography into that context. The difference in Faith's and Michael's identities is apparent here as well; however, it does not become the basis of a joke; Mrs. L "turns non-instruction into instruction" (Tharp, 2005) by giving a meta-level message about the importance of organization and keeping up with the class.

The dominant activity in this episode is school-going. This bears on Faith's and Michael's differing identities, their shared knowledge of which is not used as a resource for a joke but becomes solidified in the resolution of the dilemma—Michael requires remedial work and Faith does not. Peer social relations are subordinated to school-going (i.e., the dilemma is resolved through school-going practice and not peer practice—e.g., joking about one's identity).

Episode 6

1. Sarah: So far we have six questions, so that's two questions for each person.
2. Faith: Umm...we are looking at one [unclear]
3. Faith: What were some...we have so many follow up questions. I'm just not sure if
4. that's enough. There's four of us.
5. Sarah: I don't know. I know we are going to have a lot of other questions [unclear] and
6. we have six questions. If we get two more questions 'cause like just in case it's like we
7. need something extra.
8. Faith: Umm...
9. Sarah: So I really doubt that but...
10. Faith: I just don't, I like I don't want to like be caught, like at least she can say, "well
11. he'll talk a lot [unclear] but like I just feel like, I don't want like [unclear] us and being done with
12. our questions like and be like "what do we ask now!"
13. Sarah and Faith: [laughter]
14. Sarah: Yeah.

Students are making progress on their interview worksheet and are starting to determine how many questions they will need not only to complete the interview but to establish an equitable division of labor within it. Two dilemmas emerge in this episode: the first concerns balancing the participation structure that working in a group represents, which constrains the number of questions (keeping things roughly equal among members); the second concerns the social norms of demonstrating adequate preparation for an interview. These are related dilemmas and the goal of practically satisfying one affects the goal of satisfying the other. Faith and Sarah both grasp each of the dilemmas—Faith correcting Sarah and preventing a miscalculation; Sarah recognizing the need for "something extra" in line 7 and Faith not wanting to "be caught" and in a situation "like, *what do we do now?*" This shared concern suggests that doing history—which is partly constituted by the practice of conducting biographical interviews in the context of major social movements and political events—might be emerging as the dominant activity for Sarah and Faith, superseding school-going which would have defined the dilemma as, perhaps, how many questions would it take to fill boxes on the worksheet. This further suggests that the students understand the nature of the object of interviewing, grasp its motive (i.e., are "motivated" to conduct it in a way that generates good responses), and are independently managing resources for this purpose. Here the academic content (background knowledge) that could have been used as a resource for school-going (completing the worksheets) will have increasing value for doing the interview well, that is, academic concepts have use-value in learning.

Excerpts 7–8: Getting Ready for Interview
By now students have developed their interview questions and are preparing for the actual interview itself. Attention has shifted from completing worksheets and refining questions to the imminent performance of the interview. On this day, Faith was absent due to illness and there was some doubt whether she would be well enough to return for the interview.

Episode 7

1. Juan: You think you can type it all?
2. Michael: What?
3. Juan: You think you can type it all?
4. Michael: A what?
5. Juan: Do you think you type it all?
6. Michael: I don't know. I thought we were going to have to do our separate ones, but
7. I can make three.
8. Juan: What about Faith?
9. Michael: Oh, Faith? Oh, Faith. *Oh, Faith....*
10. Juan: Just like print out an extra one.
11. Michael: Aiight.
12. Juan: Just in case she does come.
13. Michael: Aiight son. So... [15 second pause]
14. Michael: Do I have to have the introduction crap stuff?

15. Juan: You wanted it. No, you should put it. Just put 'intro.' This back part don't type it.
16. Michael: I know, it's already typed. It'd be like wasting my time.

With Faith absent and the interview impending, Michael and Juan are both faced with the task of executing the final steps involved in preparation and preparing for the possibility that she will or will not come on the actual interview day. Juan presses upon Michael to take the final steps in preparing the master question sheet, and on line 6 Michael figures out that this is the task at hand, not doing individual worksheets as before. On line 12 Juan reminds Michael that Faith could arrive in time, and it is unclear whether Michael jokes about the fact that she might let them down by not coming or is, in effect, pleading for her help. Either way, the comment signals again their identities and the central dilemma here—she as the more capable student who often helps him because he is disorganized and often unprepared in many of his classes. Without her, Michael embraces the crucial task of finalizing the group's interview questions.

The dominant activity remains doing history and the object of conducting a successful interview subordinates both the activities of school-going and peer social relations. Michael's willingness to type up the interview sheet, and his joke/plead about Faith, suggests that the social dilemma is solvable because of his growing competence as a lay historian and his increasing trustworthiness as a group member (he might expect that Faith will evaluate his performance upon her return). Conversely, though, Juan's comment "you wanted it" on line 15 suggests Juan is sympathetic to the fact that Michael has just taken on more work, indicating the ongoing salience of both school-going and peer social relations—specifically the comparable identities of Michael and Juan in the wider school, which are likely shaped by their mutual participation in school-going. There is a weak dilemma between tasks constituting school-going and doing history, revolving around the question of whether or not the task should be approached like completing a worksheet (getting it done) or to produce a tool with use-value during the interview. Michael's decision not to "waste his time" by retyping "the introduction crap stuff" indicates his understanding of the object of the interview and the independence and confidence to economize labor and not merely comply with a teacher's directive.

Episode 8

1. Juan: Well, once we get to follow ups and we have a follow up and he answers the good
2. questions [unclear] like should the follow up be *after* he stops talking or…
3. Michael: Well, so, I think it should be like after I ask anything else, um, you would
4. like to share with us, um, I don't know.
5. Juan: So, should the follow ups be *after* the questions?
6. Sarah: Yes, well, if you have, um, a follow up a question while he's writing – not
7. writing, while he's talking – um, and there's another questions that's already on the
8. list afterwards we'd ask the follow up question after the question on the list because
9. it's more important: we're staying on the same subject.
10. Juan: What if we *all* get the same follow up question?
11. Sarah: Then someone could just say the question.
12. Michael: So, like we have it down on stickies and then after we ask him "anything
13. else you would like to share with us" he shares whatever he has to share, we pause –
14. Juan: But, what if we have a follow up question for what he has to share?
15. Michael: Yeah, that pause should be for follow up questions. Wait a second and
16. then like whoever wants to go, goes and stuff.
17. Sarah: OK.
18. Michael: So, yeah.
19. Juan: So follow ups at the end?
20. Michael: Yeah…

Here students are deciding how to handle asking follow-up questions. Juan presses on the issue, in likely anticipation of the fumbling around that could occur during the interview if they did not have a plan worked out in advance. Mrs. L has reinforced the value of both staying organized and asking follow-up questions. An additional factor here is the collaborative format of the unit, which complicates how asking follow-up questions should occur (see line 10). Michael's suggestion to insert a pause after questioning is over is taken up by Sarah and Juan, helping reach the resolution that follow-ups will occur at the end.

The central tension here is between school-going and doing history. This creates a dilemma that must be resolved: Mrs. L's directive to stay organized and group-like questions together introduces the problem of how to insert follow-up questions, which is not only a confounding directive but a problem that is compounded by the ongoing issue of conducting the interview as a group. Moreover, Mrs. L's directive to keep like questions together is informed by her awareness of the next-level object in the progression of the unit: writing up the interview thematically. Therefore, the directive *as such* is part of school-going and it establishes the grounds for use-value of the interview data and is therefore also part of the activity doing history, which later involves collating themes based on interview data. Sarah, who may or may not yet fully envision the next-level object in the unit, proposes that "staying on the same subject" should determine the strategy. This suggests that school-going could be a dominant activity for her, while for Juan and Michael, who anticipate the social embarrassment this could cause during the interview, performing well by staying fluidly organized in situ establishes the grounds for the resolution. Michael's incorporation of "stickies" (line 12)—a common organizational tool/practice in the classroom—into the solution suggests that practices from schooling have become useful at solving problems that arise in their work as lay historians.

Dilemmas Within and Between Activities as Goal Structures: Issues for Development

Motivating children to learn is a central issue in schools; however, it is not a straightforward problem of designing clever lessons, adjusting the kind of messages one gives as a teacher, or threatening to penalize children if they fail to comply with directives. It is ultimately a developmental process of changing children's subjective orientation to life activities through participation in social practices of schooling. These same social practices, however, also structure children's social relations in ways that often coincide with a learning motive—either as subjects oriented to learning as a dominant activity, school-going as a dominant activity (probably occasionally producing learning as intended), or resisting school-going as a dominant activity.

These activities shape one another and largely constituted classroom motivation in the classroom under study.

Peer Social Relations, Motivation, and Development

Elkonin's (1972) developmental framework of *periodization* and recent elaborations on it by Polivanova (2006) and Hedegaard (2011) help us understand the significance of the relations between school-going and peer social relations (we discuss the potential for collaboratively "doing history" to alter these relations shortly). The particular phenomenon we are interested in here is what these relations say about motivation to learn, from a developmental standpoint, and how curricular designs shape situations by introducing a new socially significant activity in a way that alters these relations.

Working to overcome dualistic theories of development and building on activity-theoretical work by Vygotsky, Leont'ev, and others, D. B. Elkonin proposed a developmental scheme based on periods of development that are structured by dominant social activities at various age ranges. Elkonin (1972, p. 231) cited Leont'ev as follows:

> At a given stage some types of activity will be more prominent and more significant for the further development of the personality; others, less so. Some types will play a minor role. That is why we should speak of the dependence of mental development not on activity in general, but on the dominant form of activity. In accordance with this we might say that each stage of development is characterized by one dominant activity within that given stage. … The indication of a transition from one stage to another is precisely a shift in the dominant type of activity, the dominant relationship of the child to his surroundings. (1965, pp. 501–502)

Elkonin outlined modern developmental periods roughly as *play–school (learning)–work* (see also Beach, 1995). At the transitions between these periods, individuals undergo qualitative transformations—the emotional and psychological conditions for adaptation within a stage having begun in the previous stage. In these periods, the need-motivational and cognitive or intellectual spheres are dialectically related, not opposed or parallel, and transitions are marked by crises where these spheres come into contradiction and define one another. It is the period "school learning" and the particular cognitive and need-motivational processes involved in it we are concerned with here.

In Elkonin's (1972) formulation, play establishes the conditions for adaptation within *learning* by fostering in young children a theoretical attitude to reality and an early orientation to adult division of labor. As children approach school, formal learning starts to predominate, and "it is this activity that mediates the whole system of the child's relations with surrounding adults (down to personal contact with the family)" (p. 244). Early formal schooling thus establishes the dominant motive for children's activity, that is, *learning*. Incompatibility between family or community and schooling practices presents special difficulties for children. Moreover, the introduction of schooling practices into children's activity can create changes in family and community routines, effectively incorporating adults into the activity that now dominates (Fleer, 2011; Hedegaard, 2011; Rogoff, 2003).

As children approach adolescence, however, a new motive emerges. Elkonin notes the difficulty of detecting the emergence of this motive, in large part because "the primary activity is still school studies ...for adults, success or failure in school continues to serve as the principal criterion for evaluating adolescents," and "the transition to adolescence is not accompanied by any substantial outward changes" (p. 244). In other words, it looks to observers as if adolescents are still either "doing school" or engaged in "formal learning." What emerges as the dominant "special" activity in this period, Elkonin argues, is "the establishment of intimate personal relations between adolescents," or "the activity of social contact ... Its principal content concerns another adolescent as a human being with definite personal qualities" (p. 245).

In play, young children learn by separating concrete activity from the *social meaning* of objects and relations. For example, children playing "dinnertime" not only learn their relationship to *things*, they learn the social roles of adults participating in ritualized community and economic activity. This establishes the conditions for successful (or unsuccessful) participation in situations characterized by practices of formal learning or learning *as such*. As for what happens as children approach adolescence, Elkonin is worth quoting here:

> In all forms of collective activity among adolescents, we can observe how relations are subordinated to a "code of friendship." ...the code of friendship reproduces in its objective content the most universal forms of interrelations

> that hold for adults in society. . . .it is reasonable to assume that the dominant activity during this period is social contact, the activity of building relations with friends on the basis of definite moral and ethical norms that mediate the actions of adolescents. (p. 245)

In young children's play, the relations between participation in social situations and leading activity are *discontinuous*—children play at specific things (e.g., "mommy and baby") but orient themselves within social objects of adult activity. Polivanova (2006) calls this "nonidentity of content and plot" (p. 81). This disjuncture establishes the grounds for theoretical conceptions of reality which are crucial for learning. At adolescence, the relations between participation in social situations and leading activity are *continuous*—children's immediate social relations to one another are what orient them to social objects and relations in adult activity. Thus, at a crucial age in the institutional organization of schooling, children start to learn through their concrete social relations with one another that they are particular types of people with respect not only to their peers but to the activity of schooling which constitutes much of their activity and to adult activity which chronologically follows schooling. This process, Elkonin argues, establishes the need-motivational grounds for subsequent orientation to "vocational or career-oriented activity," which includes further identification with learning activity as it is conducted in school. Following this period is the point at which learning activity will emerge as the dominant motive for some, through which they will find and express their subjecthood. In other words, the specific way in which children experience the special activity of social contact in adolescence can establish *learning* as a leading activity and *motivation to learn* a relatively stable cognitive property of persons entering later adolescence and early adulthood.

Elkonin's formulation informs our discussion about "goal structures" and motivation in two key ways. First is the possible "nonidentity" between practical conduct in school situations and children's leading activity. This bears on the consideration of actions as "on task" or "off task" as evidence of motivation per se. Categorical inclusion or rejection of on- or off-task behavior as indicative of motivation does not serve our understanding of motivated behavior. Second is the recognition of *multiply motivated activity* as the determinant of intermediate goals that direct children's actions and which may create dilemmas that resolve in favor of conservation or expansion of one or more of the elemental activities. This bears on curricular designs that incorporate varying social and institutional practices. These are discussed below.

Inferences About Motivation from On- and Off-Task Behavior

Previously, we presented excerpts in which the pervasive tensions among various activities were most evident. At other times, group members talked more directly about their friends and social relations in the school, or they participated continuously in classroom lessons, or "did real history" by studying archives at the local library. All these activities, we are arguing, predominated at various times and also subordinated elements from one another in concrete social situations. All of them were constituted by learning and motivation; however, only at key times relatively late in the unit did the motive of *learning activity* become socially significant for many children.

It can be very difficult, therefore, to make inferences about motivation from empirical data if one assumes its source either to be an individual goal orientation or a particular set of surface-level classroom cues. Moreover, relating children's actions only to schooling practices—either in the form of a "performance" or a "mastery" response—is likely to continually reproduce a favorable bias to institutionalized schooling in fundamental conceptualizations of motivation, while also causing analysts to overlook the way schooling practices are implicated in other developmentally significant activities. Take, for instance, this short example from excerpt 1:

1. Mrs. L: [to the whole class] If I am hearing conversation with your group I am
2. going to be confident that it's going to be on task. Maybe you could start by sharing
3. what you've learned so far since you haven't been working together.
4. Faith: I haven't learned very much. [said to her group]
5. Michael: *I have.*
6. Faith: Well, *you* can share Michael.
7. Mrs. L: There's some links out there... [said to the whole class]
8. Michael: *Yeah,* Faith.

At the surface level, it might appear that the teacher is establishing conditions for collaborative work among students, a positive contributor to a "mastery climate." It would be erroneous though, in our estimation, to infer that Faith and Michael are either complying or not complying with Mrs. L's directive. Instead, we are arguing, they are incorporating the school practice of "complying with a directive" and "sharing" into their leading activity of *social contact*, which has as its object the working out of peer relations as they reproduce the world of adult social relations and thus forms a dominant motive. Moreover, this interaction signals Faith and Michael's varying orientations to *learning activity*—Faith as a good student who is generally motivated to learn and Michael as a reluctant participant in schooling who occasionally surprises and impresses adults with his intellectual capabilities and ability to produce high-quality work. It is therefore possible to see Michael at a crossroads with respect to the development of motivation to learn and the necessity of understanding what constitutes meaningful activity for him, if not school. His relationship to "motivation to learn," then, is critical to understanding his later opportunities and challenges he will likely experience. Omitting "off-task behavior" in conceptualizations of classroom/school motivation, especially at various developmental periods and age ranges, is therefore a serious omission, particularly in studies making claims about the "situated" nature of motivation.

Objects, Goals, and Practices

Leont'ev's (1978) decoupling of motives, goals, and conditions makes an important contribution to understanding how "real world" projects may function to motivate children to learn. Returning to Dewey, organizing school in the form of *occupations* would function by establishing intermediate goals that would link children's collaborative work with *both* the objects of various "forms of work carried on in social life" *and* learning *as such;* children's classroom activity would, for Dewey, be doubly motivated. He explains: "Children doubtless go to school to learn, but it has yet to be proved that learning occurs most adequately when it is made a separate conscious business. When treating it as a business of this sort tends to preclude the social sense which comes from sharing in an activity of common concern and value" (1916/1944, p. 42). Children's emotional investment in the outcomes of their practical conduct would increase the likelihood that they would recognize the need to apply concepts and skills in service of common aims not yet realized, exercising control of their own activity (Roth, 2011). "Learning" is a function of this process.

In the context of the question of how children can become motivated to learn in this manner, Roth (2011) discusses and explains a study by Leont'ev which examined children's interest and engagement in a flight lesson, finding that it increased when the goal was not to learn principles of flight but to make a model airplane fly a specified distance. The intermediate goal creates a "homology" of individual partial interests (getting a model plane to fly) and the collective, general interest (getting children to learn scientific principles of aerodynamics):

> The object/motive creates the children's orientation toward action, which, because of its dialectical relation to activity, provides for the sense of what the children do. Leont'ev points out that some types of object/motives such as those of gnostic [theoretical/school] nature, require complex forms and relations of actions that go beyond what the learner can do. Thus, to stimulate interest in gnostic goals, one should not exhibit those goals by telling students that it is important to know this or that. Rather, Leont'ev recommends creating an object/motive such that the possibilities arise for the (gnostic) goal to emerge in the pursuit of a concrete content. Because knowing enhances what a learner can do, s/he will be interested inherently in learning. (p. 55)

Dewey understood that conjoining school activity and "real world" activity functions to promote *learning* primarily through the coordination of motives and intermediate goals. The intermediate goals of socially meaningful activity cultivate *interest* that is both oriented to larger motives of social activity and can be interpreted by the teacher as an indication of children's emerging capabilities—the development of motivation. This is the methodological basis for Hedegaard's (2011) developmental theory of practice, which would analyze changing participation in practices across recurrent activity settings. Primary in this chapter are school-going, doing history, peer social relations, and later, learning.

Conclusion

Educators have long believed that engaging children in socially meaningful projects is "motivating" (Blumenfeld et al., 1991; Roth, 2011); however, researchers are only starting to fully grasp the contradictions between historical forms of activity and their influence on individuals' classroom motivation. This has recently led to academic interest in videogames

(Barab, Gresalfi, & Ingram-Noble, 2010), simulations (Jurow, 2005), and "real world" design features such as writing for an audience (Magnifico, 2010) as worthwhile educational activities and not merely as "devices of art to cover up the imposition" of institutional goals (Dewey, 1938, p. 19). But, such curricular models also need to be understood in their full complexity. In the cases we present, children were *neither* students in the conventional sense nor were they professional historical researchers since the overriding object was for them to *learn*. In addition, we have questioned whether either of these were leading activities for children we studied, suggesting instead that social contact with peers was the dominant motive in many instances. In terms of curriculum design, engagement in the learning activity that serves as the focus of the curriculum, or what some would call motivation to learn, can occur as a result of the compatibility and conflation of multiple motives—learning, interest, usefulness, social engagement—of the learner. Curriculum, explicitly or implicitly, engages students in multiple activity settings which may include compatible motives at different levels of proximity to the learning goal and which may be valued in the classroom setting. A motivation to learn is the result of the resolution of dilemmas between and within these multiple activity settings.

References

Ames, C. (1992). Classrooms: Goals, structures, and student motivation. *Journal of Educational Psychology, 84*(3), 261–271.

Ames, C., & Archer, J. (1988). Achievement goals in the classroom: Students learning strategies and motivation processes. *Journal of Educational Psychology, 80*(3), 260–267.

Barab, S. A., Hay, K. E., & Yamagata-Lynch, L. C. (2001). Constructing networks of activity: An in-situ research methodology. *The Journal of the Learning Sciences, 10*(1&2), 63–112.

Barab, S. A., Barnett, M., & Yamagata-Lynch, L. (2002). Using activity theory to understand the systemic tensions characterizing a technology rich introductory astronomy course. *Mind, Culture, and Activity, 9*(2), 76–107.

Beach, K. (1995). Sociocultural change, activity, and individual development: Some methodological aspects. *Mind, Culture and Activity, 2*(4), 277–284.

Blumenfeld, P. C., Soloway, E., Marx, R. W., Krajcik, J. S., Guzdial, M., & Palincsar, A. (1991). Motivating project-based learning; sustaining the doing, supporting the learning. *Educational Psychologist, 26*(3), 369–398.

Boekaerts, M., & Cascallar, M. (2006). How far have we moved toward the integration of theory and practice in self regulation? *Educational Psychology Review, 18*(3), 199–210.

Ciani, K., Ferguson, Y., Bergin, D., & Hilpert, J. (2010). Motivational influences on school-prompted interest. *Educational Psychology, 30*(4), 377–393.

Dewey, J. (1899). The school and social progress. In J. J. McDermott (Ed.), *The philosophy of John Dewey* (pp. 454–467). Chicago: University of Chicago Press.

Dewey, J. (1912/1990). The child and the curriculum. In J. Dewey (Ed.), *The school and society/The child and the curriculum* (pp. 181–209). Chicago: University of Chicago Press.

Dewey, J. (1915/1990). The psychology of occupations. In J. Dewey (Ed.), *The child and the curriculum/The school and society* (pp. 132–138). Chicago: University of Chicago Press.

Dewey, J. (1916/1944). *Democracy and education.* New York: Free Press.

Dewey, J. (1934). Dewey outlines utopian schools. In J. A. Boydston (Ed.), *John Dewey, the later works Volume 9: 1933–1934* (pp. 136–140). Carbondale, IL: Southern Illinois University Press.

Dewey, J. (1938). *Experience and education.* New York: Macmillan.

Eckert, P. (1989). *Jocks and burnouts: Social categories and identity in the high school.* New York: Teachers College Press.

Elkonin, D. B. (1972). Toward the problem of stages in the mental development of the child. *Soviet Psychology, 10*(3), 225–251.

Elliot, E. S., & Dweck, C. S. (1988). Goals: An approach to motivation and achievement. *Journal of Personality and Social Psychology, 54*(1), 5–12.

Engeström, Y. (1987). *Learning by expanding: An activity-theoretical approach to developmental research.* Helsinki, Finland: Orienta-Konsultit Oy.

Engestrom, Y., Puonti, A., & Seppanen, L. (2003). Spatial and temporal expansion of the object as a challenge for reorganizing work. In D. Nicolini, S. Gherardi, & D. Yanow (Eds.), *Knowing in organizations: A practice-based approach.* Armonk, NY: Sharpe.

Esmonde, I., Takeuchi, M., & Dradakovic, N. (2011). Getting unstuck: Learning and histories of engagement in classrooms. *Mind, Culture, and Activity, 18*, 237–256.

Fallace, T. D. (2008). John Dewey and the savage mind: Uniting anthropological, psychological, and pedagogical thought, 1894–1902. *Journal of the History of the Behavioral Sciences, 44*(4), 355–349.

Fleer, M. (2011). Motives as a central concept for learning. In D. M. McInerney, A. R. Walker, & G. A. D. Liem (Eds.), *Sociocultural theories of learning and motivation.* Charlotte, NC: Information Age Publishing.

Gresalfi, M. S. (2009). Taking up opportunities to learn: Constructing dispositions in mathematics classrooms. *Journal of the Learning Sciences, 18*, 327–369.

Hedegaard, M. (2011). The dynamic aspects in children's learning and development. In M. Hedegaard, A. Edwards, & M. Fleer (Eds.), *Motives in children's development: Cultural-historical approaches* (pp. 9–27). Cambridge, UK: Cambridge University Press.

Hedegaard, M., & Lompscher, J. (1999). *Learning activity and development.* Aarhus, Denmark: Aarhus University Press.

Hickey, D. (2003). Engaged participation versus marginal nonparticipation: A stridently sociocultural approach to achievement motivation. *The Elementary School Journal, 103*(4), 401–429.

Hickey, D. T., & Zuiker, S. J. (2006). Engaged participation: A sociocultural model of motivation with implications for educational assessment. *Educational Assessment, 10*(3), 277–305.

Järvelä, S., Volet, S., & Järvenoja, H. (2010). Research on motivation in collaborative learning: Moving beyond the cognitive-situative divide and combining individual and social processes. *Educational Psychologist, 45*(1), 15–27.

Jurow, A. S. (2005). Shifting engagements in figured worlds: Middle school mathematics students' participation in an architectural design project. *The Journal of the Learning Sciences, 14*(1), 35–67.

Lave, J. (1988). *Cognition in practice: Mind, mathematics and culture in everyday life.* Cambridge, UK: Cambridge University Press.

Lave, J. (1990). The culture of acquisition and the practice of understanding. In J. W. Stigler, R. A. Schweder, & G. Herdt (Eds.), *Essays on comparative human development* (pp. 309–329). Cambridge, UK: Cambridge University Press.

Lave, J., & McDermott, R. (2002). Estranged labor learning. *Outlines, 1*(1), 19–48.

Lave, J., & Wenger, E. (1991). *Situated learning: Legitimate peripheral participation.* Cambridge, UK: Cambridge University Press.

Leont'ev, A. (1965). *Problems of the development of the mind* (2nd ed.). Moscow: Progress.

Leont'ev, A. N. (1978). *Activity, consciousness, and personality.* Englewood Cliffs, NJ: Prentice-Hall.

Magnifico, A. M. (2010). Writing for whom? Cognition, motivation, and a writer's audience. *Educational Psychologist, 45*(3), 167–184.

Matusov, E., Bell, N., & Rogoff, B. (2002). Schooling as cultural process: Shared thinking and guidance from schools differing in collaborative practices. In R. Kail & H. Reese (Eds.), *Advances in child development and behavior* (Vol. 29, pp. 129–160). New York: Academic.

Meece, J. L., Anderman, E. M., & Anderman, L. H. (2006). Classroom goal structure, student motivation, and academic achievement. *Annual Review of Psychology, 57*, 487–503.

Miettinen, R. (2003). Transcending traditional school learning: Teachers' work and networks of learning. In Y. Engestrom, R. Miettinen, & R.-L. Punamaki (Eds.),

Perspectives on activity theory (pp. 325–344). Cambridge, UK: Cambridge University Press.

Miettinen, R. (2005). Object of activity and individual motivation. *Mind, Culture, and Activity, 12*(1), 52–69.

Morrone, A. S., Harkness, S. S., D'Ambrosio, B., & Caulfield, R. (2004). Patterns of instructional discourse that promote the perception of mastery goals in a social constructivist mathematics course. *Educational Studies in Mathematics, 56*(1), 19–38.

Nolen, S. B., Ward, C. J., & Horn, I. S. (2011). Motivation, engagement, and identity: Opening a conversation. In D. M. McInerney, R. A. Walker, & G. A. D. Liem (Eds.), *Sociocultural theories of learning and motivation* (pp. 109–136). Charlotte, NC: Information Age Publishing.

Ochs, E., & Taylor, C. (1992). Science at dinner. In C. Lramsch & S. McConnell-Ginet (Eds.), *Text and context; Cross-disciplinary perspectives on language study* (pp. 29–45). Lexington, MA: Heath.

Oelkers, J. (1998). Empirical research in progressive education. *International Journal of Educational Research, 27*(8), 715–722.

Packer, M. (2001). The problem of transfer and the sociocultural critique of schooling. *The Journal of the Learning Sciences, 10*(4), 493–514.

Packer, M., & Greco-Brooks, D. (1999). School as a site for the production of persons. *Journal of Constructivist Psychology, 12*(1), 133–151.

Paradise, R. (1998). What's different about learning in schools as compared to family and community settings? *Human Development, 41*, 270–278.

Patrick, H., Anderman, L. H., Ryan, A. M., Edelin, K. C., & Midgley, C. (2001). Teachers' communication of goal orientations in four fifth-grade classrooms. *The Elementary School Journal, 102*(1), 35–58.

Pintrich, P. (2000). An achievement goal theory perspective on issues in motivation terminology, theory, and research. *Contemporary Educational Psychology, 25*, 92–104.

Pintrich, P. R., Marx, R. W., & Boyle, R. A. (1993). Beyond cold conceptual change: The role of motivational beliefs and classroom contextual factors in the process of conceptual change. *Review of Educational Research, 63*(2), 167–199.

Polivanova, K. N. (2006). On the problem of the leading activity in adolescence. *Journal of Russian and East European Psychology, 44*(5), 78–84.

Poortvliet, P. M., & Darnon, C. (2010). Toward a more social understanding of achievement goals: The interpersonal effects of mastery and performance goals. *Current Directions in Psychological Science, 19*, 324–328.

Popkewitz, T. S. (2007). Alchemies and governing: Or, questions about the questions we ask. *Educational Philosophy and Theory, 39*(1), 64–83.

Rogoff, B. (1990). *Apprenticeship in thinking: Cognitive development in social context.* New York: Oxford University Press.

Rogoff, B. (2003). *The cultural nature of human development*. New York: Oxford University Press.

Roth, W.-M. (2011). Object/motives and emotion: A cultural-historical activity theoretic approach to learning and work. In D. M. McInerney, R. A. Walker, & G. A. D. Liem (Eds.), *Sociocultural theories of learning and motivation* (pp. 43–64). Charlotte, NC: Information Age Publishing.

Ryan, A. M., & Shim, S. S. (2008). An exploration of young adolescents' social achievement goals and social adjustment in middle school. *Journal of Educational Psychology, 100*, 672–687.

Säljö, R., & Wyndhamm, J. (1993). The school as a context for problem solving. In S. Chaiklin & J. Lave (Eds.), *Understanding practice: Perspectives on activity and context* (pp. 327–342). Cambridge, UK: Cambridge University Press.

Seaman, J., & Nelsen, P. J. (2011). An overburdened term: Dewey's concept of *experience* as curriculum theory. *Education & Culture: The Journal of the John Dewey Society for the Study of Education and Culture, 27*(1), 2–25.

Sutter, B., & Grensjo, B. (1988). Explorative learning in the school? Experiences of local historical research by pupils. *The Quarterly Newsletter of the Laboratory of Comparative Human Cognition, 10*(2), 39–54.

Tharp, R. (2005). *Activity setting observation system rule book*. Berkeley, CA: Center for Research on Education, Diversity, and Excellence.

Tharp, R., & Gallmore, R. (1988). *Rousing minds to life: Teaching, learning, and schooling in social context*. Cambridge, UK: Cambridge University Press.

Thorndike, E. L. (1913). *Education psychology*. New York: Routledge.

Thorkildsen, T., & Nicholls, J. G. (1991). Students' critiques as motivation. *Educational Psychologist, 26*(3–4), 347–368.

Turner, J. C. (2001). Using context to enrich and understand and challenge our understanding of motivational theory. In S. Volet & S. Järvelä (Eds.), *Motivation in learning contexts: Theoretical advances and methodological implications* (pp. 85–104). Amsterdam: Pergamon Press.

Turner, J. C., & Patrick, H. (2008). How does motivation develop and why does it change? Reframing motivation research. *Educational Psychologist, 43*(3), 119–131.

Vygotsky, L. S. (1963). Learning and mental development at school age. In B. Simon & J. Simon (Eds.), *Educational psychology in the USSR* (pp. 21–49). Stanford, CA: Stanford University Press.

Wardekker, W., Boersma, A., Ten Dam, G., & Volman, M. (2011). Motivation for school learning: Enhancing the meaningfulness of learning in communities of learners. In M. Hedegaard, A. Edwards, & M. Fleer (Eds.), *Motives in children's development: Cultural-historical approaches* (pp. 153–169). Cambridge, UK: Cambridge University Press.

Willis, P. E. (1977). *Learning to labour: How working class kids get working class jobs*. Farnborough, UK: Saxon House.

CHAPTER 13

Expeditionary Learning, Constructivism, and the Emotional Risks of Open-Ended Inquiry

Amy L. Heath and Peter Smagorinsky

In this chapter, we examine the experiences of Cathy (a pseudonym), an African American student attending a public charter middle school, whose curriculum emerged from the *Expeditionary Learning* (EL) philosophy. This pedagogy has been adapted to public schools that hope to engage students in activity-oriented, inquiry-based learning. EL was founded on the concept of an expedition, commonly understood as a group journey undertaken to explore new territory for discovery, research, conquest, or other goals. When adapted to schools, EL tends to be oriented to learning-directed quests and activities. The infrastructure of EL allows for constructivism to flourish in a variety of ways, as we report, but can also be thwarted in a number of ways.

Expeditionary Learning

The sense of discovery engrained in the assumptions behind EL appears well aligned with the progressive ideas of Dewey (1902). Knowledge, rather than being fixed and established, is understood in this conception as a

A.L. Heath (✉) • P. Smagorinsky
Department of Language and Literacy Education, The University of Georgia, Athens, GA, USA

D.W. Kritt (ed.), *Constructivist Education in an Age of Accountability*,
https://doi.org/10.1007/978-3-319-66050-9_13

socially mediated construction of the learner, who seeks new understanding through the process of inquiry and investigation in relation to undertaking complex tasks within social boundaries. Not only is the activity constructivist in design, the concepts that emerge are social constructions available to the students through agency and control over their growth and learning (Smagorinsky, 2013).

Expeditionary Learning as Comprehensive School Reform

Sociocultural perspectives on power and cultural diversity (Vossoughi & Gutiérrez, 2017) suggest the importance of examining the historical context of the development of EL, which went from being a boutique program to a funded charter school program model in spite of being at odds with the sort of centralized, reductive reform gripping the US since the 1980s. Its constructivist emphasis appears to be the antithesis of federal educational policies of US for nearly four decades, with the 2000s providing a radical turn toward standardization and uniformity in curriculum, instruction, and assessment.

EL became incorporated into US educational practice during a period of Comprehensive School Reform (CSR). EL was bolstered by Title I and New American Schools Corporation funding (Farrell & Liebowitz, 1998, pp. 14–15) beginning immediately after the founding of the US Department of Education in October 1979. CSR has been described in terms of three eras, which focused on different aspects of schooling. The initial focus of school reform was on fixing schools through state government intervention (Murphy & Datnow, 2003). From 1980 to 1987, during the first era, presumably failing schools were attributed to ineffective teachers and materials, as suggested by the alarm of a "rising tide of mediocrity" that the Reagan-era *A Nation at Risk* (National Commission on Excellence in Education, 1983) warned of in precipitous terms. This reform era produced many new textbooks and curriculum materials designed to help teachers make greater demands on students, under the assumption that their own low standards had produced this presumed crisis to begin with. Centrally developed "teacher proof" materials were included in the instructional tool kit provided by policymakers, textbook companies, and university researchers and education entrepreneurs to save education from the teachers and open a new education market for corporate intervention (Bennett, 2013).

The second era of CSR ran from about 1987 to 1995. A lack of test-score improvement raised questions about the government's ability to change the performance of schools. As a result, CSR philosophy underwent a shift in impetus from centralized experts to local initiatives. Under local control, teachers and parents were considered capable of promoting student achievement. The focus turned from classroom instruction to the bureaucratic structure of schools, which required a shift from mechanistic reinforcement strategies to a professional approach to reform that treated teachers as authorities, and from regulation and compliance monitoring to mobilization of institutional capacity. As a result, decisions were to be made in school by the teachers, and families were in many cases given the opportunity to choose their child's school (Murphy & Datnow, 2003).

This shift toward local control, however, was undermined by its centralized authority and its view that only "scientific, evidence-based" results from the experimental paradigm would be consulted to inform practice (see U.S. Department of Education, 2004). In other words, local control was complicated by federal mandates that eliminated access to the complex, detailed, situated knowledge available through open-ended qualitative studies of the sort that are compatible with investigating constructivist education as a situated practice. Instead, the reliance on experimental research mapped well onto the standardized testing regime preferred by policymakers and many university researchers whose work became magnified by these policies. Local control was thus only possible within federal superstructures that limited local educators' vision and imagination, leaving the two imperatives fundamentally at odds and yet simultaneously demanded.

The third era of CSR was characterized by holding schools responsible for student outcomes, typically through achievement test scores that teachers often found inadequate measures because of their narrow emphasis on tests at the expense of broader concerns with producing knowledgeable, caring, civic-minded citizens (Kastenbaum, 2012). This discontent remains today, as testing has increasingly discouraged schools from teaching in more constructivist ways (Ravitch, 2013).

Amidst this national obsession with standardization and centralized curriculum, instruction, and assessment, counter-movements emerged that were more student oriented. Some were general, such as the movement toward emphasizing learning processes during instruction (e.g., the writing process movement and transactional reading theories in English/Language Arts instruction). Others were specific, such as the development of EL as a school-wide theme and the persistence of the Montessori curriculum. These approaches, however, were limited to special environments such as charter schools and independent schools. Most public schools were required to submit to testing regimes that have occupied instructional time, school resources, internet bandwidth, teachers' planning periods, students' and teachers' emotional capacity, and other casualties of the drive to dedicate the school to increases in standardized test scores.

With EL's approach founded on a sense of mission rather than one of meeting market demands (Farrell & Liebowitz, 1998), the approach sits quite uncomfortably in relation to national policies, even as EL students tend to do well on standardized tests. What remains unclear is whether EL itself produces this salutary effect on policymakers' sensibilities, whether schools adopting it recruit from families whose parents position their children well to succeed in school and on its testing regimens (UMass Donahue Institute Research and Evaluation Group, 2011), and other factors contributing to single-score measures of complex educational processes.

The CSR initiatives coincided with EL rather than generating it. The CSR infused education with funding that had previously been unavailable. President Carter's founding of the Department of Education was generously funded to jumpstart promising programs that helped schools meet its goal of improving education or at least improving test scores. EL benefitted from the availability of funding, even if it departed from the narrow, prescriptive, reductive vision of education that the US Department of Education has funded over time.

Expeditionary Learning and the Constructivist Tradition

EL is a national reform movement for schools characterized by the co-construction of community by students and faculty through "school structures and traditions such as crew, community meetings, exhibitions of student work, and service learning," a quote found on many EL school websites (e.g., Manara Academy, 2017). Its pedagogy is designed to provide engaging and purposeful work with and for authentic audiences, opportunities for students to talk and think with teachers who listen, and a school-wide culture of trust and collaboration (Expeditionary Learning, 2011, p. 5).

EL originated in the Outward Bound (OB) organization founded by educator Kurt Hahn, who was born in 1886 (Neill, 2008), within a generation of a host of progressive educators including Cecil Reddie (b. 1858), John Dewey (b. 1859), Rudolf Steiner (b. 1861), Maria Montessori (b. 1870), and Virginia Estelle Randolph (b. 1874), and a decade before the 1896 birth of both Lev Vygotsky and Jean Piaget, architects of constructivist paradigms. In 1930, Kurt Hahn provided the groundwork for OB by founding the Gordonstoun school in Scotland, with an enrollment of two students. In 1934, the third pupil, Prince Philip of Greece, who ascended to the title of His Royal Highness the Duke of Edinburgh, signed up as well. Gordonstoun allowed Hahn to integrate his philosophy in a curriculum focused on athletics, outdoor survival, and classroom learning (Outward Bound International, 2013).

Hahn relocated the school to Wales, enlisting the help of British shipping baron Sir Lawrence Holt, who was recruited to help teach the boys skills to survive World War II. Together, their training program aimed to develop the "tenacity and fortitude" needed by sailors to "survive the rigors of war and shipwreck" (Outward Bound International, 2013, n.p.). This curriculum embodied Hahn's belief that team-oriented character development forged through challenging experiences in nature was a top educational priority. Hahn found that people developed "confidence, redefined their own perceptions of their personal possibilities, demonstrated compassion, and developed a spirit of camaraderie with their peers" when placed in "challenging, adventurous outdoor situations" (Outward Bound International, 2013, n.p.). This Hahn and Holt partnership blossomed into the first official OB course in Europe in 1941.

The name Outward Bound refers to the nautical term for leaving a safe port for the rigors of sailing. Although the courses that Hahn originally created were designed to ensure the survival and rescue of sailors, subsequent OB programs were open to non-sailing enlistees seeking to develop as leaders through multiday excursions into a variety of wilderness settings. Courses included an array of activities such as mountain climbing, kayaking, and trekking, carrying a significant price tag, and being available for college credit (McQuillan et al., 1994).

The first OB course in the US was offered in 1962. While OB continued to offer wilderness experiences for youth and adults focused on developing leadership skills, OB also set up urban centers designed to recruit a more diverse student body in the 1980s. In these centers, OB courses included team-building events for corporations, young people, and people in various recovery programs following alcoholism, arrest, or other socially unacceptable behavior that might benefit from team-centered wilderness challenges. All courses emphasized reflection, community, success, acquisition of skills, and engagement with the natural world, in which participants were challenged but supported on their adventures.

OB's influence in the classroom continued to grow through a 1998 partnership with the Harvard Graduate School of Education. OB brought experiential learning to Harvard, and Harvard brought its reputation for academic rigor to OB. In the 1990s, OB focused on becoming an educational reform model and received funding from the New American Schools Development Corporation to put its theory into practice. Expeditionary Learning Outward Bound (ELOB) started with ten demonstration schools in 1993. At that time, there were 165 schools in 30 states and Washington, DC, serving 45,000 students and employing 4000 teachers (EL Education, 2017). In these schools, the original OB notion of challenge expanded to include the ways in which students and teachers perform and conceptualize education in the classroom setting. ELOB as a reform model promoted the belief that the core of learning and growth involves the interaction available through groups who take on challenges in new environments, providing them with knowledge that is presumed to carry over to other educational and workplace settings and their demands (Pearson, 2002). The name was revised to Expeditionary Learning, and the EL network grew into 165 EL schools across the nation during the time of Heath's (2013) study.

Today, EL schools emphasize learning by doing through a multiyear professional development plan with instructional materials and technical assistance. This approach is designed to promote changes in school culture, teaching practices, and student achievement scores (Pearson, 2002). Teaching and learning in an EL school involves work in and out of the classroom to allow students to investigate topics of their choice and interest, to engage with content experts, to have opportunities to develop critical thinking abilities, and to develop student agency, character, connection, and voice. The American Institutes for Research's (2006) review of reform models noted that the EL model eschewed a prescribed curriculum, allowing individual schools to create their own programs aligned with the governing philosophy.

The Expeditionary Learning Middle School

EL design principles and benchmarks were used as guiding philosophies for the Expeditionary Learning Middle School (ELMS), the school we feature from Heath's (2013) study. These principles were taught explicitly to students and were distributed to the students on a bookmark on the first day of school, displayed in the hallways, and included in the school handbook. These principles emphasize self-discovery, the fostering of curiosity through the cultivation of "wonderful" ideas, students' personal responsibility for learning, the development of empathic and caring dispositions, experiences with success and failure, opportunities for collaboration and competition, the promotion of diversity and inclusion, engagement with nature, and occasions for solitude and reflection.

Learning expeditions structure the academic year, designed to provide extended investigations on topics of interest outside formal classrooms that typically have value for the local community. Through these inquiries and projects, the students provide service to the community, engage in adventurous thinking and acting, and have a public dimension (ELMS Pamphlet, 2010a, 2010b, 2010c). The curriculum is interdisciplinary, involving Math, Science, Language Arts, and Social Studies, and requires projects that display student progress and knowledge (ELMS website, 2010d).

Students, administrators, and teachers in the school were a part of a crew comprising a small group of students (10–15) and one teacher who met every day, every week, over the three years that the student was enrolled at ELMS. The crew was an essential component of the EL model and in some ways looked similar to a teacher advisory meeting, a group counseling session, a book club, or a homeroom. According to the American Institutes for Research's (2006) review of middle- and high-school comprehensive reform models, EL crews helped to produce positive relationships among students and between students and their teachers.

The notion of "expedition" suggests a general destination, the pathway toward which may be navigated in a number of ways, including those conceived emergently in relation to exigencies. This voyage is undertaken in the team-centered manner that typifies sociocultural versions of constructivism, which emphasize social mediation as a critical factor in human development (Smagorinsky, 2011). The case study presented (Heath, 2013), Cathy's expedition, was the planning of a school Halloween Dance rather than a wilderness voyage. As in the original conception, however, this activity required the student to draw on knowledge from prior experiences and to develop new understandings through both social interaction and response to challenges in the social and material environment of the school. In wilderness expeditions, this knowledge is applied to a task with potentially deadly consequences, making the knowledge immediate, real, and urgent. The EL environment was designed to move school learning beyond the abstractions of classrooms and put students in the position of solving authentic, real-world problems within the realities of the school context.

In EL, collaborative reflection is assumed ideally to emerge spontaneously during the lulls in challenge. This reflection in turn allows the reconsideration and reconstruction of possible ways that the situation could have been addressed and might be addressed in the future. The students themselves thus become critical sources of knowledge construction under material conditions that have potentially threatening effects, making this knowledge quite authentic for those involved. This knowledge then gets continually refined through additional experience and reflection, making the students expert learners about teamwork, natural phenomena, human interventions, and whatever academic requirements for science, mathematics, literacy, history, or other formal knowledge they might use to inform their ongoing developments of new understandings.

Cathy, the Dance Planner

Cathy, a seventh-grade African American girl, lived with her mother, father, and younger sister in what she called an "African American suburb." Her parents were both college graduates; her father studied law, and her mother worked in the medical field educating patients at the university hospital. Cathy reported that she had been picked on because of her large body frame and dark skin tone, but she decided to be strong and stop caring about people's opinions. She wrote and printed the proposal, which she used as the basis for her presentation. She said that once she decided to be herself, other people met her on her own terms and that at the time of the dance project, she felt that she was liked and accepted by her classmates.

She was in her second year at ELMS and it was her second year of being involved with the Halloween Dance, which may be considered a well-defined yet open-ended project. Cathy felt passionately about investing herself intensively in making the dance a success. Planning the school dance required following several necessary general steps, including writing a proposal and presenting it on stage to the entire school at one of the weekly meetings, a step that had discouraged less confident students from proposing projects. She wrote and printed the proposal, which she used as the basis for her presentation. The proposal required Cathy to communicate her vision in terms of scheduling, budgeting, and party planning. She needed to anticipate the timing, communication, and coordination of multiple factors and how to execute each stage on schedule. School started in August, and planning an October dance was a big undertaking.

After reading and explaining her proposal to the school, which included over 100 teachers and students, Cathy took questions from the audience about her proposal. She came to the public proposal session prepared with chart paper and a marker to capture the audience's questions and the names of the students who wanted to help. She worked with a teacher on questions that were beyond her authority to decide, such as whether students from other schools could attend, if she could enlist bands to play, and if the price could be adjusted to encourage attendance.

Cathy used the morning crew meetings and tried to schedule other meetings to talk with teachers and administrators about moving the proposal forward. Planning was a struggle, but she persisted for months. She drafted a variety of plans for the dance, created posters to promote the event, put together committees and established rules for participation on them, gathered more signatures from students than required, drafted a formal proposal to school members to proceed with the dance, and conceived of and anticipated an exhaustive set of possibilities that would make the dance a memorable experience.

Factors That Undermined Cathy's Experience

Faith in Cathy's ability to engage in the full range of leadership activities to plan and carry out the dance rested upon a set of assumptions about her knowledge and resources. It was assumed that Cathy knew how to type and that her family had a computer and printer in their home so she could type and print her proposal. Because her family did not, in spite of being college-educated professionals, this became a multiday ordeal at school.

Although Cathy was enthusiastic thinking about balloons filled with fake blood and the playlist for the night's soundtrack, it was also assumed she was able to run committee meetings with other students during her lunch period. Cathy made a good attempt at running the meetings, requiring her classmates to sign in and list the items they were bringing to the dance. Field notes of observations reveal that most of the students were playing, talking, painting their nails, and inattentive during the meetings. Afterwards, Cathy reported being extremely disappointed that her own diligence was not met by a similar commitment from her teammates. She felt as if she had been "listened to but not heard" and that "someone else could do it" next time. Cathy felt that her classmates lacked sufficient commitment to the project, leaving her to take on many demanding jobs with only token peer contributions.

In addition, the teachers in her school were overextended and struggled to follow through in supporting her leadership on the project. The school established roles for teachers that involved guidance rather than explicit direction. This guidance came in the form of setting up challenges and serving as a resource to help the students achieve a worthwhile end. Ideally, they would be accessible to student planners throughout their project undertakings. Yet for Cathy, faculty support was largely unavailable because the teachers were still learning the EL philosophy and spread too thin to give her the levels of support she needed. Given the scope of planning and carrying out the dance, the process became overwhelming for a middle-school girl undertaking the management of her first major social event. As a result, Cathy had to take social and academic risks that she found emotionally and motivationally threatening, ultimately becoming so prohibitively imposing that she elected to withdraw from further leadership roles and the school's EL mission.

A second set of adults provided too much uninvited and disruptive assistance. As the dance approached, her classmates' parents took an interest in the event and, apparently under the assumption that they needn't consult with and work under the authority of a middle-school girl, commandeered the project with their own ideas. Recruited by a letter sent home by the school, the student's family members joined a volunteer organization meeting after school a few weeks before the dance. A number of volunteer opportunities were listed and Cathy said that she was glad to see "her" Halloween Dance included, but she was also frustrated that she could not attend and direct the portion of the meeting where the adults would be talking about the dance. Her mother attended the adults-only meeting to help make Cathy's voice heard. According to Cathy, it was at this meeting that well-intentioned volunteers began to disregard her ideas and take control of the planning. She felt uninvited stakeholders hijacked the project to meet their own goals. Cathy was frustrated because, although she was the designated leader of the dance activity, she was thwarted by unwanted interventions, insufficient faculty involvement, and a lack of wholehearted participation by other students whom she had recruited to assist her in labor-intensive aspects of planning the event.

Cathy's role as the planner of the dance was affected by a variety of factors. The school itself was implementing the new EL curriculum, with teachers having to learn on the fly how to put the philosophy and its accompanying curriculum and instruction into practice. This was less than ideal support for Cathy's leadership role. She had to manage committees, meetings, supplies, decorations, entertainment, contests, promotions, permissions, transportation, staffing, and other facets of planning the event for over 100 students. This responsibility was well beyond her entry-level skills and knowledge. The dance was well attended and those attending participated enthusiastically in a dance contest, a rap performance, a costume contest, a raffle, and a buffet in an atmosphere enhanced by a smoke machine and light effects. Despite appearing successful in her efforts, she felt frustrated and discouraged by her experience to the point where she disengaged from further leadership in school activities.

What Worked, What Did Not

Cathy accumulated a great deal of useful experience in the process of planning the dance. Rather than building on this experience, however, she subsequently withdrew from participation as a leader of school events. She had hoped, for instance, to open a school store, but decided that she could not endure another round of frustrations and abandoned the idea. The Halloween Dance had exhausted her emotional investment to the point where she could not bring herself to rally her classmates with another proposal.

Despite the school's stated commitment to mutual collaborative efforts to survive and discover one's strengths through a challenging ordeal, the potential of these intentions was not borne out in Cathy's experiences. It's one thing to ride a raft down a set of rapids, but quite another to ride one over Niagara Falls. Cathy simply was not prepared for the magnitude of the job, and in executing it, she got insufficient help from teachers and students and was subject to too many uninvited parental efforts to change the course of her expedition. She was thus denied the opportunity to have the measured support that she needed to feel that she had been the captain of a journey in which all hands were on deck.

The notion of risk-taking is central to the idea of the expedition and is central to many notions of constructivism (Hills, 2007). Engaging in open-ended projects covering unfamiliar terrain involves taking risks. In her planning of the dance, Cathy opened herself to what she felt were a few too many. As the project's official leader, she had responsibility for the performance of the students whom she enlisted to become involved. Their lack of dedicated engagement created tremendous anxiety for her throughout the process. If the dance had failed, she would have been the person accountable. The uninspired performance of her peers amplified her fears of failure right through the evening of the event.

Perhaps the dance's ultimate success could have taught her that taking on big, complex jobs is satisfying, because they require the overcoming of obstacles. Initiating and leading a project, even one that does not succeed, can teach a student how to meet and address difficulties. Some might regard her project as a successful activity through which she grew into new states of competence and achievement, gained in stature, and prepared herself for further leadership roles, because ultimately the dance was a success. However, she appeared to become embittered and disengaged rather than empowered as a result of her experience, because the task overwhelmed her and left her feeling isolated among peers and overruled by parents.

As Csikszentmihalyi (1998) might note, the "flow" of an activity—the point at which engagement is so great that a participant has no conception of passing time—is available when there is a good match between ability and challenge. Too great a challenge for one's present abilities produces anxiety and frustration, too little a challenge produces boredom. An appropriate constructivist activity would produce neither extreme. Rather, the challenge would be just within the outer limits of, or possibly slightly beyond, one's abilities to help the student to stretch into new levels of competence and confidence. Cathy's project was admirably ambitious, yet not sufficiently supported. Despite her hard work on this project, Cathy ultimately reported seeing herself as an "okay" student rather than a producer, a leader, a reader, a writer, a visionary, a change maker.

We see inconsistencies between the theory and practice of the EL observed in this school due to what might be a romanticized notion of both the child and the educational system and their potential for collaborative, civic-minded conduct. The assumption that becoming a team or crew member automatically confers on the students a sense of fairness and equal opportunity may in fact reify social inequity by leaving it unmonitored (Lewis, 1997). In Hahn's founding conception, EL builds on the idea of crews embarking on sea voyages to rescue lost sailors, create leaders, and defeat opposing fleets, all motivated by a missionary sense of salvation. This noble sense of purpose, however, does not anticipate that crews composed of children or youth may lack the maturity, group investment, and sense of equity, among other factors, that affect the success of disparate people who work collectively toward a group goal.

We believe in the general goals of EL and offer several suggestions. Schools should not expect too much too quickly. They should build project expectations gradually. Without sufficient support, they run the risk of creating too much uncertainty. Teachers should provide greater guidance to students who propose projects in terms of the scope of the work and complexity of the tasks and do so without hijacking their expeditions. The wrong kind of guidance for a complex, uncertain inquiry may leave student project leaders in overly vulnerable places and undermine the developmental possibilities.

It is critical to infuse the school with a sense of common purpose and mutual accountability as well as personal responsibility. If students are allowed to think that only the designated leader is accountable, they may take their responsibilities lightly and shift them disproportionately to the leader, who may not be mature or skilled enough to manage so much work and the pressures of sole answerability for a project's outcome. Adult involvement is necessary to help student leaders make fellow students accountable for being responsible participants.

Perhaps foremost is emphasizing what it means to take on a role in a group activity. In naval crews, there are severe consequences for failing to pull one's weight and potentially horrific consequences for crews whose members perform indifferently. If students believe that there are no consequences for not carrying out their responsibilities, then they only have the incentive of personal satisfaction to motivate their contributions. Not all students are driven by the intrinsic motivation to love learning—a romanticized notion about children that can allow constructivist possibilities to go awry (Goodyear & Ellis, 2007). Teachers must devise ways to encourage crew members to be accountable to one another and to their student leaders. Teachers must also serve as a firewall between students tasked with leading expeditions and parents who impose themselves in school projects. Schools often hope to involve parents, yet need to make sure that this involvement is supervised, monitored, and limited so that students who are entrusted with leadership roles are not undermined by parent groups. We feel teachers and other adults should provide formative feedback, support, and guidance without taking over the students' work.

Constructivist programs like EL have great potential that can be undermined by the assumptions that things will take care of themselves, that adults should stay entirely out of the way so that kids control their own learning (e.g., Graves, 1983), and wholly relying upon social processes not mediated by adults. The realities of adolescent conduct point to the importance of adult guidance and monitoring when students undertake new challenges involving the orchestration of diverse people toward a unified end.

References

American Institutes for Research. (2006). *CSRQ center report on middle and high school comprehensive reform models.* Retrieved January 18, 2013, from http://www.air.org/sites/default/files/downloads/erport/MSHS_2006_Report_Final_Full_Version_10-03-06_0.pdf

Bennett, T. (2013). *Teacher proof: Why research in education doesn't always mean what it claims, and what you can do about it.* New York: Routledge.

Csikszentmihalyi, M. (1998). *Finding flow: The psychology of engagement with everyday life.* New York: Basic Books.

Dewey, J. (1902). *The child and the curriculum.* Chicago: University of Chicago Press.

EL Education. (2017). *EL education.* Retrieved April 8, 2017, from https://eleducation.org/

Expeditionary Learning. (2011). *Core practices. Expeditionary learning outward bound* [PDF]. Retrieved April 19, 2011, from www.elschools.org

Expeditionary Learning Middle School. (2010a). *Advancing student achievement: Now enrolling grades 6, 7, and 8* [Brochure]. Columbus, OH: ELMS.

Expeditionary Learning Middle School. (2010b). *ELMS: Enrollment update* [Brochure]. Columbus, OH: ELMS.

Expeditionary Learning Middle School. (2010c). *Expeditionary learning design principals* [Brochure]. Columbus, OH: ELMS.

Expeditionary Learning Middle School. (2010d). *ELMS: Expeditionary Learning Middle School.* Retrieved November 1, 2010, from school website.

Farrell, G., & Liebowitz, M. (1998). *Expeditionary learning outward bound in year five: What the research shows.* Cambridge, MA: ELOB.

Goodyear, P., & Ellis, R. (2007). Students' interpretations of learning tasks: Implications for educational design. In ICT: Providing choices for learners and learning. *Proceedings ascilite, Singapore 2007.* Retrieved April 12, 2017, from http://www.ascilite.org.au/conferences/singapore07/procs/goodyear.pdf

Graves, D. H. (1983). *Writing: Teachers & children at work.* Portsmouth, NH: Heinemann.

Heath, A. L. (2013). *We are crew, not passengers: Middle level students' experiences of the Expeditionary Learning school reform model and its relationship to literacy, agency, and diversity.* Unpublished doctoral dissertation, The Ohio State University, Columbus, OH.

Hills, T. (2007). Is constructivism risky? Social anxiety, classroom participation, competitive game play and constructivist preferences in teacher development. *Teacher Development, 11*(3), 335–352. Retrieved April 11, 2017, from http://www2.warwick.ac.uk/fac/sci/psych/people/thills/thills/hillsteacherdevelopment2007.pdf

Kastenbaum, S. (2012, May 17). The high stakes of standardized tests. *CNN Schools of Thought*. Retrieved February 16, 2017, from http://schoolsofthought.blogs.cnn.com/2012/05/17/the-high-stakes-of-standardized-tests/

Lewis, C. (1997). The social drama of literature discussions in a fifth/sixth-grade classroom. *Research in the Teaching of English, 31*, 163–204.

Manara Academy. (2017). *We are an Expeditionary School*. Retrieved April 8, 2017, from http://manaraacademy.org/academics/el/

McQuillan, P., Kraft, R., O'Conor, A., Timmons, M., Marion, S., & Michalec, P. (1994). *An assessment of outward bound USA's urban/education initiative*. Boulder, CO: University of Colorado School of Education.

Murphy, J., & Datnow, A. (Eds.). (2003). *Leadership lessons from comprehensive school reforms*. Thousand Oaks, CA: Corwin Press.

National Commission on Excellence in Education. (1983). *A nation at risk: The imperative for educational reform*. Washington, DC: Author. Retrieved February 13, 2017, from https://www2.ed.gov/pubs/NatAtRisk/index.html

Neill, J. (2008). *Dr. Kurt Hahn*. Retrieved April 10, 2017, from http://www.wilderdom.com/KurtHahn.html

Outward Bound International. (2013). *History*. Retrieved April 10, 2017, from http://www.outwardbound.net/about-us/history/

Pearson, S. S. (2002). *Finding common ground: Service-learning and education reform. A survey of 28 leading school reform models*. Washington, DC: American Youth Policy Forum.

Ravitch, D. (2013). *Reign of error: The hoax of the privatization movement and the danger to America's public schools*. New York: Knopf.

Smagorinsky, P. (2011). *Vygotsky and literacy research: A methodological framework*. Boston: Sense.

Smagorinsky, P. (2013). The development of social and practical concepts in learning to teach: A synthesis and extension of Vygotsky's conception. *Learning, Culture, and Social Interaction*, *2*(4), 238–248. Retrieved April 10, 2017, from http://www.petersmagorinsky.net/About/PDF/LCSI/LCSI_2013.PDF

U.S. Department of Education. (2004). *About CSR*. Washington, DC: Author. Retrieved April 10, 2017, from https://ed.gov/programs/compreform/2pager.html

UMass Donahue Institute Research and Evaluation Group. (2011). *Impact of the expeditionary learning model on student academic performance in Rochester, New York*. Amherst, MA: Author. Retrieved February 14, 2017, from http://www.copperpointschools.org/wp-content/uploads/Expeditionary-Learning-UMDI-Rochester-Impact-Study.pdf

Vossoughi, S., & Gutiérrez, K. D. (2017). Critical pedagogy and sociocultural theory. In I. Esmonde & A. N. Booker (Eds.), *Power and privilege in the learning sciences* (pp. 139–161). New York: Routledge.

PART III

Implications for the Future of Public Education

CHAPTER 14

Learning, Teaching, and Social Justice: Eleanor Duckworth's Perspective

Yeh Hsueh

In a talk in 2012, Eleanor Duckworth clearly stated the values she brought to her education theory and practice: "As a teacher, and as a member of the human community, I make certain assumptions. I assume that we want students to come to feel the power of their minds, and of their creative capacities. I assume we want students' understanding to be deep, confident and complex and their means of expression to be varied and nuanced. I assume we want students to develop a sense of community responsibility, democratic commitment, and social justice" (Duckworth, 2012). She formed these convictions over a long and distinguished career that continues to inspire educators.

Eleanor Duckworth first studied with Piaget in Paris in 1957, and the next year, joined his research team in Geneva. She entered the field of education as a psychologist/piloting teacher in 1962, and went on to become recognized for her accomplishment as a scholar and practitioner in teacher education at Harvard University. Not only did she translate for Piaget for 15 years during his many visits to the United States, but she also draws on Piaget and Inhelder's work as a major source of inspiration in the field of learning and teaching (Duckworth, 2006).

Y. Hsueh (✉)
Educational Psychology and Research, University of Memphis, Memphis, TN, USA

D.W. Kritt (ed.), *Constructivist Education in an Age of Accountability*,
https://doi.org/10.1007/978-3-319-66050-9_14

The title of the then well-known publication *Piaget Rediscovered* (Ripple & Rockcastle, 1964) originated from her personal struggle and rediscovery of making connections between her research experience with Piaget and her involvement in developing an elementary science curriculum (Hsueh, 2005a, 2009). About those struggling years, Duckworth (1996) recalls, "Not only did Piaget seem irrelevant, I was no longer sure he was right" (p. 2). However, after she rediscovered the relevance of Piaget's theory to education, specifically to teaching and learning, she emphasized that, apart from stages and apart from specific children's ideas, many aspects of Piaget's theory are important for education. For example, "the whole idea of assimilation, the educational ideas I developed ever since" (Duckworth, 2000).

Many people believe that Jean Piaget's work has contributed to contemporary advocacy and practice in various constructivist movements in education since the 1970s. It might be surprising that someone like Duckworth, who worked closely with Piaget, had to struggle to see its connection with education. During her early education career, she had expressed doubts about the usefulness of Piaget's work in education. What, then, are her rediscovered connections?

In this chapter, I will present a few of Duckworth's educational ideas about teaching and learning in the larger context of schooling and school reform. These ideas embody her three assumptions in the opening of this chapter and reflect the continuous development of her own research on teaching and learning, which she later called "critical exploration in the classroom" (Duckworth, 2005b; for a brief history, see Hsueh, 2005b); interestingly, she has not specifically called her approach to education "constructivist." However, as an outstanding teacher educator, Duckworth's education method, which prioritizes learners' engagement with the subject matter, runs against the widely observable top-down school reform priorities. Her educational ideas place high values on learners as creative individuals living in a classroom that reflects a changing society. The materials cited below are from both published sources in different media and interviews I conducted with her in 2000 and 2016.

Education as Socialization

Education is a process of socializing the citizens of a society, particularly the young. Formal schooling has been the major form of such socialization in industrialized and post-industrialized societies. Since the early 1900s, the European-based system of formal Western schooling, including age-segregated classrooms, has continued to spread due in part to industrialization, urbanization, waves of immigration, population growth, and globalization (Rogoff, 2003). Bureaucratic efforts to maintain and improve school systems have also stepped up to implement various top-down policies. For the past three decades since the publication of the well-known report *A Nation at Risk*, an increasing number of state and federal policies have appeared to propel school reform movements (Gordon, 2003).

Each wave of school reform has formulated new rules, regulations, and school policies governing the school life of teachers and students. A recent example is the enhanced testing culture in school systems around the country, which developed as part of the massive standardized testing movements. "The number of standardized tests U.S. public school students take has exploded in the past decade" (Layton, 2015, para 1). One study of 66 school districts found that students had to take 112 such tests on average between pre-K and grade 12 (Council of the Great City Schools, 2015). However, what is largely missing in these policy-driven reform movements regarding children's schooling and teachers' professional work is an understanding of "how people learn things and what anyone can do to help," the central questions Duckworth has asked over her entire teacher education career.

In Duckworth's view, every specific act in teaching, such as selecting curriculum materials, listening to learners' explanations, and engaging different views with one another, has a complex dual goal of socializing the learner into becoming an innovative and complex thinker in the classroom on the one hand, and on the other, becoming an active and empathic participant in the changing society. In John Dewey's (1916) view, this kind of learning and teaching in education should be the one and same reconstruction process by which human individuals improve their living and by which human institutions improve societal living. If education can be a vehicle of social reform toward this dual goal, then the so-called school reform in a democratic society should value learners' contributions to their own learning and to one another's learning in school. However, a high-stakes testing environment works against this educational function to diminish children's and teachers' learning and teaching, and impedes the process of socializing them to engage with a "democracy of ideas" and the "social justice of ideas," two of Duckworth's educational notions that are discussed later in this chapter.

Diminishing Learning and Teaching in School

Duckworth has found the growing number of educational policies in the name of "school reform" profoundly disturbing because they demand "more and more time taking tests, less and less time learning; more and more simple right answers, less and less complexity; more and more intellectual orthodoxy, less and less diversity" (Duckworth, 2012).

On the "more and more" side, the high-stakes testing movement has created a culture in which achievement test scores are interpreted as a reflection of children's learning and the quality of teachers' teaching. This kind of test-driven schooling offers an education that reduces or rejects diverse creativities of human learners, but elevates or enhances the values of uniform thinking toward correct answers. The high-stakes testing movement pivots on various forms of testing mandated by each state or by the Common Core Standards across states. For nearly two decades, the consistently mounting political pressure for this type of educational accountability measure can be seen in the federal programs, "No Child Left Behind" and "Race to the Top." Along with everything else, Duckworth (2012) finds these two slogans blatantly—and hilariously—contradictory! Racing without leaving anyone behind! However, what is entirely missing is the students' right to a good education, an education in which students are active learners, complex thinkers, and confident human beings.

Duckworth (2016) lamented, "Politicians keep meddling with education. Education is no longer in the hand of educators, no longer in the hands of teachers, parents and communities." This observation echoes a wide range of discussions on school reform and school learning in which teachers have tried to have their voices heard (e.g., Au, 2011, 2013; Cochran-Smith, 2000; Darling-Hammond, 2015; Hilliard, 2000; Hursh, 2013; Nichols, Berliner, & Noddings, 2007). Regardless of the growing strength of these professional voices against standardized testing, they do not seem to slow the top-down push of the standardization movement. Educators have less and less say about how to teach and what to learn. Duckworth observes, "To the extent that the testing has prevailed, what education should be has not happened" (Duckworth, 2016).

Educational Constructivism

For many people, constructivist education may be a vital movement that falls on the "less and less" side in the face of school reform movements such as high-stakes testing. In an interview in 2016, I asked Duckworth whether she could define what educational constructivism was. She found it hard to answer the question even though she was no less familiar than anyone else with constructivism in the tradition of genetic epistemology. In the field of education, the word "constructivism" is used in so many ways she felt uncertain what people are asking when they ask what educational constructivism is. "It wouldn't be easy to answer. Constructivism is a word that I see can legitimately apply to Piaget's theory. Then, in education, there are so many different ideas about constructivism. The variety of *practices* that are called constructivist keeps me from using the term" (Duckworth, 2016).

Although Piaget and Inhelder's work has been the most significant source of theoretical and methodic inspiration for her educational innovations, Duckworth (1973) struggled in the field of education for years to ask questions about whether their work could inform learning, and how their work could be useful to teachers. Reflecting on Piaget's theory while working in the trenches for decades, she has observed various beliefs and attempts to apply Piaget's constructivism to education that are detached from the intellectual development that teachers and students should have. "Piaget's constructivist ideas have not had the great impact on education that they should have because people did not understand them. Some people tried to teach kids to do Piaget interviews better. So that was not what he had in mind. Some people encourage kids to come up with their own ideas, but make sure those ideas are replaced by 'right' ideas in the end. They try to make sure that children do not go home at the end of the day with 'wrong' ideas. So that is not very useful in giving learners a sense of confidence in their own ideas. Learners don't get to learn to be confident in their own ideas because they still check out their ideas against whether the teacher says they are right or wrong" (Duckworth, 2016).

Critical Exploration in the Classroom

Although the constructivist education movement quietly arose in the 1970s (Hsueh, 1995) and caught on in the 1990s, as seen in official statements by a variety of professional education organizations,[1] Duckworth rarely uses the word constructivism to characterize her work, but "I can talk about my own principles of teaching" (Duckworth, 2016). This approach has inherited the name of "critical exploration"—the name Inhelder, Sinclair, and Bovet (1974) gave to the Genevan research approach (also see Duckworth, 2005b; Hsueh, 2005b). Duckworth combined this name with the phrase "in the classroom." She said, "Because I believe that that very research approach can be a productive classroom teaching approach" (Duckworth, 2016). The learner is engaged in learning the subject matter while the teacher learns about the learner's thinking in order to understand the student's grasp of the subject matter.

"I am going to talk about our work in Critical Explorers." By "our work," Duckworth referred to her recent involvement with a group of former graduate students who are currently university professors, public school teachers, and school administrators. This work of critical exploration has a central principle, that is, "We work on trying to have teachers not come between students and the subject matter. The teacher's job, our job, is to get the learner right into the midst of the subject matter. That means, the primary material, the curriculum material, has to be very well selected so that it captures the attention of a variety of learners, and also – in the course of the curriculum study – it offers a way for the learners to find the big ideas in the subject matter. That means that a lot of good work has to be put into the curriculum so that learners themselves can form ideas without the teacher saying, 'Here is the idea you should be getting from this one'" (Duckworth, 2016).

A good number of studies have documented how teachers and students have done critical exploration in the classroom. In addition to some of her publications of late (Duckworth, 2001, 2005a, 2005b, 2009, 2010), interested readers can find specific examples in the studies by many others who have helped to advance the critical exploration approach (e.g., Auger, 2014; Cavicchi, 2007, 2008a, 2009; Chiu, 2009; Hughes-McDonnell, 2009; Rauchwerk, 2003).

Many Wonderful Ideas in Progress Versus a Few Right Ideas in the End

Following Duckworth's work over time, one can find a clear approach to learning and teaching that had already emerged in the year of *Piaget Rediscovered*: The teacher can best engage learners by following the learners' ideas and keeping the ideas in direct interaction with the subject matter. Prioritizing the students' own ideas is also to acknowledge and honor the diversity of ideas in the classroom. With a range of ideas in one classroom, both the teacher and the students can move their ideas forward by engaging with one another's ideas about the subject matter. This early emphasis pivots on the teacher's sensitivity to learners' ideas, or as Duckworth (1973) noted, "The sensitivity to children in classrooms continued to be central in my own development" (p. 262). This thinking runs against the perennial baffling issue of applying Piaget's stage theory to education and educational psychology, an effort that is still prevalent in many colleges of education. In an essay entitled "The having of wonderful ideas," Duckworth (1973) offered her hard-earned insight as follows:

> I am suggesting that children do not have a built-in pace of intellectual development. I would temper that suggestion by saying that the built-in aspect of the pace is minimal. The having of wonderful ideas, which I consider the essence of intellectual development, would depend instead to an overwhelming extent on the occasions for having them. (p. 275)

The occasions for having wonderful ideas is essential for the learner's continuous intellectual engagement with the subject matter, and for all students in the classroom to engage with one another's ideas about the subject matter (Duckworth, 2005a, 2005b, 2010). Central to both the curriculum and the pedagogy is the teacher's conscious effort to help learners continually happen upon these occasions. In other words, it is essential for learners to have their own ideas; it is also essential for the teacher to be sensitive to the rise and development of these ideas in order to be part of these intellectual occasions, to notice them, to join with the learner, and to follow along with the progress of the ideas.

In contrast, an activity in the classroom that leads to a set of "correct" ideas not only promotes a narrow sense of learning, but also promises a time-tested negative consequence in learners' loss of interest in the subject matter, and loss of confidence in their own ability to learn. Regarding this common phenomenon in school, Duckworth observes, "Making sure that learners come to the right answer is destructive most of time. You want learners to keep having questions, not to get simple answers which make them think they know it. I find that students can be very involved in some matter, struggling with making sense, and then if someone tells them 'this is the answer,' they lose interest. And then, also, they develop less and less confidence in their own thinking abilities" (Duckworth, 2016). Consider that when students make earnest efforts to learn something and then an authority figure concludes with established ideas that largely override the students' own developing ideas, this inevitably minimizes their interests and disrespects students' intellectual development.

What Materials Are Suitable for Critical Exploration?

"Wonderful ideas" cannot come out of the blue. They originate from what learners discover in their environment and experiences, such as they find meaningful and connectable to the activity in the classroom. In order to make it possible for all learners in the classroom to have their own wonderful ideas, a thoughtful selection of curriculum materials is key. What materials are considered to be suitable for critical exploration in the classroom in order to help students develop their own wonderful ideas? Duckworth (2016) answered this question by examining the intended materials based on the principles that they are accessible to everyone and rich in possibilities. She said, "[The materials] have to allow many routes in – and be full of interest once you are in there. There have to be enough materials backing up the activities so that learners can go deeper and deeper in the subject matter. Different people will get different things. Material that makes people do the same thing is not very valuable" (Duckworth, 2016).

However, it is not always realistic for classroom teachers to go out to look for such materials. Designated educators who are well versed with teaching and learning principles like those in critical exploration should come to help. Duckworth suggests, "It's not the only way to help teachers, but it is a very important thing. What educators who are not classroom teachers should do is develop curriculum materials for teachers. Teachers do not have time to do all the searching that is needed for good curriculum – for curriculum in which students are historians who work from primary sources; scientists who explore first-hand phenomena; mathematicians who invent their own ways to solve problems, and so on. We need curricula that put learners in touch with subject matter. If I were a superintendent, that is what I would hire people to do: Find curriculum materials and questions that put teachers and learners in touch with subject matters" (Duckworth, 2016).

Encounter Between Materials and Students

Once the carefully selected materials for critical exploration become available to the teacher, how should the teacher use the materials? Pedagogically, there are many specifics worth mentioning, but one principle is foundational: The teacher should not get in between materials and students but instead must place students directly in touch with the subject matter by working arduously to keep them connected with it. "I consider teaching to be helping people learn, not telling people what you know. The key as I have seen is to aim for putting learners directly in touch with the subject matter, *not with words about* the subject matter. It's not a matter of mediating between the subject matter and the learners. It's not a matter of telling them how to think about it. But keeping learners directly in touch with the subject matter itself and the subject matter becomes the authority" (Duckworth, 2012, italics added).

In stark contrast to Duckworth's approach, the ubiquitous instructional approach in school is telling students the correct answers and explaining what they should learn. It is a norm for teachers to explicate widely accepted mathematical formulas, laws of physics, equations of chemistry, and grammatical rules, that is, to use words to impart knowledge. To illustrate her own approach, Duckworth (2012) cited an example of a 9th grade English teacher teaching poetry in a Boston high school to students of English as a second or third language, who were enrolled in the lowest of four tracks in school. Lisa Schneier (2001), the teacher, worked with these students by helping them expand and deepen their own encounter with the text of the poem. To do this, the teacher stood to one side in the encounter between students and text, not in the midst of it. In so doing, Schneier noted the growing interest of the students and "the palpable intelligence that creates those ideas and propels them into new ones as the students create their own deep and secure knowledge of this poem" (p. 46).

Duckworth (2012) reiterates this position: "I want to emphasize how the poem was the authority here, not the teacher. The teacher had hard work to do, but it wasn't the work of explaining her own ideas, or those of a textbook, or the literary authorities. It was the work of keeping the students connected to the poem itself. She had faith in the power of a good poem, and she had faith in the power of her students' minds, and that double faith brought the students to the very heart of the matter, the very nature of poetic use of language."

Democracy of Ideas in the Classroom

Students' direct encounters with the subject matter allow them to forge their own routes into the material to bring forth their ideas. Then, how do the teacher and other students treat these ideas? In the test-driven method, only "correct" answers are honored. Duckworth found this troubling because it does two injustices to learners: to their ideas and to their citizens' rights.

In our recent interview, Duckworth shared her current view on education as she thinks it ought to be. It was the first time that I heard her discussing her new phrase "democracy of ideas." The phrase itself seems simple to grasp but it is not an easy educational practice to implement in the classroom. First, here is the meaning of the phrase:

> In the classroom, an idea should not get greater attention because it is the teacher's idea, the smart kid's idea or the idea in the book or on Google. My view of democracy of ideas in the classroom, also my thought about social justice in the classroom, is that no matter who puts forth an idea, that idea gets attention. Maybe it does not hold up, but if it is submitted with a serious intent, it has to be dealt with and considered as whether it will stand up with other ideas we have had so far. Do we need further evidence to see if it will work or not? Does it contradict something else? If so, what will it be that settles that contradiction? Or it could easily be dismissed quickly because everybody agrees that couldn't be the case because of X, so that the idea could be dropped and the person who proposed could realize, "Oh I see it has to be dropped." But as long as an idea has got some possibility to it, it is on the table for a continuing discussion, and the discussion needs to consider it before dropping it to go on to some other topic. Teaching this way, learners get to develop respect for their own ideas – which is of central importance to many students; and they get to develop respect for each other's ideas – which is of central importance for all students and for society at large. (Duckworth, 2016)

It is worth noting that most schools do not practice or promote such democracy in their classrooms. Although students' ideas can be considered as their starting points in learning, they are not given a chance to be engaged with others' ideas, and not necessarily treated as valid in the end. The officially correct ideas will rule; the high-stakes testing environment does not allow diverse ideas to interact with one another to work themselves out, but demands that systematic efficiency govern students' own development. Little room is available for a socially engaging intellectual process.

This process acknowledges every individual's idea in his or her learning effort as a serious foray into the subject matter, and into a shared experience among learners present. It also calls for learners to make connections to ideas already shared. All ideas from learners, just like all learners are human beings, are on equal footing. Thus, the bottom line in teaching is that "an idea is not to be discarded because of the person it came from. It will be considered no matter who says it – unless the person who puts it forward is not taking it seriously" (Duckworth, 2016).

Where can people find democracy of ideas in classroom practice? There could be a long list of examples, and Duckworth mentioned a few in her interview: Constance Kamii's (1982) arithmetic classes; Elizabeth Cavicchi's (e.g., 2008b, 2009) history of science and contemporary science learning; Alythea McKinney's (2005) history classes in elementary school; and Lisa Schneier's (2015) graduate course on teaching and learning. "So what I call the democracy of ideas seems to me an important element of the climate in the classroom. As ideas are accepted democratically, the *person* also tends to be accepted democratically. We will get more respect for people along with all these respected ideas" (Duckworth, 2016).

Teaching and Learning: A Way of Living for the Present

Critical exploration in the classroom prioritizes the ideas of all learners because such ideas are the essence of intellectual development. Trying to figure things out often means struggles, confusion, and uncertainty along with playfulness, openness, and readiness to embrace the complexity of the subject matter. All these are the important characteristics of genuine learning and teaching that derive from that starting point of learners and teachers figuring things out (Duckworth, 2012).

However, politicians and educational bureaucrats often set their eyes on education to prepare students for the next grade and for future employment. For example, on the eve of the statewide annual standard tests in Tennessee schools, called TNReady, the governor sent out a warm and encouraging letter to every student in the state with a B2 pencil and this opening statement: "Whenever I visit a Tennessee classroom, I am impressed and inspired by the hard work our students and teachers are doing. Across the state, I see students learning what they need to know for the next grade and for success in life after high school" (Haslam, 2017).

Important as these future goals are, there is little concern about how students should value their own learning and respect one another's ideas; about what teachers do to help students learn; and about the social justice of allowing everyone's ideas about the subject matter to be considered in the classroom.

In her address to a large audience, Duckworth (2012) responds to the increasingly difficult situation in which teachers find themselves in school: "I'd like to say that teachers are being deprived, not only of their professional dignity, but for me, even more regrettable, of knowing the joy that their work could bring them." If teachers are not respected for their professional dignity and their joy in teaching and learning, can we expect students to be socialized to respect one another's ideas and value one another's creative minds?

Concluding Remark

Recall the three assumptions Duckworth states at the start of this chapter: teaching and learning in the classroom are all about developing the power of students' minds, and of their creative capacities; about helping students become confident and complex thinkers; and about building in them a sense of community responsibility, democratic commitment, and social justice. In contrast to what learning is supposed to be in the high-stakes testing environment, Duckworth (2012) calls for a different kind of reform in education, a return of joy to learning and teaching:

> Drawing students into your subject matter, seeing what their ideas are, witnessing the struggles, the insights, the perseverance, the playfulness, often enriching your own point of view with theirs. It is engrossing, and fascinating, and exhilarating. I wish it for you, and I wish it for children and teachers in our schools right now.

Note

1. In the United States, professional education organizations issued guidelines incorporating different shades of constructivism, such as *the Curriculum and Evaluation Standards for School Mathematics* (NCTM, 1989), *The National Science Education Standards* (National Research Council, 1996), and *Innovations in Science Education Survey Instrument* (BSCS, 1994). In other

Western countries, "The New Zealand National Science Curriculum is heavily influenced by constructivist theories and ideals. . . .Comparable documents in Spain, the UK, Israel, Australia, and Canada bear, to varying degrees, the imprint of constructivist theory" (Matthews, 2002, p. 122).

References

Au, W. (2011). Teaching under the new Taylorism: High-stakes testing and the standardization of the 21st century curriculum. *Journal of Curriculum Studies, 43*(1), 24–25.

Au, W. (2013). Hiding behind high-stakes testing: Meritocracy, objectivity and inequality in U.S. education. *International Education Journal: Comparative Perspectives, 12*(2), 7–19.

Auger, J. L. (2014). The author has the last word: Buddy editing in a first-grade classroom. *Harvard Educational Review, 84*(3), 367–384.

Biological Science Curriculum Study. (1994). *Innovations in science education survey instrument*. Colorado Springs, CO: Biological Science Curriculum Study.

Cavicchi, E. M. (2007). Mirrors, swinging weights, lightbulbs...: Simple experiments and history help a class become a community. In P. Heering & D. Osewold (Eds.), *Constructing scientific understanding through contextual teaching* (pp. 47–63). Berlin, Germany: Frank & Timme.

Cavicchi, E. M. (2008a). Opening possibilities in experimental science and its history: Critical explorations with pendulums and singing tubes. *Interchange, 39*, 415–442.

Cavicchi, E. M. (2008b). Historical experiments in students' hands: Unfragmenting science through action and history. *Science and Education, 17*(7), 717–749.

Cavicchi, E. M. (2009). Exploring mirrors, recreating science and history, becoming a class community. *The New Educator, 5*(3), 249–273. https://doi.org/10.1080/1547688X.2009.10399577

Chiu, S. M. (2009). The ancient master painted like me. *The New Educator, 5*(3), 229–248. https://doi.org/10.1080/1547688X.2009.10399576

Cochran-Smith, M. (2000). Gambling on the future. *Journal of Teacher Education, 51*(4), 259–261.

Council of the Great City Schools. (2015). *Student testing in America's great city schools: An inventory and preliminary analysis*. Washington, DC: Council of the Great City Schools.

Darling-Hammond, L. (2015). Can value added add value to teacher evaluation? *Educational Researcher, 44*(2), 132–137.

Dewey, J. (1916). *Democracy and education*. New York: Macmillan.

Duckworth, E. R. (1973). The having of wonderful ideas. In M. Schwebel & J. Raph (Eds.), *Piaget in the classroom*. New York: Basic Books.

Duckworth, E. R. (1996). *"The having of wonderful ideas" and other essays on teaching and learning* (2nd ed.). New York: Teachers College Press.
Duckworth, E. R. (2000, March 11). Interview by Y. Hsueh. Cambridge, MA.
Duckworth, E. R. (Ed.). (2001). *"Tell me more": Listening to learners explain.* New York: Teachers College Press.
Duckworth, E. R. (2005a). A reality to which each belongs. In B. S. Engel (Ed.), *Holding values: What we mean by progressive education* (pp. 142–147). Portsmouth, NH: Heinemann.
Duckworth, E. R. (2005b). Critical exploration in the classroom. *New Educator, 1* (4), 257–272. https://doi.org/10.1080/15476880500276728
Duckworth, E. R. (2006). Introduction. In *"The having of wonderful ideas" and other essays on teaching and learning* (3rd ed.). New York: Teachers College Press.
Duckworth, E. R. (2009). Helping students get to where ideas can find them. *The New Educator, 5*(3), 185–188. https://doi.org/10.1080/1547688X.2009.10399573
Duckworth, E. R. (2010). The soul purpose. *Learning Landscapes, 3*(2), 21–28.
Duckworth, E. R. (2012, February 16). *Confusion, play and postponing certainty.* Cambridge, MA: Harvard Thinks Big. Retrieved from http://news.harvard.edu/gazette/story/2012/02/confusion-play-and-postponing-certainty-eleanor-duckworth-harvard-thinks-big/
Duckworth, E. R. (2016, April 26). Interview by Y. Hsueh. Memphis, TN.
Gordon, D. T. (2003). Introduction. In D. T. Gordon (Ed.), *A nation reformed? American education 20 years after A Nation at Risk.* Cambridge, MA: Harvard Education Press.
Haslam, B. (2017, April 10). *Letter to Tennessee students.* Nashville, TN: State Capital.
Hilliard, A. (2000). Excellence in education versus high-stakes standardized testing. *Journal of Teacher Education, 51*(4), 293–304.
Hursh, D. (2013). Raising the stakes: High-stakes testing and the attack on public education in New York. *Journal of Education Policy, 28*(5), 574–588.
Hsueh, Y. (1995). *From Piaget to pedagogy: A brief history of constructivist teaching movements.* Qualifying paper. Cambridge, MA: Harvard Graduate School of Education.
Hsueh, Y. (2005a). The lost and found experience: Piaget rediscovered. *The Constructivist, 16*(1). (Refereed electronic journal of the Association for Constructivist Teaching).
Hsueh, Y. (2005b). Critical exploration in the classroom: Its past and present. In D. Wallace (Ed.), *Education arts, and morality: Creative journeys* (pp. 121–141). New York: Kluwer Academic.
Hsueh, Y. (2009). Jean Piaget in the United States, 1925–1971. In U. Müller, J. M. Capendale, & L. Smith (Eds.), *The Cambridge companion to Piaget.* Cambridge, UK: Cambridge University Press.

Hughes-McDonnell, F. (2009). I wonder how this little seed can have so much potential: Critical exploration supports preservice teachers' development as science researchers and teachers. *The New Educator, 5*(3), 205–228. https://doi.org/10.1080/1547688X.2009.10399575

Inhelder, B., Sinclair, H., & Bovet, M. (1974). *Learning and the development of cognition*. Cambridge, MA: Harvard University Press.

Kamii, C. (1982). *Number in preschool and kindergarten*. Washington, DC: National Association for the Education of Young Children.

Layton, L. (2015, October 24). Study says standardized testing is overwhelming nation's public schools. *The Washington Post*, Education Column. Retrieved from https://www.washingtonpost.com/local/education/study-says-standardized-testing-is-overwhelming-nations-public-schools/2015/10/24/8a22092c-79ae-11e5-a958-d889faf561dc_story.html?utm_term=.c027847ec710

Matthews, M. R. (2002). Constructivism and science education: A further appraisal. *Journal of Science Education and Technology, 11*(2), 121–134.

McKinney, A. (2005). *Using women working resources in schools: A case study*. Cambridge, MA: Harvard Graduate School of Education.

National Council of Teachers of Mathematics. (1989). *Curriculum and evaluation standards for school mathematics*. Reston, VA: National Council of Teachers of Mathematics.

National Research Council. (1996). *National science education standards*. Washington, DC: National Academy Press.

Nichols, S. L., Berliner, D., & Noddings, N. (2007). *Collateral damage: How high-stakes testing corrupts America's schools*. Cambridge, MA: Harvard Education Press.

Rauchwerk, S. (2003). *Incubating knowledge: A narrative account of eight teachers studying chickens*. Qualifying Paper. Cambridge, MA: Harvard Graduate School of Education.

Ripple, R. E., & Rockcastle, V. N. (Eds.). (1964). *Piaget rediscovered*. Ithaca, NY: Cornell University Press.

Rogoff, B. (2003). *The cultural nature of human development*. New York: Oxford University Press.

Schneier, L. (2001). Apprehending poetry. In E. R. Duckworth (Ed.), *Tell me more: Listening to learners explain* (pp. 42–78). New York: Teachers College Press.

Schneier, L. (2015). *T-440 teaching and learning: "The having of wonderful ideas."* Retrieved from http://www.gse.harvard.edu/course/fall-2015/t440-teaching-and-learning-having-wonderful-ideas-fall-2015

CHAPTER 15

How Documentation of Practice Contributes to Construction and Reconstruction of an Understanding of Learning and Teaching

Linda R. Kroll

Learning to teach is a lifelong endeavor, requiring constant construction and reconstruction of one's teaching, curriculum, classroom management, philosophy, and a devotion to an inquiry stance toward one's practice. In this chapter I examine how a teacher education program, founded on principles of teaching for social justice, uses constructivist-inspired instruction to help prospective and practicing early childhood and elementary school teachers to become inquiring practitioners who continually examine how they and their students are constructing understanding of content, culture, process, and themselves. To begin, I examine recent clarifications and changes in our understanding of constructivism, as a theory of learning and as an inspiration for how to teach.

I have based my teaching and my learning life for the past 45 years on the theory of constructivism—a theory about *learning* and how one learns. This chapter focuses on where I am now in my thinking about how constructivist theory can inform our teaching, and particularly, how it can inform our thinking about what we teach, how we teach, for whom we teach, and how we know what our students have learned (not necessarily the same as what we intended to teach). I will address three ideas: constructivism as I

L.R. Kroll (✉)
School of Education, Mills College, Oakland, CA, USA

D.W. Kritt (ed.), *Constructivist Education in an Age of Accountability*,
https://doi.org/10.1007/978-3-319-66050-9_15

understand it now; the principled nature of learning to teach; and documentation as research and assessment, and as a way to connect constructivist theory with how we think about and understand our teaching, our own learning, and our students' learning.

Constructivism as a Way of Understanding Knowledge and Learning

"All knowing is an action by the knower. All knowing depends on the structure of the knower. Knowledge is brought forth in doing" (Maturana & Varela, p. 34). In *The Tree of Knowledge* (1992), Maturana and Varela take us into the biology of how we know and show how knowledge itself is a biological construction. Understanding constructivism as rooted in biology and the action of the knower is not a new idea, but it has been recently confirmed and clarified by several theorists. Fosnot and Perry (2005) present a review of constructivist theory, its biological roots, and the biological, social, and cultural genesis of development and learning. "Current biological models help us understand that both the structure of the mind and the knowledge we construct of the world are a part of an open system—in fact knowledge and mind cannot be separated because one affects the other" (p. 28). Understanding these basic connections helps us to see that teaching and education are rooted in this knowledge and mind relationship. Fosnot and Perry go on to say "All cultures represent the meaning of experience in some way…Abstracting and generalizing experience by representing them with symbols (itself a constructive process) allows the creation of 'semiotic spaces' where we can negotiate meaning" (p. 30). In many ways, our focus on constructivist theory for thinking about children's learning and teachers' work has been limited, in that we tend to focus on learning what is to be measured in school. The concept of schools and teachers as accountable for children's learning, and children and students as responsible to learn particular material in a particular form is in direct contradiction to what we now know about the nature of knowledge, how we learn, and how we can be effective as teachers. In addition, the way we measure what we think our students have learned, through the traditional assessments of standardized tests, other summative assessments, and other more formative assessments limits how we think about the nature of learning and the potential of schooling.

The application of constructivist theory to issues of schooling and teaching must take into account the role of representation in how we learn and how we communicate with one another about what we "know." Fosnot and Perry (2005, p. 31) write, "learning is a constructive building process of meaning making which results in reflective abstractions producing symbols within a medium. These symbols then become part of the individual's repertoire of assimilatory schemes, which in turn are used when perceiving and further conceiving." This "individual repertoire of assimilatory schemes" may be unique to that individual, but it is neither idiosyncratic nor isolated from the community in which these schemes are constructed. Fosnot and Perry add, "Multiple perspectives may offer a new set of correspondences, and at times even contradictions, to individual constructions" (p. 31). The act of representation and re-representation requires reflection, generalization, and further abstraction of what has been constructed in action. The reflection on learning that is required to produce a representation is another constructive act. Reflection on the representations of others then leads to a re-representation and reconstruction of the individual's structures. Thus, both representation and collaborative construction contribute to an individual's understanding and knowledge, which individuals and their collaborators continue to construct and reconstruct, within a particular culture and context.

Constructivism can guide us in thinking about how and what and when we teach if we understand four essential ideas within the theory (as articulated by Fosnot & Perry, 2005, pp. 33–34).

"Learning is not the result of development, rather learning is development." When we understand this, we move away from either a behaviorist or maturationist perspective on development, and understand that development is not linear, nor is it prescriptive. It is the result of reorganization of understandings on the part of an active learner in interaction with context and culture. It is a recursive process, where structures are continually disturbed and reconfigured or rebuilt.

"Disequilibrium facilitates learning." Learning occurs when a person's structures or understandings are disturbed by a contradiction, by "errors" that are welcomed and examined. Rather than correcting learners, teachers can encourage learners to explore contradictions and recognize that confusions can lead to restructuring and further learning and development.

"Reflective abstraction is the driving force of learning." Learning takes time to consider and reconsider the contradictions or errors identified, as well as concepts that are considered to be true. Reflection is an essential part of the learning and development process. Young children can be seen to reflect in action, while older students reflect in a variety of ways that help them restructure their understandings. Representation and re-representation of ideas through writing, drawing, diagrams, sculpture, photography, movement, and other media support the reflective process and allow for generalization and regeneralization across experiences, situations, and contexts.

"Dialogue within a community engenders further thinking." This is an understatement! Thinking and learning occur within a context that inevitably includes other people, whether they are actually present or whether they are present in the form of books, tools, and other methods that support development and learning. But particularly in schools, the understanding that a community can support the identification of contradictions, the raising of questions, and the restructuring of understanding is essential. Rogoff (2003) talks about participation in a community of learners and the participatory appropriation which leads to new understandings. While this is a different conception than the reflective abstraction described by Fosnot and Perry (from Piaget originally), together these two ideas help us to understand how learning occurs, both within the individual and across individuals in collaborative contexts.

Constructivism, then, is a theory that can help us understand how people learn. It can then help us to think about how we might construct contexts in which our students can learn—always recognizing that what we hope they will learn might look different from our own constructions. That does not mean that what the students learn is *less correct* than what we are trying to teach them; it means that we, too, as teachers, must continually be constructing and reconstructing what we need to teach prospective teachers about how to teach!

I will return to the importance of representation and re-representation as an essential piece of applying constructivist theory when I discuss documentation as research and the possibility of using documentation as assessment for understanding what students and teachers are learning. But first, we must consider ethical issues in schools and how constructivism can contribute to schools that serve a social justice purpose, to support the development and learning of all children and youth, their teachers, and their families.

Principled Practice

The Mills College Teacher Education programs where I teach are founded on a set of six principles, under the umbrella of working toward social justice, excellent outcomes and opportunities for all students (Kroll & Galguera, 2005). Keeping these principles in mind as we teach prospective teachers and as they learn to teach their students is a powerful holistic way to think about the art of teaching and its obligations. Briefly, I review these principles as they underlie the constructivist nature of our programs.

Teaching Is a Moral Act Guided by an Ethic of Care

Above all, teaching is about relationships, between teachers and students, teachers and other teachers, teachers and families, students with one another, school personnel and teachers, students and families. These relationships must be grounded in the premise that we all are looking out for one another and have in mind the best outcomes for each of us, as we are all learners together (Richert, 2005). We must recognize the moral nature of the dilemmas we encounter on a daily, if not hourly basis. Keeping in mind the centrality of relationship to a learning-teaching encounter is essential.

Teaching Is Based on Reflective Practice

Because teaching is a lifelong learning proposition, what happens in the classroom is subject to active and systematic investigation. The uncertainty of teaching and learning can be mitigated by an inquiry stance, which embraces that uncertainty and welcomes it with curiosity and passion (Donahue, 2005). This perspective is tied to a constructivist view of learning, articulating clearly the role of reflection and reflective abstraction in constructing new understandings.

Teaching Is Collegial and Collaborative

It is not just friendly relationships among colleagues and students, but teaching well reflects an understanding that what we know and what we learn are constructed together, in social contexts and as a social construction. Colleagues and community are central. Again, we return to the idea that teaching is based on relationships, in a relationship. Working together ensures a context for both support and critique, for questioning our practices and testing out our ideas with one another as we seek to construct classroom contexts that are democratic and equitable (Cossey & Tucher, 2005). This principle emphasizes the social constructivist nature of learning and, consequently, of what occurs in the classroom. While teachers have traditionally felt isolated, behind their closed doors, more and more collaboration between teachers, and between teachers and their students, is recognized as essential to a productive and moral learning environment.

Teaching Is a Political Act

Teaching and professional practice are political; teaching is concerned with matters of change that are neither neutral nor inconsequential. Each lesson, each interaction, each curriculum is a political act, reflecting, whether we intend it or not, a stance toward students' and teachers' abilities, rights and goals (Galguera, 2005). The political nature of teaching is very much about power and how that power is distributed and used by teachers; there are political implications for every action we take as teachers, and also for every action we fail to take to ensure social justice and equity for all students.

Knowledge is power. As children become better learners, they gain power within the society in which they want to become full-fledged participants. Knowledge also gives one authority; if one is an expert in a subject, then one has power to help society and others and also to abuse that power. A teacher's main responsibility is to create a context in which children can learn, can develop the knowledge they need to succeed in life and participate in society. But teachers, too, are subject to regulations and requirements that may or may not support the full development of the children they are teaching. Thus, teachers must make political decisions about how to follow directed curriculum and testing mandates, while ensuring that the children they teach are learning to their full potential. Because teachers are also subject to these mandates, they are often forced to make uncomfortable choices. These choices are the result of political decisions, whether or not teachers are conscious of the political nature of them (Kroll, 2008).

When We Teach, We Teach "Something": Content Knowledge Is Central to Our Teaching

Our professional work is deeply connected to the content of our work; our central goal is to prepare others to acquire deep understandings of the content of their practice (LaBoskey, 2005). Understanding the constructivist nature of knowledge is imperative to having a curious, tolerant, and passionate attitude toward both our subject matter and how our students learn this subject matter. Being open to the errors learners make and the contradictions that learners encounter in the process of learning content as opportunities for deeper learning is essential. While we are teaching about a content, we are not so interested in the right answer, as we are in the deep construction of understanding of a subject or content.

Learning Is a Social, Developmental, and Constructive Process

Our understanding of the learning process is supported by our understanding of constructivist theory and the social and cultural nature of how people learn (Kroll, 2005). This understanding is at the heart of how we understand constructivist theory and how we think about our practice. This understanding of how people learn is reflected in the way we organize our individual classes, how we organize our program strands and concentrations, and in how we think about the responsibilities we have undertaken to educate our students to be teachers focused on issues of social justice for all students.

These six principles are touchstones for every decision we make. We use them to relate back to our central question of how we can prepare educators to work for social justice, equitable opportunities, and excellent outcomes for the children they teach, the teachers they supervise, and their colleagues. They underlie the ethical nature of our endeavor. While constructivist theory helps us to understand how people learn, and how contexts and cultures support different kinds of learning, an ethical stance that supports these understandings enables us to be respectful and welcoming of individual and cultural differences. The multiethnic, multilinguistic, and multicultural nature of our society requires that we be open to a variety of ways of knowing. We need to recognize the genius of each of our students and of ourselves in order to support their construction of new knowledge.

Documentation as Research: A Way of Knowledge and Making It Public

Documentation (e.g. Edwards, Gandini, & Forman, 2012; Krechevsky, Mardell, Rivard, & Wilson, 2013) is a complex and deep process of teacher research and inquiry which refers to "any record of performance that contains sufficient detail to help others understand the behavior recorded" (Forman & Fyfe, 2012, p. 250). Its goal and effect is to make visible and explain the learning processes of the students and teachers within a learning community. Its process is to gather a variety of data through different media, including written observational notes, audio recording of student and teacher conversations, student work (such as drawings or writing), photographs, and video, as a basis for communal reflection and conversation. Each medium provides a unique glimpse into the learning process and together this systematic data collection makes learning visible. Uniquely among teacher research processes, documentation is inclusive of not only the teachers examining their practice, but also of the students and community who are both participants in and audience for the documentation and the documentation process. Documentation is not an end in itself (Krechevsky et al., 2013); rather it is both a retrospective and prospective process. It allows teachers and students to reflect on what happened, on what was learned, and on what questions were asked, in an effort to decide what to do next. Thus, documentation does not simply show others what happened, but makes visible learning to the benefit of the learners (adults and children) as they move forward. Such reflection and progression makes teacher research and inquiry a recursive process where documentation can serve as powerful assessment and make public both the content and process of learning. Documentation makes teaching and learning truly democratic processes, including all participants—teachers, children, and families (Kroll & Meier, 2018).

Key practices of documentation include *observation, recording, interpreting* and *sharing* (Krechevsky et al., 2013). *Observation* can be purposeful when observing an activity, practice, or child with intention and, also, curiosity. *Recording* creates tangible artifacts with different media, serving as the memory of the group, and allowing for revisiting: "documentation lends relevance to what comes next and, when what comes next emerges directly from learners' own questions and ideas, learners see they are contributing to the direction of their learning" (Krechevsky et al., 2013, p. 81). *Interpreting* provides a forum for reflection and interpretation of the artifacts and other data: "When the purpose is to uncover assumptions, know learners better, and examine teaching practices, teachers need to articulate their thinking and compare their interpretations with those of others (including students)" (IBID, pp. 82–83). In Reggio Emilia, educators refer to documentation as "visible listening." *Sharing* makes learning and teaching visible to others.

Forman and Fyfe (2012) differentiate between *display* (which shows) and *documentation* (which explains). Documentation makes learning and teaching visible to others. It can establish a forum for discourse (rather than talking) about learning and teaching. It can engage families beyond their concerns for their own child and create public exhibitions. The most well-known of these public exhibitions are the international traveling exhibitions from the municipal infant toddler centers and preschools of Reggio Emilia (*The Hundred Languages of Children; The Wonder of Learning*); and these international exhibitions have inspired local ones. Documentation creates a context for children and adults to come together in a civic forum, giving each child, teacher, and school a public voice and a visible identity. Other forms of going public can be more local, where documentation panels are available for view within the school public spaces.

In addition, in all cases, documentation panels are visible to the children and their families within the classroom, providing vehicles for reflection and clarification for everyone. Because documentation includes not only the students and teachers, but also the community in which learning occurs, there is a democratic and participatory aspect to the process. By making public what is happening in a classroom and a school, by inviting the perspectives of all participants, and by continuing to raise questions that are generated by the documentation, the educational context of the classroom becomes a democratic space listening to everyone's voice.

Documentation of practice in a variety of media (e.g., audio, video, photo, written notes) provokes reexamination of one's learning and teaching, giving both teachers and children the opportunity to take a second or third look at teaching and learning experiences. This second look allows teachers to reexamine their beliefs and understandings of what they think happened in their teaching and students the opportunity to examine their own learning. The purpose of documentation is to make learning visible (Rinaldi, 2006), the learning of the students involved in what is being documented and also the learning of the teachers involved in the learning exchange. Thus, documentation attempts to make visible the construction process of learning. It provides the forum for reflection and can provoke reflective abstraction resulting in further learning and development.

In the Mills College early childhood teacher education program, student teachers learn to use documentation as research to investigate their practice and to assess the learning of the children with whom they work. To that end, they use a variety of documentation techniques, including documentation panels, learning stories, videographic records of students' learning and teachers' teaching, and other media. In learning to do these sorts of investigations, a most challenging aspect is determining a question that will focus the investigation, using that question to filter evidence that illustrates children's learning, and ultimately realizing what further questions there are to continue pushing the learning forward.

Student teachers often have difficulty understanding the difference between documentation and child observation. Their initial questions almost always center on a particular child in the classroom who puzzles them, who intrigues them, with whom they feel a particular affinity. Their questions are often connected with a notion of learning about the child in order to 'fix' the child. Of course, they do not articulate their question in quite that way; but often that is what it comes down to. This is a perversion of the purpose of documentation, which is to see the child clearly for who she or he is and to celebrate the learning and brilliance they demonstrate. However, through the process of documentation, of reflecting on the different representations that they collect, the student teachers who have begun with wondering about a particular child come to recognize that children have a purpose for what they do, a reason for the actions they take, and that young children in particular are always trying to figure out the nature of the world in which they find themselves. In a context where they are encouraged to pursue their interests and their questions, their knowledge construction becomes clear. Documentation through a variety of media helps the teacher to see that construction process more clearly.

I recently finished teaching a class on documentation as research. The students produced a visual (and often auditory) presentation of what they had been investigating all semester, making visible the learning of the children with whom they were working. Inadvertently (on their part, but not mine), they also made visible their own learning. One after another they realized that they had come to view children as powerful learners, as competent, as exercising agency in their work, as having multiple ways of demonstrating what they understand, are learning, and are thinking about. Studying how to do documentation, trying it out for themselves, and then reflecting on it together with their classmates revealed to them in powerful ways what they had been saying but not particularly understanding. Of course, this understanding will be subjected over and over again to a rethinking and representation, because learning never stands still. But their development as thoughtful teachers, constructing their own understanding of the teaching and learning processes, was mightily affected by this way of inquiring into their practice. It allowed them to be both up close and personal with the children's learning and to take a reflective stance *along with the children* about what was happening in their classrooms. The projects led them to examine their own assumptions, biases, and beliefs in significant depth. The documentation project reflects the application of the six Mills principles (presented earlier in this chapter) to the curriculum taught in our program.

In addition, documentation contributes to the participatory and democratic possibilities inherent in classroom teaching. Because documentation makes learning visible, and because documentation is made public (in however small or large a venue), the voice or language of the students and the teacher become evident to the local and (possibly) the greater community. In addition, because documentation reveals the local and particular nature of the learning and investigations occurring in a school or classroom, the *power* of the students' and teachers' learning is evident. In contrast to standardized assessments, which are anonymous (except when they demonstrate the 'deficiencies' of certain students or student groups), documentation shows what students have learned, how teachers have taught, and celebrates the achievements and knowledge created within the local context. By recognizing these achievements, the community accords both gravitas and power to the students and the teachers, and in turn to the communities in which they are situated.

Documentation as Assessment: Constructivism Can Redefine Accountability

Let us return to the notion of representation and re-representation. Fosnot and Perry remind us that it is through constructing symbolic representations that we go beyond the "immediacy of the concrete, to cross cultural barriers to encounter multiple perspectives that generate new possibilities, to become conscious of our actions on the world in order to gain new knowledge with which to act" (2005, p. 31). We ask students to represent their thinking primarily through language, both spoken and written, although we use graphic representations for some content as well. However, most of these representations are for the benefit of the teacher, to assess the student's learning. What if we were to use representation and re-representation for students to reflect on their own ideas and understandings? Through different modes of representation, we can come to understand something in a more complex way.

For example, if we ask a five-year-old to take a photograph of a flower, to sketch the flower from life, to draw the flower from the photograph, to create the flower using clay or wire and tissue paper, to make a diagram of the life cycle of the flower, to keep a diary of the growth of the flower, and so forth, then by the end of this long study of the flower, the child will have noticed and learned many things about this flower, about flowers in general and about many things to do with plant growth. If in between each iteration of representation, the five-year-old discusses what she has done with her friends, if some of the time she makes some of these representations with other children, then what they all observe and think about flowers will be constructed and reconstructed. These modes of representation lead to reflective abstraction about that flower and flowers more generally, knowledge that can be applied in other (horticultural) contexts. They develop theories about flowers. "For adults and children, understanding means being able to develop an interpretive theory, a narrative that gives meaning to the world around them…in Reggio these theories are extremely important in revealing how children think, question, and interpret reality, and their own relationships with reality and with us" (Rinaldi, 2012, p. 234).

The opportunity to represent one's understanding in multiple media provides opportunities for others to listen carefully to those ideas and respond to them and to assess them in a variety of ways. In the infant toddler centers, preschools, and elementary school in Reggio Emilia, documentation is used to support the learning of children, teachers, and communities. "Documentation …does not mean to collect documents after the conclusion of experiences with children, but during the course of these experiences…Documentation is part of the daily life in the schools. It is one of the ways in which we create and maintain the relationships and the experiences among our colleagues and the children. …In the process of learning through documentation, we become aware of learning and its value; we assess it. Therefore, we believe that assessment is also an integral part of the learning and teaching process" (Rinaldi, 2012, p. 238). Listening is seen as the pedagogical basis of teaching and learning. Rinaldi says "listening becomes not only a pedagogical strategy but also a way of thinking and looking at others. Listening is an active verb that involves giving meaning and value to the perspectives of others, a form of assessment" (Rinaldi, 2012, p. 236). Documentation is a form of making listening, as well as learning, visible.

Accountability and quality are two terms that impact the US educational system from care and education of infant toddlers through the education of graduate students at the university level. The public sector demands that those who educate be accountable for the results of their work—that is the successful education of students no matter what level. I just completed my annual report demonstrating how our student teachers have accomplished the goals we set out for them in our program documents. This is not an uncommon experience for any teacher, at whatever level. Moreover, educators are expected to account for and prove that what they are doing results in a quality education for the students they serve, no matter what their age. The implication of this expectation and demand is that there is one destination at which we want all students to arrive. This implies that development or learning has a linear path and common goal. Constructivism would have us understand that it is otherwise. As Maturana and Varela (1992) explain:

> as part of human social dynamics, mind and consciousness operate as selectors of the path which our ontogenic structural drift follows. Moreover, since we exist in language, the domains of discourse that we generate become part of our domain of existence and constitute part of the environment in which we conserve identity and adaptation. ...either we generate a linguistic domain (a social domain) through what we say and do, wherein our identity as scientists is conserved, or we disappear as such. (p. 234)

Constructivism as a post-structural psychological theory (Fosnot & Perry, 2005) would urge us to take a different stance toward assessment. Documentation as a form of assessment can show us children (and students) learning in action and in reflection. It captures through representation and re-representation the different structures that students construct as they participate together in learning encounters. A constructivist perspective challenges us to find assessments that demonstrate the wonder of learning, the extraordinary brilliance of all students. When learning is wondered at and celebrated, when we look for what the students have learned, ask them to think about what it is they have learned and to further question that learning, we create a more equitable, just, and more interesting context for teaching and learning.

References

Cossey, R., & Tucher, P. (2005). Teaching to collaborate, collaborating to teach. In L. R. Kroll, R. Cossey, D. M. Donahue, T. Galguera, V. K. LaBoskey, A. E. Richert, & P. Tucher (Eds.), *Teaching as principled practice: Managing complexity for social justice* (pp. 105–120). Thousand Oaks, CA: Sage.

Donahue, D. M. (2005). Preparing and supporting the reflective practitioner. In L. R. Kroll, R. Cossey, D. M. Donahue, T. Galguera, V. K. LaBoskey, A. E. Richert, & P. Tucher (Eds.), *Teaching as principled practice: Managing complexity for social justice* (pp. 35–56). Thousand Oaks, CA: Sage.

Edwards, C., Gandini, L., & Forman, G. (Eds.). (2012). *The hundred languages of children: The Reggio Emilia experience in transformation*. Santa Barbara, CA: Praeger.

Forman, G., & Fyfe, B. (2012). Negotiated learning through design, documentation and discourse. In C. Edwards, L. Gandini, & G. Forman (Eds.), *The hundred languages of children: The Reggio Emilia experience in transformation* (pp. 247–272). Santa Barbara, CA: Praeger.

Fosnot, C. T., & Perry, R. S. (2005). Constructivism: A psychological theory of learning. In C. T. Fosnot (Ed.), *Constructivism: Theory, perspectives and practice* (2nd ed., pp. 8–38). New York: Teachers College Press.

Galguera, T. (2005). Learning to see the invisible: Power, authority, and language in the classroom. In L. R. Kroll, R. Cossey, D. M. Donahue, T. Galguera, V. K. LaBoskey, A. E. Richert, & P. Tucher (Eds.), *Teaching as principled practice: Managing complexity for social justice* (pp. 121–142). Thousand Oaks, CA: Sage.

Krechevsky, M., Mardell, B., Rivard, M., & Wilson, D. (2013). *Visible learners: Promoting Reggio-inspired approaches in all schools*. San Francisco: Jossey-Bass.

Kroll, L. R. (2005). Constructivism in teacher education: Rethinking how we teach teachers. In L. R. Kroll, R. Cossey, D. M. Donahue, T. Galguera, V. K. LaBoskey, A. E. Richert, & P. Tucher (Eds.), *Teaching as principled practice: Managing complexity for social justice* (pp. 57–80). Thousand Oaks, CA: Sage.

Kroll, L. R. (2008). *Teaching as principled practice. Managing complexity for social justice and beyond. The inclusion of human rights in learning to teach*. In the symposium, T. Russell, chair, Principles to guide learning to teach: Lessons from research and experience. Paper presented at the annual meeting of the American Educational Research Association, New York.

Kroll, L. R., & Galguera, T. (2005). Teaching and learning to teach as principled practice. In L. R. Kroll, R. Cossey, D. M. Donahue, T. Galguera, V. K. LaBoskey, A. E. Richert, & P. Tucher (Eds.), *Teaching as principled practice: Managing complexity for social justice* (pp. 1–16). Thousand Oaks, CA: Sage.

Kroll, L. R., & Meier, D. R. (2018). *Documentation and inquiry in the early childhood classroom*. New York: Routledge.

LaBoskey, V. K. (2005). Preparing to teach content: "Not just a series of fun activities". In L. R. Kroll, R. Cossey, D. M. Donahue, T. Galguera, V. K. LaBoskey, A. E. Richert, & P. Tucher (Eds.), *Teaching as principled practice: Managing complexity for social justice* (pp. 105–120). Thousand Oaks, CA: Sage.

Maturana, H. R., & Varela, F. J. (1992). *The tree of knowledge: The biological roots of human understanding* (R. Paolucci, Trans., Rev. ed.). Boston: Shambhala.

Richert, A. E. (2005). Learning to negotiate the moral terrain of teaching. In L. R. Kroll, R. Cossey, D. M. Donahue, T. Galguera, V. K. LaBoskey, A. E. Richert, & P. Tucher (Eds.), *Teaching as principled practice: Managing complexity for social justice* (pp. 17–34). Thousand Oaks, CA: Sage.

Rinaldi, C. (2006). *Dialogue with Reggio Emilia: Listening, researching and learning*. New York: Routledge.

Rinaldi, C. (2012). The pedagogy of listening: The listening perspective from Reggio Emilia. In C. Edwards, L. Gandini, & G. Forman (Eds.), *The hundred languages of children: The Reggio Emilia experience in transformation* (pp. 233–245). Santa Barbara, CA: Praeger.

Rogoff, B. (2003). *The cultural nature of human development*. New York: Oxford University Press.

CHAPTER 16

Reimagining Research and Practice in Education

Stanton Wortham

In some educational policy circles, a comparison with the medical profession generates both breathless admiration and paternalistic scolding. The profession of teaching could be like medicine, we are told, and all would be well. Unfortunately, however, stubborn or self-interested teachers, teacher educators, administrators, unions, and others refuse to behave like doctors. Before we follow unreflective advocates of the medical model too far, we should examine the assumptions made by this simple account. Many aspects of the analogy between medicine and education deserve scrutiny. In this short chapter, I examine one: education should not be conducted like medicine because the dominant model of the relationship between research and practice in medicine does not fit what should happen in education. In order to improve education, we must imagine and implement a different kind of relationship between research and practice.

Over the past decades, "implementation science" has become a central concern of policymakers, researchers, and practitioners in medicine and public health—leading to thousands of journal articles and the field's own journal, *Implementation Science*. Advocates of this new field hope to facilitate the effective use of research evidence in health care. The first sentence of the opening editorial in the first issue of the journal defines the field: "Implementation research is the scientific study of methods to promote the

S. Wortham (✉)
Boston College, Chestnut Hill, MA, USA

D.W. Kritt (ed.), *Constructivist Education in an Age of Accountability*,
https://doi.org/10.1007/978-3-319-66050-9_16

systematic uptake of research findings and other evidence-based practices into routine practice, and, hence, to improve the quality and effectiveness of health services and care" (Eccles & Mittman, 2006). This and similar definitions of "implementation" presuppose at least three important things: there is a gap between "research" and "routine practice"; this gap is qualitative, because "research findings" are a different kind of entity from "health care"; and the ideal movement between research and practice is unidirectional, with research findings used to improve practice.

I agree with the journal editors and others that practice in both medicine and education would be improved if researchers and practitioners collaborated more to incorporate relevant research findings into hospitals and schools. But I disagree with the three assumptions above, which undergird most conceptual, empirical, and practical work on the use of research evidence in medicine and education. I argue that there is no qualitative gap between research and practice, because both researchers and practitioners engage in practical activities that involve theories, evidence, and action—often different types of activities, but not qualitatively different. That is, researchers don't deal exclusively in knowledge and practitioners don't deal exclusively in action. It follows that theories, evidence, and guidelines for action can productively move from practice to research as well as the other way around.

This chapter develops an alternative to the dominant account of research and practice. I make no further claims about how research and practice do or should relate in medicine. Perhaps the commonsense account presupposed in "implementation science" works in medicine, or perhaps not. Either way, this model should not be adopted in education. My proposed reconceptualization of "implementation" in education has important consequences. Mistaken assumptions about a qualitative gap between research and practice can impede well-intentioned advocates of implementation as they try to improve practice. If we misunderstand the nature of both research and practice, we are less likely to use research evidence productively. Accurate understanding is particularly important at this historical moment, when researchers, policymakers, and practitioners are attending closely to "evidence-based" practice.

Beyond the Gap

The prevailing view—exemplified in the *Implementation Science* editorial and many other accounts (e.g., Haines & Donald, 1998)—is that researchers and practitioners each have a distinct set of goals, concepts, and activities, producing a gap between research and practice. This idea is accurate in some respects but misleading in others. Researchers and practitioners habitually participate in different types of activities, but there is no qualitative difference between the two domains. Researchers do have things to offer practitioners, but not through the transmutation of decontextualized knowledge into practical action nor through the deductive "implementation" or "application" of general knowledge. My reconceptualization of the relationship between research and practice focuses on four terms: "activity," "repertoire," "movement," and "evaluation."

Activity

Most accounts of "implementation" assume a difference in kind between the two domains: researchers discover relatively decontextualized knowledge, and practitioners use this knowledge to change the world. But researchers and practitioners both make knowledge claims and take action in the world. For instance, as Nelson, Leffler, and Hansen (2009) and Honig and Coburn (2008) show, practitioners regularly consult a range of evidence in making decisions, even though they do not always use the types of evidence that researchers trust the most. Both researchers and practitioners participate in *activities* that combine knowledge and action in sociocultural context. They may habitually be involved in different mixes of activities, but both make knowledge claims, gather evidence, and act to change the material world. Knowledge cannot be created or implemented except through activities, which are inevitably amalgams of knowledge and action in social context.

This argument is based in cultural-historical activity theory (Cole, 1996), a perspective on learning and development that builds on Vygotsky (1934/1987). This tradition makes a compelling case that humans are not by nature disembodied thinkers. The basic unit of analysis for human conduct is "activity," an event in which individuals use resources to act in context. Individual knowledge is essential to activity, but so are the "mediational means" or tools that we use to formulate and accomplish action (Wertsch, 1998). These mediational means often include other people, with whom we communicate, but even solitary action is mediated by language and other artifacts that have been developed by others. An analysis of even the most intellectual activities—such as science, for example (Knorr-Cetina, 1999), or intellectual discussion (Wortham, 2006)—must describe the practical dimensions of human action: the goals, relationships, politics, tools, and so on, that partly constitute the activity.

Accounts of a qualitative gap between research and practice generally assume that research discovers decontextualized knowledge, which can then be applied or implemented. This implementation is often assumed to take what Weiss (1977), Walter, Nutley, Percy-Smith, McNeish, and Frost (2004), and Davies and Nutley (2008) criticize as a too-simple "linear" form, with knowledge moving in a line from research to practice. From a cultural-historical perspective, I agree with these authors that decontextualized knowledge is not often a useful unit of analysis. Research findings are developed in activities, and those activities depend on goals, relationships, politics and tools that mediate them. The results of research cannot be neatly excised from these mediators and passed on to practitioners, because the mediators partly constitute those results. Research can certainly influence practice—sometimes productively and sometimes not—but this involves the movement of knowledge together with mediational means, together with pieces of the activities in which it was developed, into another domain of activity in which it is recontextualized and partly transformed. The use of research evidence involves the incorporation of research activities—or products of those activities that contain traces of their activity-based origins—into an ongoing set of "practical" activities.

Repertoire

Like everyone else, researchers and practitioners engage in various activities as part of their jobs. They reason and act in a range of ways, depending on the task and the context. Researchers regularly engage in instrumental actions intended to achieve concrete results—like getting a grant, having a manuscript published, receiving approval from peers, being recognized by scholarly or popular audiences, and so on. Practitioners often make decontextualized knowledge claims and analyze evidence—as when teachers give quizzes or ask questions and infer from the responses what students have learned. Neither research nor practice involves or produces a pure type of knowledge or action. The domains of research and practice are heterogeneous, in two senses. First, researchers and practitioners develop various types of theories, analyze various types of evidence, and engage in various types of action. Both domains involve people who participate in diverse activities, not people who do only one thing. Second, both researchers and practitioners develop theories, analyze evidence and act in the world. Research is not simply "pure," and practice is not simply "applied." The heterogeneous mix of activities that researchers do involves both reflection and action, both discovery and application, and the same is true for practitioners.

In other words, researchers and practitioners have diverse *repertoires*. Rymes (2010) traces the concept of "repertoire," as it has been used in linguistic anthropology to account for people's capacity to communicate in various settings. Many people are capable of talking sports with fans in a bar, talking science with colleagues in a lab, talking about a relationship with a partner, and so on. On the other hand, no one can participate coherently in every type of verbal interaction, even in one's native language (many of us cannot converse with theoretical physicists, for example, or ice climbers, and some of us do not talk about relationships well, either). We each have overlapping but partly divergent repertoires—involving phonological, morphosyntactic, semantic, and pragmatic capacities as well as background knowledge. Rymes and others use this approach to explain language learning, arguing that all learners can manage some types of speech even in a new language and that educators must build on these existing capacities to expand learners' repertoires.

The concept of repertoire helps explain the more general capacity to participate in activities. Each of us can participate in various activities because we have knowledge and skills, dispositions and habits that let us coordinate with other participants, and because we know how to use tools to make progress in a given activity. No two people have exactly the same repertoires, although there is significant overlap in many cases. Educational researchers, for instance, will have overlapping repertoires, with some central activities familiar to everyone and others less so. Some educational researchers are deeply experienced with educational activities, while others have no contact with children. Educational practitioners in the US overlap with researchers in some parts of their repertoires (literacy in English, for example, and understanding the importance of controlled experiments). Some educational practitioners are quite adept at research activities, publishing articles and having advanced degrees, while others are not. The core of researchers' and practitioners' repertoires may differ, but there is substantial overlap.

The typical activities of research are distinct from those of practice. But even for researchers these activities involve both knowledge and action. Researchers and practitioners each perform some activities that involve data analysis and knowledge development and some that involve acting more directly to change the material world, even though the prevalence of these activities differs across the two domains. Individuals and groups vary in their repertoires: some researchers' repertoires overlap more significantly with practitioners', and vice versa. On this account, moving research evidence productively into practice requires deeper understanding of the activities in each domain and the variability in repertoires across practice settings, plus knowledge of how evidence can be recontextualized in applied activities in heterogeneous local settings. I thus agree with Davies and Nutley (2008) that we must study the contextualization of research evidence in practice, but I add an emphasis on the heterogeneous repertoires found in both domains.

Movement

Both researchers and practitioners engage in activities that involve theory, evidence, and action. They participate in heterogeneous activities while doing their jobs, with some activities more decontextualized than others. To participate competently in these activities, researchers and practitioners have heterogeneous repertoires. And these repertoires overlap significantly across the domains of research and practice. Furthermore, both individuals and activity settings change over time: individuals periodically stop doing some activities, and they learn new ideas and techniques; theories, evidence and guidelines for action come and go across settings. The knowledge, skills, tools and dispositions that constitute researchers' and practitioners' repertoires *move* across space and time.

Contemporary accounts of culture have shifted from containers to flows as the central metaphor (Appadurai, 1986; Urban, 2001). A culture has traditionally been conceptualized as a bounded group of people who share certain knowledge and habitual actions. More recent accounts speak instead of flows, in which beliefs and actions move across space and time, circulating densely in some areas but spreading unevenly and eventually being diluted or replaced. Instead of studying a stable set of beliefs and activities, anthropologists now study how beliefs and activities stabilize within subsets of a group, then break up or reorganize as further movement occurs and new forms emerge (Agha, 2007).

It is distorting to conceptualize researchers' and practitioners' activities and repertoires as stable properties of individuals or groups. At any given time, researchers and practitioners participate in heterogeneous but characteristic activities and tend to have certain repertoires. But the ideas, evidence, and habits of individuals and groups change, with established ones spreading or contracting and new ones appearing. This means that research evidence moves into practice in the context of other motion. Practitioners adopt new ideas, consider new evidence and develop new habits at the same time as they and others introduce research evidence into the local practice context. The question becomes: How does research evidence intersect with the changing, heterogeneous activities and repertoires of practice contexts? How can we expand practitioners' repertoires by creating productive intersections between the changing mix of activities engaged in by researchers and practitioners?

Evaluation

As ideas, evidence, and templates for action move across contexts, people always *evaluate* them. These evaluations are social facts that also move across space and time. Bakhtin and others have shown how, when we introduce a new idea or action, we cannot help but take a stance on its value (Bakhtin, 1935/1981; Wortham, 2001). When an educational intervention enters a new setting, for example, practitioners might evaluate it as "impractical," "inappropriate," "successful," and/or "research-based." As Davies and Nutley (2008) argue, the introduction and use of research evidence is always a political matter, and evaluations are part of the political struggles that can accompany such evidence. An evaluation of some idea or protocol as "research-based" might be valued differently by different constituents. Some front-line practitioners might see it as ill-informed meddling by researchers who do not understand practice, while others might see it as proven to be effective. Nelson et al. (2009) describe how many practitioners evaluate research evidence as irrelevant or limited. Such evaluations will often circulate along with the idea or tool in question, as practitioners discuss it among themselves or consult other experts.

It is important to see that evaluation goes beyond the cognitive processes involved in "sensemaking" and related activities (Klein, Moon, & Hoffman, 2006; Weick, Sutcliffe, & Obstfeld, 2005). Evaluations involve tacit positioning as well as explicit evaluation—they are mediated by cultural artifacts and embodied stances, not limited to explicit mental representations

(Csordas, 1994). Whenever we speak or act, we do something and we simultaneously frame or comment on the action (Agha, 2007). If we attend only to the level of what a reformer says or what an intervention proposes, we miss the framing activity that gives our action meaning and direction. Evaluations matter because the same idea or technique will be interpreted and used differently depending on the prevailing evaluation. To investigate how research moves into practitioners' activities, we must also investigate how associated evaluations move with and influence the use of that research.

Implications

According to "implementation science," we should follow the medical model and overcome the alleged gap between research and practice by enticing or coercing educators to implement "evidence-based" techniques. Researchers discover what works, and then practitioners should implement their recommendations. This approach has various moral, conceptual, and practical problems, many of them described by Cochran-Smith and Lytle (2009) and Hargreaves and Shirley (2012), among others.

In this chapter I have argued that an "implementation" approach also presupposes an unrealistic account of research and practice. Researchers and practitioners rely on changing, heterogeneous repertoires of ideas, activities, and tools, as well as evaluations of those ideas, activities, and tools. Both researchers and practitioners make knowledge claims, gather evidence, and act to change the world in various ways, and they use overlapping repertoires to do so. There is no qualitative gap between research and practice. Research can be useful to practitioners, but not as a set of decontextualized knowledge claims or general techniques that differ completely from practitioners' own repertoires.

Instead of asking how we can get practitioners to do what researchers say, we should be asking how we can work with practitioners to expand their repertoires, such that they incorporate some of the dispositions, habits, and assumptions that characterize good educational research. In order to do this successfully, we will need to do a different kind of research on implementation. We must study how ideas, tools and activities can productively move from the heterogeneous domain of research into the heterogeneous domain of practice. How are research evidence and evidence-based strategies inserted into practitioners' ongoing activities, which themselves already involve knowledge claims, evidence and practical techniques? How do research evidence and evidence-based strategies move into practitioner repertoires, amidst the movement of other claims, evidence and techniques that is already occurring? How do practitioners evaluate these "evidence-based" techniques, and what other evaluations influence their adoption and modification of researchers' ideas and proposals? How can researchers and practitioners together expand practitioner repertoires in ways that improve practice?

We also need changes in policy and practice. Some top-down policy changes are necessary, along the lines suggested in Hargreaves and Shirley (2012), to treat teachers like professionals. But repertoire expansion will happen most effectively if we change our activities. One promising example is the practitioner inquiry movement, which empowers teachers to do research on their own practice, sometimes with researchers available as coaches (Cochran-Smith & Lytle, 2009). Another is design-based implementation research, which involves partnerships between researchers and practitioners (Penuel, Allen, Farrell, & Coburn, 2015). New kinds of activity like these challenge the assumptions behind "implementation," in practice. It will take both reimagining and redoing the relationship between research and practice if we hope for educational research to be productive.

References

Agha, A. (2007). *Language and social relations.* New York: Cambridge University Press.

Appadurai, A. (1986). *Modernity at large.* Minneapolis, MN: University of Minnesota Press.

Bakhtin, M. (1935/1981). *The dialogic imagination.* Austin, TX: University of Texas Press.

Cochran-Smith, M., & Lytle, S. (2009). *Inquiry as stance.* New York: Teachers College Press.

Cole, M. (1996). *Cultural psychology.* Cambridge, MA: Harvard University Press.

Csordas, T. (1994). *The sacred self.* Berkeley, CA: University of California Press.

Davies, H., & Nutley, S. (2008). *Learning more about how research-based knowledge gets used: Guidance in the development of new empirical research.* New York: William T. Grant Foundation.

Eccles, M., & Mittman, B. (2006). Welcome to implementation science. *Implementation Science, 1*, 1–3.

Haines, A., & Donald, A. (1998). Getting research findings into practice: Making better use of research findings. *BMJ, 317*, 72.

Hargreaves, A., & Shirley, D. (2012). *The global fourth way.* Thousand Oaks, CA: Corwin.

Honig, M., & Coburn, C. (2008). Evidence-based decision-making in school district central offices: Toward a policy and research agenda. *Educational Policy, 22*, 578–608.

Klein, G., Moon, B., & Hoffman, R. (2006). Making sense of sensemaking: Alternative perspectives. *IEEE Intelligent Systems, 21*, 70–73.

Knorr-Cetina, K. (1999). *Epistemic cultures*. Cambridge, MA: Harvard University Press.

Nelson, S., Leffler, J., & Hansen, B. (2009). *Toward a research agenda for understanding and improving the use of research evidence*. Portland, OR: Northwest Regional Educational Laboratory.

Penuel, W., Allen, A.-R., Farrell, C., & Coburn, C. (2015). Conceptualizing research-practice partnerships as joint work at boundaries. *Journal for Education of Students at Risk, 20*, 182–197.

Rymes, B. (2010). Classroom discourse analysis: A focus on communicative repertoires. In N. Hornberger & S. McKay (Eds.), *Sociolinguistics and language education* (pp. 528–546). Tonawanda, NY: Multilingual Matters.

Urban, G. (2001). *Metaculture*. Minneapolis, MN: University of Minnesota Press.

Vygotsky, L. (1934/1987). *Thought and language* (Trans. A. Kozulin). Cambridge, MA: MIT Press.

Walter, I., Nutley, S., Percy-Smith, J., McNeish, D., & Frost, S. (2004). *Improving the use of research in social care practice*. London: Policy Press.

Weick, K., Sutcliffe, K., & Obstfeld, D. (2005). Organizing and the process of sensemaking. *Organization Science, 16*, 409–421.

Weiss, C. (1977). Research for policy's sake: The enlightenment function of social research. *Policy Analysis, 3*, 531–545.

Wertsch, J. (1998). *Mind as action*. New York: Oxford University Press.

Wortham, S. (2001). *Narratives in action*. New York: Teachers College Press.

Wortham, S. (2006). *Learning identity*. New York: Cambridge University Press.

CHAPTER 17

School Learning as Compliance or Creation

David W. Kritt

For almost two decades, since the advent of No Child Left Behind, test performance has been the paradigmatic metric of learning. Teaching-to-the-test, a phrase that originated as a denigrative epithet, has become entrenched as standard operation procedure in classrooms and schools across the country. Critiques of testing (e.g., Au, 2009; Taubman, 2009) have laid bare false assumptions and biased implications. Many veteran teachers despair of what their profession has become, but their opinions have been cast aside and they have been targeted as villains in the tale of what has gone wrong with public schools. The centrality of testing in American education has proven resilient, able to weather all critiques. Both conservative (G.W. Bush) and liberal (Obama) administrations have supported testing practices through funding incentives. Politicians are cowed into being tough, insisting on results. Parents are discouraged from questioning, pressured to acquiesce. And so, the prominent place afforded testing is now a well-entrenched fact of life.

Perhaps because tests are so familiar from our own school days, and also because they are cloaked in the authoritative-sounding technicalities of psychometric certainties, their power to provoke fear and awe is mostly unchecked and unexamined. Standardized Army mental tests, claiming to

D.W. Kritt (✉)
School of Education, College of Staten Island, City University of New York, Staten Island, NY, USA

D.W. Kritt (ed.), *Constructivist Education in an Age of Accountability*, https://doi.org/10.1007/978-3-319-66050-9_17

measure aptitude, came into widespread use during World War I, when large numbers of military conscripts had to be sorted and placed as quickly as possible. Other early uses included identification of "mental defectives"; these efforts were sometimes aligned to the eugenics movement (e.g., Galton, 1904). Current uses are cast in a more acceptable rhetoric.

Just as square pegs don't fit round holes, divergent thinkers have difficulty passing some crucial tests. By smoothing off the edges of variability to achieve quantifiable performances, schools from K-16 have become sites that promote intellectual uniformity for the sake of measurable standards. Careful consideration must be given to the very notion that the proverbial wheat should be separated from the chaff. Social hierarchies (e.g., Bourdieu & Passeron, 1977/1990) and prejudices (e.g., Alexander, 2010) are, of course served. In terms of individual thought, it abets homogeneity. Citing examples of singular artists (e.g., Ornette Coleman in jazz, Jorge Luis Borges in literature, Mark Rothko in painting) is one way of arguing for the merits of the unconventional; many less vaunted talents make the case equally well. Early and repeated screenings that exclude, discourage, and channel youthful effort in only the most conventionally accepted directions may facilitate meeting workforce needs but does a disservice to those seeking to create, as well as far greater numbers pursing fulfilling lives.

Most education has been oriented toward the ability to replicate procedures currently in use rather than creating new ones. A constructivist approach often starts with a focus on the student's understanding and works to move it toward greater sophistication. This requires careful observation to reveal how a person understands a problem. This observational approach appears, albeit in different forms, in Socratic instructional dialogues, Piaget's interviewing, and Vygotsky's Zone of Proximal Development.

Instruction narrowly oriented toward right answers and recognizing only the most straightforward, logical, or conventionally accepted route to solutions may help many students pass a class or a test. But learning to replicate optimal performances precludes challenges that, when used as an impetus for further exploration, catalyze thought about how and where ideas and formulas work and when they do not. Although antithetical to covering the greatest amount of material as quickly and efficiently as possible, a focus on the learner provides the opportunity for deep and flexible understandings that may eventually contribute to the creation of new knowledge.

There has been a good deal of partisan bickering, characterizing Piagetian discovery learning as haphazard and undisciplined cognitive meandering, or deriding guided instruction as focused on replicating socially promoted, culturally valued practices, rather than true cognitive growth. With discovery learning, the question arises how standard practices are constructed. Social construction approaches must grapple with how novelty arises.

A primary tension lies between how much guidance, and what type, is used. Theoretical differences can be productively put aside in the interest of achieving shared goals of producing engineers who not only compute but also ask new questions and derive fresh answers, and artists who synthesize technique, broad-based inspiration, and imagination. Solving problems involves much more than applying a procedure. Ellen Langer discussed the presentation of a block building task under two different conditions, one where a few solutions were demonstrated, another where it was suggested that there are many ways to construct a bridge (1997, pp. 85–87). Participants in the first condition tended to replicate what they were shown. In the other condition, a substantially greater range of creative solutions was generated.

A set task, as might be encountered on a factory assembly line, can be taught in a procedural way. Although many jobs require enacting routines, few that are currently available provide a living wage. Perhaps now more than in the past, when factories, farms, and mines employed vast numbers, skilled workers must often figure out what the problem is before they can begin to solve it. A very different kind of education is needed to encourage posing new questions (Riegel, 1976), devising ways to approach old ones, and addressing emerging problems as they arise.

Scaffolding

A brief look back at Woods, Bruner, and Ross (1976), the article that introduced "scaffolding" to the English-speaking world, both provides insight into differences in basic assumptions about learning and suggests ways of integrating the insights of often divergent camps. Although Vygotsky is not cited in the article, similarities to instruction suggested by the Zone of Proximal Development have been acknowledged by subsequent analyses (Berk & Winsler, 1995; Rogoff & Wertsch, 1984). The general issue for teachers is how to assist a student.

Woods et al. combine theoretical discussion with descriptions of "how children respond to different forms of aid" (1976, p. 91). In order to make these descriptions systematic, the problem presented to children was well-defined in terms of objectives and design of materials. Although a good research method, it skews the conception of learning and teaching; it is a task where the instructor knows precisely what the student should do and how to solve the problem. It is assumed that success requires combining component acts and identifies instances where "it is matching (and the correction of mismatching) that is at the heart of problem solving" (p. 90). Further, it is asserted that "comprehension of the solution must precede production" (p. 90), because recognition of a solution is essential for successful use of feedback on the means to an end. These assumptions are seldom questioned, but it must be acknowledged that this is a very specific type of learning situation, calling for a particular type of intelligent performance.

The children were given an initial five minute period to acquaint themselves with the materials prior to the tutoring sessions reported. To their credit, the authors acknowledge, "They did not always enjoy giving up imaginative play for the more constrained task of building a pyramid" (p. 93). This contrasts greatly with the structured instruction, where there was always a definite desired solution and standard verbal feedback to a child was "make some more like that one" (p. 92).

The tutoring process itself is premised on these biased preferences: "This scaffolding consists essentially of the adult 'controlling' those elements of the task that are initially beyond the learner's capacity, thus permitting him to concentrate upon and complete only those elements that are within his range of competence" (p. 90). In this way, focus and choice are restricted. Furthermore, the tutor is clearly placed in the role of confirming whether something has been done correctly. The importance of being right is strongly communicated, often resulting in a loss of confidence in one's own thought and feeling. Satisfying the teacher becomes much more important than satisfying one's own curiosity. Spontaneity is all but extinguished, as is student initiation of inquiry (Oyler, 2006). We see this peculiar sort of relationship in virtually every classroom, with students insecure about what they are doing without frequent and clear confirmation by an adult, creating a crippling dependency for some.

In practical terms, educators as theoretically disparate as Duckworth (1973/2006), Wells (1999), and Arievitch (2017) prescribe actually doing very similar things: encouraging children to do as much as possible on their own; determining where a child is encountering difficulty and using this as a guide to instruction, directing attention, and starting with broad clues, providing more detailed cuing only if the child cannot successfully use previous cues. But this is not to deny differences in employing verbal cues and manipulating objects. One is how the thought involved in problem solving is conceptualized—as "combining component acts" (Wood et al., 1976, p. 90) or coordinated action (Piaget 1971). The former is oriented toward the acquisition of discrete skills, while the later emphasizes understandings and operations where the whole is more than the sum of its parts; meaning arises from the relations between the parts (whether acts, facts, simple ideas, or cognitive operations). Another difference is the frequent overuse of the demonstration of materials and techniques. Reference to a model as a standard to be imitated differs greatly from exploring the use of symbolic representations (Edwards, Gandini, & Forman, 1993) and physical models to work through conceptual understandings (Passmore, Gouvea, & Giere, 2014; Forman, this volume). These fundamentally differ, both in terms of the cognitive processes promoted and desired outcomes. Emphasizing observational learning and replication of what has been demonstrated or even attempting to direct a child's field of attention to features of an already solved problem narrows possibilities rather than opening a variety of types of elaboration (cf. John-Steiner, 1985/1997).

Such considerations could fundamentally change the place of scaffolding in the discourse of the field (J. Becker, personal communication, March 12, 2017). Instead of an innocuous, universally accepted central method of teaching and learning, it should be recognized as inherently focused on compliance with predetermined procedures and reproduction of outcomes instead of creative engagement in exploration and innovation.

A Disciplined Mind

It is widely thought that children need to be disciplined in three distinct ways. One is punishment for transgressions. A second is guidance into the attentional foci and accumulated wisdom of academic subjects. The third is a multileveled matrix of coaxing, steering, and incentivizing of consciousness (cf. Foucault, 1977) in certain directions (e.g., love of classical music, respect for business-like entrepreneurship, compliant conformity) rather than others (e.g., rebellious outrage, wildly unconventional and idiosyncratic artistic expressions by outsiders crafting detritus and feeling).

True learning is not and never was about filling children's heads or efficient coverage of essential knowledge. But neither is it acceptable to place our faith in children running naked through the wilderness, innocently and naturally discovering the wonders of the world. The young do not magically possess truth, only to be perverted by society. Children need guidance. Teachers need orientation on how to provide it. It is a matter of balance, and now the balance is extremely tilted. Students' misunderstandings, curiosity, and insecurity provide prime opportunities for interventions (i.e., "teachable moments") that nurture deepening understanding, expanding horizons, and grounded approximations of certainty.

Dewey's (1916/1997) intent was teaching children skills valued by their society. It is difficult to argue with this. No parent wants their child to be a misfit; even rebels value charm, persuasiveness, and the analytic prowess to dissect societal hypocrisy. Yet to teach valued skills, teachers frequently rely upon demonstrations so that students might imitate (i.e., the common teacher practice of modeling) and restrictive correction of the way students work through problems. No doubt these practices contribute to the large numbers of children prone to just giving up until an adult guides them step-by-step.

A pivotal issue separating a broad array of constructivist approaches is a focus on individual mental activity, epitomized in exploration and discovery, or emphasis on the communal basis of human activity. This is not at its heart a dispute about how much of a role social, cultural, and material context plays; it is a fundamentally different conception of thought and feeling. Nonetheless, it is possible and worthwhile to work toward psychological and educational approaches that are fully cultural while preserving individual identity and subjectivity (Cole & Wertsch, 1996; Kritt, 1993; Stetsenko & Arievitch, 2004). Participation in a cultural milieu does not preclude individual invention, and cultural acquisition need not be a context-based mimetic process; there is transformation during use, as well as internal transformation (Vygotsky, 1934/1987). In this way, learning can be invention while also being participatory.

Constructivist education is very difficult to do right; it is infrequently taught with perseverance and depth, and more often presented as one technique in a bag of tricks including flashier use of technology for "sharing" in various ways. It is inadequately acknowledged by the profession because it is not new and does not fit the accountability narrative. Innovations arouse excitement and lately this has been almost exclusively ideas surrounding tests and materials for standardized curriculum, as well as moves toward privatizing public schools. This is accentuated by a lack of sustained support by schools, administrators, communities, and politicians for teaching for understanding and helping students reach their potential. The devaluing of constructivist approaches and teacher wisdom, and the low social prestige and pay of teachers are part of a circular causality.

Teachers are publicly vilified and not trusted to do much more than comply with a scripted mandate to get results and produce uniformly reliable output in terms of the thinking of individuals who pass through their classrooms.

Learning in Schools and Out

Especially early in their careers, teachers are frequently reviewed by supervisors and so must be concerned with planning lessons in relation to Common Core requirements and test preparation. They are pressured (by mandated curriculum, by administrators) to race through a large number of topics, introducing each quickly and superficially. The best of their students can keep up and the rest invariably fall behind. Confronting new material without an adequate framework for understanding, too often they have to fake their way through classes. Even students who get good grades do not necessarily have a good grasp on the material. When the criterion for success is doing more and doing it faster, successful surface performance is confused with understanding.

"The basics" are frequently taught in a rote manner with the expectation they will subsequently be used (Langer, 1997), yet neither multiplication tables nor declensions of nouns in a foreign language are useful in themselves. Thinking is not the conscious application of rules or following guidelines for task completion. Faith in freezing memories of basic principles and relying on retrieval for application results in vast numbers of students who can repeat the Pythagorean theorem but not understand how it works, know scales but have little feel for music, have command of several components of a language but are unable to speak or read it. Functioning in the world requires understanding situations and conditions and making adjustments where needed.

The emphasis in schools is on students arriving at the right answers, not improving a student's thought. Teachers feel they don't have time to allow students to build on what they know, adjust an initial solution when it is inadequate, and figure out the answer in their own way. Students working through their confusion and everyday epiphanies are not as easily documented as immediate successes.

The presumption "that the goal of the educational process is to equip students to achieve specific, desirable outcomes" (Langer, 1997, p. 121) is both an almost ubiquitous disposition toward teaching and a rationale for testing that has persisted as such a truism that it is seldom stated. Teachers often take the approach: Here's what we want to do and here is how to do it. Common Core instruction perpetuates this long unexamined pedagogical tradition by prescribing optimal logical steps toward solution. Even approaches ostensibly emphasizing "critical thinking" or "learning how to learn" frequently tell students what their objectives are and supply a set of tools for how to achieve them. Of course, there are real-world incentives for students. A student must demonstrate passable levels of performance in a range of academic subjects to graduate high school, and higher levels to graduate with distinction and gain admission to a competitive college. Most parents are concerned that their child must clear a number of hurdles in order to get a good job and have choices in life. And so, they find it difficult to question rigidly imposed educational imperatives ostensibly ensuring well-rounded students.

In the popular imagination, a concept of the average child is granted legitimacy by high-stakes tests (cf. Gould, 1981). Because of rampant grade inflation this is not necessarily a student who consistently receives grades of "C" in coursework. Gould (1996) expressed doubt that individuals ever were uniform in abilities. It is more likely that students vary widely depending upon type of thought required and context (e.g., Kritt, 2004). Nonetheless, it is the widespread expectation within schools that everyone should demonstrate competence in a wide range of pursuits, ranging from quantitative ability to physical fitness.

If, however, we look at real children in classrooms and their lives outside of school, we see that a dialectic emerges so that interests develop and guide an individual toward certain aspects of the world and the modes of thought relied upon by practitioners of related craft (e.g., engineers and social workers, would-be sports stars and rappers; cf. John-Steiner, 1985/1997). Children have, and seek, widely different experiences. Student interests could be encouraged and interrelations explored if that were truly valued (e.g., Renninger, Kensey, Stevens, & Lehman, 2015). Instead, even well before the latest round of educational reforms, students were routinely denied the opportunity to develop their own ideas about a topic (Duckworth, 1973/2006, p. 64); they were presented with problems rather than encouraged to formulate their own questions. Working out solutions has been streamlined almost to extinction with the ease of looking up answers to virtually everything online. Obtaining answers is not a substitute for critical thinking and problem solving.

Children's curiosity seems to diminish, their scientific speculations, storytelling, and artistic creations become reluctant, clumsy and less interesting as they advance through school. One explanation is that intuitive understandings must be replaced if thought is to progress (cf. Gardner, 1991; Vygotsky, 1934/1987). Naïve sophomoric attempts to comprehend, ignorant of all that has come before, tend to lead to self-indulgently solipsistic railings. Accordingly, youthful enthusiasms are held in abeyance as students are introduced to academic traditions of knowledge and modes of inquiry. Only after regimented immersion in disciplinary conventions over a span of years (often until college and sometimes lingering until completion of postdoctoral placement in someone else's lab) is a degree of true individuality in thought encouraged.

In this way, thought is disciplined. The molding and shaping that we call education is primarily oriented toward reproducing itself. Mutatis mutandis, we make what is makeable, with substantive innovation occurring at a glacial pace. There are internal psychological reasons for this, as well as the conservative bias of society's structural constraints. A period of disorganization occurs before new understandings and achievements are consolidated into a more sophisticated coordination (Strauss & Stavy, 1982; Uttal & Perlmutter, 1989). Teachers also conform to social norms (Brown & Gilligan, 1992), often unwittingly constraining the full development of their students. The result is that few individuals ever emerge to do something better; most become disenchanted and withdraw, left with an imposed orthodoxy and thwarted imaginations.

Education for the Future

A wide range of educators expound with a rhetorical flourish that we must prepare students for a rapidly changing world. This will not be achieved by training mastery of a set of skills; it requires flexibility, an education that will equip students to ask new questions about things we cannot even anticipate. An unsung constructivist sage, Heinz Werner (1926/1948) long ago reminded us that there is more than one answer to many questions and also multiple pathways to the same answer.

Recognition of the variety of backgrounds, interests, and ways of learning students bring to any topic or understanding paves the way for heightened awareness of their misconceptions. Traditional teachers just ignore them and concentrate on the right answer. More enlightened teachers realize that obtaining answers is not everything. It is better to make a mistake than to be afraid to think. Having a wrong idea and then figuring out where it went wrong can be an opportunity for further exploration that leads to real understanding. Duckworth (1973/2006, p. 68) notes, "What you do about what you don't know is, in the final analysis, what determines what you will ultimately know." Accordingly, constructivist approaches to learning prescribe taking a longer time with fewer topics and encouraging students to explore them more completely. This sort of education requires authentic issues and rich problems that are multifaceted. Topics should be presented with multiple entry points (Gardner, 1983, 1991) so that students who think and learn in a variety of ways can proceed in a fully engaged way.

It is widely acknowledged that children cannot learn things well beyond their understanding. On the other hand, attempting to match instructional materials too closely to the child's mental level (perhaps as indicated by test results) may lead to instruction that is not challenging. Genuine intellectual involvement is unlikely to emerge from either alienation and bewilderment or functioning within a comfort zone. Nor is it likely to be inspired by problems devised to demonstrate application of a particular formula or principle. Engagement with real activities lessens the gap between learning and application (e.g., Arievitch, 2017; Arievitch & Haenen, 2005; Lave & Wenger, 1991; Rogoff, 1990; Salomon, 1993; Scribner, 1984).

The case against the types of assessment that are currently in the foreground of education is multifaceted. These assessments are based on a naïve understanding of learning and thinking and are used punitively instead of to improve classroom learning. The standards are often low, with passing rates adjusted as a political expediency; it has been reported that at times school personnel cheat to meet criteria. Probably the most detrimental effect is that test performance pressures dominate instruction, as if achieving a score is a truly meaningful goal rather than a purely instrumental one.

There are, of course, alternative approaches to assessment. Instead of looking for what the student does not know, the emphasis could be on letting students demonstrate what they know. Tests yield numerical summaries of the static endpoint of a performance. These are used in comparisons of individual performance to group performance, criterial standards, or, more rarely, one's own prior performance. Such analyses yield some perspective, but many of the questions asked and answered are wrongheaded and too often used to penalize low-scoring individuals and schools. A primary orientation toward obtaining information that could directly contribute to the intellectual development of specific children would lead us to proceed quite differently. We could value students' points of view, try to figure out how they understand, and use this as a jumping-off point for personalized interventions or group instruction.

In contrast, most testing situations focus on answers. Students get credit only for what they do correctly; near misses and valiant attempts don't count. For Vygotsky (1978, Chap. 6), determining what a child can do on her own was only the first step of assessment. He proceeded to work with the child, partially completing a solution and leaving it to the child to do more. He concluded that the difference between what can be accomplished with assistance and what can be done independently reveals where instruction should be focused to reach the next step of a child's functioning. This Zone of Proximal Development (Grigorenko and Sternberg, 1998; Kozulin, 2005; Vygotsky, 1978) can be used as a guide to working toward the child's potential.

Prior to the complete takeover by high-stakes testing, there was much interest in another promising alternative approach to assessment, portfolios. The standard portfolio includes a selection of work in a variety of areas (e.g., in various artistic media, literary genres or styles, or in several school subjects—English, Math, History, and Science). Providing a sampling of what a student can do is similar to what testing does, but the works were produced in a meaningful context and are authentic in that respect. Furthermore, the selection process may involve reflection upon one's own work, strengths, and weaknesses. But when used only in a workman-like way, they are just a collection of work and students fill in the slots to fulfill requirements. And since it is intended as a social display, presented for purposes of receiving a grade or sometimes shown to prospective employers, its value for further learning and development is often subordinated.

A further refinement, with greater potential to contribute to further learning and honing one's craft, is the process portfolio (e.g., Wolf, 1989; cf. Kroll, this volume). Inclusion of evidence of one's progression—initial attempts, intermediate steps, mistakes, and poor choices made along the way, as well as "masterpieces" produced—provides a record of how thought has developed. It can be encouraging to see how far one has come, even if the goal is to go further. Looking at earlier work can provide insight into current performance, sometimes illuminating whether persistent tendencies have limited what is attempted or how a distinctive style emerged. Paths not taken can be reconsidered. New challenges might be suggested. Process portfolios are an opportunity for a very personalized and authentic assessment of what has been produced and what still requires work. But they are not prone to easy quantification, so they do not currently receive a great deal of attention in schools.

On Creativity

We have all encountered the trope of parents who think that their young child paints like Paul Klee or Jackson Pollock. The child's creation might be vibrant and uninhibited, but children do not have the control of their mode of expression that an adult artist can achieve. Most artistic creation involves working with the constraints and affordances of materials or forms (e.g., in sculpture or film, music or literature). This requires exposure to a wide variety of works of art, as well as techniques, broad experience wielding paint brushes and chisels, arranging forms in space and tones in time, and reflecting upon what has been created. But the process is more than fulfilling prerequisites and moving on to the next step.

It is unfortunately the case that few adult artists, even those who receive an excellent arts education and work tirelessly, create works that are original, expressive, truly shocking, or timelessly beautiful. Most are conventional in one way or another. Discovering something new or changing the way we see is extremely rare. We are all so immersed in the correct way to do things and cultural normalcy that it is indeed difficult to move beyond it. This is probably natural, in the same way that regression to the mean cannot be faulted as either willful or forced conformity. Yet there are powerful forces in the community of educators that strive for a smooth consistency and uniformity. It is not that this is inherently bad, but that it is achieved in a way that precludes everything else.

Similarly, certain types of thought are favored, particularly the sciences, mathematics, and skills useful for business. Collateral damage includes the arts, which are inadequately supported in schools. Regrettable in itself, this is also symptomatic of pervasive skewing of the entire educational enterprise toward an insistence upon measurable results and an emphasis on outcomes rather than process, spawning the ubiquity of rubrics for scoring a wide range of student work in colleges as well as K-12 classrooms. In common use, students are provided specifications of necessary features of their productions (e.g., written assignments). Some of my borderline college students find this very useful; it helps them to produce workman-like papers that cover all the bases, but even with this specific guidance, they are seldom among the better papers.

Although students learning to write are very different than accomplished authors, it may be instructive to consider whether favored methods of instruction encourage or thwart expressiveness and originality. As a case in point, the novelist Cormac McCarthy, not unlike many of his contemporaries, sometimes writes in a way that is technically ungrammatical. In his novel, *The Road* (2006), he uses this to poetic effect:

> Woodsmoke on the damp air. (p. 83)
> The still poured shape of a river. The dark brick stacks of a mill. Slate roofs. ...No smoke, no movement of life. (p. 78)

If he were a high school student writing these sentences for a class assignment or test, it is likely that these faux sentences would be cited as incorrect. Everything about schooling would encourage the usual and punish divergence. The complete sentence that might be composed would not be as evocative. His art would be lost, his confidence to persevere crushed, if his writing were judged by conventional rubrics or test scoring criteria. Furthermore, his post-apocalyptic theme and imagery would be dismissed as inappropriate; a caring teacher might guide him toward more conventional topics and treatments. Certainly McCarthy has abundantly demonstrated proper usage elsewhere. He might well pass, combining his best efforts with his putative mistakes. But he is not average in ability.

A Playful Mind

From pre-K onward, educating youth is a serious business. Play is seldom given adequate attention by school administrators and policy makers, despite its importance to human development (Bruner, Jolly, & Sylva, 1976; Garvey, 1977/1990; Hirsh-Pasek, Golinkoff, Berk, & Singer, 2009; Paley, 1986). The focus is on learning new content and skills and development of abilities that seem to have tangible value.

But play is not simply a childish waste of time; it is a symbolic achievement (Piaget, 1945/1962) that helps children step away from the here-and-how and deal with unrealized desires (Freud, 1920/1972). Piaget (1945/1962) believed that peer play offers something different and superior to adult-directed activities. In their interactions, children negotiate roles and social expectations, engage in problem solving, and sometimes resolve disagreements; they co-construct plans, interpret scenarios, and imaginatively expand understandings (Goncu & Gaskins, 2011).

Vygotsky (1967, 1978) contended that children perform at a higher level during play than during other activities. The imaginary play of young children "reconfigures reality," so that meanings come to mediate perception of a situation. Following the implicit rules of a fantasy situation transforms relationships between meaning and action in a way that prepares the child for the symbolic substitutions and changes of frame required by study within many academic subjects (e.g., in mathematics, the conventions of literary genres), where disciplinary concepts dominate over concrete situations and initial understandings (cf. Vygotsky, 1934/1987, Chap. 6). It also prepares individuals to continue to play with ideas in adolescence and to engage in hypothetical thought and see beyond current realities.

Unfortunately, the types of play that are developmentally important are at risk of becoming an endangered species. Unsupervised play in parks and various neighborhood sites, once widespread, is now less prevalent because of parental safety fears. And, too often technology structures play on its own terms, not the child's (Kritt, 2000; Kritt & Winegar, 2007). Parents marvel at the toddler who can use an iPad, seldom questioning if anything is learned beyond procedures to make interesting sights and sounds appear. Although computer games can, at best, offer much greater complexity and flexibility (see Polin, this volume), the exchange of photos and videos of cute animals and obsessive social networking do little to provoke imaginative thought.

By the time a person reaches adolescence, certainly during adulthood, play usually consists of athletic activities, organized sports with authoritative referees, competitive online games, or structured social games with written rules. Often absent are real creativity and a sense of wonder. It has been replaced by challenges centered on sophistication of skill or strategy (e.g., in poker, chess, or golf). There is precious little play that breaks the frames of our everyday reality and does artful rearrangement, even if just for a moment. Seeing beyond well-prescribed societal boundaries (Mills, 1967; Weber, 1904/2008) or conceiving of transformative possibilities for individuals and society (Greene, 1995/2000; Stetsenko, 2017) is difficult.

Impassioned arguments for the importance of a liberal arts education (Deresiewicz, 2014; Nussbaum, 2010; Roth, 2014) have cautioned that the current emphasis on career preparation does not well serve the needs of young people. The combination of high costs for education and economic insecurity favor vocational and technical specialization, improving employment opportunities in the short run, but setting the stage for obsolescence in a few years when newer graduates come along with more up-to-date skills, willing to work for lower starting salaries. Yet schools are primarily dedicated to producing well-trained workers to fill slots in corporate and bureaucratic institutions.

Political socialization in schools begins early, including an emphasis on following rules, fulfilling the specifications of rubrics, and a focus on doing what is needed to get good grades. When entering a classroom, it is fairly clear whether curiosity is nurtured or discouraged. If presumptive necessary knowledge takes the foreground, active minds, while not wholly denied, are accorded a clearly secondary role. Certainly disciplined, conventional thinking is valued in most workplaces, and so perhaps it should be increasingly emphasized as the end of schooling and transition to the workforce approaches. But it is strange that it should be so strongly infused in education from early childhood onward. A generation ago, it was argued that childhood is not valued for itself; rather, it is primarily viewed as preparation for adult life (Elkind, 1981/2001). In the interim, the disappearance of childhood (cf. Postman, 1982/1994) has only accelerated. The test scores of third grade children are valued as a predictive indicator of future economic productivity. By eight years of age, childish things must be put aside.

A prospective early childhood teacher in my class concluded her initial report on a classroom observation by stating the three-year-old target child "just needs to understand how to follow orders and do what he is told." In this case I had lost my semester-long effort to dissuade her of this foremost concern. Despite the initial biases of students entering a course of study to become teachers (and too many of their professors as well), emphasizing classroom management and content knowledge is an impoverished view of what is most important about teaching. A young mind should not be corralled.

Even amidst bureaucratic attempts at quality control and teacher-proofing, there is a counter narrative for education where teachers assume a role as public intellectuals nurturing the next generation to not only get good jobs, but to also lead fulfilling lives and participate in a democratic society. This is not a straightforward process. Learning involves divergences and teaching requires improvisation for both the eager and prepared and those bringing mostly resistance to the classroom. That, quite simply, is why constructivist learning principles should continue to play a vital role in an age of accountability.

References

Alexander, M. (2010). *The new Jim Crow: Mass incarceration in the age of colorblindness*. New York: The New Press.

Arievitch, I. M. (2017). *Beyond the brain: An agentive activity perspective on mind, development, and learning*. Rotterdam, Netherlands/New York: Sense Publishers.

Arievitch, I. M., & Haenen, J. P. (2005). Connecting sociocultural theory and educational practice: Galperin's approach. *Educational Psychologist, 40*(3), 155–165.

Au, W. (2009). *Unequal by design: High-stakes testing and the standardization of inequality*. New York: Routledge.

Berk, L. E., & Winsler, A. (1995). *Scaffolding children's learning: Vygotsky and early childhood education*. Washington, DC: National Association for the Education of Young Children.

Bourdieu, P., & Passeron, J. C. (1977/1990). Reproduction in education, society and culture. Thousand Oaks, CA: Sage.

Brown, L. M., & Gilligan, C. (1992). *Meeting at the crossroads: Women's psychology and girls' development*. Cambridge, MA: Harvard University Press.

Bruner, J. S., Jolly, A., & Sylva, K. (1976). *Play: Its role in development and evolution*. New York: Basic Books.

Cole, M., & Wertsch, J. (1996). Beyond the individual-social antinomy in discussions of Piaget and Vygotsky. *Human Development, 39*, 250–256.

Deresiewicz, W. (2014). *Excellent sheep: The miseducation of the American elite and the way to a meaningful life*. New York: Free Press.

Dewey, J. (1916/1997). *Democracy and education: An introduction to the philosophy of education*. New York: Free Press.

Duckworth, E. (1973/2006). *"The having of wonderful ideas" and other essays on teaching and learning* (3rd ed.). New York: Teachers College Press.

Edwards, C., Gandini, L., & Forman, G. (1993). *The hundred languages of children: The Reggio Emilia experience in transformation*. Westport, CT: Ablex.

Elkind, D. (1981/2001). *The hurried child: Growing up too fast too soon* (3rd ed.). Cambridge, MA: Perseus.

Foucault, M. (1977). *Discipline & punish; The birth of the prison*. New York: Vintage.

Freud, S. (1920/1972). *A general introduction to psychoanalysis*. New York: Pocket Books.

Galton, F. (1904). Eugenics: Its definition, scope, and aims. *American Journal of Sociology, 10*(1), 1–25. Retrieved January 10, 2017 from http://galton.org/essays/1900-1911/galton-1904-am-journ-soc-eugenics-scope-aims-htm

Gardner, H. (1983). *Frames of mind: The theory of multiple intelligences*. New York: Basic Books.

Gardner, H. (1991). *The unschooled mind: How children think and how schools should teach*. New York: Basic Books.

Garvey, C. (1977/1990). *Play*. Cambridge, MA: Harvard University Press.

Goncu, A., & Gaskins, S. (2011). Comparing and extending Piaget and Vygotsky's understandings of play: Symbolic play as individual, sociocultural, and educational interpretation. In A. Pellegrini (Ed.), *Oxford handbook of the development of play* (pp. 48–57). New York: Oxford University Press.

Gould, S. J. (1981). *The mismeasure of man.* New York: Norton.

Gould, S. J. (1996). *Full house: The spread of excellence from Plato to Darwin.* New York: Three Rivers Press.

Greene, M. (1995/2000). *Releasing the imagination: Essays on education, the arts, and social change.* San Francisco: Jossey-Bass.

Grigorenko, E. L., & Sternberg, R. J. (1998). Dynamic testing. *Psychological Bulletin, 124*(1), 75–111.

Hirsh-Pasek, K., Golinkoff, R. M., Berk, L. E., & Singer, D. (2009). *A mandate for playful learning in preschool: Presenting the evidence.* New York: Oxford University Press.

John-Steiner, V. (1985/1997). *Notebooks of the mind: Explorations of thinking.* New York: Oxford University Press.

Kozulin, A. (2005). Learning potential assessment: Where is the paradigm shift? In D. B. Pillemer & S. H. White (Eds.), *Developmental psychology and social change: Research, history, and policy* (pp. 352–367). New York: Cambridge University Press.

Kritt, D. W. (1993). *The subjective meaning of shared representations: Television characters and self.* Unpublished doctoral dissertation, City University of New York Graduate Center.

Kritt, D.W. (2000). Loving a virtual pet: Steps toward the technological erosion of emotion. *Journal of American and Comparative Culture, 23*(4), 81–87.

Kritt, D. W. (2004). Strengths and weaknesses of bright urban children: A critique of standardized testing in kindergarten. *Education and Urban Society, 36*(4), 457–466.

Kritt, D.W., & Winegar, T. W. (2007). Technological determinism and human agency. In D. W. Kritt & T. W. Winegar (Eds.), *Education and technology: Critical perspectives, possible futures* (pp. 3–29). Lanham, MD: Lexington.

Langer, E. J. (1997). *The power of mindful learning.* Cambridge, MA: Perseus.

Lave, J., & Wenger, E. (1991). *Situated learning: Legitimate peripheral participation.* New York: Cambridge University Press.

McCarthy, C. (2006). *The road.* New York: Vintage.

Mills, C. W. (1967). *The sociological imagination.* New York: Oxford University Press.

Nussbaum, M. (2010). *Not for profit: Why democracy needs the humanities.* Princeton, NJ: Princeton University Press.

Oyler, C. (2006). *Learning to teach inclusively: Student teachers' classroom inquiries.* Mahwah, NJ: Lawrence Erlbaum Associates.

Paley, V. G. (1986). *Mollie is three: Growing up in school.* Chicago: University of Chicago Press.

Passmore, C., Gouvea, J. S., & Giere, R. (2014). Models in science and in learning science: Focusing scientific practice on sense-making. In M. R. Matthews (Ed.), *International handbook of research in history, philosophy and science teaching* (pp. 1171–1202). Dordrecht, Netherlands: Springer.

Piaget, J. (1945/1962). *Play, dreams, and imitation in childhood.* New York: W.W. Norton.

Piaget, J. (1971). *Genetic epistemology.* New York: Norton.

Postman, N. (1982/1994). *The disappearance of childhood.* New York: Vintage Books.

Renninger, K. A., Kensey, C. C., Stevens, S. J., & Lehman, D. L. (2015). Perceptions of science and their role in the development of interest. In K. A. Renninger, M. Nieswandt, & S. Hidi (Eds.), *Interest in mathematics and science learning* (pp. 93–110). Washington, DC: American Educational Research Association.

Riegel, K. F. (1976). From traits and equilibrium toward developmental dialectics. In *1975 Nebraska symposium on motivation* (pp. 349–407). Lincoln, NE: University of Nebraska Press.

Rogoff, B. (1990). *Apprenticeship in thinking: Cognitive development in social context.* New York: Oxford University Press.

Rogoff, B., & Wertsch, J. (Eds.). (1984). *Children's learning in the "zone of proximal development".* San Francisco: Jossey Bass.

Roth, M. S. (2014). *Beyond the university: Why liberal education matters.* New Haven, CT: Yale University Press.

Salomon, G. (Ed.). (1993). *Distributed cognitions: Psychological and educational considerations.* New York: Cambridge University Press.

Scribner, S. (1984). Studying working intelligence. In B. Rogoff & J. Lave (Eds.), *Everyday cognition; Development in social context* (pp. 9–40). Cambridge, MA: Harvard University Press.

Stetsenko, A. (2017). *The transformative mind: Expanding Vygotsky's approach to development and education.* New York: Cambridge University Press.

Stetsenko, A., & Arievitch, I. M. (2004). The self in cultural-historical activity theory: Reclaiming the unity of social and individual dimensions of human development. *Theory and Psychology, 14*(4), 475–503.

Strauss, S., & Stavy, R. (Eds.). (1982). *U-shaped behavioral growth.* New York: Academic Press.

Taubman, P. (2009). *Teaching by numbers: Deconstructing the discourse of standards and accountability in education.* New York: Routledge.

Uttal, D. H., & Perlmutter, M. (1989). Toward a broader conceptualization of development: The role of gains and losses across the lifespan. *Developmental Review, 9,* 101–132.

Vygotsky, L. S. (1934/1987). Thinking and speech (N. Minnick, Trans.). In R. Rieber & A. Carton (Eds.), *The collected works of L.S. Vygotsky: Volume 1, Problems of general psychology* (pp. 39–285). New York: Plenum.

Vygotsky, L. S. (1967). Play and its role in the mental development of the child. *Soviet Psychology, 5*(3), 6–18.

Vygotsky, L. S. (1978). *Mind in society*. Cambridge, MA: Harvard University Press.

Weber, M. (1904/2008). *The protestant ethic and the spirit of capitalism*. New York: Norton.

Wells, G. (1999). *Dialogic inquiry: Toward a sociocultural practice and theory of education*. New York: Cambridge University Press.

Werner, H. (1926/1948). *Comparative psychology of mental development*. New York: International Universities Press.

Wolf, D. P. (1989). Portfolio assessment: Sampling student work. *Educational Leadership, 46*(7), 35–39.

Wood, D. J., Bruner, J. S., & Ross, G. (1976). The role of tutoring in problem solving. *Journal of Child Psychology and Psychiatry, 17*(2), 89–100.

Index

A

Accountability, 3, 4, 9, 12–16, 34, 37, 39, 50, 66, 67, 98, 106, 107, 127–138, 192, 211, 213, 214, 218–221, 223, 225, 226, 249, 279, 288, 311, 332, 341
Active learning, 5, 79
Activity
- classroom, 11, 12, 16, 106, 108, 221, 260
- learning, 15, 81, 82, 120, 123, 131, 232, 237, 247, 258–260, 262
- system, 105, 106, 108, 247

Activity theory
- cultural-historical, 16, 232, 319
- sociocultural, 165

Alternative
- assessment, 336, 337
- conceptions, 74–76, 79, 82, 83
- frameworks, 74

A Nation at Risk, 268, 287
Arts, 67, 78, 135, 145, 149, 150, 233, 262, 305, 338–340
Assessments, 8, 12–14, 16, 62, 63, 66, 67, 74, 80, 81, 84–86, 89, 97, 127, 169, 170, 175, 179, 190–195, 219, 221, 249, 268, 269, 302, 304, 308, 311–313, 336, 337
Authentic
- education, 78, 79, 336
- inquiry, 106, 107

B

Best practices, 8, 200

C

Child-centered, *see* Learner-centered
Collaborative learning, 116, 118, 124n4, 185, 239, 249
Common Core State Standard, 5, 180, 192, 194, 198, 200–202, 218, 219
Community, 5, 30, 39, 40, 42, 43, 48, 50, 51, 61, 64, 67, 77, 79, 90n1, 99, 101, 103, 105–108, 122, 129,

Note: Page number followed by 'n' refers to notes.

D.W. Kritt (ed.), *Constructivist Education in an Age of Accountability*,
https://doi.org/10.1007/978-3-319-66050-9

131, 134, 143–159, 164–166, 173, 174, 178, 180, 184, 189, 190, 201–205, 212, 216, 218–221, 236, 241–243, 257, 270, 271, 273, 285, 288, 296, 303–305, 307–309, 311, 312, 338
Community of practice, 99, 137, 165, 233
Complex (complexity)
  subject, 295
  thinking, 287, 288
Confucius, 13, 57–64, 68, 69n1
Confusion (uncertainty), 12, 59–61, 99, 105, 106, 197, 279, 295, 303, 305, 333
Context, 4, 5, 7, 9, 10, 14, 25–28, 30, 35, 44, 60, 61, 63, 65–68, 74, 76, 80–87, 89, 98–100, 102, 103, 106, 113–116, 124n2, 128, 130, 131, 134, 136, 137, 147, 148, 164, 165, 170, 173, 174, 176, 177, 183, 199, 200, 218, 219, 221, 223, 225, 231–262, 303–307, 309–313, 319, 320, 323, 332, 334, 337
Cooperative learning, 116, 117
Correct
  answers, 12, 288, 293, 294
  ideas, 291, 294
Creative (creativity), 14, 21, 26, 77, 85, 88, 89, 99, 102, 106, 144, 148, 151, 153, 155–158, 170, 174, 179, 207, 215, 225, 285, 286, 288, 296, 329, 331, 338–340
Critical
  exploration, 286, 289, 290, 292, 293, 295
  literacy, 148, 195
  thinking, thought, 5, 191, 218, 225, 227n5, 272, 334
Culture (cultural), 6, 10, 12, 14, 27, 30, 37, 38, 40–45, 51, 65, 67, 68, 99, 100, 106, 107, 122, 129, 131, 133–136, 146, 148, 149, 151, 153, 157–159, 163–165, 175, 179, 185, 206, 216, 217, 219, 225, 227n4, 232, 233, 235–237, 240–243, 249, 268, 270, 272, 287, 288, 301–303, 307, 311, 320, 322, 323, 329, 332, 338
Curriculum
  English, 179, 199
  Language Arts, 196, 243
  science (scientific), 43, 73, 97, 174, 286
  social science, 196, 199, 242

D

Darwin, Charles, 21, 24, 25, 30, 31, 34–36, 46
Deficit discourse, 107
Democracy (democratic), 15, 22, 23, 37, 43, 45–51, 130, 131, 189, 190, 202, 203, 206, 285, 287, 294–296, 305, 308, 309, 311, 341
Democracy and Education (Dewey, John), 21, 29, 36, 40, 47, 48
Development
  cognitive, 9, 87, 98
  intellectual, 238, 239, 289, 291, 292, 295, 336
  social, 307
Deweyan, 205
Dewey, John, 6, 9, 13, 21–52, 191, 205, 206, 233–235, 237, 241, 260–262, 267, 270, 287, 332
Dewey School (Laboratory School at the University of Chicago), 29, 34–36, 39, 41–45, 47, 49, 50, 52n1
Dialogic, 79, 83, 105
Dialogue, 4, 14, 68, 132, 143, 169, 170, 174, 178, 183, 219, 243, 304, 328

Difference, 5, 6, 9, 10, 13, 15, 30–34, 36, 41, 46, 59, 90n1, 90n2, 113, 114, 143, 176, 177, 196, 232, 233, 235, 246, 247, 250, 307, 310, 319, 329–331, 337
Disciplinary norms, 105
Diversity, 7, 14, 50, 131, 134, 136, 137, 158, 169, 174, 178, 203, 268, 273, 288, 291
Duckworth, Eleanor, 9, 16, 285, 330, 334, 335

E
Educational research, 34, 74, 76, 117, 171, 324, 325
Eugenics, 21, 31, 32, 34, 328
Expeditionary learning, 267–279

F
Freire, Paolo, 6, 147, 152, 191, 195, 196

G
Galton, Francis, 31, 328
Games
  computer, 163, 167, 182, 340
  making, 181–183
  videogames, 163, 171, 180, 182, 261
  virtual reality, 170, 184
Glasersfeld, Ernst von, 75, 218
Goal
  achievement, 232, 235, 237–240
  learning, 108, 232, 233, 237, 242, 246, 262
  mastery, 237
  performance, 237
Greene, Maxine, 159, 191, 340
Guided instruction, 80
  See also Scaffolding; Zone of Proximal Development (ZPD)

I
Identity
  personal, 14, 145, 156, 157, 173, 217
  social, 146, 148, 149, 155, 158
  student, 14, 15, 67, 131, 133, 136, 144, 145, 149–151, 153, 156–159, 217, 226, 250
Imagination, *see* Creative (creativity)
Inhelder, Bärbel, 9, 103, 285, 289, 290
Inquiry (enquiry), 14, 16, 21, 23, 34, 37, 51, 73, 78, 102, 106, 107, 118, 152, 169, 175–177, 213, 221, 235, 240, 267, 301, 305, 307, 308, 310, 325, 330, 335
Inquiry-based learning (IBL), 118–120, 123, 124n5, 267
Interaction, 10, 11, 61, 64, 65, 75, 145, 146, 164, 165, 168, 169, 171, 178, 197, 218, 235, 236, 239, 246, 260, 272, 273, 290, 303, 306, 321, 339

J
James, William, 21–26, 28, 29, 34, 38

K
Kuhn,Thomas, 74, 77

L
Learner-centered, 9, 61, 64, 65, 69
Learning
  community, 61, 64, 67, 220, 307
  theory, 6–8, 97–108, 116, 164, 168, 170

M
Middle school, 15, 174, 175, 198, 203–205, 231, 235, 244, 267, 272–274, 276

Misconception, 12, 169, 335
Mistake, 12, 167, 171, 183, 335, 337, 339
Misunderstanding, 146, 332
Model, 6, 64, 76, 78, 81, 82, 86, 98, 100–106, 131, 133, 144, 165, 168, 176, 181, 190, 198, 212, 213, 216, 217, 240, 241, 261, 262, 268, 272, 273, 302, 317, 318, 324, 331
Model-based, 102, 103, 107, 108
Modeling, 6, 11, 14, 98–106, 108, 332
Motivation, 30, 40, 41, 51, 63, 115, 136, 196, 202, 231, 279

N

No Child Left Behind (NCLB), 4, 5, 12, 192–195, 288, 327

P

Pedagogy, 8, 14, 47, 76, 79, 81, 82, 88, 103, 106, 107, 128, 136, 144, 164, 170, 179, 184, 185, 203, 207, 212, 216, 219, 267, 270, 291
  constructivist, 79, 83, 89, 207
Perspective, 11, 13, 14, 16, 59, 64, 66, 68, 69, 73–75, 77, 82, 90n1, 97, 107, 131, 136, 149, 153–155, 163–185, 189–191, 212–214, 217, 221, 232, 268, 285, 303, 305, 309, 311–313, 319, 320, 336
Piaget, Jean, 6, 9, 10, 38, 40, 74, 103, 218, 271, 285, 286, 289, 291, 304, 328, 331, 339
Play, 8, 14, 15, 41, 42, 44, 58, 59, 61, 66, 138, 148, 154, 163, 166, 167, 170–172, 174–180, 182, 192, 205, 226n1, 256–258, 275, 330, 332, 339–341
Positivism, 43, 99
Pragmatism, 23, 36, 38
Preservice, 185
Professional development, 174, 184, 185, 191, 272
Progressive
  education, 6, 13, 225
  era, 46, 50
Project, 11, 15, 42, 46, 143–159, 164, 174, 176, 177, 179, 203, 217, 236, 238, 242, 247, 260, 261, 273–279, 310
Project-based, 191, 231, 236, 242

R

Race to the Top (RTTT), 5, 12, 190, 195, 288
Representation
  scientific, 100
  symbolic, 100, 311, 331
Respect
  for ideas, 294–296
  for others, 319
Right answers, *see* Correct, answers
Risk (risk-taking), 14, 38, 44, 152–155, 226, 267, 340
Rogoff, Barbara, 11, 99, 165, 233, 240, 257, 287, 304, 329, 336
Role playing
  games, 182
  and understanding, 182

S

Scaffolding, 80, 106, 118, 165, 167, 329–331
School reform, 16, 268–270, 286–289
Science education, 13, 14, 73–76, 82, 87, 97
Science, Technology, Engineering, and Mathematics(STEM), 13, 14, 113–124, 164, 175, 176

Scientific method, 32, 34, 44, 51, 99, 105, 107
Small-group learning, 15, 116–120, 123, 124n4
Social constructivist, social constructivism, 43, 164, 165, 184, 185, 305
Social justice, 7, 16, 33, 129, 147, 148, 158, 190, 285–296, 301, 304, 306, 307
Social learning theories
  social constructionist, 164, 169, 305
  vs. cognitive constructionist, 165
Standards, 3–5, 13, 65, 67, 85, 88, 89, 97, 98, 129, 133, 137, 144, 166, 176, 180, 190–195, 197, 198, 200–202, 207, 211, 212, 218, 219, 221, 225, 226, 226n3, 243, 268, 288, 295, 327–331, 336, 337
Structuralism, 10

T
Teacher education, 4, 83, 98, 103, 107, 285, 287, 301, 304, 309
Teaching
  with games, 166, 172–174
  pedagogy, 8, 14, 47, 73–89, 103, 106, 107, 128, 136, 147–149, 164, 165, 167, 168, 170, 171, 179, 181, 184, 185, 203, 206, 207, 216–218, 223, 225, 267, 270, 291, 312
  with virtual worlds, 185
Test (resting)
  achievement, 269, 288
  intelligence, 33
  standardized, 5, 7, 65, 130, 131, 193, 225, 269, 270, 287, 288, 302
Thorndike, E. L. (Edward Lee), 13, 21, 234

U
Understanding, 5, 6, 8–16, 42, 60, 61, 63–66, 73, 76, 78–80, 82, 85, 98, 101, 104–107, 115, 127, 149, 158, 165–169, 171–173, 175, 181, 182, 185, 191, 192, 195, 198–200, 202, 203, 238–240, 244, 247, 253, 258, 260, 268, 273, 274, 285, 287, 301–313, 318, 321, 322, 328, 331–336, 339, 340

V
Videogames, 163, 171, 180, 182, 261
Virtual worlds
  commercial, 184, 185
  educational, 171, 174–177, 184
Vygotsky, L. S., 6, 8, 10, 163, 168, 191, 233, 256, 271, 319, 328, 329, 332, 335, 337, 339, 340

W
Wonderful ideas, 273, 290–292

Z
Zone of proximal development (ZPD), 328, 329, 337

Zeitfracht Medien GmbH
Ferdinand-Jühlke-Straße 7
99095 Erfurt, Deutschland
produktsicherheit@kolibri360.de